CJ Hinke was the last man arrested for America's Vietnam draft. In order to prepare for becoming a conscientious objector in prison, he started to interview war resisters who had served time from World War I to the war on Vietnam, in the United States and beyond.

Resistance today, a chronicle of objectors, the historical background to war refusal, and the author's activist autobiography, *FREE RADICALS: WAR RESISTERS IN PRISON* has the stories of brave men and women who risked their freedom and often their lives for peace. They are our heroes and veterans.

FREE RADICALS: WAR RESISTERS IN PRISON details the military draft in all 100 countries where conscription is in effect, including the USA. CJ Hinke encourages and counsels draft refusal and shows you the whys and hows. *FREE RADICALS* provides all the international legal treaties and recommendations applicable to conscientious objectors both for absolutist war refusers and selective objectors to particular wars.

FREE RADICALS: WAR RESISTERS IN PRISON tells about religious war refusers, moral war refusers, and political war refusers. This book tells the story of deserters in every war throughout history. If you're already in the military, *FREE RADICALS* wants you to desert to disable the world's war machinery.

We have met the terrorists, and they are us.

The only sensible choice is to ignore your government: Don't register when you turn 18! *FREE RADICALS: WAR RESISTERS IN PRISON* tells you why and how. Moving to Canada, also, bears second thoughts.

In these violent times, with drums of war beating all around us, the nuclear doomsday clock at three-and-a-half minutes to midnight, and trillions of dollars being spent on senseless slaughter, *FREE RADICALS: WAR RESISTERS IN PRISON* is timely, practical, and essential.

CJ Hinke is a lifelong peace activist, co-founder of Nonviolence Conflict Workshop (NVCW) and sits on WikiLeaks' international board of advisors.

i sing of olaf glad and big
whose warmest heart recoiled at war:
a conscientious object-or
his wellbeloved colonel(trig
westpointer most succinctly bred)
took erring Olaf soon in hand;
but – though an host of overjoyed
noncoms(first knocking on the head
him)do through icy waters roll
that helplessness which others stroke
with brushes recently employed
anent this muddy toiletbowl,
while kindred intellects evoke
allegiance per blunt instruments –
Olaf(being to all intents
a corpse and wanting any rag
upon which God unto him gave)
responds,without getting annoyed
"I will not kiss your fucking flag"

straightway the silver bird looked grave
(departing hurriedly to shave)

but – though all kinds of officers
(a yearning nation's blueeyed pride)
their passive prey did kick and curse
until for wear their clarion
voices and boots were much the worse
and egged the firstclassprivates on
his rectum wickedly to tease
by means of skilfully applied
bayonets roasted hot with heat –
Olaf upon what were once knees)
does almost ceaselessly repeat
"there is some shit I will not eat"

our president,being of which
assertions duly notified
threw the yellowsonofabitch
into a dungeon,where he died

Christ(of His mercy infinite)
i pray to see;and Olaf,too

preponderatingly because
unless statistics lie he was
more brave than me:more blond than you.

e.e.cummings

CJ Hinke (below left) marching at the front on the National Mobilization to End the War in Vietnam October 16, 1967, in New York City. The "RESISTERS" box is full of returned draft cards.

SUPPORT DRAFT REFUSERS

RESIST! RESIST! RES

SUPPORT IN ACTION

RESISTERS

FREE RADICALS

War Resisters in Prison

C.J. Hinke

Free Radicals: War Resisters in Prison
Copyright © 2017 C.J. Hinke All Rights Reserved

Published by:
Trine Day LLC
PO Box 577
Walterville, OR 97489
1-800-556-2012
www.TrineDay.com
publisher@icloud.com

Library of Congress Control Number: 2017944381

Hinke, C.J.
  – 1st ed.
p. cm.
Includes references
Epub (ISBN-13) 978-1-63424-063-5
Mobi (ISBN-13) 978-1-63424-064-2
Print (ISBN-13) 978-1-63424-062-8
1. Draft resisters. 2. Conscientious objectors -- United States. 3. Conscientious
objectors -- World. 4. World War, 1914-1918 -- Draft resisters -- United States. 5.
World War, 1939-1945 -- Draft resisters -- United States. 6. Vietnam War, 1961-
1975 -- Draft resisters. I. Hinke, C.J. II. Title

First Edition
10 9 8 7 6 5 4 3 2 1

Printed in the USA
Distribution to the Trade by:
Independent Publishers Group (IPG)
814 North Franklin Street
Chicago, Illinois 60610
312.337.0747
www.ipgbook.com

कालो 'स्मि लोकक्षयकृत्प्रवृद्धोलोकान्समाहर्तुमहि प्रवृत्त
Now I am become death, the destroyer of worlds.

– J. Robert Oppenheimer,
nuclear physicist and Sanskrit scholar,
quoted Bhagavad-Gita XI.32 in 1945
after seeing the first atom bomb test
…called Trinity.

☮☮☮

*Six time Socialist Party candidate for president, Norman Thomas,
wrote of his brothers in 1923:*

To
The Brave
Who Went For Conscience' Sake
To Trench Or To Prison
This Book Is Dedicated

my book is dedicated to the revolution.

☮☮☮

TABLE OF CONTENTS

Dedication v

CJ Hinke, The Last Draft Dodger: We still won't go! 1

CJ Hinke, The View From 1969 15

Thomas and Marjorie Melville, Preface.. 21

Daniel Berrigan, Foreword...25

CJ Hinke, The World at War in the 21st Century.. 27

CJ Hinke with Koozma J. Tarasoff, Shaking, Quaking, and Spirit-Wrestling, Uncompromising pacifists: Shakers and Doukhobors.. 47

CJ Hinke with Andrei Conovaloff, Russian Spiritual Christians In America: The Innocence of Lambs 59

CJ Hinke, Russia's Jewish Draft Pogroms... 69

WORLD WAR I
The Conscientious Objector and the Military Prison

Eugene V. Debs, My Prison Creed... 73

Earle Humphreys, Four Hutterites In Military Confinement 83

Carl Haessler, In Camp 95

CJ Hinke, AWAKE! Jehovah's Witnesses and War..105

CJ Hinke, Should I Stay Or Should I Go? Conflicted Christians: The Seventh-Day Adventists...111

CJ Hinke, NOT Universal Soldiers: Unitarian Universalist COs 115

CJ Hinke, Mormon COs: Adhering to the Bible and the Book 119

CJ Hinke, Pentecostals & Pacifism: Charismatic COs...123

WORLD WAR II
The Conscientious Objector and the Federal Prison System

Bureau of Prisons, Federal Prisons and the War 131

Lowell Naeve, "Envelopment" 133

Philip Jacob and Mulford Q. Sibley, Prosecution, Trials and Imprisonment of Conscientious Objectors...135

Howard Schoenfeld, The Danbury Story..145

Jim Peck, Ending Jim Crow: Two Wars Later 157

Lowell Naeve, 1969 – I've Changed My Mind.....................................163

Wally Nelson, I Don't Close Jail Doors 167

Ernest Bromley, The Story Of Corbett Bishop 175

Lowell Naeve, "Written after two years in Upper Hartford Cell House, Danbury Federal Prison"..179

CONSCIENTIOUS OBJECTORS IN THE 1950s
A Study in Repression. The Selective Service Act of 1948, Multiple Prosecutions, Nonpayment of War Taxes, and the Smith Act Victims

Karl Shapiro, "The Conscientious Objector" 182

Letters from the Four Doty Brothers 183

Arlo Tatum, The Second Time Around...191

THE CONSCIENTIOUS OBJECTOR IN THE 1960s
Direct Action for a Warless World. Omaha Action; the Golden Rule and Everyman I, II, and III; Polaris Action; and the Draft

Karl Meyer, The Nonviolent Revolution and the American Peace Movement....199

CJ Hinke, PEACE – What (some) Muslims Want, Muhammad Ali: 'Float like a butterfly, sting like a bee'..205

Julian Beck, Letters From Jail 211

Marjorie Swann, Experiences At Alderson...217

Arthur Harvey, Prison and Me 227

1970s PRISONERS
From Witness to Resistance

John Phillips, How I was carried to a cell in a wheelchair and evicted from prison in a laundrycart, with some observations made in the intervening period 233

F. Paul Salstrom, A Prison Journey..251

Darryl Skrabak, What Will It Be Like When You Get Out?................259

Michael Vogler, The Scene At Springfield..263

Robert Gilliam, To Stand Where One Must Stand..............................265

Mike Wittels, Stockade Life 275

Suzanne Williams, The New Absolutist..291

Jeffrey Segal, Jail is a Bummer..303

Dorothy Lane, "2 Monologues"..307

Simon Townsend, Objector In The Guardhouse 309

THE RESISTANCE TODAY
Happening now, wherever you are

Phil Ochs, "Draft Dodger Rag" 319

Peter Harvey, Buddhism and Conscientious Objection to War.......................323

Netiwit Chotiphatpaisal, My Declaration on My 18[Th] Birthday.....................331

CJ Hinke with Scott Harding & Seth Kershner, Military Lies In Our Schools: "Hey, teacher, leave them kids alone!" 333

AFTERWORD

CJ Hinke, Simple Facts – The Cost of Killing 343

APPENDICES

CJ Hinke, Each Stone a Prison 361

Winifred Mary Letts, The Deserter 362

CJ Hinke, Lock 'em all up: Spinning money from misery...............................363

CJ Hinke, Military Conscription Worldwide...365

The War Resisters' International Declaration...381

CJ Hinke, Desertion: A Long Proud Tradition...383

CJ Hinke, Imagine there's no army… 389

Freedom Now, A Guide to Writing Prisoners of Conscience 393

Draft Law Group, The Personal Effects of Resistance 395

Jackson MacLow, Jackson, "Jail Break" (for Emmett Williams and John Cage)...401

EPILOGUE

The Rosenburg Fund for Children 406

"I don't want to be drafted. What should I do?" 408

Albert Camus, Neither Victim Nor Executioner..411

Mohandas K. Gandhi, Fear of Imprisonment...413

Supporting US prisoners for peace 414

Supporting US deserters in Canada 420

Supporting international conscientious objectors, deserters, and prisoners of conscience 421

Bibliography..435

Acknowledgments 437

Refuse to Register
NO REGISTRAR
CONSCRIPCION NO

Fred Moore (1941-1997)

☮ ☮ ☮

THE LAST DRAFT DODGER: We *Still* Won't Go!

CJ Hinke

My father, Robert Hinke, was not political. Nor was he religious. Nevertheless, he was a complete pacifist.

When I was a very small boy, he took me to one of the many demonstrations opposing the death penalty for the accused atomic spies, Ethel and Julius Rosenberg. He was passionate and outspoken his whole life against the death penalty, a mistake which could never be undone.

My father was of draft age when the US threw itself into World War II. If he knew about conscientious objectors, I never heard him say so. Nor did I ever see him vote.

He was a football player at Rutgers. When he was called for a draft physical, he goaded another player to break his nose by insulting his mother. When the draft authorities told him he was still able to fight, he goaded the same football player to bust him in the nose again. He failed the second physical – a deviated septum meant a soldier who could not wear a gas mask.

I come from the 'duck and cover' generation. We were taught in school that to hide under our desks and cover our heads would save us from the bomb!

I was not a particularly rebellious boy. Pledging allegiance to the flag is still the method I use to determine right from left. But, on joining the Cub Scouts, appearing at assembly to take the pledge, I knew I could not wear a uniform and follow orders; I threw down my pin in disgust and stalked off the stage.

I was 13 in 1963, when the National Committee for a SANE Nuclear Policy marched through my hometown of Nutley, New Jersey, led by pædiatrician Dr. Benjamin Spock (1903-1998). I read SANE's leaflet about mutually-assured destruction.

Without a moment's hesitation, I joined SANE's march to the United Nations in support of the Nuclear Test Ban Treaty, formally the Treaty Banning Nuclear Weapons Tests in the Atmosphere, in Outer Space, and Under Water. This was my first arrest for civil disobedience. In New York City's Tombs, I met my first transsexuals and learned to play blackjack using tobacco for currency.

From this point, I read everything I could find about Hiroshima and Nagasaki, and nuclear weapons testing. I began to study Japanese language the next year in order to get closer to this issue and the terrible crime which America had perpetrated on the Japanese and the world.

Family friends introduced me to Friends' silent meeting for worship and the their peace testimony, seeing the Light in every person. Quakers are a traditional peace church but my attender friends were not religious nor was I. It did not take a great deal of reflection by age 14 to decide I would not register for the Vietnam draft.

Simply put, conscription feeds the war machine. If you don't believe in war, you must refuse the draft.

It was about this time I began to refuse to pay war taxes from my part-time job. These acts led logically to becoming a vegetarian: If I will not kill, why should I pay anyone to do my killing for me. I didn't know any vegetarians; I actually had never heard of any but it was a question of making nonviolence work for me. I'm still a vegetarian today.

I began to devote all my free time to the pacifist groups at 5 Beekman Street in lower Manhattan. I started out in the Student Peace Union national office and was mentored by the dean of American pacifists, A.J. Muste. I put my efforts into the War Resisters League and the Committee for Nonviolent Action, often working on their newsletters and helping with mailings.

This period saw much draft card burning as political protest. Draft card burnings and returnings had taken place since the beginnings of the "peacetime" SSA in 1948 but destruction of draft cards was not made illegal until a special act of Congress was passed in 1965. Among the first to burn, in 1965, was my friend, Catholic Worker David Miller, at New York's Whitehall Street Induction Center. 30,000 draft refusals in July 1966 rose to 46,000 by October.

November 6, 1965: (L-R) Tom Cornell, Marc Edelman, Roy Lisker, David McReynolds and Jim Wilson burn their draft cards at Union Square in New York City.

A small group of us, including Dr. Spock, was arrested that day for chaining shut the doors of the center. I was, however, determined I would never have a draft card to burn. I did, however, get to enjoy this singular act of rebellion when one of my draft counselees gifted me with his own! This action was followed by the Fifth Avenue Peace Parade Committee, chaired by Norma Becker, which I helped organize in March 26, 1966 with Sybil Claiborne of the Greenwich Village Peace Center.

We brainstormed into being a new group of draft-age young men, The Resistance. I worked full-time for The Resistance and was eventually chosen the liaison with the many disparate groups forming the Mobe in planning the Spring Mobilization to End the War in Vietnam on April 15, 1967.

That fall, our pacifist coalition marched across the border to Montréal where the 1967 World's Fair, Expo '67, was being held in the capital of French Canada. The U.S. had commissioned a giant geodesic dome designed by futurist architect Buckminster Fuller for its national pavilion. We wore t-shirts painted with antiwar slogans under our street clothes into the fair and stepped off the escalators to climb into its structure. We were arrested by ladder and removed, and held the night before being re-

leased without charge from the 1908 Prison de Bordeaux. Of course, we made international news. Welcome to Canada!

The Resistance was the yeast that grew the Mobe; we raised the bread to make it happen. The Spring Mobe evolved into the National Mobilization Committee to End the War in Vietnam, chaired by Dave Dellinger, which spearheaded the 100,000-strong Confront the Warmakers march on the Pentagon on October 21, 1967.

Six hundred and eighty-two of us were arrested at the Pentagon, the largest civil disobedience arrest in American history. (Yes, some people put flowers into the barrels of the rifles of the National Guardsmen keeping us at bay and some soldiers joined us – I saw it!)

The Mobe was composed of many traditional lefties but also much of the 'New Left', like Students for a Democratic Society and other stakeholders against the war such as the Student Nonviolent Coordinating Committee, the Black Panthers, the Congress of Racial Equality, the Industrial Workers of the World, and the Yippies.

As a movement representative, I attended the first national convention of the Wobblies and the first American Communist convention since McCarthy's Red scare. I saw my job as holding the movement coalition to nonviolence. Violence was the self-defeating tactic of big government.

I was doing a great deal of counseling of draft-age young men for The Resistance. Many of my pacifist pals were going to prison, sentenced to three to five years under the Selective Service Act. I could honestly not expect less. My father was not happy about this probability but never tried to dissuade me, either. I started to draft counsel in Canada, so-called draft 'dodgers' and military deserters as well, and he was delighted when I fell for a Canadian Quaker girl while editing Daniel Finnerty and Charles Funnell's *Exiled: Handbook for the Draft-Age Emigrant* for the Philadelphia Resistance in 1967.

On May 6, 1968, five days after my 18th birthday, we held a demonstration in front of the Federal Building in Newark, New Jersey, where physicals and inductions were scheduled. However, that day more than 1,500 people, entertained by the Bread and Puppet Theater and General Hershey Bar, (parodying Selective Service director, Gen. Lewis B. Hershey), showed up to celebrate my refusal to register. There were no inductions or physicals that day. The Feds were spooked and turned away all draftee appointments.

General Hershey Bar, 1968

More than 2,000 of my supporters signed a statement declaring they had counseled, aided and abetted me to refuse the draft, an act carrying the same legal penalties of five years in prison and a $10,000 fine. We turned ourselves in to the Federal Marshal in Newark who simply refused to arrest me. And I'd packed a toothbrush!

The word 'evader' has an ignoble ring to it, as if one were a coward. We need to change the perspective because the only thing resisters are evading is injustice. COs also get called, pejoratively, 'shirkers' or 'slackers'. The only thing we shirk is shrugging off the chains of militarism.

I had already planned to move to Canada. However, I had a few more things to do to end the war.

My summer of 1968 was spent at the Polaris Action Farm of the New England Committee for Nonviolent Action, centered around a

Bread and Puppet Theater, 1968

1750 farmhouse in rural Voluntown, Connecticut. During this summer, a paramilitary right-wing group calling themselves the Minutemen were plotting to attack the CNVA farm and murder all the pacifists. The police knew about the plot but did not inform us because they thought (rightly) that we would warn the Minutemen.

The five right-wingers arrived in the dead of an August night and set up an automatic weapon on a tripod in the field. At that point, the Connecticut State Police ambushed the Minutemen into a firefight. One of the rounds blew a hole into the hip of one of our residents, Roberta

Trask; she needed extensive surgery and rehabilitation. For some years, I wrote to one of the Minutemen in prison. New England CNVA lives on as the Voluntown Peace Trust.

My summer of 1969 was spent working with Arlo Tatum, George Willoughby, Bent Andresen and others at the Central Committee for Conscientious Objectors in Philadelphia, counseling draft-age men and editing the 11th edition of CCCO's Handbook for Conscientious Objectors. I was fortunate to live with veteran peace activists Wally and Juanita Nelson. I have never met more positive committed activists nor anyone more in love.; they celebrated life in every way possible.

New England CNVA chose me as their representative to the Japan Socialist Party's annual Conference Against A and H Bombs in 1969 due to my research on the atomic bombings and Japanese language skills. I was one of eight international delegates and certainly the youngest.

Nothing could have prepared me for Hiroshima at 8:15 am on August 6th at the epicenter of "Little Boy"'s atomic blast; there is no greater call to peace. Working with the World Friendship Center founded in 1965 by Barbara Reynolds, I spent much of my time in both the Hiroshima and Nagasaki Atomic Bomb Hospitals where people are still dying from nearly 70-year old radiation illnesses.

Outside the U.S. military base in Naha, Okinawa, I gave a speech in Japanese. Then I turned around the speakers to blast the giant U.S. base with instructions for deserters.

In September 1969, I found myself living in Canada. My gainful employment was working with the massive collection of archived papers of British pacifist vegetarian philosopher Bertrand Russell at McMaster University. Russell was of enormous support to conscientious objectors as were Henri Barbusse, Albert Einstein, and H.G. Wells.

I was greatly supported by Toronto Quaker pacifists, Jack and Nancy Pocock, who opened their Yorkville home and hearts to many draft exiles, later Vietnamese boat people and again for Latin American refugees.

My experience as a draft counselor led me to work with Mark Satin of the Toronto Anti-Draft Programme to edit and revise the fourth edition of his Manual for Draft-Age Immigrants to Canada, published in 1970. The book's publisher, House of Anansi Press, began my association with the alternative education of Rochdale College in Toronto, where I became both resident and part of the administration.

My gainful employment at the time was for Toronto's prestigious Addiction Research Foundation, walking distance from The Rock, from one drugstore to another! I ferried drug samples from Rochdale dealers to ARF's doctors for testing, protecting the safety of the youth community. Eventually I migrated from ARF to the province's Whitby Psychiatric Hospital where I hosted radical British psychiatrists, R.D. Laing and David Cooper. We disabled the electroshock machines there and took a lot of psychedelics.

It was during this period that I was most active in a sort of latter-day underground railroad which arranged transportation to Canada and Sweden for American military deserters and draft resisters already charged.

I have to mention that life in the supercharged peace movement was a hard act to follow. But nonviolent activism requires constant reinvention. Specific noncoöperation has an expiry date and then one must move on to new issues, new tactics. Unlike many of my activist contemporaries who remained in the U.S., moving to Canada was, for me, like Lowell Naeve in these pages, a refreshing reset which enabled me to remain true to my conscience and ethical values but still remain on the cutting edge of critical thinking and analysis.

It would be remiss of me not to credit wide use of LSD among young people for encouraging draft resistance. It's pretty hard to be one with everything when harming anyone is just like killing yourself. I hope the spiritual self-exploration made possible by psychedelics comes back to us. We need it ...

Over the intervening decades, I have honed and sharpened what nonviolent direct action means to me. My definition has broadened considerably. I now fully embrace the concept of economic sabotage and destruction of the machinery of evil. I no longer think an activist needs to do so openly and thus be sacrificed. Better to do so secretly and live to plant another monkeywrench where it will do the most good at stopping violence.

Draft "exile" may have altered my circumstances but not my life. In Canada, I never failed to inform the FBI of my changes of address. However, after I was indicted in 1970, they didn't notify me. I was aware of my illegal status when traveling to the US but I was not burdened with it.

In the autumn of 1976, I rented a retreat cottage in the bucolic farmland of Point Roberts, Washington. Point Roberts is American solely because of its location below the 49th parallel. It can only be reached via American waters or by road ... through Canada.

The American war had been over for more than a year. However, one dark December evening, a knock on the door announce US Marshals, local police and sheriff's deputies. When I told them I was Canadian and would simply get out of their car when we reached the border, they advised me to dress warmly.

Shackled and handcuffed, they rowed me in a tiny aluminum boat to a 70-foot Coast Guard cutter with a crew of 15 men. When these boys, all younger than I, asked what I had done, they were amazed; to a man, they thought the draft was over. It was thus I arrived at Whatcom County Jail. In order to confuse my supporters who were gathering around the jail, they moved me incommunicado to King County Jail in Seattle. I fasted until the new President was inaugurated.

I had just become the last American arrested for the Vietnam draft, and the first pardoned.

Jimmy Carter was elected President in November of 1976. The day after he took office, January 21, 1977, Carter's first official act as President was Proclamation 4483 which pardoned unconditionally all those accused of draft law violations from 1964 to 1973. Including me – I walked! A huge celebration of supporters was held at the Capitol Hill Methodist Church.

Due to my central position in the American peace movement, I started these interviews in 1966 when I was 16 years old. I fully expected to go to prison for the draft and I wanted to be forearmed. I soon saw that these interviews would be of the same inspiration and encouragement to other draft resisters as they were to me.

Moreover, my friendship with these fearless activists convinced me that conscience led to commitment, commitment to defiance, defiance to refusal, and refusal to noncoöperation. Radical pacifists seasoned me from a principled teenager into a lifelong radical.

I decided to make this body of work into a book to share. Pacifist friend, poet Barbara Deming, was published by Richard Grossman in New York. With her introduction, Dick agreed to publish this book. Dick gave me a $3000 advance and let us live in his Lower East Side apartment for a month. However, I was in process of moving to Canada, the manuscript was lost, and I ran away with Grossman's money. (Sorry, Dick!) My sister only recently rediscovered it in my boxes of family archives, after more than 40 years.

Sometimes I feel like the Forrest Gump of the modern pacifist movement. I met everybody, I demonstrated everywhere, I got arrested frequently. I have been privileged to have been made family to three generations of well-known refuseniks. Today I do my best to impart those teachings of conscience to my students.

I wanted to know if these writings were purely of historical interest or if they had relevance to today's antiwar activists. In working again with these interviews, I find that these refusers sowed the seeds of my lifetime philosophy of anarchism, socialism, and pacifism, justice equality, civil liberties. They are no less moving now to me as an old man as they were when I was a teenager. These peace activists still teach us all the true meaning of courage.

I agonized over the title for this book in 1966. I used Thoreau's quote and called the manuscript, "In Quiet Desperation...". I think now, however, that title was a product of its time, when young men felt a little desperate about going to prison – jail was a last choice. I don't believe that anymore. I think nonviolent civil disobedience in the 21st century should be our first choice... if we are committed to genuine and meaningful change. And CD needs to have a sense of humor! Better still, don't get caught and live to act another day. That is revolutionary nonviolence...

Voting with my feet by no means dampened my personal activism. I was arrested with 1,500 others at the Nevada Nuclear Test Site in 1983; Quakers were my "affinity group" (sheesh!); we locked arms and ran as fast and as far as we could get over the fence, making Wackenhut goons play whack-a-mole chasing us among the cacti with SUVs. When asked by state police, I gave my name as "Martin Luther King."

Nevada Nuclear Test Site, 1986, 65 miles north of Las Vegas.   Connie L Sheehan

I hand-built a cabin in Clayoquot Sound off the west coast of Vancouver Island in 1975. First Nations people have lived here for 10,000 years. They arrived with the cedars as the last ice age receded. From 1984 to 1987, I defended the 1,500-year old Pacific temperate rainforest, first at Meares Island, my front-yard view.

My strategy was taken from native loggers. I supported driving big spikes into the most valuable trees to make them worthless to an industry producing toilet paper and copy paper. In all, 12½ square miles of proposed logging were spiked on Meares Island, more than 23,000 old-growth trees. I followed this up with contributions on tree-spiking to the Earth First! book, Ecodefense: A Field Guide to Monkeywrenching by EF! co-founder Dave Foreman.

Sulphur Passage on the Clayoquot mainland of Vancouver Island was also threatened by old-growth clearcut logging. My daughter and I pitched a tiny puptent in the logging road to stop its progress. Who speaks for the trees, so far up the evolutionary ladder from ourselves? After being arrested by helicopter, I acted in my own defense in B.C. Supreme Court and served 37 days for civil contempt in provincial prisons.

The largest Antipodean corporado, controlling 20¢ of every New Zealand dollar, was behind the clearcutting on the westcoast. I traveled to New Zealand with a group of Clayoquot Sound natives to make our voice heard at the 1990 Commonwealth Games in Auckland. We also managed to shut down the loggers' company tower and send its robber baron to flight.

I was again arrested at Oakland, California for blocking munitions trains to the Concord Naval Weapons Station in 1987. A small group of us covered the tracks with tenting. Inside the tent, we'd brought heavy tools and were busy removing the rails.

Freedom Against Censorship Thaiand, 2006.

Upon moving to Thailand, secret, extensive, irrational censorship was impacting my academic research and hobbling the ability of my students to produce internationally-competitive papers. I started Freedom Against Censorship Thailand (FACT) with a petition to the National Human Rights Commission. No one was publicly talking about Thai censorship where, to date, government has blocked more than a million webpages. FACT turned knowledgeable conversations about censorship from taboo to trendy. Censorship remains a hot-button issue here.

FACT posted leaked government blocklists as some of the first documents on WikiLeaks in 2006. Early in 2007, Julian Assange invited me to serve on WikiLeaks' international advisory board, a position I still hold.

Currently, I am a founder of the Nonviolent Conflict Workshop in Bangkok and the spark behind Thailand Peace Pledge.. We hope to secure

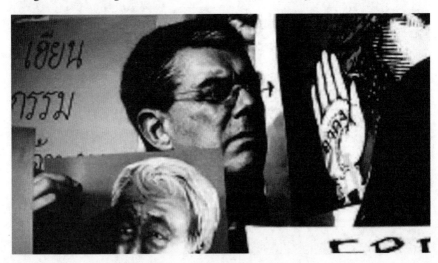

recognition for conscientious objection under Thailand's military draft with the long-range goal of ending conscription entirely. Ω

Editor's Note: I wish especially to acknowledge with the deepest gratitude and fondness the pacifist luminaries who mentored me at 5 Beekman Street: A.J. Muste (1885-1967); Dave Dellinger (1915-2004) (*Liberation*); Karl Bissinger (1914-2008), Grace Paley (1922-2007), Igal Roodenko (1917-1991), Ralph DiGia (1914-2008), Jim Peck (1914-1993), David McReynolds (War Resisters League); Bradford Lyttle, Peter Kiger, Marty Jezer (1940-2005), Maris Cakars (1942-1992) & Susan Kent, Barbara Deming (1917-1984), Keith & Judy Lampe, Paul Johnson (died 2006, Eric Weinberger (1932-2006), Allan Solomonow (Committee for Nonviolent Action, New York Workshop in Nonviolence and *WIN Magazine*); Joe Kearns (Student Peace Union). In our wider pacifist circle, Max & Maxine Hoffer (Montclair Friends Meeting); Marjorie (1921-2014) & Bob Swann, Neil Haworth (New England Committee for Nonviolent Action); Wally (1909-2002) & Juanita Nelson, Ernest (1912-1997) & Marion (1912-1996) Bromley, (Peacemakers); Arlo Tatum (died 2014), George Willoughby (1914-2010), Bent Andresen, Lawrence Scott (Central Committee for Conscientious Objectors). These brave pacifists remain my resistance family. They were gentle and forceful in making a better world for everyone. They gave me the best peace education a 'Murrican boy could have. It's lasted to this day.

It would be remiss of me not to include my wider peace movement influences and inspirations: Radical pro bono movement lawyers, (and often mine): Bill Kunstler (1919-1995), Gerry Lefcourt, Len Weinglass (1933-2011), and Lenny Boudin (1912-1989). They were often cited for contempt in our defense. Timothy Leary (1920-1996); Allen Ginsberg (1926-1997); A.C. Bhaktivedanta Swami (1896-1977) (Krishna Consciousness); Michael Francis Itkin (1936-1989) (Gay Bishop); Paul Krassner (*The Realist*); Stokely Carmichael (Student Nonviolent Coordinating Committee); Gary Rader (1944-1973) (Chicago Area Draft Resisters); Peace Pilgrim (1908-1981); Mario Savio (1942-1996); Jim Forest (Catholic Peace Fellowship); Aryeh Neier (New York Civil Liberties Union); Abie Nathan (1927-2008) (Voice of Peace); Abbie Hoffman (1936-1989) (Yippie!); Bob Fass (WBAI); Dee Jacobsen (Students for a Democratic Society); and Walter Dorwin Teague III (U.S. Committee to Support the National Liberation Front of Vietnam). The antinuclear activists: Grey Nun Dr. Rosalie Bertell; Australian physician Dr. Helen Caldicott; Sister Megan Rice, Michael Walli, Gregory Boertje-Obed (Transform Now Plowshares); Catholic Worker Sisters Rosemary Lynch and Klaryta Antoszewska (Nevada Desert Experience). And our philosophers: Richard Gregg (1885-1974), Gene Keyes, George Lakey, Gene Sharp, Paul Goodman (1911-1972), Howard Zinn (1922-2010), Dwight Macdonald (1906-1982), Noam Chomsky.

☮ ☮ ☮

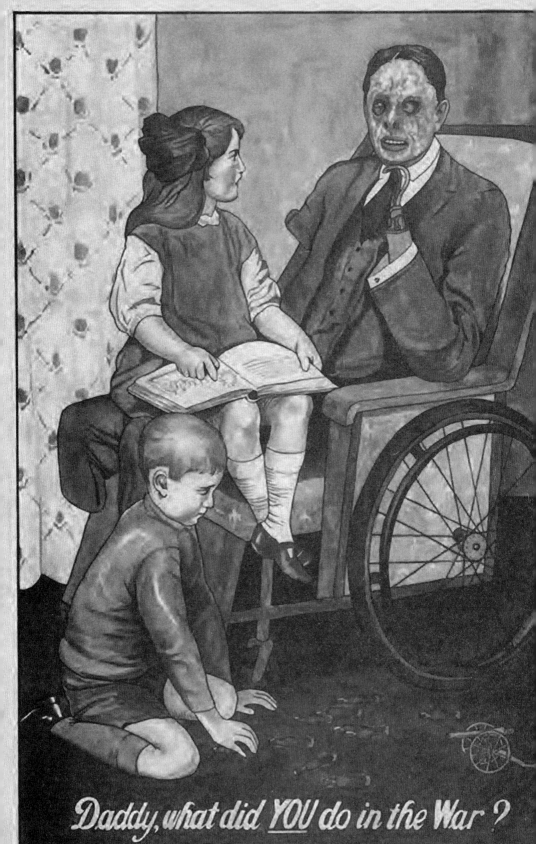

Daddy, what did _YOU_ do in the War?

☮ ☮ ☮

THE VIEW FROM 1969

As I stood considering the walls of solid stone, two or three feet thick, the door of wood and iron, a foot thick, and the iron grating which strained the light, I could not help being struck by the foolishness of that institution which treated me as if I were were flesh and blood and bones, to be locked up.

— Meltzer, Miltoo and Harding, *A Thoreau Profile*, 1962

Thus spoke Thoreau. I began the research for this volume nearly two years ago in response to a need in our movement. As more and more of us are taken to prison for resistance to the warfare state, draft refusal, tax resistance, the destruction of draft files, aiding desertion and emigration, resistance on every level in this society, this need today is more acute than it has ever been in the past.

The need for demystification of the prison system within the movement and prison education – what prison means to us – for both the public and our support, is growing in political terms. The fact that many of us will be taken to prison in the months to come because of this system, because of its illegitimate authority and our resistance to it, brings forth the need to ease the fear of those institutions of higher learning. The fact that we are all afraid of prisons and the prison experience must be discussed and shared.

The United States has a long, peculiar history of conscientious objectors in prison, more than in any other country. The conscientious objector here has been more than a political prisoner alone for, more often than not, political prisoners have been in prison for a great act of personal violence against the government, whereas, the conscientious objector has acted nonviolently and stood quietly alone.

Many instances of nonviolent resistance can be cited in support, for example, against British colonialism, such as the Boston Tea Party, and, on the other hand, members' of the Society of Friends refusal to pay taxes in support of the American Revolution. Henry David Thoreau's historic and eloquent single night in county jail for tax refusal against the Mexican-American war has been backed up by hundreds during every war, including thousands today, many of them members of one or another of the historic peace churches.

In addition to these numbers, there have been deserters from all our wars, runaway slaves, conspiracy trials, censorship, subversion, sedition, espionage, and treason laws. Countless other individuals have been imprisoned for aiding and abetting, for counseling, for advising, for giving men of conscience sanctuary when they could safely go nowhere else.

In 1968, there are more than 2,000 conscientious objectors in prison. Others refuse to pay war taxes. Many more of us wait in the courts and many, many more stand outside ready to support us with their actions and take our places.

If we are to build a better, healthy society in which to live, there will be many more put in prison because of their actions. Those now destroying Selective Service System records, for example, are indicative of a new age, an age that enlists freedom, an age that says that property is robbery, and that some property has no right to exist. This book is a salute to the resistance. This movement stands with them. Many more of us will follow them.

The young men and women who choose prison today are part of a resistance to war, rather than just the isolated phenomena of the religious, practising their faith in a moral witness against war. This in many ways changes the historical perspective of this book. However, the true believers who went to prison for their conscience in the past have much to share with us today. They were not afraid of the prison experience because of their faith in God and merely recognized their action and the subsequent prison experience as something that they had to do – an act of pure faith.

Some of us today feel the same way about the revolution (and make no mistake, that is what we are fomenting in American society through our resistance on many levels) because that revolution would be based on purity of faith and spirit as well. That form of dedication is often very difficult to come to grips with in the course of a politically radicalizing experience. Most who have that particular kind of dedication are quiet within their faith and yet, it seems to me that our goal must be to remain active throughout the course of this revolutionary experience. Religion in this situation for us does not always provide that.

If we are able to view the prison as a revolutionary institution, an institution in which we can learn and practice the human values required of the resistance movement. If it is possible to organize a revolutionary consciousness in these, the very victims of this system, then fear becomes education and the prison experience takes on new and more meaningful dimensions to those of us in the movement.

I find the educational potential of the prison institution to be staggering. Within the micro-cosmic prison society, one is able to see overtly the coercion used in American society today, the directed channeling of employment, forced labour, censorship, and total control over the individual citizen. Those who are taken to prison with a conscience but without a radical consciousness, (the elements which unquestionably form the two basic facets of a revolutionary), emerge from the prison chrysalis with a greater perspective on our society and have a greater chance of joining us in the resistance movement.

For the past few years I have counseled young men confronting the military system. Some of them have been deserters, some expatriates, some draft dodgers, and some have been draft resisters. The point is that I have been able to help them get away from this system and fight it, grant one less body to the machinery of war, and you can do the same. In the course of draft and military law counseling I was often asked for my personal counsel and advice. My advice to young men, like Tolstoy, has been to listen to your conscience and follow its call.

I can no longer advise young men to leave the country when we are confronted with the most massive use of illegitimate power since Nazi Germany. It is worldwide power and there is no escape for us in Canada or Europe. To escape a prison sentence in a country where there exists no alternative for radical social change, least of all in terms of a movement, is the very highest compromise of conscience.

So often I hear the argument that one or another young, middle class, white boy is psychologically incapable of prison. I ask you, is any black ghetto teenager any more capable of a term in an institution that is even more impoverished than home? No, of course not, but the black ghetto teenager is the one who will inevitably be put there.

White boys have that choice, and we must make it wisely. I am afraid that the revolution will be here and that my advice to young men is to desert, to lay down their arms and refuse to serve, and not go to registrations or physicals or inductions and, most of all, not to go to jail. When they take me to prison, they're going to have to take me first.

It was over three years ago when I decided I would not register for the draft when the time came, during the first Peacemakers Conference on Noncoöperation with Conscription in New York in 1966. This was where I first really got to know A.J. Muste. There were only a few of us then, from witness, to draft refusal, to non-coöperation, to resistance.

Two years later the time came and I refused to register before U.S. Marshal Leo Mault amid flowers and black balloons in a large public celebration on May 6, 1968 in Newark, New Jersey. Bread & Puppet Theater and General Hershey Bar made sure 1,500 supporters were well entertained and more than 2,000 signed the petition we delivered stating they had counseled, aid and abetted me to refuse the draft. Best of all, we so spooked the military, they refused to allow draftees in for physicals or induction, thinking they might be part of our conspiracy!

That day, the Marshal refused to arrest me or my supporters. However, how long will it be before I, too, am in prison? Or, is the question really, is anyone in our society really outside of prison?

I began to study the prison phenomenon in 1967 when large numbers of men began to refuse the War on Vietnam draft in the United States. By this time, I had already been imprisoned in numerous local lock-ups, detention centers, jails, correctional institutions, and prisons more than 35 times for many and varied acts of civil disobedience. Most of the charges were made up, of course: I certainly didn't feel mischievous or petty let alone trespass, or damage any property that I know of. Well, just maybe I did conspire with others! When activists ask you how many times you've been arrested, the only right answer is, "Not enough!"

I entered this study to eliminate the need for prisons and to abolish the prison institution. I began as one who could never coöperate with the system that puts men in cages: I will not stand before a man who calls himself my judge; I will not stand before a jury of men and women who are so obviously not my peers; I will not bear my own body into prison, nor will I eat or drink while I am imprisoned. Quakers may have been behind the first penitentiaries; likewise they will also be behind their demolition.

Like Corbett Bishop, I simply feel that there are absolutes to conscience and here is where I draw the line. Perhaps this must be our approach today, as during World War II, so that one does not become a part of this system. I tried to study the prison experience as a convict although I have spent no exceptionally long period inside. I found that our movement was not fulfilling the needs of the conscientious objectors in prison, nor were the prisons filling an educational need in our movement. I began to visit the prisons (my hair was shorter then and, when required, I sometimes dressed as a clergyman) in support of the prisoners and to take notes on the system, on prison life, to talk with the prisoners and the administrators, in the hope of being able to provide some insights to my counseling.

I discovered that a guidebook for resisters to the federal prison system was needed and set out to prepare one. Several other such projects were subsequently initiated by other organizations and individuals while this editor began to find an entirely new perspective on prison life opened up by the personal experiences of war resisters in prison. The usual facts on prisons are already available. Several guidebooks have been prepared in the movement, the Prisoners' Information and Support Service (P.I.S.S.) has been very effectively developed, and even the Bureau of Prisons now permits "visitations" by supporters and will circulate their catalogues on each institution, but still I found an emotional need to be filled.

This editor has tried to fill that gap with this book. I have attempted to present personal testimonies and accounts of experiences in prison and maybe some of them will resonate for you. Some of these prisoners have come out radicalized and enlightened and others of them have been crushed and shattered by the weight of their experience. This is up to you. This is prison.

This book is only the first step. What the reader can glean from the literacy of these prisoners is to be forearmed, and each of us can prepare himself for the prison experience. We must set up discussions, raise questions, and begin programs to train ourselves for the long prison days that are sure to follow. We must find the strength for prison in each other, within our resistance community.

I initially tried to present these accounts in the most comprehensive historical and international perspective for the movement and for the wider radical intellectual community. This finished volume falls slightly short of these goals and it is my hope that the reader, especially in the international community, will be able to aid me in the preparation of some future, more complete study and assist me in my counseling of young war resisters. I would be most pleased to receive information and addenda and to reply to queries by email.

The earlier accounts attempt to demonstrate that we are not really alone in this struggle and this experience, that others have gone before us, and many, many more will follow. In many cases, the former prisoners whom I was able to contact were too busy with their own valuable work to write for this volume. Thus, the 1950s, for example, is rather sparsely represented, although individual actions of resistance during that period were numerous.

Unfortunately, I was not able to represent political prisoners and international prisoners of conscience as adequately as I had hoped. I hope that soon we can fill that gap. On the title page for each period, I have attempted to present an outline of the major conscientious actions during that period which resulted in imprisonment. Unfortunately, you will not find each prison represented, nor each period, nor each country.

This is a book about going in committed and coming out whole. I ask you here to let many things about this book speak to you. To let these actions and these experiences and these lives speak to you...

The choice is ours. Resist. Ω

C.J. Hinke
Direct Action Farm
New England Committee for Nonviolent Action
Voluntown, Connecticut
Autumn, 1969

Editor's Note: I wish to thank the following conspirators for aid and comfort in the long months of preparation that this volume has seen:

*Richard L. Grossman, my publisher, and the contributing authors to this book, for their patience, understanding, and vision. They saw it through.

*The Resistance and Resist in New York City, where I worked many long hours and took on many difficult draft and desertion cases in perspective for this book.

*The Central Committee for Conscientious Objectors for their indulgence in my work there.

*The New England Committee for Nonviolent Action, where I completed a great deal of this manuscript.

*Grace Paley (1922-2007) and Karl Bissinger (1914-2008), Fred Moore (1941-1997) and Suzanne Williams, Chuck Matthei (1948-2002), Bradford Lyttle and Mary Suzuki, Ernest (1912-1997) and Marion Bromley, Wally (1909-2002) and Juanita Nelson, Arlo Tatum, Marjorie Swann, Tom and Marjorie Melville, Daniel Berrigan, and John Phillips, for providing the sustenance, discipline and criticism it took to make this work a book.

*My wife, Frances, for being able to love me even through long nights of aloneness while I put my body on the line for peace.

It has taken all of us to make this movement live. Peace.

Not me, not you!

☮☮☮

☮ ☮ ☮

PREFACE

Tom and Marjorie Melville

Our personal prison experience consists of a one week sojourn in the Towson County Jail in Maryland, after having burned some draft files last May [1968]. We do expect that in the near future the government is going to offer us the opportunity to expand this penal experience and broaden our understanding of its correctional institutions despite the fact that we would prefer not to. Furthermore, our familiarity with the CO and his political orientation, has been much more superficial than we would have desired. This too, the government insists we remedy. Lacking on both these counts, the reader may judge us bold for writing, a conclusion that our recent activities are not likely to contradict. Nevertheless, we do have some thoughts on the matter that this offer enables us to express publicly, and we hereby do so gratefully.

Prison has been part of the personal experience of the CO in this country for generations. For most, those of us who heard that such a breed of men exists, neither they nor their experiences were of more than academic interest. But in the past few years, namely during the escalation of the Vietnam war: prison, COs, pacifism, non-violence and other esoteric concepts that most Americans associated with an unwashed minority, are pushing their way out of our subconscious and unconscious, no longer remaining theoretical determinations of a disloyal morality, but becoming first- and second-hand personal confrontations between our souls and society. As we ourselves now face some years in prison, (an idea that would have been a mad proposition not very long ago), what do these words, these concepts mean to us?

All societies have prisons. All societies proclaim the basic premise that they have the right to defend and maintain themselves. Prisons are for curtailing the activities of those individuals that society considers a threat. Prison is a logical extension of the instinct of self-preservation, except that on the societal level it may be less instinctive and more calculated. These calculations are formulated by a group of men called legislators whose function it is to decide where the heart of their society lies and what course its life's blood should follow.

The substitution that sometimes occurs of these men's own vital parts for those of their society is the understandable consequence of human fallibility and frailty. Nevertheless, someone has to decide on what are the basic requisites and needs of his society and then to enact laws to fulfill them. The sad thing is that the individuals occupying this position are often selected for reasons extraneous to their ability and sensibility, thus multiplying the resulting confusion. When this happens, the effect is degeneration and eventually self-destruction and as with the law of gravity on physical bodies, so here the momentum becomes more and more rapid as it approaches the end of its fall.

There are two types of men in our prisons, if we will discount those who gave been lost behind the walls as innocent victims of a fallible juridical system. Both these classes of men are threats to our society and thus we feel the need to lock them up. Indeed, most of them know in their heart of hearts that they should be in prison. For want of a better denomination, I'll refer to the first group as "criminals" and to the second as "prophets." The former group are men who for some reason or another put their own interests above those of society, and go to extreme lengths to obtain those interests. This is not to say that all such men are in prison. If they are educated, they can consider going into any number of professions, not the least of which is politics, where they may operate unhindered by laws and the appellative "criminal" particularly in a culture such as our own.

Where our culture emphasizes individualism an extreme degree, deifying them who progress at the expense of their peers, and making a sacrament of competition and conflict, it is natural that our society produces a mass of criminals, or people excessively interested in personal gain even at the expense of a healthy society. It is necessary therefore that we be concerned with "law and order," so that we can control this tendency toward self-destruction and keep it within workable bounds.

In such a nation as ours, it is evident that the difference between a criminal and a law-abiding citizen, between a prison inmate and a multimillionaire, depends often upon the education of the individual in question, as well as who our legislators are and where their interests lie. Alas, in this digression we nearly forgot our second category of prison inmates, the "prophets." These are the men who refrain from violating society as the criminal violates it, and who even refuse to allow society to violate itself, its members, or other societies. In times of great crisis, their number and daring may increase, though not necessarily their audience.

All too often in the past, society has felt obliged to still their voices forever, thus only sounding its own death knell and hastening the disintegration the prophet foretells. Most downfalls of great societies in history have been preceded by the imprisonment or execution of some of its finest citizens. Perhaps this is the price that God asks, or it is the birthpangs required by nature, to bring forth the new. From Socrates, through Jesus Christ, to Abraham Lincoln on down to Martin Luther King, all societies manage to quiet those who would forge a new structure and revitalize her life. The less vocal and therefore less dangerous, but nonetheless prophetic, often disappear behind bars. A good measure of a society's degeneration is obtained by examining the quality of the men in her prisons.

It must be obvious that we have been referring to the Conscientious Objector in the foregoing paragraphs. We prefer to call him a prophet rather than a CO, his legal classification.

We do not necessarily agree that all wars are intrinsically evil for this could violate the right of self-preservation. We do accept that more often than not, wars produce more injustices than they eradicate. If nothing else, the CO is constantly pointing out this less than profound but often obscure truth to the rest of us. We ourselves would prefer to engage in the struggle on the side of justice and attempt to ameliorate the injustices that might be committed. This obliges us to combat actively the wrongs perpetrated in the name of justice, even if performed by our own government or society. This leads us from conscientious objection to active resistance in our attempts not only to avoid injustice ourselves but to heal its wound and prevent its multiplication. We recognize that such a course is fraught with dangers as one confronts the possibility of personal excesses, losing one's way, becoming a false prophet. But the alternatives are more frightening yet and the consequences more devastating.

Today, as 1968 comes to a close, as nine of us go on trial for burning draft files in Catonsville, Maryland and fourteen more are now imprisoned for the same "crime" in Milwaukee, as our prisons fill with the finest minds and hearts in our country, and others no less fine but perhaps less farsighted flee to Canada, America finds herself in a real sociological crisis. From this point in history is hard to see if we are going to resolve this crisis or break under it and collapse.

Some anthropologists, historians and sociologists, noting the speed with which we have developed, the speed with which we complete all our accomplishments, tell us that it is with speed that we are destroying ourselves.

We who feel obliged to play the role of prophet with our freedom and our lives, while in no way harboring messianic accretions must be prepared not only to say these things but also to try to stop our society from destroying others in what may be its death convulsions. Our own deaths or at least imprisonment is the toll which will be exacted from us for such a role. Would that it could be otherwise.

Washington, D.C
5 October 1968

Editor's Note: Thomas Melville has been an ordained Maryknoll priest for eleven years. He was sent to Guatemala in 1957 as a parish priest and was made a pastor in 1961. He founded four coöperatives between 1962 and 1964, as well as the National Federation of Credit Coöperatives in 1965.

Tom began to work in land reform and was expelled from Guatemala in December, 1967 by religious and civil authorities for teaching and advocating the use of armed self-defense on the part of the peasants to protect their rights in carrying out their struggle for social betterment.

He then travelled to Mexico where he married Sister Marian Peter in January, 1968.

Marjorie Bradford Melville was born in Mexico of American parents. She entered the Maryknoll order as a nun in 1949. After completing her education, she was sent to Guatemala in 1954, where she worked for 13 years, teaching both elementary school and college sociology and teacher education.

Marjorie began to work with university students and founded a university student group, CRATER, dedicated to labour organization and literacy programs, and was expelled from Guatemala for being involved in the "internal politics" of that country.

Tom and Marjorie returned to the United States in April, 1968 and in May used homemade napalm from a recipe in the Special Forces handbook to destroy 800 draft files from the Selective Service System offices in Catonsville, Maryland along with seven others. Jesuits Daniel Berrigan, S.J., his brother Philip Berrigan, S.S.J., Thomas Lewis (both Phil Berrigan and Tom Lewis began serving their six-year sentences at the Federal Prison Camp at Allenwood, Pennsylvania for pouring their blood on the same files earlier in the year and are presently out on appeal bond), David Darst, John Hogan, George Mische, and Mary Moylan, to demonstrate their conviction that the military system is one of oppression of the poor in other countries and in their own.

All nine were convicted on October 10, 1968 in Baltimore and were sentenced to terms from two to three-and-a-half years, Tom receiving a three year sentence and Marjorie, two years. "We are always searching..." Ω

☮☮☮

☮ ☮ ☮

FOREWORD

Daniel Berrigan, S.J. (1921-2016)

1.

In Baltimore as we came in for trial
a butterfly came to rest on our big Boeing wing
pulsing there, a hand in ballet motion, a heartbeat.
I wished the little tacker luck. He was
technologically innocent, flying
by grace of the US Air Control Command
because his wing spread
(I checked this)
lay somewhere below the danger area of the breadth
of minor aircraft.

2.

At 7 a.m. on trial day
courtesy of warden Fester,
the San Jose vineyards
and a common baking shop
we took
in a workman's cracked cup
at a slum table
prisoner's pot luck.

3.

We sit or walk our cage
day after day;
at night, the moon
striped like a tiger
leaps on us with a cry,

Unlikely men, white, black
sweating with rage and grief
our diet decreed
our own prophetic guts –
the prison poems of Ho,
the sayings of Chairman Jesus.

Catonsville Nine – Napalming the draft files, May 16, 1968.

Editor's Note: Daniel Berrigan, S.J., was born in northern Minnesota and his early schooling was completed at St. John the Baptist in Syracuse in 1939, at which time he entered the Society of Jesus, the Jesuits. He completed his philosophical studies at Woodstock College in Maryland and was assigned to teach in St. Peter'a Preparatory School in Jersey City, New Jersey from 1946 to 1949. Dan was ordained in Boston in 1952, studied the following year in France, and returned to teach at the Brooklyn Preparatory School, LeMoyne College in Syracuse, and then spent a sabbatical year in Europe for 1963 and 1964. He has travelled extensively in Central Europe, Russia, and Africa and recently returned from North Vietnam. He has also taken an extended tour of Latin America for a year and is presently Associate Director for Service at Cornell United Religious Work at Cornell University in Ithaca.

Dan received his M.A. from Georgetown University and then a Licentiate of Sacred Theology (S.T.L.).from the Gregorian University in Rome. He has published extensively in periodicals, especially The Atlantic Monthly, Poetry, The Saturday Review, Commonweal, and was an Associate Editor of Jesuit Missions in New York. His books include *Encounters, Love, Love at the End: Parables, Prayers and Meditations, America Is Hard To Find, Words Our Savior Gave Us, Prison Poems, Hole in the Ground: A Parable for Peacemakers, Stations: The Way of the Cross* (with Margaret Parker), *And the Risen Bread: Poems 1954-1997, Daniel: Under the Siege of the Divine, Uncommon Prayer: A Book of Psalms, The Bride: Images of the Church, To Dwell in Peace: An Autobiography, Absurd Convictions, Modest Hopes, Geography of Faith, Time Without Number,The Dark Night of Resistance, Night Flight to Hanoi, Trial Writings* (with Tom Lewis),*The Raft Is Not the Shore: Conversations Toward a Buddhist/Christian Awareness* (with Thich Nhat Hanh), *Swords into Plowshares: A chronology of plowshares disarmament actions 1980-2003, Prayer for the Morning Headlines: On the Sanctity of Life and Death* (with Howard Zinn), *The Trouble With Our State, and Jeremiah: The World, The Wound Of God*. He also reads his poetry, lectures and has written several television plays.

What brings Dan Berrigan to this book is his covenant with God. He is one of the Catonsville Nine and is under three year sentence for destruction of government property. These nine extraordinary people have reached out with their own hands to all the world. It is only fitting to call then nonviolent revolutionaries. Ω)

☮☮

THE WORLD AT WAR IN THE 21ST CENTURY

CJ Hinke

One soldier too many! (You ...)

The lines of resistance to war take many forms as these stories of resisters in prison in World Wars I ("the Great War," "the war to end all wars") and II ('the good war"), the Cold War, the undeclared Korean "conflict," the 'Red Scare' of the McCarthy period, the 1960s and, finally, the US war against Vietnam, demonstrate. More than 20,000 young men were arrested for the Vietnam draft and at least 3,250 served prison sentences.There are as many reasons and methods to refuse war as there are refusers. The Department of Justice classified WWII resisters as religious, moral, economic, political, neurotic, naturalistic, professional pacifist, philosophical, sociological, internationalist, personal and Jehovah's Witness.

Why are some awake and aware, why do some feel their conscience so strongly they cannot ignore it? As A.J. Muste proclaimed, "If I can't love Hitler, I can't love at all." Why isn't that spirit inside all of us? Most of us have unconsciously shut up the voice of our troublesome conscience to make our lives easier. I assure you, however, the world would be immeasurably better if we all learned to listen to even its faintest of stirrings.

The reason The Resistance was so effective against the draft is that meetings listened to *everybody*. This stratagem was learned *in vivo* from Quakers, SNCC, and CNVA. The Resistance functioned because of its underlying commitment to principled consensus. Many of us – (does not play well with others) – went ahead to devise our own actions out of frustration with this long and often tedious performance. Sometimes others joined us seeing its value and sometimes they did not. If there were "leaders" of The Resistance, I never met any!

Consensus is not easy but it works. Consensus is a process rather than a conclusion. Consensus never succeeds by filibuster. Consensus works in precisely the way that majority rule and voting never do. Voting ends up with a large disaffected, unsatisfied group of constituents. Do you really want to vote for some second-best, had-to-run, mealy-mouthed, forked-tongue liar anyway?!?

Consensus is experiential. Voting is adversarial. Consensus builds community. Voting makes enemies, creates outsiders. So just *listen* already.

There are a hell of a pile-up of people on this planet and I may just be too idealistic. But in an ideal society, we would all be making decisions through participatory democracy rather than the essential disenfranchisement that is at the core of majority voting.

The pre-Saxons used sanctuary laws from the fourth century BC. Fugitives were legally immune from arrest in sanctuary from the fourth to the 17th centuries in England; legal sanctuary was abolished in 1623.

Among other tactics, the Resistance proposed employing the ancient Judæo-Christian and Mediæval law concept of sanctuary – a place of safety, a refuge – to military deserters and draft resisters under indictment. One of the first to open its doors for sanctuary was the Washington Square Methodist Church, home to the Greenwich Village Peace Center.

More than 500 churches coast to coast, including Lutherans, United Church of Christ, Roman Catholics, Presbyterians, Methodists, Baptists, Jewish, Unitarian Universalists, Quakers, Mennonites, and some universities, also declared themselves safe havens. Arresting war resisters in a sanctuary was a chilling image.

Another tactic which provided us great inspiration was the destruction of draft board files to make the induction of soldiers impossible. This was followed by the destruction of corporate records for major war profiteers such as Dow Chemical, producers of napalm, and General Electric, producer of bomb components. Remember, if you can, this was decades before computerization; without those files, meat could not be fed into the maw of the war machine.

Staughton Lynd documents at least 15 actions against draft boards and war corporations from 1966-1970 resulting in the destruction of from a few hundred to more than 100,000 records. In 1969 the Women Against Daddy Warbucks not only destroyed draft files but removed all the '1' and 'A' keys from New York draft board office typewriters so draftees could not be declared fit for duty.

Jerry Elmer, Esq., a year my junior to refuse to register, may hold the record for this tactic. He burglarized 14 draft boards in three cities! Jerry became Harvard Law School's only convicted felon in the class of 1990.

The Internet offers a vast new world of opportunities for nonviolent activists, including networking with others for action in the real world. The practice of evil now requires computers and we can easily interrupt the processes of evil and greed. You can fuck up the system without ever leaving the couch.

Since 2010, American boots were on the ground in military incursions into Pakistan, Afghanistan, Iraq, Libya, Jordan, Turkey, Yemen, Somalia, Uganda, Chad, the Central African Republic, Sudan, and Mali. Threats to US national security were the reasons given. Be afraid. Be very afraid. Our "commander-in-chief" tells us America has "the greatest army the world has ever known" – and that's a good thing?!?

In 2016, the United States will spend $1 *trillion* dollars a year on its current military misadventures – almost two million dollars *a minute* – four-point-six times its nearest competitor, China, and greater than China, Saudi Arabia, Russia, United Kingdom, France, Japan, India Germany, Brazil, Italy, South Korea, Australia, and Canada *put together*. No other country comes close. This mammoth figure, however, fails to include the the debt for past war spending. In all, 54% of the US budget is spent in war, 4.4% of our Gross Domestic Product, 73 cents of every US dollar. America's military is a parasite.

That's a trillion and a half dollars in total from $20 trillion in US debt. Think of all the good in the world that inconceivable amount of money could do.

The United Nations estimates only $265 billion annually would end poverty and hunger worldwide, less than 13% of military budgets. Another $240 billion, 12%, would realize universal primary and secondary education everywhere. Four per cent would guarantee agriculture and food security; three per cent universal clean water and sanitation 11% for energy; 12% for telecommunications.

We'd rather slaughter around the globe and decimate other countries. To put this in perspective, it would cost less than 1/10 of the U.S. military budget, $62.6 billion, to provide every American tertiary education for free!

If one examines history, it is easy to be overwhelmed because history is primarily the history of war. Although 619 million human beings have been slaughtered, there is not a war in humankind's long history which would not have been "won" by attrition sooner rather than later.

Can anyone think black slaves would not have been freed and attained at least the level of "equality" seen in the 21st century if young American brothers and neighbors had not massacred each other in America's bloodiest war of all time, the US Civil War?

Can anyone think Germany's imperialist Nazi regime would not have collapsed on its own? Which course generates more suffering, waiting or slaughter?

Although the U.S. Constitution requires Congress to declare war, as does, more recently, the 1973 War Powers Resolution, it has not done so since World War II. Thus, the unilateral military incursions made by the U.S. military into Korea; Vietnam; Laos; Cambodia; Grenada; Panama; Iraq and Kuwait ("Desert Storm"); Afghanistan ("Enduring Freedom"); Iraq ("Iraqi Freedom") were clearly illegal wars.

U.S. wars on terror are really nothing more than wars *of* terror. They come at a terrible human cost, of course, but also are costing Americans $120 million *an hour*. Of course, I have only touched on the high points – there are dozens more minor military actions in sovereign nations. They call these military *theaters*, where real people die onstage. The USA bombs hospitals. To paraphrase Pogo, we have met the terrorists and they are us.

As Noam Chomsky states, "If the Nuremberg laws were applied, then every post-war American president would have been hanged."

Perhaps I should not be so hard on the United States but, after all, it's my country. In all six millennia of recorded human history, that human history records a grand total of merely 300 years of peace! But, of course, that doesn't make war right …

The U.S. Constitution created a fine system for control of government powers, checks and balances from government's three branches. However, government has spiraled out of control unchecked and unbalanced. The U.S.A. has existed for more than 240 years; in all that time, we have only seen, generously, 16 years of peace! Nearly every one of America's wars have been wars of aggression and against self-determination deemed not in America's national interest.

Schools, hospitals, wedding parties,, funeral processions, refugee camps, and civilian neighborhoods are our specialties and those "allies" who have been trained by the US. Remember "*pacification*"? We are a nation with at least three separate kill-lists for "targeted" assassinations decided on "Terror Tuesdays." Is this *your* America? U.S. soldiers are not only terrorists to ordinary citizens but murderers without sanction. By any test, there are U.S. war criminals at every level. The acid test for war is to imagine its reverse, war happening to us, at home.

Tell me, please, which are the "good" wars? Neither politicians nor their sons are often soldiers. How long would a war last if all the 80-year old senators from both sides had to fight each other?!? As in gladiatorial contests. Bring on *The Hunger Games* for the 1%!

In the decades since America's war on Vietnam, widespread support for conscientious objectors has diminished despite continued requirements for Selective Service registration. The U.S. government has also succeeded in minimizing public advocacy and peace activism against its so-called wars on "terrorism" domestically and overseas.

War is just terrorism with a bigger budget.

However, the War Resisters League still actively supports military objectors along with the Center on Conscience and War. War Resisters' International and the Peace Pledge Union in the United Kingdom also support international resisters and document cases of military conscription in over 100 countries.

Every single person must ask themselves the seminal question, "What would be worth dying for?" because there is certainly nothing worth killing for. At most, only about five percent of humans have ever killed another. Everyone knows the difference between right and wrong: human beings are both hardwired and programmed not to kill. War turns soldiers inside-out, both literally and figuratively.

Militaries the world over torture and brainwash young soldiers to overcome their nature not to kill by objectifying other young men as "the enemy." War remakes the soldier as cipher then as casualty. The result is almost always a very damaged man or woman. 22 U.S. veterans commit suicide every day, more than 8,000 each year. America has used them up and thrown them away. Not only untreated, nearly 60,000 veterans are homeless.

Of course, we make our "enemies" out of nothing, both personally and by government policy. Radical, sensible concept: stop viewing any "others" as enemies! Dialogue, conversation, mediation, negotiation, compromise, conciliation, peacemaking, makes friends out of "enemies."

The very terms applied to war, the "winners" and the "losers" can be equally applied to the courtroom. The atomic bomb and the death penalty are governments' idea of victory. Wars and prisons are simply not a lasting solution precisely because they fail the most basic test of compassion for one's fellow man. No war and no prison sentence has ever achieved a permanent solution for society's problems. War and prison both are simply treadmills ending in turnstiles.

The first woman elected to the United States Congress, in 1916, Jeanette Pickering Rankin declared before the U.S. entry into World War I:

"You can't win a war any more than you can win an earthquake." We obviously needed more of this kind of sentiment – full women's suffrage was not enacted until 1920.

The United States is also world leader in weapons sales, including guns, ammunition, missiles, drones, military aircraft, military vehicles, ships and submarines, electronic systems, and much more. 2.7% of the world's Gross Domestic Product is spent on weapons; however, the US GDP share is almost five percent. America rakes in $36.2 billion on arms sales, rising 35% in 2014, 50% of the world's total. As with military spending, this is nearly than four times its nearest capitalist competitor, Russia. The USA sells antipersonnel weapons, cluster bombs, drones, and landmines to any country with money and calls its drones "Hunter-Killers," their soft (read human) targets determined by "military intelligence." Pop quiz: Which country deserves economic sanctions?

Prior to the Second World War, President Roosevelt declared, "The time has come to take the profit out of war." President Eisenhower, a decorated World War II general, on his last day in office, warned of "a military-industrial-congressional complex," linking the armed forces with corporations and politicians.

NATO Countries Military Spending (billions)

USA	$596
Turkey	$42
UK	$36
Italy	$21
Canada	$19
Albania	$17
Spain	$13
Romania	$10
Netherlands	$8
Croatia	$5
Norway	$5
France	$5
Greece	$5
Czech Rep	$4
Estonia	$4
Poland	$4
Belgium	$4
Germany	$4
Portugal	$3
Denmark	$2
Bulgaria	$1
Slovakia	$1
Lithuania	$0.4
Slovenia	$0.4
Hungary	$0.3
Latvia	$0.3
Luxembourg	$0.3

Perhaps this destructive trend could have been stopped by leaders in 1961; instead, they exploited it for gain. The US is profiting from the suffering of the victims of this heinous trade. I remember palmier days when America gave foreign aid and disaster relief to needy countries and exported education and manpower for development. Now we just export destruction.

Nine nations now are part of the nuclear "club" which spends over $100 billion on nuclear weapons every year. Russia has a few more warheads than the USA (8,500/7,700) but is busy selling off its plutonium cores to power nuclear reactors.

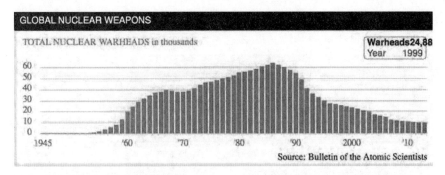

America's nuclear strategy is far more aggressive, spending eight billion, 600 million dollars on maintaining nukes in readiness each year. Obama's wrote his senior thesis at Columbia on the arms race and a nuclear freeze. However, his 2015 budget includes maintenance, design, and production of nuclear weapons, the highest figure ever, due to rise by seven per cent in 2016. This will include the production of 'smart' nuclear weapons for battlefield use. The real question is why there need be any battlefields at all!

We've certainly all seen what abject failures 'smart' bombs and 'smart' drones are. Now we can add smart nukes to our list of failures with far more devastating consequences, human, environmental, and political. America used A-bombs first; will we now use them a second time? Obama's White House refused to present the Comprehensive Test Ban Treaty to the U.S. Senate for ratification ... under two Secretaries of State.

The US has housed launch-ready nukes in South Korea since at least 1958. When North Korea tested in 2013, America decided to play chicken with them. And Israel's got the bomb – yikes!

The fact we haven't yet destroyed all life on Earth is not the result of high morals or political restraint – it's been a lucky accident ... so far. South Africa is the only country to have developed nuclear weapons and then dismantled them entirely. America is again recklessly gambling with our lives by spending $100 billion to build a new fleet of Trident nuclear submarines, updated from the subs on which I was arrested at Groton.

Although the Peace Prize President pledged in 2010 no new nukes, he is leaving office with a legacy budget of $3,000,000,000 (that's trillion) to 'upgrade' nuclear weapons, plus $11 billion on American nukes in Belgium, the Netherlands, Germany, Greece, Italy, and ... Turkey. Scary, huh? 157 states have ratified the UN's Comprehensive Test Ban Treaty:

not Egypt, India, Iran, Israel, North Korea, Pakistan, and ... the United States. Shameful.

Here in Thailand where I live, I found myself in one of my life's greatest pacifist's dilemmas. In March 2008, Viktor Bout, a Russian alleged 'illegal' arms dealer, was lured to Thailand by the US Drug Enforcement Administration. Bout was fictionally portrayed by Nicholas Cage in the Hollywood blockbuster, *Lord of War*. The DEA agents were posing as Colombian People's Army FARC guerrillas buying arms to entrap Bout for providing material support to foreign 'terrorists', "conspiring to kill Americans," and, of course, that old standby, 'money laundering'. Oops, FARC are not listed as "terrorists" in Thailand.

As soon as Bout met with the agents, he was arrested, on Thai sovereign soil, by US foreign agents. A Thai court of first instance found Bout was entrapped for political purposes and arrested illegally. The court denied extradition but a US motion ensured Bout was not released. Throughout this process, 30 months, the USA had a jet waiting on the tarmac at Don Muang airport to fly Bout to an American prison.

Bout's Court of Appeal hearing ruled for extradition, upheld by appeal to the High Court, and ... he was gone, sentenced to the minimum 25 years in the US in 2012. Although then-US Secretary of State, Hillary Clinton, made Bout's extradition 'a top priority', Bout's Federal judge stated Bout was entrapped by a 'sting' operation in giving the minimum sentence possible.

I simply find myself unable make any distinction between 'illegal' arms sales and legal ones. If sales are 'legal', corporations and governments reap the profits, if 'illegal', no taxes are paid and entrepreneurs line their pockets. Like, so what?

I defended Viktor Bout on principle. He was lured and entrapped and deserving of my support. During my defence of Bout, I got to know his wife, Alla, a very fine woman who loves Viktor dearly. The worst people in the world, of course, have wives and mothers and children who love them.

Viktor's only real crime was being America's competitor in the arms trade. If he really was an arms dealer, his weapons killed no more efficiently than America's. The pot calls the kettle black.

Here's a laugh: a 2007 book called *Bout, Merchant of Death: Money, Guns, Planes, and the Man Who Makes War Possible.* Tacitus told us in the first century, "Corruptissima re publica plurimae leges." ("The more corrupt the state, the more numerous the laws.") Who really makes wars possible?

Prisons are always used with malicious intent; they are carrion birds – they feed on the bodies of the living dead. Prisons trade in misery. Like wars, prisons are simple, blunt instruments of revenge, the antithesis of human civilization. The offender simply cannot offend again for the period of time he or she is locked up.

WWI. The injured from Gallipoli.

The irony is that the U.S. prison population remained stable, at around 250,000 prisoners, from 1930 to 1960. Only war, no less destructive to society than any war fought with weapons, escalated those numbers for the U.S. to become that largest prison system in the history of the world – the war on drugs. In 2010, there were 13 million people arrested in the United States; five years later, that number has certainly only increased. Some 500,000 of these accused can't afford to pay bail or fines and remain caged.

And there are 140,000 Americans serving life sentences, 41,000 of them without possibility of parole. As Stalin's chief of secret police said, "Show me the man and I'll show you the crime." Government has created a climate of public fear, sown seeds that we all need to be protected by … locking people up and throwing away the key.

James V. Bennett was the US government's director of the Bureau of Prisons for 34 years. Appeals by COs went to Bennett. These were somewhat more civilized times, when prisons made minor attempts at rehabilitation and education. Today, the Bureau has 38,000 employees.

Today's prison-industrial complex is a fully operational slave labor industry raking in millions for publicly-traded corporations such as the Orwellian-sounding Corrections Corporation of America, the GEO Group, and Community Education Centers. In capitalist America, government even shares the living dead with private prisons, using investment capital from the Bill and Melinda Gates Foundation, in regions far from the prisoner's family and community.

US prisons today hold 2.6 million prisoners in more than 4,500 jails fueled by mandatory minimum and three-strikes sentencing. This figure amounts to 25% of all the prisoners in all countries combined. The US has 700,000 more prisoners than China, a country with four times its population. While there may be no generalized systematic torture, racial violence is endemic. Barely a noticeable occurrence for prisoners in any other country, in 2012 alone there were 216,000 incidences of reported prison rape, 10% of all US prisoners. Of course, the vast majority go unreported.

American prisoners are still vindictively stripped of their civil rights such as voting. Nearly seven million Americans are under some sort of 'correctional' supervision. That's 2.9% of all Americans, the largest number of disenfranchised citizens in history, anywhere. 75% are nonviolent offenders. 26 million people have been incarcerated for marijuana!

Adding to this human misery, 34,000 are arrested by the U.S. Immigration and Customs Enforcement (ICE) squads as illegal "aliens" *every single day*, denied the due process guaranteed by the U.S. Constitution. ICE detention facilities are administered by the Department of Homeland Security, treating the detainees as terrorists just because they happen to be foreign-born. Most of these detainees face deportation or indefinite incarceration for simply seeking a better life with more opportunity, doing jobs like picking strawberries or tobacco or cleaning swimming pools, that few native-born Americans would even consider. These are secret prisons: no one is notified of one's arrest.

It costs $53.3 billion dollars to incarcerate the citizens of this disenfranchised country. In fact, the great state of California proposes to spend fully 10% of its budget on locking up its citizens. It costs up to $24,000,000 from arrest to execution for each prisoner sentenced to death. The population of America's prisons is overwhelmingly the poor, people of color. It is therefore even more striking that the current director of prisons in a black man, Charles E. Samuels, Jr. Orange is the new black.

1 9 3 4 COLLECTION

BOSS
HUGO BOSS

The director's job would suit Nazi Adolf Eichmann, himself director of the Reich's national network of gulags. Samuels, like Eichmann, directs a legal enterprise of soulless barbarity. Both bureaucrats merely meekly follow orders, what Hannah Arendt calls "the banality of evil." British philosopher George Bernard Shaw commented in 1907 that prisons are like smallpox, "the thoughtless wickedness with which we scatter sentences of imprisonment."

The Bureau of Prisons' principal war crime is the use of solitary confinement, often for decades. No natural light, no fresh air, no sun or moon or stars or sea – *for decades*. In a concrete tomb. As of 2012, over 81,600 U.S. prisoners were in solitary. However, it is rather unlikely Samuels will be tried for his war crimes, the inevitable conclusion to be executed by hanging. Samuels is just as surely a major organizer of the American prison holocaust, a crime against humanity.

Three past directors of the BoP, war criminals Harley Lappin, Michael Quinlan, and Norman Carlson, have moved on to executive positions with private prison corporations, Corrections Corporation of America and the GEO group. Each of these publicly-traded companies profits with revenues of nearly two billion dollars made from human suffering. Private prisons are fast becoming a profitable US export, beginning with Colombia, followed by Mexico, Honduras, and South Sudan.

The crime against humanity is even more irrevocable in the case of the death penalty, a mistake which can never be undone. The USA ranks fourth in total number of executions, behind China, Iraq, and Iran. There are 3,095 prisoners on death rows in the United States. America legally murdered 43 people in 2012, halved by happenstance from 98 in 1999.

In the four decades 1974-2014, 144 death row prisoners were exonerated and freed. During the Great War, 17 American COs were sentenced to death. More than 50% of executions in 2013 took place in Florida and Texas. Texas claims 38% of all U.S. executions; two percent of U.S. counties are responsible for all death sentences. Victims' families can watch …

Obama has the worst record of any president in history regarding clemency. He's issued all of 39 pardons and no – zero – commutations of sentence. We have impunity for the powerful and imprisonment for the powerless.

All prisoners are political prisoners.

In 2014, the United States no longer has a military draft. But the Selective Service Act is still in place and young men are still required to register five days after their 18th birthdays.

More than 20 million American men of draft age have violated the Selective Service Act of 1980 by failing to register at age 19, failing to complete registration details such as Social Security number, late registration, and failing to keep Selective Service informed of their current address until age 26, making any effort to raise a standing army in the event of war unfeasible.

All these acts are punishable by five years in prison with the fine now raised to $250,000. (Good luck with that!) The statute of limitations on SSA violations expires when one turns 31. Further social penalties for noncompliance are ineligibility for student loans, government jobs and naturalization as citizens.

I myself still counsel, aid, and abet these acts and conspire with others to do so.

There have been only 15 prosecutions so far and only nine prison sentences, between 35 days and five and a half months. Only a few outspoken activists were prosecuted. Government may have finally realized such a strategy could never be implemented.

As radical pacifist Roy Kepler observed about COs in prison, " … The biggest single mistake the government made was introducing us to each other. They helped build the pacifist network."

However, over 100 countries around the world still conscript young people for military service and only a handful of Western "democracies" permit conscientious objection. In recent years, I have been working for the recognition of conscientious objector status and an end to conscription in Thailand which has been my home for more than two decades.

11,700 U.S. high schools administer the Armed Services Vocational Battery Test, given to 11,700 secondary students in 2013 without any parental consent. America's "volunteer" military volunteers for three reasons. The young and poor and badly educated join the military because they are at a dead end with no opportunities for further education or jobs with a living wage. Military recruiters hoodwink the young and inexperienced with promises of basic paychecks and "education." "Drone pilot" might not be such a marketable skill after leaving the military! We now have the videogame generation fighting America's wars onscreen and in the electronic cockpits of America's police cars. The dehumanization was easy to accomplish: they think you can shoot someone, they just get up and you can get to the next level of play.

However, it appears such 'training' does not ineluctably produce effective, unquestioning killing machines. Studies of soldiers finds that 50% of recruits choose to shoot into the air or over the heads of the "enemy" and the other 50% are psychopaths. Obedience to orders seem not to be enough for voluntary consent to killing.

Young men also volunteer because of a constant brainwashing for patriotism which begins with a kid's first flag salute. Others join up for kicks or because it's a tradition in their military families. The volunteer army has resulted in thousands of AWOLs and desertions and refusal to fight. American veterans have no support network nor does government provide them effective medical care or housing. We have an army of damaged, traumatized and often homeless trained killers wandering our streets.

American anarchist Emma Goldman said it best, "If voting could change anything, it would be illegal." I've never voted. I've always found the choice is voting for the lesser of two evils and that just doesn't sound like democracy to me. The vote is gamed by politicians just as in an Atlantic City casino. The vote is rigged, the ballot box already stuffed. I wouldn't vote if they paid me!

There can be no better example of this than Obama's campaign under the slogans, "Hope" and "Change." As a black man, we hoped he was able to identify with and raise up to real equality poor people and people of color and provide fair play for all immigrants legal and illegal. Blacks in America learn humility from a billy-club or an attack dog. Obama missed those lessons.

As a Constitutional legal scholar, we hoped he would uphold those guarantees of our liberties enshrined in the Bill of Rights. As one of the youngest U.S. presidents, we hoped he would be open-minded, strong, and honest.

As a man, we hoped he would draw down America's senseless wars and military misadventures spearheaded from 1,400 US bases in more than 175 countries, including … at least 194 golf courses for troop morale, 2,874 holes. Secret operations by U.S. special forces have carried out secret military missions in 147 countries. They cost social programs $100 billion a year.

The U.S. provides some form of military assistance to 150 countries, more than 80% of the world. U.S. companies reap the spoils from suffering.

"Change you can believe in"??? Try Honest Abe: "You can fool all the people some of the time, and some of the people all the time, but you cannot fool all the people all the time." Change? For the worse: well over 600,000 Americans are homeless. 1,500,000 households and three million American children live on less than $2.00 a day. The World Bank calls this poverty in third-world countries; in the U.S., these figures have more than doubled since 1996.

Obama sends his daughters to a Quaker school but assassinations, torture, and kidnapping are now free America's stock in trade. Our nation is made of *schadenfreude*. History will not forgive you, Barry.

However, Obama has proved to be no commander-in-chief; we are, in fact, unsure just what secret powers are actually allowing him to command. All the American public got was the impunity occasioned by the arrogance of power. Obama's one campaign promise was to close the extraterritorial prison at Guantánamo, a stain on freedom since 2002. His legacy is to place American troops everywhere in the world ... forever. Since he was awarded the Nobel Peace Prize in 2009, the American president has started new wars on seven Muslim nations: Afghanistan, Iraq, Libya, Pakistan, Somalia, Syria, and Yemen. Hitler and Stalin killed 40 million – they were nominated, too!

Change? Why nothing's changed at all. Think the next one will be any better? Politicians are lying liars – it's part of the job description. Governments are flim-flam snake-oil smoke and mirrors. Bush Jr.'s and Obama's regimes are the best examples I know for refusing to pay war taxes or, for that matter, any taxes. And *Hillary's* up next?!?

The mass media is tasked with concealing the lie. Our society has devolved into one of *panem et circenses*, bread and circuses as in Ancient Rome, a diversion designed to nullify citizens' sense of civic duty. Corporate media propaganda distracts us from the killing with sports scores, celebrity gossip, and unreal reality TV.

Let's face facts: Nobody *wants* to be an activist! We all want to be sitting in front of the box watching reruns and drinking Blatz. But sometimes there are issues that so tweak your conscience that you simply can't walk by them – it feels exactly like new shoes that bite or the beginnings of a toothache, impossible to ignore. The results of such principled opposition are often pretty scary. That's what makes us even more stubborn. When you listen to the stories in this book with an open mind, it's the conscience saying, "Is *that* all you got?!?"

The root of civil disobedience is the word, 'obey'. Soldiers must be *taught* to kill, to blindly obey without thinking. These don't come naturally to sentient beings. Humans are the only species in nature with an intention to kill one another. Disobedience puts the thinking part first.

The point is, just one person can be a dynamic force for social change. It doesn't take a mass movement. It only requires listening to your conscience and picking your issues. Gandhi called such individuals *satygrahis*, people who demand the truth. We can *all* be Gandhi!

As a small example, Thailand, which drafts one-third of all its 18-year old young men into military servitude, except of course, for those who can pay tea-money, records 25,000 draft evaders. This is a quiet and growing resistance.

This brings us up to today. America conducts its wars in secret. As British Prime Minister David Lloyd George said in 1917: "If people knew the truth, the war would be stopped tomorrow. But of course they don't know and they can't know." It is illegal even to photograph the returning, flag-draped coffins of dead soldiers; dead soldiers' loved ones grieve in secret.

CCTVs, with facial recognition, and domestic drone surveillance follow all of us everywhere. Data harvesting throughout all electronic media makes privacy and anonymity impossible, except for a committed few. The homeland security state is responsible for the PATRIOT Act; anyone who questions or dissents is, by default, not patriotic.

As Cicero wrote, "Inter arma silent leges" [During war, the laws are silent.]

Yet we still resist. I am inspired by the Occupy and anti-globalization/anti-'free' trade movements, campaigns against America's drug wars and

for legalization of all drugs, Silk Road, the Darknet, Bitcoin, psychedelics researchers, prison abolitionists, Ships to Gaza to break Israel's blockade of Palestine, The Pirate Bay and other creative anti-copyright efforts, Sea Shepherds' defense of the oceans, drone and nuke protesters, anti-frack-ing activists, tar sands and pipeline blockades, the tree-sitters, the mining blockaders, the native activists of Idle No More and the Sacred Peace Walk, Ruckus Society, Raging Grannies, the weekly peace vigils, The Onion Router, the hacktivists of Anonymous, and WikiLeaks.

I applaud Sister Megan Rice, at 84 described as "the world's most hardcore bad-ass nun," who with a couple of youngsters (63 and 57) – the Transform Now Plowshares – walked past security to pour their own blood on nuclear weapons production at Oak Ridge, Tennessee in 2012. Thank you Megan, Greg, Michael.

The US calls its whistleblowers traitors. Daniel Ellsberg, Chelsea Manning, serving 30 years, Edward Snowden, in exile, and scores of others are evening the playing field between citizens and their governments at great personal sacrifice and gaining traction for resistance to oppression. We all need to honor them. Censorship and surveillance ensure conformity. Whistleblowers secure our freedoms.

I *love* Russia's kick-ass art collective, Pussy Riot, and Ukraine's activists in the FEMEN movement. And I am heartened by the growth of jury nullification; the juries who refused to convict runaway slaves are now saving drug war victims.

In particular, I am inspired by the grassroots Mexico's nonviolent guerrillas, the Ejército Zapatista de Liberación Nacional. The Maya in Chiapas, shook the power elite to its core in 1994 from behind their balaclavas. Traditional Mayan village life integrated with libertarian socialism, anarchism, and Marxism to produce a working radical democracy. "*Aquí manda el pueblo y el gobierno obedece.*" – "Here the people govern and the government obeys."

Zapatistas' grassroots village organizing for land reform, full gender equality, public health, anti-globalization and revolution schools have been effectively eroding the status quo with little fanfare for nearly two decades. The EZLN communiqués cut precisely to the heart of social change and how to effect it. Inspired by the Zapatistas, the Piqueteros are now spreading nonviolent grassroots revolution to Argentina.

Canada has deported American military deserters to certain U.S. prison sentences in recent years. However, on June 3, 2013, the Canadian Parliament voted to cease all deportation and removal proceedings against such military resisters and started a program to normalize their status by applying for permanent residence in Canada.

The Western world celebrates its military holidays as occasions for beer and hotdogs and fireworks. Even the American national anthem, "The Star-Spangled Banner," revels in its "bombs bursting in air." Americans are sure good at blowing shit up.

However, only peace activists truly remember the meaning of war and their fallen soldiers on Memorial Day, originally called Decoration Day to commemorate fallen soldiers of the U.S. Civil War, and Veterans Day or Remembrance Day, originally called Armistice Day in recognition of the end of World War I – never again! Just say no to war. Wear a *white* poppy! No more slaughter! *No pasaran!*

The advent of technology has made the world a very small place. There are some 300 billion webpages, growing by a billion *a week*. People everywhere are now able to have conversations with each other. This scares the shit out of every big government on the planet and so they grow ever more repressive.

This repression is like the Berlin Wall – it won't hold for long. We're taking back our privacy. All we need is a Declaration of Independence, to act on "Life, liberty and the pursuit of happiness." Spread the love around fearlessly. And governments will lose their iron grip on us. Nationalism poisons us all. And it's a dead horse.

If you have any doubt of this, you haven't listened to John Lennon singing "Imagine" enough yet. Time to play it again!

It's only fitting to end this essay remembering Norman Morrison, the young Quaker who, in 1965, brought his infant daughter, Emily, to the Pentagon where he immolated himself under the office windows of the Secretary of War. Anne Morrison Welch: "I think having Emily with him was a final and great comfort to Norman... [S]he was a powerful symbol of the children we were killing with our bombs and napalm--who didn't have parents to hold them in their arms." Mo Ri Xon is still a hero in Vietnam. The American War on Vietnam lasted ten years more; the last US soldiers were withdrawn on my birthday in 1975.

Only thing that we did right. Was the day we refused to fight.

We activists who take great personal risks for the good of all and end up imprisoned by the state also suffer for our children. It lifts a great burden to know that others care enough to look out for them. Our humble thanks to the Rosenberg Fund for Children.

Prison is only the beginning. Julian Assange's motto:

"Courage is contagious." Ω

Editor's note: Sadako Sasaki was two years old in Hiroshima a mile from the real Ground Zero. Japanese legend has it that anyone folding 1,000 paper origami cranes will be cured by the gods. Sadako only managed 644 before succumbing to leukæmia in 1955.

These are our real heroes…

☮☮☮

$\oplus \oplus \oplus$

Shaking, Quaking, and Spirit-Wrestling, Uncompromising Pacifists: Shakers and Doukhobors

CJ Hinke
(with thanks to Koozma J. Tarasoff)

E arly Christian theologians and mystics, some of whom were later canonized, Justin the Martyr, Tatian, Clement of Alexandria, Tertullian, Cyprian, Origens Adamantius, Ambrose, Irenaeus, Chrysostom, Jerome, and Cyril all declared that war could not be waged by Christians.

The earliest surviving record of conscientious objection to war occurred in 274 AD. Maximilianus, son of Fabius Victor, was executed by beheading in Thagaste, Numidia (now Tébessa, Algeria), for his refusal to be inducted into the Roman Army. He was 21 years, three months, and 18 days old. He was later canonized a martyr saint by the Roman Catholic Church; as he was executed on March 12, that day has become the saint's feast day. St. Maximilian is reputed to be buried at Carthage. An antiwar clergy group, the Order of Maximilian, has taken his name.

The traditional peace churches are considered to be the Quakers, the Mennonites, and the Brethren. However, the United Society of Believers in Christ's Second Appearing, or Shakers (for "Shaking Quakers"), were both pacifists and vegetarians during and after the U.S. War of Independence.

SHAKERS

S hakers appeared to draw their inspiration from the French 'prophets' called Camisards who fled France for England in 1706. Many Camisards had been shot, burned at the stake, or broken on the wheel as heretics against Catholicism following an edict against Protestantism in 1685.

The Protestant movements of Quakerism, Camisardism, and Shakerism were unique during these times in accepting female ministry finding men and women equal before the Fall from grace in the Garden of Eden.

THE SHAKERS HARVESTING THEIR FAMOUS HERBS

Shaker leader, Mother Ann Lee or Ann the Word, and several of her followers were arrested as British spies and sympathizers. Quakers were shaking at their meetings for worship a century earlier, trembling in the sight of God. Shakers accepted Mother Ann as the second coming of Christ.

Ann Lee's ideas were so revolutionary, she commented, "We are the people who turned the world upside down.";Shakers were certainly far too unconventional for the mainstream.

Shakers were routinely beaten, whipped, stoned and jailed. Mother Ann served terms in the 'Lunatick Ward' and the Manchester House of Correction. Both she and her father were sentenced to seven-year terms of transportation to the American colonies, arriving in New York harbor in 1774, nine Shakers in all, aboard the condemned schooner *Mariah*.

During the Civil War, President Lincoln exempted Shakers from military service and both Union and Confederate soldiers found their way to Shaker communities where they were cared for equally. Shaker principles refuted "bearing arms, paying fines, hiring substitutes, or rendering any equivalent for military services." Despite their pacifism, the New England Shaker communities grew poppies and produced most of America's opium which they supplied to the Union army along with horse blankets and other medicinal herbs..

Shaker Brother Frederick Evans was co-founder, with Quaker Alfred Love, of the Universal Peace Union in 1866. Shaker pacifism peaked with a Believer-sponsored Peace Convention at their community in Mount Lebanon, Maine.

Even the non-pacifist Mormons consider all their members to be serving missionaries. They deferred large numbers of young LDS men as divinity students during the Vietnam War. In Utah, the numbers proved too great for government's liking but young Mormons in other states had no difficulties getting such deferments, including 2008 and 2012 presidential candidate, Mitt Romney.

The churches of the Moravian Brethren, founded in the 1500s; Dunkard Brethren or Tunkers; Brethren: Plymouth Brethren and Gospel Hall; Inspirationalists; Anabaptist Amish; Hutterites; and Mennonites founded in the 1600s and having a current membership of a million and a half believers; Schwarzenau Brethren; Bruderhof communities, loosely affiliated with the Hutterites; American Schwenkfelders; Spiritual Christians in Old Russia: Doukhobors; Molokane; Prgyny; Subboniki; and others; Rogerenes, associated with Friends; Nazarenes; Charismatics; Seventh Day Adventists; Community of Christ; Jehovah's Witnesses; Unitarian Universalists; Pentecostals of nearly all sects; Christadelphians; Blessed Hope Abrahamics; Muggletonians; The Truth, really, unwilling to name themselves but often described as Two by Twos or Cooneyites; Worldwide Church of God; Catholic Workers and Pax Christi; Greek Orthodox; Anglicans; Methodists; Baptists; Lutherans; Presbyterians; Jews; Muslims; Sufis; Hopi Indians; Raëlists; and Rastafarians have all stood against war and defied military conscription.

Russian Doukhobors burning their arms, June 29, 1895.

DOUKHOBORS

The pacifist convictions of many of the dissident Protestant sects emerged in similar circumstances to those of the Doukhobors who officially arose in Russia in the 1700s. They were labelled as 'Spirit-Wrestlers' by the church hierarchy saying that these people wrestled against God. The dissidents adopted the title, saying "We wrestle with the spirit of truth and love that is within each of us as human beings'.

In fact, one principal Doukhobor hymn asks the question, "What manner of man art thou?" The simplistic answer is: "All governments are founded in violence" and "are maintained by armies, courts, prisons, and the police." Many Doukhobors believe that even national flags lead to violence.

The Kootenay Valley in British Columbia has long been home to many of the pacifist vegetarian Doukhobors, the Spirit-Wrestlers, formerly also known as the Christian Community of Universal Brotherhood. 7,500 of them were given sanctuary by Canada in 1899. Doukhobors were first exiled to Transcaucasia (including the present-day Georgian Republic, Azerbaijan and Armenia) from their origins in the Ukraine and southern Russia in 1826 for their refusal to fight in Tsar Nicholas I's army in the lead-up to war against the Ottomans in the 1840s.

Four thousand, nine hundred and ninety-two Doukhobors were exiled to what is now Georgia between 1841 and 1845. Georgia's Romanov Grand Duke ordered the Doukhobors into military service during the Russo-Turkish war in 1878 despite the fact that Peter the Great established liberty of conscience in Russia in 1717.

Romanov's alternative was forced conscription, looting Doukhobor villages, and raping their women. Doukhobors of that day compromised by transporting arms, ammunition, and other supplies to the soldiers using their own resources, sparing them further harassment.

Although Nicholas founded Kiev University, he was one of Russia's most autocratic and reactionary monarchs. His plans for consolidating the Russian Empire led to the Crimean War. "Bloody" Tsar Nicholas II was hardly better than his ancestor. He initiated military conscription in his lead-up to the Russo-Japanese war.

The number of Doukhobors in Transcaucasia reached some 20,000 by 1886. Following a law in the Caucasus requiring universal military service in 1887, Doukhobors reasserted their pacifist beliefs resulting in harsh reprisals.

Some Doukhobors submitted to the government's demands for military service. However, a single Doukhobor soldier, Matvei Vasilyevich Lebedev, on Easter Sunday in 1895 in what is now Azerbaijan bravely stated that the war and Christianity are incompatible, and laid down his rifle. Soon all 60 Doukhobor conscripts in locations throughout the Russian Empire followed his example; they were arrested, beaten, and tortured after returning their arms and refuting their oath of allegiance to the tsar. Many of them were put in solitary confinement. In total about 400, including protesting village elders, were jailed. Several were sentenced to death. Lebedev was sentenced to three years.

Doukhobors from ten villages in present-day Georgia, Azerbaijan, and six villages in Turkey continued their revival of conscience. At midnight on June 28-29, 1895, St. Peter's Day, the Russian dissident Doukhobors simultaneously set ablaze their government-issued firearms, pistols, and swords, kept for protection. Nearly 7,000 Doukhobors from their scattered settlements in the Caucasus participated in three gun bonfires. As they held a prayer, 200 government Cossacks in Bogdanovka attempted to put the fires out, unsuccessfully, and in the process trampled many attenders with their horses. However, the Doukhobors refused to bow to the governor by removing their hats.

At this point, one young Doukhobor, Feodor Tschakoff, returned his red military reserve documents to the governor followed by others. The governor ordered the Cossacks to gun down the dissidents, but an administrative chief, Prince Kospinsky, ordered them to hold their fire. However, the beatings continued and women were raped, including a girl of 16. Theft of food and household items was commonplace.

This simple act of rebellion was met with arrests and beatings by the Cossacks; 36 young men of military age received 100 lashes with thorny acacia rods and were sentenced to two years. Occupation of Doukhobor villages by Cossacks resulted in numerous deaths from starvation and exposure. The Doukhobor men were judged by military courts and sentenced to penal battalions under harsh conditions. In all, 300 Doukhobor men returned their military reserve documents.

Originally sentenced to death, three Doukhobor leaders were imprisoned in Siberia following the intercession of Count Lev N. Tolstoy and the Society of Friends (Quakers). The eldest was imprisoned in 1897 for inciting young men to refuse the draft. He was exiled to Siberia but died en route. His son Peter V. Verigin was exiled the same year for refusing to serve; he was not released until 1902.

Following prison sentences of two years, about 150 Doukhobors were exiled to Siberia. They walked 528 miles over the Urals to Aleksandrov prison, near Irkutsk, in 45 days. By the time they reached Alekseyevsky prison farm in Kirensk, they had walked 800 miles. Doukhobors were not the only religious dissidents exiled to Siberia; they joined far more numerous Skoptsy and Khylysts who were exiled for life rather than fixed terms.

The government agreed to allow "Tolstoy's people" to leave Russia on condition they never return, would finance their own passage, and that those Doukhobors in prison serve out their remaining terms. In 1899, some 7,427 Doukhobors fled Nicholas' draft for Canada (1,300 more arrived by 1930) to build a present-day population there of 40,000.

Their passage was paid for by Tolstoyans and Quakers, and supported by anarchist Peter Kropotkin and James Mavor, University of Toronto political economist. Tolstoy's efforts alone, along with his Quaker assistant, Aylmer Maude, raised half the emigration funds for which he is called *Dedushka* (Grandfather) to this day by Doukhobors. The Friends petitioned Queen Victoria to allow the migration of the Russian dissidents to

Doukhobors from the first ship to arrive at Halifax

Canada. Tolstoy wrote the Nobel Committee in Sweden, nominating the Doukhobors for the first Peace Prize.

Two Doukhobor immigrants were born at sea but six died of smallpox in the close quarters of shipboard on the last Doukhobor freighter, the *S.S. Lake Huron* after 28 days passage. On arrival in Canada, 2,275 Doukhobors were quarantined at the Grosse-Isle Quarantine Station in the St. Lawrence River. 43 Doukhobors were hospitalized with smallpox. Seven Doukhobors died at the hospital of various causes during their internment.

Canada amended the Dominion Military Act in 1898 to exempt Doukhobors from military service. In its nation-building, Canada needed strong backs to cultivate the soil, build railroads, and create settlements in order to prevent their U.S. neighbor to the south from occupying Canadian territory as it had with Mexico and Hawai'i. The new Russian migrants aptly filled this need with their strong work ethic and coöperative structures. (Doukhobor communities emulated the Russian coöperative *mir* system for decades.) In Canada, lacking horses in the first year, some women hitched themselves to a plough and cultivated the soil for the first crop of potatoes. Some men (who were not occupied with employment outside pulled their wagons themselves to the central town.

Some 100 Doukhobors migrated to the U.S. where they had no such military exemptions: sons and fathers were subject to the World War I draft.

Alfred Nobel, the Norwegian chemist who became immensely wealthy for his invention of modern dynamite and association with the Bofors armaments company, endowed the prize in his will to be awarded to those who "shall have done the most or the best work for fraternity between nations, for the abolition or reduction of standing armies and for the holding and promotion of peace congresses." Nicholas II, responsible for the exile of the Doukhobors, was also nominated in 1901. (Neither won.)

A radical sect of some 2,000 people, calling themselves the Sons of Freedom, broke away from the wider Doukhobor community in begin-

ning in 1902 to oppose Canadian private property, taxation, oaths of allegiance to the Crown (required later by the Homestead Act), the flag salute and singing the national anthem, government education, vital statistics records of birth, marriage, and death, and the census (starting in 1911). An anarchist mediator sent from England, Alexander Bodyansky, soon acted as their spokesman, stating, "...We wish to be citizens of all the world, and do not wish to register our children in the Royal Crown Government books..."

Their initial protest was nonviolent: the protesters released penned livestock, burned their own property, houses, possessions, and money to avoid paying taxes and marched naked, eschewing materialism, including undressing in court when they were arrested. They also "went from house to house, collecting horse-collars, harness, leather footwear, and fur coats," all of which they burned to renounce the slavery of domestic animals.

The protesters' first nude protest was a walk to Yorkton, Saskatchewan from their settlements there in 1903. 28 Freedomites were sentenced to three months in Regina jail. The Sons refused to coöperate in prison and were mocked, abused, and tortured by their jailers. Tolstoy himself began to speak in defense of those who had disrobed and wrote in a letter, "The nudes will come to the rescue..."

When land ownership issues became a problem in Saskatchewan, two-thirds of Doukhobors led by charismatic Peter V. Verigin moved to British Columbia beginning in 1908. One third, known as Independent Doukhobors, stayed behind and purchased their land.

Verigin's first skirmish in B.C. occurred when five were sentenced to three months in prison for failing to register a death in 1909. This caused

Doukhobors to remove their children from B.C. public schools. A young Community Doukhobor boy stated, "We've been attending school during the eleven weeks it was in session, but we no longer wish to go to school again, because the teacher, though very kind, belonged to the people who had put our friends in prison."

The government assessor was William Blakemore, Nelson publisher of the local newspaper *The Week,* and a B.C. Conservative Party stalwart. In his 1911 report, he recommended a moderate approach using compromise but also suggested that Doukhobor exemption from military service be canceled. Starting in May 1923 and in the months which followed, nine schools were torched by unknown arsonists.

In 1925, following the arson of three more schools resulting in the arrest of two protesters, 55 men and 49 women were sentenced to six months for indecent exposure. In 1929, protesters withdrew their children from school. This resulted in ten arrests which, in turn, led to a nude protest.

The Canadian Parliament responded by criminalizing public nudity in 1931. The test of this law came in May 1932 when a group of 117 community members were expelled for non-payment of dues. In protest, they went to Thrums, B.C. where they were arrested in April 1932 for marching nude along the highway. By the end of the month more parades took place, and 745 men, women, and children were arrested and housed in an improvised detention camp of tents and makeshift buildings within a barbed-wire enclosure near Nelson.

Smaller marches continued until the end of June, by which time a total of 600 adults were sentenced to the mandatory term of three years imprisonment. In addition, 365 children were taken into custody when their parents were arrested. These were the largest number of arrests in Canada.

Over 1,000 radical Doukhobor men, women, and children were arrested for nude protests. To accommodate this large number, the adults were sent to a specially-built penal colony created for them on Piers Island near Victoria where they were allowed to cook their own vegetarian meals, while their children were taken into group homes in Vancouver.

One elderly lady was reported to have said that she was not naked, she was married to Christ and had worn the bridal clothes. At the "Doukhobor penitentiary" the protesters adopted non-coöperation and passive resistance such as work stoppages and hunger strikes to prison demands such as wearing prison numbers or standing for count, including disrobing, particularly among the older women prisoners.

Although newborns were allowed to stay with their convict mothers for their first six months, there were some allegations that three babies died from neglect by prison staff. 357 protesters' children were placed in foster care, orphanages, industrial and residential schools for the duration of their parents' sentences. The prison camp was abandoned in 1935 following the release of all Piers Island prisoners.

Despite exemption from military conscription and service in Canada, military authorities before World War II sent orders for medical examinations to draft-age Douhobor men. Although officials stated this was a mere formality, there was great resentment in the Doukhobor community. Beginning in the 1940s, many of the most zealous of the protestors named themselves the Sons of Freedom. The Freedomites in particular were deeply opposed to government registration of any kind but especially military.

In 1940, the Canadian Parliament passed the National Resources Mobilization Act requiring universal registration as a prelude to military conscription, followed in 1943 by the War Services Act which required conscientious objectors to perform four months of alternative service in lieu of military training. Half of the Doukhobors were willing to go to jail rather than be conscripted, considering alternative service to be merely another form of militarist strategy, while the other half accepted the alternative service provisions under the War Measures Act. Many eligible Freedomites chose jail but most fled to the B.C. wilderness and escaped conscription.

About 12,000 Canadians sought alternative service as conscientious objectors. In contrast, in two conflicting reports, 92 Doukhobors were prosecuted in Alberta alone for failing to report and another 70 accepting civilian alternative service and another 90 in Saskatchewan. Another report has 56 Doukhobors in Saskatchewan and Alberta combined failing to report and only 37 accepting alternative service.

Most absolutist objectors were sentenced to four months in prison, the term of required alternative service. However, others received sentences of a year. Upon release, COs were still subject to further calls from National Selective Service and required to pay a monthly 'donation' to the Red Cross.

Due to such high rates of noncompliance, this effort was only carried out for a single season. In any case, these provisions provoked such resistance that no attempt was even made to enforce them in British Columbia.

One Doukhobor CO noted, "I have learned one great lesson: laws and promises, made by governments or man, cannot only be 'bent' but unashamedly broken or altered, and their reliance, as a result, to me parallels, in a sense, weather forecasting."

British Columbia's Social Credit government decided to enforce its Compulsory Education Act 1953. 46 Freedomite families in British Columbia refused to send their children to government public schools. After being arrested, they were confined in buildings which, 20 years earlier, had been used to intern Japanese-Canadians following the attack on Pearl Harbor. In mid-1950, 400 male Sons were sentenced to the British Columbia Penitentiary, Oakalla, near Vancouver, and the few Daughters women to Kingston Penitentiary in Ontario.

However, in 1960 the Federal government opened a new special prison at Agassiz, B.C., 60 miles east of Vancouver, near the city of Chilliwack, for the 400 Sons. Sons of Freedom lodged a complaint with the United Nations under the Convention on Genocide against the forcible removal of children from their families.

The Freedomites clearly stated their beliefs: that public education results in the militarization of youth, "schools are nurseries of militarism and capitalism," that schools offer nothing of practical value, and that they alienate children from their families and communities. Compulsory public education has largely proven these beliefs true. By 1959, the New Denver school was closed and 170 children returned to their released parents. The confrontations continued into at least the 1970s.

The last Freedomite radical, Mary Braun, 81, was not allowed matches under the terms of her release. However, in 2001, she burned down a portable college building which had been used to house Doukhobor children forcibly taken from their families. In October 2001, her Canadian judge called her an addicted terrorist when sentencing her to six years just after 9/11. Mary Braun suffered 15 convictions and more than 25 years in jail.

Canada never apologized to the Doukhobors for their mistreatment, including the kidnapping of more than 170 of their children into abusive residential schools, as politicians did to First Nations, only issuing a statement of regret in 2004. The Pete Seeger song, "The Doukhobor Do," chronicles the Sons' protests.

In all, some 1,000 Freedomites were jailed with sentences totaling 4,000 years. At least some of the instigators were police spies and *agents provocateurs*. This strategy cost B.C. taxpayers more than ten million dollars.

The Doukhobor mainstream considers the Sons of Freedom ceased to be Doukhobors when they participated in destruction of proper-

ty as protest. However, most Canadians might never have heard of the Doukhobors at all if the Freedomites had not hijacked crucial issues.

In 2011, a peace memorial named the Wall of Remembrance was dedicated in Winkler, Manitoba to recognize all 3.021 Manitoba conscientious objectors in World War II. Two Doukhobors from Benito, Manitoba have places on the Wall. One chose civilian alternative service and the other, Walter W. Latkin, rejected it. He went to prison and his CO draft status was revoked.

Between 1964 and 1984, the Doukhobors were principal organizers of anti-war and anti-arms demonstrations in Canada, including a 50,000-kilometer Peace and Friendship Caravan, from B.C. to the U.S.S.R. Sigurd Askevold, a Creston, B.C. high school teacher, Quaker, and lifelong pacifist, took three years and 2,000 letters to organize the trip.

The honorary sponsor was 1963 Nobel Peace Prize laureate Dr. Linus Pauling and the official sponsor, the Argenta Friends Meeting. The caravan was endorsed by the Quakers, the Doukhobors, the Mennonites, and the moderator of the United Church of Canada and included two Doukhobors, five Quakers, two Mennonites, and one Jew, all from the U.S. and Canada with one Norwegian. Traveling by car through 22 European countries, over three months, billeting in local homes, getting to know our "enemies."

Ironically, up to 30,000 communitarian Doukhobors remained in Russia, eschewing private property and materialism, after the Revolution: they proved to be the real "communists." Unfortunately, many Russian Doukhobors have assimilated into the greater society.

Yet, to this day, Doukhobors worldwide remember the first mass demonstration against the institution of militarism and war. In Canada, Doukhobors celebrate Peace Day, St. Peter's Day, June 29, the day remembered for the Burning of the Arms in 1895. Ω

☮☮☮

RUSSIAN SPIRITUAL CHRISTIANS IN AMERICA: The Innocence of Lambs

CJ Hinke
(with thanks to Andrei Conovaloff)

Радение «корабликом»

Patriarch Nikon of the Russian Orthodox Church introduced revisions to ritual in liturgy to correct discrepancies with Greek Orthodoxy in 1652. The revisions codified the church's relationship to government and forbade such practices as drunkenness among the clergy, while promoting education, and protection from tax collectors.

The church adopted Greek as the language of learning in this convocation called by Tsar Ivan IV and the patriarchs of Antioch, Alexandria, Jerusalem, and Constantinople examined nearly every aspect of church life and ritual. Some scholars contend the visiting patriarchs each received 20,000 *roubles* in gold and furs for their participation and, perhaps, for their agreement. Certainly, the changes standardizing the Eastern rite had far-reaching political and economic benefits for the state. By the end of the 19th century, these practices became known as 'new rite'.

Old Ritualists (sometimes referred to as Old Believers), who preserved Church Slavonic rites and language, venerated *typikons*, and practiced congregational song as well as liturgical song sung by antiphonal choirs, schismatized with the church over this issue in 1666 and 1667, rejecting the changes. Their holidays originated from the *Subbotniki*, non-Jewish Russians who adapted them from the Old Testament holidays and those of Jews in Old Russia. The Subbotniki had a close relationship with the Old Ritualists despite religious differences and some even followed the Molokans when they emigrated to Los Angeles in 1910.

Books were also venerated, making for a largely literate population, even though they wrote on birch bark! The first printed bible, the Ostrog Bible was made in 1580 with corrections in 1581, translated from the Greek Septuagint into Old Church Slavonic and uses the Cyrillic alphabet. The Ostrog was patronized by Prince Konstantin Ostrozhskiy during the reign of Ivan the Terrible and was the first bible in the entire Eastern Orthodox sphere. An Orthodox bible in Greek did not appear until 1821 and even that was printed in Moscow!

The Old Ritualist sects preserved councils called sobor and formed the basis for evangelical democracy in selection of leadership and decision-making, from the wider issues to the most trivial. The separation of the Russian and Greek orthodox branches was decided by a sobor over joining the Roman church.

The dissidents' books and rites were anathematized in a 1666 synod. They began to be persecuted over trivial rituals and all civil rights were removed. In 1682, some of the most vocal deniers were executed as heretics. In 1685, torture was added to the persecutions which included kidnapping, banishment, and death.

The Old Ritualists received military exemption from the tsar in exchange for colonizing new territories, expanding the reach of empire.

Those Old Ritualists who did not flee Russia at this time grew impregnable by force of numbers in their local areas. By 1910, Old Ritualists constituted about 25% of Russian Orthodox faithful, up to a present-day 10 million. Most were scattered by the pogroms following the Russian Revolution in 1917. However, it was not until 1971 that the Moscow Patriarchate revoked the anathemas set in the 17th century.

The pacifist sect customarily known as Molokans after it was named in 1765, is more properly known as one variety of Spiritual Christians and was founded by Simyon Uklein. The Biblical commandment, "Thou shalt not kill" is central to Molokan belief and they were intensively persecuted for their pacifism and refusal of military service.

Molokans were decreed religious freedom by Tsar Alexander in 1805. That freedom, however, did not mean acceptance.

Molokans observed nearly 200 fasting days, taking only milk, including the Great Fast during Lent. Molokan means 'milk-drinker' in Russian. Russian Orthodox faithful abstain from milk during Lent.

The *Pryguny* (Jumpers') were founded about 1833 in South Ukraine. Their worship service involves raising hands, prancing, skipping, and leaping as the innocent lambs and calves, and prophesying. One congregation of this sect was led by Maksim Rudomyotkin in 1854 in what is now Armenia. Rodomyotkin referred to his sect as "the new Israel," "jumpers and leapers," and "the new Zion"; his followers were variously referred to as *Maksimisty, noviy Israil, pryguny, skakuny,* and *noviy sion,* in English, as Maksimists.

Tsar Peter I abolished the patriarchate in 1721 and appointed the Eastern Church's bishops. In 1855, Rudomyotkin was arrested for his declaration against czarism and calling for its abolition. He was sentenced to life imprisonment, beaten and tortured for 22 years until his death in 1877. During his imprisonment, Rudomyotkin's niece smuggled out his writings on the paper wrappings for tea, 4 x 3½ inches in size. These writings were first compiled by Valov and Kobseff in Arizona in 1915. Heated competition produced two more versions which were rejected prior to a fourth version edited by Ivan Samarin in 1928, called *Book of the Sun, Spirit, and Life.* Today, only a few *Dukh-i-shizniki* believe Rudomyotkin never died and are awaiting his return to lead them to Mount Ararat.

Like the Doukhobors, Molokans also come from the dissident Central *ikonobortsy*, the iconoclasts.

Pryguny also emigrated to Baja California Norte in Mexico in 1905 where they are still called los Rusos despite being heavily intermarried into the local community which now includes *mestizo* children from marriages with local Indians and other races. The *Prygun* immigrants were given asylum and land grants by dictator Porfirio Diaz who was deposed by the Mexican Revolution just a year later. These sturdy Russian farmers started out growing table grapes but by the 1930s some became expert wine growers, on Highway 3, *La Ruta del Vino,* from Ensenada to Tecate. The valley produces 90% of Mexican wines and one man whose grandparents were *Prygun* settlers still produces very fine wines in Mexico, notably the Bodegas Valle de Guadalupe-Vinos de Bibayoff winery, on Rancho Toros Pintos. Vinos de Bibayoff won gold medals for its wines in 2008 and 2009. Electricity didn't arrive in the valley until 1949. From an original 104 families, 800 *Pryguny*, around 100 remain. Exemption from military conscription does not appear to have presented moral issues to the immigrants.

Although a 1906 effort of 110 *Pryguny, Maksimisty,* and Molokane to build a settlement in Hawai'i failed as did an attempt to emigrate from the

U.S. to establish colonies in Uruguay and Brazil, by 1940 most Spiritual Christian immigrants from Russia settled in California, Arizona, Oregon and Baja California. "While *Maksimisti* failed to return to Mt. Ararat, *Klubnikinisty* failed to find a land of refuge, and *Novyi izrail'* failed to move to Israël. By default their promised land transformed into a kingdom in the city." – Los Angeles.

Most Pryguny are settled in Los Angeles and Baja; most Molokane in San Francisco and Oregon. About one-third of Spiritual Christian Doukhobors from Russia moved to Canada to settle. 32 emigrated to Australia and were scattered widely. Within such a small community, endogamous marriages proved problematical and there was intermarriage among the various Spiritual Christian faiths. However, since the 1980s, *Dukh-i-zhizniki* have had little official contact with any outside faiths.

Some remain as collective farms in Ivanovka, Azerbaijan. At least 10,000 in the former U.S.S.R. identify with the original Spiritual Christian Molokan faith, fewer for *Dukh-i-zhizniki* and *Prygun* faiths. However, their diaspora is thinly-populated and has an increasingly difficult time maintaining its distinct identity.

Today, only one congregation of Molokane in central Stavropol uses Old Slavonic during service, and only for part of their service, because only a few members learned how to read it. Spiritual Christian historian Andrei Conovaloff visited this meeting house and interviewed the presbyter. Today Molokane have no direct relationship with Old Ritualists. However, some Molokan-Subbotniki moved to the vicinity of the Molokan community in Stavropol. In central Oregon, several *Dukh-i-zhizniki* are friendly with neighboring Old Ritualists, who divided into 12 different confessions in close proximity, some churches less than 100 feet from one another.

All Russians were subject to attack, just as all blacks were subject to discrimination. Spiritual Christians in America became targets of zealous, xenophobic police efforts using the 1903 Anarchist Exclusion Act, Naturalization Act of 1906, 1907-1911 Dillingham Commission, 1913 California Alien Land Act, Immigration Act and Espionage Act of 1917, 1917-1919 Committee on Public Information, Immigration Act and Sedition Act of 1918, 1918 'Slacker' Raids, Overman Committee1918-1919, 1919 California Criminal Syndicalism Act and Red Flag Law, 1919-1920 First Red Scare and Palmer Raids, 19th Amendment 1920, 1920-1933 Prohibition, 1920 second California Alien Land Act, 1921 Emergency Quota Act, Immigration Act of 1924, 1930s "Red Squad" of the Los Angeles Police Department, 1947-1991 Cold War.

This unjustified harassment was exacerbated as the *Pryguny* sect had some collaboration with the Doukhobor splinter group of zealots [*svobodniki*] later to be translated as Sons of Freedom. The Freedomites petitioned to resettle in the U.S. in 1905, Hawai'i in 1906, and return to Russia in 1957.

Community Doukhobors were confused by the Americans with the zealots when they proposed communes with the American Molokane in Hawai'i in 1906, Los Angeles in 1908, Santa Barbara in 1910, Oregon in 1923, and Mexico from 1923 to 1938. *Pryguny* were investigated, reported in the news, and some arrested for illegal activity (bride selling [in Russia, a dowry of two dairy cows, in America, $200-500]), not registering marriages, disturbing the peace with loud ecstatic jumping to exhaustion, unusually long funerals, declaring the arrival of the end of the world and fleeing to the mountains, semi-nude children in public, refusing to allow children to attend school, exorcisms, failed resurrections, and more.

Prior to the U.S. entry into World War II, Molokan immigrants were registered and fingerprinted under the Alien Registration Act of 1940. This law was later used to intern both Japanese- and German-Americans for the duration of the war. All Spiritual Christian congregations in Southern California were transforming into *Dukh-i-zhizniki* after 1928 and most Molokane left their heritage faiths. Some *Dukh-izhizniki* refuse to serve on juries, file lawsuits, go to court, take oaths, or hold driver's licenses, regarding license photos as 'graven images' prohibited in the Bible. Before passage of the Homeland Security Act of 2002, 15 states allowed exemption for religious objection to photos on driver's licenses. Currently, such freedom of religion is universally denied in the United States.

The 65th U.S. Congress passed the Selective Service Act of 1917 requiring registration of young men between the ages of 21 and 31 for military conscription. *Pryguny* translator John Kulikoff went to jail in Arizona in 1917 along with 33 other young men for organizing resistance against draft registration. Due to such persecution, conscientious objectors changed their identity each generation. In 1917, during World War I, a notarized resolution and petition listed 259 "Russian Sectarians, Spiritual Christians – Jumpers" in Los Angeles who registered as required by law for the draft.

At least one or more member of each Spiritual Christian family was within that age bracket. This led to a great feeling of unity in the community, leading to meetings and spiritual revival, especially among draft-age men. This was a traditional community and the young men agreed to follow in their elders' decision.

Although the draft law provided for conscientious objection from recognized religious sects, it also stated, "but no person so exempted shall be exempted from service in any capacity that the President shall declare to be non-combatant." Russian Spiritual Christians were all pacifists but were divided by separate creeds, dogma, liturgy, and ritual. War fever was running high so the brotherhood unanimously decided to petition President Wilson for exemption from military service. The petition summarized *Pryguny* history and their emigration from Russia due to demands for military service. They asked the president to shield the approximately 4,000 Russian Christians from prosecution for noncompliance.

On arrival in Washington, the delegates prevailed upon the Russian Embassy to help establish their claim as historic objectors to military service. The Army, however, saw this as a misunderstanding: draft registration did not necessarily result in military service and was, in fact, a way of notifying the authorities of their *bona-fide* objection. The delegation mistakenly assumed Russian Spiritual Christians had been granted exemption by the U.S. Their young men registered.

Russian Spiritual Christians in the U.S. were encouraged to buy war bonds to finance the war through their employers. However, their pacifist opposition to this effort could not be articulated well enough by the Russians so they were seen as "slackers" in the war effort. Some Spiritual Christians donated to the Red Cross in lieu of war bond purchase which satisfied the Liberty Loan Committee.

Although the Spiritual Christians were exempt from military service as "aliens" in the United States, they were still required to register for conscription. In Arizona, the Russian colony of nearly 1,000, decided that draft registration was tantamount to receiving the "mark of the beast" prophesied in Revelations. 34 *Maksimisti* and *Pryguny* young men, supported by the brotherhood, notified draft officials they would not comply with the law. The community organized demonstrations in Phoenix and Glendale. On registration day, the 34 were arrested, convicted, and sentenced to one year in the Yavapai County Jail in Prescott, Arizona.

After serving ten months of their sentences, 28 of the 34 agreed to register and were released to their farms and families. The remaining six absolutists

Fort Riley COs, 1919

were summarily inducted into the army as enlisted soldiers and sent to Fort Hauchucha in Tucson. Later they were transferred to the the Disciplinary Barracks in Fort Riley, Kansas, which already housed many and varied conscientious objectors. Upon arrival at Fort Hauchucha, they were ordered to put on the military uniform. For their constant refusal they were sprayed with a high-pressure fire hose to unconsciousness, at times hand-cuffed to their cell doors in such a position that they either had to stand on their toes or hang by their wrists for an hour, repeating the process after a short rest.

The bulk of COs were detained at Fort Riley because the War Department did not consider defining non-combatant service a priority to the war effort. Eventually, President Wilson signed executive order #28 defining non-combatant service as Army service in:

1. Medical Corps on the battlefield or in the rear area.

2. Quartermaster Corps such as stevedore companies, the laundry service, labor companies, etc.

3. Engineering service, in the front or in the rear such as railroad construction and operation, road building, preparation of rear line fortifications, docks, wharves, etc.

Some COs were willing to accept these terms. However, the six from Arizona along with other absolutists in the camp were constantly harassed to break their resistance to wearing the uniform or to army discipline.

The War Department remained unaware of these "absolutists." A 1918 Board of Inquiry was established in the War Department " to inquire into and determine the sincerity of conscientious objectors." The Board set out to examine and interview every conscientious objector throughout the county.

The Board had the option of assigning a CO to a farm or industry or to the Friends Reconstruction Unit in France. The Board also had the option of forcing a CO into the Army. Meanwhile, the harsh camp discipline continued unabated. The Board found the Spiritual Christians, not because of their number, but because of their novelty, to be "among the most perplexing cases of what the War Department has had to deal."

The Board was told the Spiritual Christians were on a hunger strike, absolutely refusing to take food or drink, and were in the base hospital being force-fed. He was asked by the camp authorities how, in his opinion, they were to be treated. The Board made the suggestion to place food and water within their easy reach.

"The Board was informed by one of the six who spoke English [Ivan W. Kulikoff] that they did not wish to embarrass the government in any way. Their reason for the strike was that they were vegetarians and their desire was that they be allowed to prepare their own food in their own way. He was told that they would not take part in the war in any way and would not accept farm furlough as that too was under military control. When Major [Walter] Kellogg informed them that such refusal would undoubtedly subject them to further imprisonment, they replied that they would rather be shot to death than participate in war." the Major found, "They very probably were good fathers and model husbands whose good citizenship could hardly be questioned until they and their exotic religion were brought plumb against the grim realities of war."

All the absolutists refused farm furlough. They suffered military courts-martial resulting in J. D. Conovaloff and F. F. Wren getting sentences of 25 years; A. F. Shubin, Ivan W. Kulikoff, Ivan W. Sussoyeff and Morris E. Shubin 15 years, to be served in the U.S. military prison in Leavenworth, Kansas. However, in April 1919 all draft prisoners were subjected to Presidential amnesty and release.

Of an estimated 4,000, only three members took part in the war and these volunteered for fun. Those who registered for the draft were legally exempt as aliens, having declared themselves in their questionnaires not only as objectors to military service on religious grounds but also as "resident aliens who had not declared their intention to become citizens of the United States"; their classification was 5-F. This was considered to be a better classification than 1-O as COs because this classification was required to serve in as non-combatants.

One *Prygun*, M.J. Bolotin, however, had begun the process to claim U.S. nationality. His sons were unable to claim exemption as aliens. His eldest son's refusal led to a court-martial at Fort McArthur in San Pedro, California where he was sentenced to 12 years. The 34 Arizona boys, too ,would have been eligible for classification as aliens.

During World War II, more than 740 "Russian Molokans" (Spiritual Christians) enlisted in the military, although only about 172 or 23% were Molokane from San Francisco. 76 were recorded in Civilian Pubic Service, of which only one was Russian Christian from San Francisco. 13 were absolutist COs who chose prosecution, but three of those eventually enlisted. In the records of the Swarthmore College Peace Collection, only one, Pete A. Wren, is shown as "Young Russian Christian Spiritual Jumpers [Molokan]." After World War II, 76 professed *Dukh-i-zhiznik* COs refused to pay half of their fees of $30 a month for CPS camp. To avoid jail, they cheated and scammed the National Service Board of Conscientious Objectors and three peace churches for $17,024.

In 1957, Nick Allen Klubnikin, failed to appeal his draft status in US 9th District Court of Appeals as "member of a sect called Molokan Spiritual Jumpers" (227 F.2d 87 (1955), Case No. 14628). Klubnikin was granted full CO status but wanted to take care of his widowed mother and pregnant wife. Accordingly, he refused to perform civilian service. The court ruled that his pay for service would allow him to support his wife and mother without undue hardship. However, even when offered higher paying civilian work, Klubnikin offered no interest.

No *Dukh-i-zhizniki* went to jail over conscription during the U.S. wars on Korea or Vietnam. A majority of young men filed as conscientious objectors.

On September 25, 2001, the U.S. Selective Service System received a letter from a Los Angeles *Dukh-i-zhizniki* asking to be recognized as "Russian Molokan Christian Spiritual Jumpers," which is the only single use of the term "Jumpers" in "The Young Molokan and Military Service," compared to use of "Molokan" 41 times. (Letter taken off-line in 2012.)

Presently there are about 20,000 people who "ethnically identify themselves as Russian Spiritual Christians. There are also approximately 200 Spiritual Christian meeting houses, 150 of them in Russia and Azerbaijan. Approximately 25,000 Russian Spiritual Christians reside in the United States, of which only about 5,000 "ethnically identify" with the faith; most of whom reside in California, Arizona, Oregon, Washington, Montana, and Wyoming. Settlement of Molokans in southern Alaska during the 1960s was well documented. Molokans are said to be numerous in Canada; over 1,000 reside in the province of British Columbia and hundreds more in Alberta with their traditional communal lifestyle remaining intact.

Significant numbers of Russian Spiritual Christians live in Armenia, Azerbaijan, Kazakhstan, Ukraine and throughout Russia. To a lesser extent, Spiritual Christians can also be found in Mexico, Brazil, Argentina, Uruguay, Australia, Indonesia, Malaysia, Mongolia, and in northwest China. In 1995, the Smithsonian Folklife Festival featured Russian Spiritual Christians as one of their peoples. Ω

☮☮☮

Russia's Jewish Draft Pogroms

CJ Hinke

Shtetl life in the Pale

Of course, Spiritual Christians were not the only religious to suffer under Tsar Nicholas' draft pogroms. Jews were already forced by imperial decree to live in provinces called the Pale of Settlement established by Russian Empress Catherine the Great in 1791. The 'pale' or line of demarcation (from the Latin *palus*, meaning boundary stake or fencepost) includes much of present-day Lithuania, Belarus, Poland, Moldova, and Ukraine, extending to the western Russian border with Germany, Austria, and Hungary. Jews were literally not allowed 'beyond the Pale'. The Pale was described by author Mark Frutkin, himself a descendant of a Russian Jewish draft émigré, as an "economic Siberia." Four million of the world's 7.7 million Jews lived in the confines of the Pale and not permitted to live in the cities.

In the reign of Tsar Nicholas I (1925-1855), Jews were forced to supply four times the recruits of other Russians. As detailed by author

Frutkin, "Half the children, taken from their parents and raised in barracks, died before they reached 18," the age to formally join a regiment. In the effort to convert them to Christianity, at St. Petersburg, conscripts were forced into hot baths and then icy holes in the frozen rivers; many died of drowning or heart failure. Frutkin: "…at a place called Orel, on a bitter winter night, more than a hundred little boys were taken to town on sledges, but on arrival they were found frozen to death."

Self-mutilation was a common way to attempt draft evasion, including year-long fasts. Frutkin: "'Experts' were hired to render boys unfit for service by puncturing their eardrums, temporarily paralyzing hands, or even removing an eye." Punishment was swiftly visited on the families of those found unfit; they had to provide two sons instead of one.

From 1820 to 1870, only 7,500 Russian Jews emigrated to the United States. "In the next ten years (1871-80), 40,000 emigrated. From 1881 to 1890, the number more than tripled to 135,000." From 1890 to 1910, there were more than a million Jewish émigrés to America. During this period, Jews of the Pale were restricted from living closer than "fifty *versts* (about 33 miles)" from Russia's western borders to prevent them disappearing abroad.

Small easements were enacted during the brief reign of Tsar Alexander II (1855-1881). The serfs were freed from bondage and the draft term was reduced to 15 years from 25 and eventually five years. Alexander was assassinated and pogroms against the Jews were reinstituted by Tsar Alexander III (1881-1894).

During the reign of Tsar Nicholas II (1894-1917), the concentration of Jews in the Pale made them easy targets for pogroms and anti-Semitic riots by the majority Russian population. Thousands of Jews were killed by ethnic cleansing in the Pale, their houses destroyed. The 1964 musical play and 1971 film, *Fiddler on the Roof,* was set in the Pale in 1905, based on stories by Sholem Aleichem, and depicts a Jewish life of deepest poverty. By imperial decree, any Jew found not carrying valid papers, was press-ganged into the Tsar's army; informers were rewarded with exemption from recruitment.

The intention of the Tsar's draft was to break young Jews from their religion. However, Jewish social services in the Pale provided kosher food to Jewish conscripts. Each village was required to supply young men from the ages of eight to 25 for 25 years of military service.

Nicholas II's reign of cruel injustice did not end well for him. He was forced to abdicate in 1917 and executed by the Russian Revolution in 1918. The tsar and tsarina, three of their daughters and their son were killed near Sverdlovsk (Yekaterinburg) along with four non-family members. They were all named martyr-saints by the Russian Orthodox Church in 1981 and confirmed in 2000. Ω

☮☮☮

WORLD WAR I:
The Conscientious Objector and the Military Prison

☮ ☮ ☮

MY PRISON CREED

Eugene V. Debs (1855-1926)

(Editor's Note. Eugene Victor Debs was born in Terre Haute, Indiana on November 5, 1855. He became a coalman for the railroad and became active in the Brotherhood of Locomotive Firemen. He led walkouts that twice were responsible for his imprisonment on federal contempt of court sentences as a leader in the union.

Debs ran three times on the Socialist Party ticket for President and then was nominated as a Congressional candidate in Indiana from prison. In 1920, he became the first man to be nominated for President from a Federal prison cell, this time serving a ten-year sentence for violating the Espionage Act of 1917 by advising young men not to join in World War I.

"The master class has always declared the wars; the subject class has always fought the battles. The master class has had all to gain and nothing to lose, while the subject class has had nothing to gain and all to lose – especially their lives."

Debs was arrested just fourteen days after delivering this speech to an enthusiastic Canton, Ohio audience on June 16, 1918. When accused of his crime before the jury, he said, "I admit it. I am proud to admit it." Ω)

> *While there is a lower class I am in it;*
> *While there is a criminal element I am of it;*
> *While there's a soul in prison I am not free.*
> — Eugene Victor Debs, *Walls and Bars*

The sentence of the law is executed with all the solemnity and ceremony of a funeral, and the culprit, with head bowed either from grief or rage, is led from the courtroom between two feelingless factotums to begin his punishment – justice is served, society is avenged, and all is well once more. But is it? Not so fast!

The victim has already suffered every torment and feels the keenest sense of shame and humiliation, but this does not count in the matter of atonement. He goes back to jail until the sheriff can arrange to take him to the "pen."

The fateful day arrives! He is manacled, sometimes hand and foot, and put on a train where everyone learns he is a convict and secretly mocks him.

He is delivered, signed for, sheds his name and receives a number. He is no longer a man but a thing. He has ceased to be a human being. He is stripped naked under the clubs of guards who hurl insults and epithets at him about his body. He is put into cheap prison garb that in itself proclaims the status to which he has been reduced. He is examined in a rude and perfunctory way by the physician's assistant, who himself may be a convict. He is made to sign a document stating where his body is to be shipped in case of death. He is handled as if he were a bag of malt as he goes through the Bertillon system. Note is taken and a record made of every mark upon his body. All his personal effects are taken from him. These are supposed to be shipped back to his home, if he has one, and if he has money to pay the charges. The chances are, however, his effects will be stolen before they leave the prison, if they have any value.

The introduction a prisoner receives and the way he is put through the initial stages of his sentence are not calculated to impress him with the fact that a prison is a human institution. The rigorous treatment he receives will not convince him that he had been placed there to redeem him from his transgressions and reclaim him as a human being. On the contrary, the process embitters him against all who had any part in his plight, estranges him from whatever kindly influences that may still be operating in his behalf, and alienates him from society which, in the first and final analysis, is responsible for him, and, perhaps in the end must answer to him.

But there was no real rejoicing from the influential and powerful side of our national life until June, 1918, when I was arrested by Department of Justice agents in Cleveland for a speech that I had delivered in Canton, Ohio. I was taken to the Cuyahoga County Jail, and when the inmates heard that 1 was in prison with them there was a mild to-do about it, and they congratulated me through their cells. A deputy observed the fraternity that had sprung up, and I was removed to a more remote corner. Just after I retired that Sunday midnight I heard a voice calling my name through a small aperture and inquiring if I were asleep. I replied no.

"Well, you've been nominated for Congress from the Fifth District in Indiana. Good luck to you!" he said.

When a jury in the federal court in Cleveland found me guilty of violating the Espionage Law, through a speech delivered in Canton on June 16, 1918, Judge Westenhaver sentenced me to serve ten years in the West Virginia State Penitentiary, at Moundsville. This prison had entered into an agreement with the government to receive and hold federal prisoners for the sum of forty cents per day per prisoner. On June 2, 1919, the State Board of Control wrote a letter to the Federal Superintendent of Prisons complaining that my presence had cost the state $500 a month for two extra guards and requested that the government send more federal prisoners to Moundsville to meet this expense. The government could not see its way clear to do this, since it was claimed that there was plenty of room at Atlanta, and if, as the State Board of Control averred, I was a liability rather than an asset to the State, the government would transfer me to its own federal prison at Atlanta, which it did on June 13, 1919, exactly two months after the date on which I began to serve my ten years imprisonment – a sentence which was commuted by President Warren Harding on Christmas day, 1922.

Strict secrecy was enjoined by the government as to my removal, and especially as to the train upon which I was to take my departure. I have since been informed that before I left Moundsville the government officials commanded the two telegraph offices in Wheeling to accept no messages from reporters or other persons about my leaving West Virginia prison until the next morning. In spite of this attempt to effect profound secrecy as to my movements, a leak occurred somehow, for 1 was interviewed by a reporter the same day at Cincinnati en route to the south.

It appears that I was too near the coal fields in West Virginia, in which I had previously spent considerable time organizing the miners who were greatly agitated over my imprisonment. At one mass meeting at Charleston, which was attended by several thousand miners and other citizens, resolutions were passed threatening a march on Moundsville if I was not released.

Debs' prison cell

Warden Terrell gave me a friendly introduction to U.S. Marshal Smith, who with his three deputies, took me in charge on arrival at Wheeling, whither the warden and his son had taken me in their automobile. The marshal and his deputies treated me with consideration over the entire journey. The marshal bore a letter from Warden Terrell to Warden Fred G. Zerbst at Atlanta, commending me on the basis of my prison record.

Shortly after the noon hour on the following day, June 14, we arrived in Atlanta. The marshal called for a taxicab.

"Where do you want to go?" asked the chauffeur.

"Take us to your best penitentiary," replied the marshal. Less than half an hour later we were landed at the gates of my new home, and I was delivered, signed for, and the marshal and his deputies took their departure, wishing me a pleasant stay.

In the massive main corridor in which I found myself I had my first view and received my first impression of the sinister institution known as the U.S. Penitentiary at Atlanta. It seemed to me like a vast sepulchre in which the living dead had been sequestered by society. Through the steel gate at the end of the corridor I could see human forms hurrying back and forth under the watchful eyes of guards with clubs, and they appeared to me with all the uncanniness of spectral shapes in the infernal regions. I was perfectly calm and self-possessed for I had made up my mind from the beginning that whatever my prison experience might be I should face it without fear or regret.

I told Mr. Zerbst that the prison as an institution and I were deadly enemies, but that within the walls I should observe the rules and get along without trouble. I gave him to understand that I neither desired, expected, nor would I accept any privileges or favors that were denied to other prisoners. All I asked was that I be treated the same as the rest, neither better nor worse. The warden assured me that on that basis I would have no cause for complaint.

It may or may not, according to the point of view, be an enviable distinction to be nominated for the high office of President of the United States while in the garb of a felon and serving a term as such in one of its penitentiaries.

I am reminded of an editorial paragraph appearing in one of the eastern dailies at the time of my imprisonment at Moundsville which read something like this: "Debs started for the White House, but he only got as far as the federal prison." I was not in the least perturbed by this comment for I knew in advance that my course led, not to the presidential mansion, but through the prison gates. I had already been the candidate of the socialist party in four previous campaigns for President – 1900, 1904, 1908, and 1912.

Having had almost a million votes cast for me in the latter campaign and as many more that were not counted, and feeling that I had been more than sufficiently honored, I concluded not to be a presidential candidate again, and in the national political contest of 1916 I did not permit the use of my name in the nominations. During the year previous to the convention in 1920 many of the party papers carried the slogan, "From the Prison to the White House," and I was told by many of my visitors and correspondents that I would be the choice of the rank and file of the party for President.

Next in order was the visit to the prison of the committee on notification, the department at Washington having granted the necessary permission for such a committee to call upon me. In due time the committee arrived, consisting of both men and women, and the ceremony occurred in the warden's office, Mr. Zerbst and other officials of the institution being interested spectators.

The nomination address was in the nature of a most complimentary tribute to which I responded in an expression of my thanks and appreciation. The occasion was altogether as impressive as it was unique and created a lively interest throughout the prison.

To have a presidential candidate in their midst was a thing the nearly three thousand prisoners had never experienced before and they seemed to feel a thrill of pride as if they, too, shared in whatever distinction was bestowed upon me, which indeed they did, for I can say in all sincerity that there is among men in prison a fellow-feeling that in some respects is less selfish and more refined and generous than that which commonly prevails in the outer world.

Never in all of my experience as a presidential candidate had I been so deeply touched and so profoundly impressed by the congratulations of friends as I was by those I received that day and in the days that followed from the inmates of the Atlanta federal prison.

The hands, black and white, were extended to me from the cells and and from all directions, while faces beamed with a warmth and sincerity that found expression from eager lips.

One of the most popular comments heard in the course of the prison campaign was that I was certain to sweep through every precinct in the penitentiary, and that neither Mr. Harding nor Mr. Cox, my political adversaries, would receive a single prison vote.

Strange as it may appear, I received but two or three uncomplimentary letters during the entire campaign. The mail of nearly every candidate for an important office is burdened during his campaign with all sorts of insulting and threatening letters. One of my correspondents said that I should be shot, and the other wrote that I was at last where I belonged, and he hoped I would not leave there alive; he concluded with the hope that the warden would have my naked back lashed until it bled every day I was there. This benevolent writer also advised me in the same letter that he had written to the warden to the same effect.

Election night is vividly recalled as a pleasant and interesting special occasion. Soon after the supper hour I was sent for and received by the deputy warden who conducted me to the warden's office to hear the returns that were being received by telephone and in the form of special messages. The warden and his wife were present as were representatives of the press. The bulletins came in rapidly and the table was soon covered with these returns.

Early in the evening I conceded the election of Warren G. Harding and my own defeat, which apparently excited no surprise among those in the office and beyond the walls; the only surprise, if not chagrin, that was felt came from the prison cells. An interesting question arose while we sat there in the warden's office as to a pardon to myself in the event of my election, and we all found some mirth in debating it. I am sure the question did not disturb my slumber in the nights preceding this particular one.

A nation-wide holiday campaign had been inaugurated for my release so that I might return home for Christmas. It has long been a custom with the pardoning power at Washington to grant a meritorious prisoner freedom as an act of grace at the season of "peace on earth and good will among men." President Wilson granted the Christmas pardon as usual, but in this instance it was not in response to the numerously signed petition representing every state in the union which had been presented to him, but the boon was granted to an Indian who was serving a life sentence for murder.

When Mr. Palmer's (the Attorney General) report was placed before the ailing President the latter had but one word to offer as signifying his attitude toward me. Over the face of the recommendation he scrawled, "DENIED."

I have been a trifle more than casually interested in the reason that prompted Mr. Wilson to arrive at that state of mind which is furnished by his former private secretary, Joseph P. Tumulty, who, in his book, *Woodrow Wilson As I Knew Him*, sets down the record of the President's comment in my case: "One of the things to which he paid particular attention at this time, the last days of his rule, was the matter of the pardon of Eugene V. Debs. The day that the recommendation arrived at the White House he looked it over and examined it carefully and said:

"I will never consent to the pardon of this man. I know that in certain quarters of the country there is a popular demand for the pardon of Debs, but it shall never be accomplished with my consent. Were I to consent to it, I should never be able to look into the faces of the mothers of this country who sent their boys to the other side. While the flower of American youth was pouring out its blood to vindicate the cause of civilization, this man Debs stood behind the lines, sniping, attacking and denouncing them. Before the war he had a perfect right to exercise his freedom of speech and to express his own opinion, but after the Congress of the United States declared war silence on his part would have been the proper course to pursue.

"I know there will be a great deal of denunciation of me for refusing this pardon. They will say I am cold-blooded and indifferent, but it will make no impression on me. This man was a traitor to his country, and he will never be pardoned during my administration."

(Christmas day, 1922) I could see their anxious eyes peering at me from all directions, and how could I turn my back on them and leave them there! They wanted me to go, to join my family, to have my liberty, while the impulse seized me to stay with them until we could walk out of the barred cells together into the sunlight of the outer world.

The grim guard simply opened the steel door in front at a signal from the Warden.

Midway in the reservation, between the prison entrance and the street, we were halted by what seemed a rumbling of the earth as if shaken by some violent explosion. It was the roar of voices – the hoarse voices of a caged human host that had forgotten how to cheer and gave vent to their long pent-up emotions in thunder volleys I never heard before and never shall again, for that overwhelming, bewildering scene, without a parallel in prison history, will never be re-enacted in my life.

The demonstration was spontaneous as it was startling and spectacular. No one could have planned or sponsored the sensational outburst. It all happened in a twinkling and gave the officials and guards a surprise that struck them dumb. They stood staring and speechless as they beheld the wild demonstration of the mob of convicts who but a moment before were the silent and submissive slaves of a brutal prison regime.

Feeling themselves free for the moment at least they let loose again and again in roars of farewell salutation. Prison rules, hard and forbid-

DEBS' RELEASE FROM WOODSTOCK JAIL

ding, as if by magic, fled the scene, while grim guards, a pitiless terror and torment of the convicts, looked on paralyzed and speechless with amazement.

Ever since leaving the prison I have been haunted by those guns on the walls, and those clubs in those clubs in the hands of the guards within the walls. Neither the guns nor the clubs should be there. To the extent that they serve at all it is in a brutalizing way which tends to promote rather than restrain attempts to escape, and causes lesser infractions of the prison discipline.

The gun and the club are the signs and symbols of the prison institution and they proclaim its cruel function to the world.

If I were inclined to lock a human being in a steel cage under any circumstances I think I should make it a penitentiary offense to send a human being to a penitentiary. The man who sends another there should know in justice to both what it is himself.

In recalling some of my fellow-prisoners and contemplating their excellent character and human qualities I am reminded of a prison incident that occurred eight years ago in which I had an humble part. The noble character of a convict revealed in this incident must be my apology for placing it on record here. There are men without number in prison, to my personal knowledge, of the same lofty character and tender sensibilities as this particular convict.

It was near the Christmas season, 1914. There was an organization known as the "Good Fellow Club" which provided toys and gifts to homeless and friendless children. A convict at a state prison at Jackson, Michigan, read of it and wrote the Club as follows:

"I don't know whether I would be considered a good fellow or not. Society has decreed that I was a bad fellow and has segregated me for a period. In spite of the fact that I transgressed the law I am being clothed and fed and taken care of while hundreds of people, especially children whose only crime is poverty, are actually suffering for bare necessities of life and through no fault of theirs are facing the Christmas season with scant hope of happiness. I am sending $2.00 which I hope you will be able to use to bring in some small measure gladness to some little one. You need have no fear of this money being tainted, for it was honestly earned at 15 cents a day. I have two little girls of my own and while I am sending them Christmas money, I am sure they will be glad that I shared with some others less fortunate.

Yours in Christmas spirit,
INMATE 9756."

The foregoing letter came under my eye in the press dispatches of a local paper whereupon I wrote 9756 (a few years later I came near having that very number myself) as follows:

Terre Haute, Ind., December 16th, 1914
Inmate No. 9756, Jackson, Mich.

My dear Brother:

I do not know who you are but I have read your Christmas letter and I send you my greeting with my heart in it. You may be a convict but you are my brother and when your message came to me I was touched to tears.

There is more of the real religion of Jesus Christ in the spirit you breathe out to the world from behind your cruel prison bars than in all the orthodox sermons ever preached. You love the little children even as He loved them, and you are in prison while He was crucified. It is well that you are patient and forgiving. The world moves slowly. It may still be said: "They know not what they do."

You had the misfortune to be born in a world not yet civilized. Jesus loved the erring into righteousness, his professed followers shut them out from God's sunlight and torture them into degeneracy and crime. The erring did not make themselves. God made thee. Let Him judge them.

The society that sent you to prison devours its own offspring. Thousands of little children are starved, stunted and ground into dividends in the mills of mammon. It is the Christian society's homeless, neglected babes to whom you, one of its condemned convicts, feel moved to send the pennies coined in your own blood and agony.

What a sermon and what a rebuke!

If you ought to be in the penitentiary I know not one who ought to be out.

Believe me with heart and hand your brother and fellow-man,

EUGENE V. DEBS

☮ ☮ ☮

☮ ☮ ☮

Four Hutterites In Military Confinement

Earle Humphreys

(*Editor's Note*: The following article was prepared as a pamphlet for the Forest River Community of the Hutterian Brethren. Although the pamphlet was undated, the article suggests that it was written shortly after the experiences of the four Hutterites, David, Joseph, and Michael Hofer and Jacob Wipf, in military confinement as conscientious objectors at Alcatraz and Leavenworth. Earle Humphreys, who wrote this account, has long since been dead, and it is one of the few accounts concerning Mennonites imprisoned as conscientious objectors.

The Forest River Community is still in existence in Fordville, North Dakota and lives as a religious community engaged in farming and stock raising. Unfortunately, no further information could be obtained, even though the widow of one of the men was still alive at the time of Humphreys' writing. She wishes that the injustice done these four will not be emphasized. Ω)

T he following remarkable narrative is based on the account of a young Hutterish Mennonite, or Huttrian Brother, named David Hofer, who related these experiences after his release from military confinement, during which his two brothers, Joseph and Michael, had died in prison.

The attitude of the Huttrian brotherhood with regard to participation in warfare is perhaps the most uncompromising of all the various branches of the Mennonite Church. Their treatment by the military authorities has therefore been unusually harsh.

When the four young men, three of whom were married, left their home in South Dakota for Camp Lewis, their troubles began on account of their beards. The other boys on the train amused themselves by jeering at the bearded objectors and even cutting their hair and beard with a clipper, to make them appear ridiculous when they would arrive at the training camp. This treatment of members of religious sects whose religion includes the wearing of a beard has been a common experience during the war.

When they arrived at Camp Lewis they were asked to sign a card, promising obedience to all military commands. Being absolute objectors to war service on religious grounds, they refused to sign. They likewise refused to take up any line of military service in the camp. They were commanded to step into line and march along with the rest to the drill ground. This they also refused, and refused to put on the military uniform in place of the peculiar home-made garb which they were wearing like all Huttrian Mennonites. They were put into the guardhouse in close confinement, and were cursed and ridiculed by the guards.

After two months in the guardhouse, the four men were courtmartialed and sentenced to 37 years, which, however, was reduced by the camp commander to 20 years. They were to be sent to the military prison on the island of Alcatraz in San Francisco bay. Chained together two and two they were sent there in charge of four armed lieutenants. By day the fetters on their ankles were unlocked, but never the handcuffs on their wrists. At night they had to lie flat on their backs, doubly chained together. They got little sleep the two nights of the trip, only moaning and weeping.

When they arrived at Alcatraz prison, they were forced to take off their outer clothes and ordered to put on the military uniform, which they again refused; whereupon they were taken to the dungeon and placed in solitary cells, down below, in darkness, filth and stench. The uniform was thrown down by their side and they were told: "There you will have to stay until you give up the ghost, if you do not yield; – like the case of the last four that we carried out of these cells yesterday." Thus they were left in their light underwear.

During the first four and a half days they received no food whatsoever, and only half a glass of water every twenty-four hours. During the night, they had to sleep on the cold, wet concrete floor without any blankets. The next one and a half days they had to stand with their hands extended above their heads, crosswise, and were in this position manacled to the bars so high that they could barely reach the floor with their feet. The strain was such, that David, the discharged man who is now at home, says he still feels the effect in his sides. At times he tried to lessen the terrible pain in his arms by working the chamber pail nearer with one foot so as to be able, occasionally, to get up on the pail with his feet and thus ease the strain. The men were not placed near enough together to be able to speak with each other; but once David heard Jacob cry out: "Oh, have mercy, Almighty God!"

At the end of five days they were taken out of the "hole" and brought into the courtyard, where a number of other prisoners were standing. Some of them were touched with compassion at the pitiful sight of the sufferers, and one of them said with tears in his eyes: "Isn't it a shame to treat men like that?" For the men were covered with scurvy eruptions, were insect-bitten, and their arms swollen so badly that they could not get the sleeves of their jackets over them. They had also been beaten with clubs down in the dungeon, and Michael had once been beaten so brutally that he fell to the floor unconscious.

When they got out of the dungeon at noon on the fifth day, they did not yet get any food; not before evening, when they got their supper. Then they were taken back to their cells for close confinement by day and by night, being allowed to speak with each other. Only on Sunday did they get one hour for exercise in the open air of the stockade, under continuous close guard. In this manner their confinement continued at the Alcatraz prison for four months. About November 24, 1918, they were transferred from Alcatraz Island to the military prison at Fort Leavenworth, chained together again, two and two, in charge of six armed sergeants.

Fort Leavenworth solitary cell

The journey went down through Texas and lasted four days and five nights. They arrived at Leavenworth at 11 o'clock at night and were driven through the middle of the street, under much noise and prodding with bayonets, as if they were swine. Chained together at the wrists, carrying their satchels in one hand and their Bibles and an extra pair of shoes under the arm, they were hurried on, in a cruel manner, up the hill toward the military prison.

When they reached the gate they were covered with sweat, so that even their hair was wet, and in this condition, in the raw winter air, they were again compelled to put off their own outer clothing, while the prison garb was being brought to them. It took two hours, till one o'clock at night, until they were taken into the prison, and by that time they were chilled to the bone. In the morning they were called at five o'clock and again had to stand and wait outside in the cold. Joseph and Michael Hofer broke down and had to be taken to the hospital, at once.

Jacob Wipf and David Hofer were sent to solitary confinement, because they refused to take up prison work under military control. They had to stretch their hands out through the bars, where they were manacled together, and thus they had to stand nine hours a day on a bread-and-water diet. This continued for fourteen days and so on alternately.

When Joseph and Michael Hofer became ill, Jacob Wipf sent a telegram home to the wives of the two sufferers, who took the next train at night, accompanied by a male friend, to go and see their husbands. Both had small children. To make matters worse the depot agent insisted that the telegram had come from Ft. Riley, not from Ft. Leavenworth, and sold them tickets to the wrong place. So they lost a day by going to Ft. Riley; and when they finally reached the military prison, at 11 o'clock in the evening, they found their husbands so near death that hardly a word could be spoken.

When they came again early in the morning, Joseph was already dead and the body was in charge of the undertaker. He could not be seen any more, it was said; but his wife, Marie, pushed the guards aside, pressed on through various doors, until she reached the Colonel, where she pleaded in tears to be allowed to see her husband once more. She was conducted to the place where the corpse had already been prepared and laid in the casket. She eagerly looked in through her tears; but, alas!, they had clad her husband's body in the military uniform, which, during life, he had so valiantly refused to don, because it was objectionable to men of his religion.

Michael died a few days later and was fitted out in his civilian clothes at the special request of his father, who had arrived meanwhile. When dying he stretched forth his hands and said; "Come, Lord Jesus, into thy hands I commend my spirit."

When the relatives had gone home with the dead, David, who had been permitted to be at the deathbed of his brother, Michael, was again sent back to his chains in the solitary cell. He says: "All the next day I stood there and wept; but I could not even wipe away my tears, as my hands were manacled to the prison bars."

No one seemed to have any pity for him. The next morning, however, one of the guards was willing to go to the Colonel to ask a favor in behalf of David. He begged to be transferred to a cell where he would nearer his friend Jacob and could at least see him, even though he be not allowed to speak to him. The guard took the message to the Colonel.

In an hour he returned and told David to pack up his things, for he had been discharged. This, however, was too sudden for him, and he could not believe it. But the guard took him along to the Colonel who affirmed to statement and gave him his discharge papers. A request to go and take leave of his friend Jacob was not granted. So he went out through the gate into the outside world. Here he again hesitated, doubts arising, whether all this were reality or only a dream.

Thus he remained standing until a guard came along and asked him what he was waiting for. "They tell me, I'd discharged, and I can't be sure of it," he said. The guard replied: "You can be sure of that, for no one gets out of here who is not discharged." David then said, that he would have liked very much to say good-bye to his friend Jacob.

The guard told him to write a few lines on paper, and he would bring the note to Jacob the same day which the guard did, as could be seen from Jacob's next letter to his wife, in which he wrote: "Kathrine, just ask David: he will be able to tell you everything better than I can write it." From this it is plain, he already knew about David's release.

The piteous funerals of the two brothers and the sympathy shown by the whole Mennonite community was something indescribable. These young brethren have been away from home and their families for six months, always in close confinement, suffering tortures of soul and body; the effect of their return as corpses, is something that pen cannot describe. The sufferers have gone to their well-deserved rest.

On Dec. 6th the Secretary of War issued an order prohibiting further handcuffing of prisoners to iron bars, and other cruel corporal punishments. When, however, some of the Hutterish Brethren about five days later went to see Jacob in his solitary cell, was still handcuffed to the bars for nine hours a day. He got his breakfast of bread and water at seven in the morning; at noon he was released from the bars for 30 minutes to eat his dinner of bread and water; and at 6:30 he was again released and given the same fare for supper. Although he still had to sleep on the concrete floor, he had four blankets now; but there were vermin (especially bedbugs) without number.

Jacob sent the following message home with his friends: "I some-times envy the three who have already been released from this misery. Then I think: Why is the Lord so so hard on me? I have always endeavored to be faithful and industrious. I have given the Brotherhood little cause for worry. Why should I now have to suffer so much longer singlehanded? But then again it is a source of joy for me, when I realize that the Lord considers me worthy to suffer for his sake. And I must concede that life here is like in a palace in comparison with our former experiences."

From this the reader can form a conception of the experiences of these men at Alcatraz prison. If standing handcuffed for nine hours a day, on a bread-and-water diet, and sleeping among vermin on a concrete floor, was like a palace by comparison, it is no wonder that Jacob finally felt that to be released by death would be preferable to a long continuation of life in that living grave of Alcatraz.

On December 12, pursuant to Secretary Baker's order above referred to, handcuffing to the bars was discontinued at the military prison. The solitary prisoners were also given planks on the floor to sleep on, which made it warmer for them at night than sleeping on the bare concrete floor. Further relief was given about New-Year, after the monster petition for the Release of the C.O.s had been laid before the Secretary of War.

About this time Jacob became ill and had to be removed to the hospital, whence his story, (which fully corroborates David's account) was first given to the outside world. Jacob was not included in the 113 conscientious objectors who were released or discharged from the Disciplinary Barracks at Ft. Leavenworth on January 27th in pursuance of an order of the Secretary of War dated December 2nd.

(Jacob Wipf was released at last, April 13, 1919.)

Meanwhile most of the Hutterish Brethren have emigrated to Canada.

The case of these Hutterish Mennonites is one of peculiar severity; but hundreds of Mennonites and other non-resistants have suffered similar indignities and cruelties in the camp guardhouses and military prisons. If anyone has the nerve to call these men "cowards," let him do so! At any rate they are living examples of what harmless religious people have to suffer in this enlightened day, because their views and convictions do not correspond with the rest.

THE HOFERS' CASE

The fellow was telling his story. His eyes – plaintive eyes – spoke eloquently of intense suffering and were fitting comrades to the tale he voiced. The story, indeed, came as a stale breath from the Inquisition – a smudge of mediaevalism hanging on through the centuries to shadow its insidious deviltry upon our Twentieth Century – a hideous jest to taunt us moderns who boast of idealism and democracy.

As this bearded man with the beseeching eyes recounted his nearly unbelievable tale of religious persecution there seemed to spring from the trite words of his narrative a vitality of Will to Believe. I saw manifested there an indomitable spiritual courage to live to conviction and to permit no coercive interference with the still small voice of conscience. Such were the virtues so evident in the man – qualities indeed which did not only define the strength of any personal religion but which essentially characterize man's progress toward all spiritual freedom. Such were the virtues that authority's persecution had violated, – and, as my sympathy and admiration surged to the man, I suddenly felt twisted into some abhorrent nightmare of a past inquisition.

Unquestionably the story should be told – and retold; for, while it probably instances one of the worst of the present war's persecutions in America – it still typifies the spirit under which the war heretics had to suffer. Words, however, seem inadequate to tell the story as related to me by this C.O., for it is, in reality, written only in the indelible characters of his terrible sufferings and in the deaths of his comrades.

Jacob Wipf and the three Hofer brothers were members of the Huttrian sect. Staunch to their religious convictions, they protested against the forced use of their bodies in war. They were remanded by the authorities to the Alcatraz prison. This prison, built on a rock island of twelve acres, contains a typical Spanish dungeon or "Hole" as it is called in the vernacular of the prisoners. It is with this chamber of punishment that our story deals.

The usual rigors of confinement that military prisoners all endure – though evil enough in themselves – are nothing as compared with the tortures suffered by Wipf and his associates. They believed, with an intense conviction, that their duty to their God utterly precluded any submission to military command.

Immediately, therefore, upon their entrance to the prison they refused to comply with any dictate of soldier authority. It must be remembered that this was no degenerate whim nor yet the stubbornness of criminals – it was the highest spiritual conviction of deeply religious men.

Upon refusing to work, they were sentenced to confinement in the "Hole," and they descended to this terror cell to suffer for five days under the most inconceivable conditions. The dungeon – a hideous reminder of past ignorance and cruelty – is located thirty feet below the base of the prison building and just at the level the sea. The thick stone walls, standing through long years, have become saturated with moisture and water continually worked through the crumbling mortar joints and trickled on to the floor. The air of the place was heavy – and always damp and stale.

Into this "Hole" the Huttrian brothers were thrown and, impotent before the uncompromising power of the officers, they could not reasonably anticipate help from any human agency. You cannot conceive the poignant isolation an individual feels behind the walls and restrictions of a military prison. A dull sodden impotence pervades one's mind and body – a deep-seated horror of the bars, the guards and the oppressive rules (regulations). Realizing the injustice of his confinement and seeing his cherished American ideals of Freedom and of the right to Honest opinion brutally ravished – there comes to the political prisoner a slow, throbbing spiritual pain. But add to this the terrors of a torture cell of the Alcatraz type and you know the acme of heinous persecution.

The four Huttrians were handcuffed by the wrists to an iron bar whose level barely allowed their feet to touch the floor. Guards stripped them of their Civilian clothing down to underwear. Blankets or covering of any kind were refused them; and they lived in shivering fear of the cold and damp of the cell.

Beside them on the floor were laid soldier uniforms. The tenets of their church forbade the wearing of military garb. The sneering guards, miscalculating the determination of these prisoners, swore that soon they would be dressed up as "regular soldiers." Wipf's eyes shone triumphantly as he told me this incident.

"But," he said, "we had decided, To wear the uniform was not what God would have us do. It was a question of doing our religious duty, not one of living or dying;" then quietly: "and we never wore the uniform."

For a full thirty-six hours, these quiet heroes remained "strung up" as it is called. Not a bite of food of any sort was furnished them and but one glass of water. They suffered – chilled to the bone, nearly naked and thirsting – and with pain and fatigue torturing their every nerve. To add to their torments, guards came to them during this 36-hour period and beat them brutally with clubs. Yet never once did they think of accepting the easy way out by succumbing to the military will.

Finally, the inhumanity – as well as the futility – of such treatment was apparent even to the authorities and they released the Huttrians who were, by this time, in wretched condition.

For the rest of the five day period, they were exempt from this "hanging up" but the other features of this punishment remained in force. They were without clothing. The cell was damp and musty. They were allowed but a single glass of water each 24 hours and not a morsel of food for the full five days. The dungeon contained no bed and their rest was taken on the water-soaked floor. Washing and toilet facilities were entirely lacking and thus they were forced to live there close to the filth of their own excrement. Frequently the sentries came in to manhandle their victims.

Full of the horror and pain of it all, these four protestants gradually became physically weaker and weaker. They felt the "death by inches" close in upon them. Sanity remained to them only by the sturdiest effort of will.

At last the authorities, fearing the consequences of their action, released Wipf and the Hofers from this ordeal. They emerged from the dungeon, broken in health, and barely managing to walk. Upon reaching the light and fresh air of the upper prison they were found to have contracted scurvy. Their skin was covered with unsightly eruptions. The effects of this disease were still evident in Wipf's face, as I talked with him.

This completes the story of the actual dungeon experience of the Huttrians and, though they were yet exposed to many petty persecutions in the California prison, their lot was softened considerably.

The immediate sequel, however, is as hideous as the actual story. Shortly after their ordeal in the underground cell, the Huttrians were transferred to another military prison where most of the C.O.s are at present in confinement. The change was from a temperate climate to one more rigorous and this was accentuated because the season was that of early winter.

With their advent to the DISCIPLINE of this other prison, the Huttrians found similar difficulties awaiting them. They again refused to submit to military duties, and as in their former place of imprisonment, they were sentenced to confinement in "Solitary." Conditions here were infinitely more favorable in respect to sanitation and the like. Still they were placed on a bread and water diet for fourteen days; "strung up" to the bars of their cell; and forced to sleep on the floor.

The consequences of such "disciplinary" treatment following so closely upon their former ordeal and combined with the sudden change from warm to cold weather are easily pictured. Cold draughts that swept across them as they slept on the floor soon took fatal effect on their weakened lungs. Within ten days two of them – two of the brothers – lay dead in the hospital. The immediate cause – the surgeon's report stated – was pneumonia.

The third brother – already in a precarious, though not serious physical condition – was granted an immediate release, to arrange for the journey home of his dead brothers. Jacob Wipf – physically the strongest of the four – stayed staunchly in "solitary" fighting down his general weakness and diminishing vitality, with never a thought of playing the coward.

Finally Wipf's physical strength became exhausted – and, as I write his story, he now lies in the prison hospital suffering the effects of the dungeon torments. I recall him as he spoke with me, patient and quiet, – though staunch in an unassuming heroism, he held neither malice nor hate against his oppressors. There was a gentle forgiveness for them. All that remained of his concern about his persecutions was a wonderment that our present system could thrive and that the social conscience could remain callous to such coercive brutalities.

This is the spirit of the man and the message of his story. It is sufficiently startling to quicken the conscience of every American to shame that he should be even a remote party to such oppression. And similar sufferings were meted out to all the objectors to war, though in many instances the coercion was not carried to such brutal extremes as in the case of the Huttrians. But all suffered much the same – Christian and Jew – Socialist and Moralist; – a thousand of them, and as clean-cut and quietly brave group of Americans as I have ever seen teamed to a common cause.

You who are caught quietly in the comfort of your library armchair or the calm of your own firesides ! You worshipers who sit softly in church and call upon the name of the Father! You workers and men of trade who are free to go and come as you will and relax in the joy of your families! To all of you – Americans! – comes the story of Jacob Wipf and the Hofers who would not let their conscience die.

Fort Leavenworth, December, 1912.

☮☮☮

☮☮☮

They are slaves who fear to speak
For the fallen and the weak;
They are slaves who will not choose
Hatred, scoffing, and abuse,
Rather than in silence shrink
From the truth they needs must think;
They are slaves who dare not be
In the right with two or three.

– James Russell Lowell, American Abolitionist
Stanzas on Freedom, 1843

☮☮☮

THE · C.O. · IN · PRISON.

☮ ☮ ☮

In Camp

Carl Haessler (1888-1972)

Editor's Note: Carl Haessler was born in Milwaukee, Wisconsin on August 5, 1888 and was listed in *Who's Who in America* prior to Volume 35. He was tried by a court-martial in the summer of 1918 under a charge of willful disobedience in time of war, under Article 64 of the Universal Code of Military Justice. Haessler was sentenced to 12 years at hard labor with forfeiture of all pay and allowances, plus a dishonorable discharge.

Haessler was transferred to the United States Disciplinary Barracks at Fort Leavenworth, Kansas in the fall of 1918 and later transferred to Alcatraz, "The Rock," in June 1919 after leading a successful general strike among the prisoners. His sentence was cut to three years as a result of the strike and he was released in August 1920 after it was further commuted.

He returned to Milwaukee after his release to resume his position with Congressman Berger's *Milwaukee Leader*, the socialist daily, leaving it in 1922 to become news editor and later managing editor of the Federated Press, an independent labor news service. The wire service folded in 1956. Haessler has edited various labour papers, including the *United Auto Worker*, the *United Rubber Worker* as well as regional and local union papers the Detroit area. He also worked in public relations for trade associations and has been a frequent speaker at forums and become a draft counsellor during the war in Vietnam. Ω

Mother took me to hear Debs in Milwaukee when I was 10. Father was a [Robert M.] La Follette [Sr.] Republican. Both had been youthful friends of Victor and Meta Berger. I was a radical in high school and in college at Wisconsin I was Secretary of the Socialist Study Club.

Arriving at Balliol in 1911, I found Senior Tutor (later Master) A.D. Lindsay, president of the Oxford Fabian Society. I joined, and also the Independent Labor Party and the Oxford Coöp. Balliol was generally quite radical even if Harold MacMillan was one of my classmates; G.D.H. Cole and Harold Laski were at New College. [Sir George Bernard] Shaw and his group were at their height.

I became an assistant in philosophy at Illinois in 1914. There I found kindred souls and an established Socialist Club, of which Paul Douglas, and then I, became president. We had a group of 20 faculty people listed who were ready to address college groups against entering the war.

When war came in April 1917, most of us stuck to our convictions and most of us were fired, or pressured to find jobs elsewhere. Even our less committed friends like Professor B.H. Bode, my intellectual (as distinguished from departmental) boss, found it prudent to go to Ohio State in 1920, I believe. I never doubted my position so there was no question of choices. I knew what to do.

Belonging to a radical group of faculty people at the University of Illinois, I wrote on my draft card, "I will not serve if drafted because I cannot patriotically approve of the war." The draft board leaked this to Professor A.H. Daniels, the philosophy department head, who fired me.

I immediately got a job on the *Milwaukee Leader* in June 1917, staying on till ordered to report to the army at Urbana and taken to Fort Thomas, Kentucky. Passing through Chicago, I had a hotel stenographer type my letter to Secretary of War Baker explaining that the U.S. should have no part in the Anglo-French-Russian imperial alliance and that I believed it best for the U.S. if every conscript followed my example.

At Fort Thomas, the dozen objectors, all Mennonite except me, were put in separate barracks and beaten up when they refused the uniform. I expected the same treatment after the quartermaster sergeant put a folded uniform on my arm. I dropped the arm letting the uniform fall to the ground. But my sergeant ordered the gang to lay off as they approached me in the barrack. When I expressed my surprise, he said, "Voted for Gene Debs every chance I got." He was called back from retirement.

The chaplain promised me a bulletproof post if I'd conform, but I knew he was a liar just putting me to the test. The post commander heard my stand and said, "Do you think you can get away with that?" I said that was my position no matter what happened. We were shipped to Camp Sheridan near Montgomery, Alabama.

In Camp Sheridan the objectors were again detailed to different companies. After several months, I was ordered to appear in uniform in the captain's tent at 1 pm the next day. I appeared with the uniform on my arm. I was reminded of his order. I said I knew it and he ordered an armed sentry to take me to the camp headquarters where the adjutant pompously said, "Now then, I order you, etc. Do you obey?"

I quietly said no and was marched to the camp stockade, courtmartialed some weeks after a trip to Camp Gordon near Atlanta where the objector commission (Harlan Stone, Judge Mack, and a colonel) heard our statements and determined our classification. Stone said my sincerity was granted, but the government could not with self-respect grant my position (deeming the government a Wall Street stooge or crook). I said I hardly expected that.

The court sentenced me to 12 years at hard labor, dishonorable discharge, etc. With a batch of prisoners, I was taken to Fort Leavenworth in October 1918 and soon was put to desk work in the mess department.

After the Armistice, unrest began to grow, primed by the influx of American men from overseas who thought they would be out of durance when the fighting ended. Unrest developed into rioting against obvious minorities – first against Negroes, and we objectors were felt and threatened to be next. So we persuaded the hard guys to team up with us for a general strike of the 3,000 prisoners, more or less.

The strike continued till Colonel Sedgwich Rice phoned, as agreed, from Washington, giving the terms of settlement, including immediate release of over 100 and reduced sentences for most of the rest. I was chairman of the strike committee. We voted to return to work.

In June (the strike was at the end of January, 1919), the strike leaders were suddenly confined in the post guardhouse and early one morning marched handcuffed under guard to the rail station and transferred to Alcatraz. I was commuted in August 1920 to time served.

The World War I radical or political objectors found to their surprise that a calm demeanor and reasonable conversation excited much interest and some sympathy among the soldiers. Expressions like, "I wish I had your guts" and "Damn right, it's a rich man's war and a poor man's fight" were not uncommon out of officer earshot. Even among officers who knew of the political objectors' position, there was some sympathy, usually expressed as, "I understand what you are doing, but it's going to be a short war and where will you be afterwards? Who will give you a job? What will your children think?"

I did the various chores assigned to prisoners in a camp cheerfully, including latrine digging, cleaning garbage cans with lye, cleaning the mule corral, etc. I was friendly and sympathetic and did not nurse a grievance, but was adamant on my position.

Provost sergeants like a willingness to work and good humor. When assigned the four garbage cans, I looked at them thoughtfully and started to feel out my sergeant guard by saying, "Looks like a morning's work." He bit eagerly with, "It'd take me all day to do it."

When we delivered coal to the company cooks, we expected a generous handout – meat sandwich, pie and coffee. Those who didn't come across were served with coal dirt next time.

Returning after work one day to the camp stockade, I saw a soldier with a heavy ball and chain "between the wires," the term used to describe the barbed wire completely fencing in the square stockade, with sentry towers at each corner. He had suffered in the blazing Alabama sun all day and the sergeant in charge refused to call a doctor, I was told by indignant fellow prisoners. He dragged himself to a tent at night, then out between the wires at daylight.

He had mistakenly been put to guard a prisoner who was his best friend and they had deserted together. He had caught a fever in the swamp where they were tracked by a plane and was awaiting sentence.

After a couple of days and still no doctor, I reported the matter at the camp medical headquarters. A doctor came out and ordered the man into the hospital where he died. I wrote up the incident and smuggled it into the mailbox at the camp YM addressed to Roger Baldwin [founder of the American Civil Liberties Union and its executive director until 1950] in New York. He took it to Washington and soon an order came down abolishing the between the wires punishment.

A few days later, my buddy and I, still on the coal, etc., detail, walked into the officers mess. A cook put fruit on the counter and a slice of pie for each of us. We had barely finished the pie, when an officer entered by one screen door as we hastily left by the other. He surely saw us, but said nothing, at least to us.

Later an officer friend told me that because of the punishment abolition order from Washington, I was regarded as Secretary Baker's intelligence undercover man to report to him how the camp observed the department's objector regulations. We kept on eating well and I once heard myself described as the guy who eats a colonel's pie before the old boy gets any.

In October 1918, half a dozen prisoners were taken by train to Fort Leavenworth, Kansas. We overnighted in Birmingham and were invited by our guards to have intercourse with a woman in the cheap hotel at a dollar a shot. I declined. Those who agreed were later treated at Ft. Leavenworth for venereal disease.

From the railroad station we were marched up the hill to the walled prison with manned turrets which reminded me of the description of ancient Troy. Enrollment wasn't much different from any college procedure – name, birth, education, denomination, etc. We radical objectors threw a little shiver across the room when we stated we were bolsheviks and atheists. That seemed rather dreadful to the simple army souls in charge.

Every freshman was ordered out of bed at 5 am and marched outdoors for setting-up exercises, then put on light work until personnel got around to finding the right slot. Our group was put at stuffing mattress bags with fresh straw. Soon I was a clerk in the mess office and not long after that, I was playing chess on some Saturday afternoons with Major Smoke, in charge of mess and a son-in-law of the Wyoming senator who headed the armed services committee or its equivalent in Washington.

The prison inside the walls consisted of a big central building (Priam's palace?), which had wings spreading out in eight directions, or maybe it was six, some of them unfinished. Most wings had open cells, only the wing door being locked.

One wing, for homosexuals and others, had locked cell doors. The open wing led to much sociability after work and weekends and this fostered the solidarity that led to the successful general strike.

The prison, after the Armistice, began filling with overseas offenders so that, though built for 1,200 men, it actually housed around 3,000 by the new year 1919. Meager food, puny visiting hours, only one letter to be written a week, some guard brutality, chafing at confinement after the war had ended, stupid work arrangements, etc., brought on mounting resentment.

It first expressed itself in a hard-guy pogrom against Negro prisoners. Some of them said we objectors would be next. We told them we weren't their enemy, the government was. We said, let's talk to the big-shots. The gangsters would not hear of it, saying they couldn't talk to the officers, all they knew themselves was to fight. Let's split it up, we suggested. We'll all go on strike. You do what fighting is needed. We'll talk to the officers. Agreed all around.

Next morning after breakfast when everyone lined up in the prison yard and the different work gangs were called out and marched away, some to shops, some to offices, some to the chicken farm, some to the clay bank and brickworks, etc., the strike began. The sergeant yelled, Second gang. These were tailor shop softies and when some of them hesitantly began stepping, the first gang rowdies threatened to break their necks. The tailors stepped back.

The sergeant called the officer of the day. All the captain heard was, Ain't no more! He called the executive officer, with the same result, the prisoners growing more hilarious and more resolute step by step.

Then Col. Sedgwick Rice, the commandant, came in his long winter overcoat. Rice had made a name for himself among penologists by running the prison (officially styled Disciplinary Barracks) as a rehabilitation center for military offenders. He walked slowly with a hand in each overcoat pocket and we knew there was a sixshooter in each.

He did not call out the gangs. He walked slowly up and down the ranks looking into the faces. He paused to start a quietly spoken, well-phrased redbaiting appeal to the prisoners. The few bolsheviks should not bring dishonor on those who had worn our country's uniform. We must not jeopardize the chance to return to the colors or to embark on civilian life with a clear good record here. So just go out to work, boys, and we'll forget about this mutiny.

The answer was a doubly resounding, Ain't no more!

The colonel wasn't stupid. He ordered everybody back into the cell wings and told them to elect committees from each wing and discuss the matter with him in the afternoon. We gleefully hurried back to the wings.

In the progressive wings, we had elected our committees some days before. When all elections had been held, the committees met to frame the demands to be negotiated. We drew up a dozen or more, beginning with immediate release and ending with more postage stamps. I was elected chairman and, after one of the best lunches we had behind the bars, we were taken to headquarters.

We found Col. Rice patriarchichly sitting behind his desk flanked by all the principal officers. He welcomed us and asked us to state our case. I said we had drawn up a number of demands about our grievances to discuss with him. He objected to the words demands and grievances. I softened them to requests and suggestions. He felt better. He said he had little power to change army regulations.

I proposed that he go to Washington and have Baker empower him to do what he thought best. We haggled quietly for about two hours. The upshot was his proposal to go and meantime we would go back to work. I caucused with the committee and they, especially the hard guys, said nothing doing.

I told Rice we would go back to work when we heard from him at Washington what the terms would be on our suggestions. He reluctantly agreed, except for one thing – he would not order the tough guys out of solitary who had been put there for roughhousing a guard. I proposed putting the case before the prisoners.

The prisoners, prompted by our lieutenants, turned down Rice's plan and he then ordered a new summary trial for each man in solitary (with an eyebrowed, but unwritten, understanding that they would be deemed to have been punished enough). We took it easy for three or four days while poor Rice sweated before Baker's aides. We held lectures, debates, ate well, rollicked in the yard and made big plans.

Word came from Rice in Washington that over 100 men would be immediately released and the rest would have sentences sharply reduced, except for felonies carrying corresponding civilian penalties. Actually, 113 were set free but all of them were religious objectors, which was considered a dirty sellout.

But my 12 years were reduced to two, a lifer got two years and quite a few, with the time already served, were due out fairly soon. Visiting hours were doubled. Letter privileges were extended. Food stayed better; guards were more tolerant.

As a precaution against strike renewal, all objectors were herded into a barbed wire cantonment built against the outer prison wall. There we had a delightful community. We held classes in philosophy, biology, mathematics, public speaking, history, etc. We started a weekly paper called *Wire City Weekly*, which went to six issues before the officers became aware of it and then only because the two issues we regularly smuggled out to Chicago and New York came under F.B.I. notice.

An F.B.I. agent was sent to the prison from Kansas City to investigate. Col. Rice said there was only one paper in the place, touchingly called, *Stray Shots*, and edited by the chaplain. Who is this editor of yours? he asked the flatfoot. He replied Carl Haessler.

I was summoned and Rice incredulously repeated what the F.B.I. had told him. You are not editing a paper here, are you? he asked me. I said I was and would lead the F.B.I. man to look it over. In Wire City, we showed him a file, but he wasn't satisfied. He must see our printing plant, especially as our masthead bore the line, "One of the 1,500 Bolshevik papers in America." However, we couldn't show him because

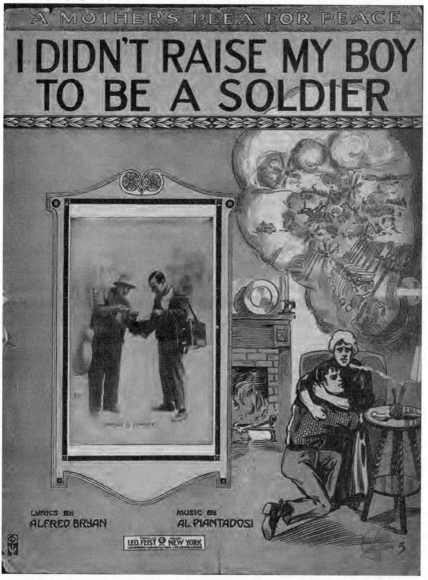

it was printed on the prison mimeograph and the cartoon cover on the blueprint machine.

After another big influx of overseas prisoners and great over-crowding, the strike leaders were whisked off to Alcatraz without notice.

The rocky islet of Alcatraz athwart the Golden Gate of San Francisco Bay was in 1919 a military prison. It had an evil name in the army and its appeal to the authorities was that each cell could be locked individually, unlike the open cell wings of Ft. Leavenworth.

We were taken by army motorboat to the dock and marched up the hill to the prison proper and registered as before. The officers were surprised to find a number of prisoners better educated than themselves and with plenty of *savoir faire*.

The chaplain proposed that these men teach in the compulsory night school, and soon I was teaching American history, others geography, grammar, etc., all with a strong radical tinge. We seemed to be respected as indeed we were. Prisoners who had passed the entrance exams came back to take the courses over again.

Our mistake was putting radical questions in the finals and getting radical answers. These in a period of sobriety were read by the chaplain, who had the same shivers as his Ft. Leavenworth brethren when we tagged ourselves as atheist and bolshevik. Academic freedom suffered another blow. We were fired, but not discharged from the institution.

My regular job was breadcutter. My cell on the second tier overlooked the strait into the Pacific and day by day I watched the sunset when weather permitted and day by day saw the sun make its circuit south from the summer solstice and back again the next year.

Conditions weren't bad for those who worked, but there were some absolutist objectors who would not obey military commands. For them, the machine shop built a cage upright to be hinged on the cell door and padlocked after the objector stepped into it upright for the length of the working day. We dubbed this punishment the iron maiden and from buddies in the machine shop an exact description and statement of purpose of the thing.

I smuggled this out to a sister in San Francisco, who mailed it to Roger Baldwin with notice that she would wire him in code as soon as an objector was so tortured. It came soon. The publicity clicked perfectly.

For weeks, papers came into the prison from all over the country with huge 'Iron Maiden' streamers on page one. Washington ordered the cages dismantled. The executive officer, Col. Johnson, told me, thinking that women visitors from Berkeley and Palo Alto had put this over, "This would be a good job if it weren't for the damned ladies from Palo Alto."

Soon, more and more objectors were being freed. I was among the last, but in August 1920, the Democrats in power, fearing the election outcome and seeking liberal votes, let the last of us out, too – foolishly believing that we and our friends would vote for the party that had commuted our sentences. They forgot that the same party had put us in.

WATCH TOWE
Herald of Christs Presence
ROCK OF AGES
Other foundation can no man lay
A RANSOM FOR ALL
"WATCHMAN!
WHAT
OF THE NIGHT?
~ THE ~
MORNING
COMETH
AND A NIGHT ALSO"
ISAIAH 21:11

⊛⊛⊛

AWAKE!
Jehovah's Witnesses and War

CJ Hinke

Very little has been written about the Jehovah's Witnesses' refusal of temporal wars and their draft resistance. This chapter will serve the reader to enlighten and sympathize.

"Ye are my witnesses, saieth Jehovah, and my servant whom I have chosen."
– Isaiah 43:10.

Charles Taze Russell, a Pittsburgh draper, was told by an atheist, accurately, that nowhere in the Judaeo-Christian Bible is there any mention of hell. He went on to build a homegrown American religion around that fact. "Pastor" Russell's followers became known as the Witnesses of Jehovah.

Russell died in 1916 and in 1917 Joseph Franklin Rutherford, the Society's legal counsel was elected his successor. In 1918, Rutherford and seven other Watch Tower executives served prison sentences for sedition against the Great War. (We just didn't know it was the 'First'.)

The sentences derived from publication of *The Finished Mystery* based upon Russell's writings on the prophecies in the Bible's books of Revelation and Ezekiel. However, the book widely criticized Christian churches for supporting the war. The book became a bestseller and was translated into six languages.

Charges were dropped against the Society's directors in 1920 after the war's end. Upon his release, Rutherford grew its Watch Tower organization through book sales and door-to-door ministry. The religion was banned outright in Canada in World War I for refusal of its members of all national service.

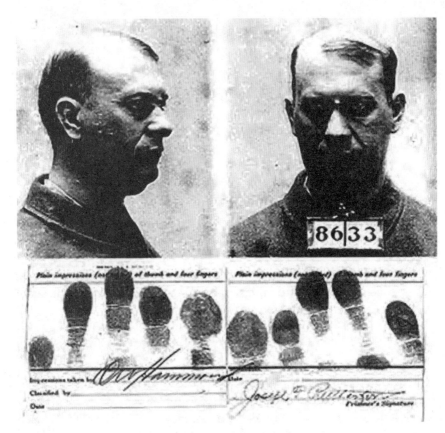

After "Judge" Rutherford's death in 1942, the Watch Tower elected Nathan Homer Knorr its president. Under Knorr's leadership, the Witnesses renounced all forms of organized religion.

Jehovah's Witnesses are politically neutral and swear loyalty only to a theocratic kingdom ruled by God. They reject any duties required by any nation's citizenship including the flag salute, pledge of allegiance, national anthem, or voting, and are conscientious objectors to any form of military service, including alternative civilian service. Many Witnesses have been jailed, fined, and beaten for their refusal to recognize temporal governments.

Forty religious groups were banned in Nazi Germany but Jehovah's Witnesses were the most extensively persecuted. There were around 20,000 JWs in Germany in 1933 and at least 10,000 were imprisoned up to 1945 for refusal to pledge allegiance to the Fürher Principle, including Witnesses from Germany, Austria, Belgium, Czechoslovakia, the Netherlands, Norway, and Poland.

Twenty-nine year old August Dickmann was the first CO to be executed, by firing squad, at Sachsenhausen concentration camp on September 16, 1939, before all prisoners, including 400 Witnesses. These last were threatened with the same fate; not one renounced their faith.

Of these, 2,500 to 5,000 were sent to Nazi concentration camps, identified by armbands with purple triangles. 1,200 died including 270 who were executed; more than 200 were executed for refusing military service – usually by guillotine or hanging, the largest number of COs executed from any victim group in World War II.

In addition, at least 860 Witness children were removed from their families. Although Witnesses could not be identified by ethnicity such as Jews and Sinti and Romani Gypsies and, unlike these groups, could easily have escaped persecution at any time by renouncing their beliefs, JWs defied torture and death in great numbers for refusing the "Heil Hitler!" salute.

In World War II, Canada banned the Watch Tower Society from 1940 to 1943 and interned entire Witness families alongside Canadians of Japanese, German, Italian, and Chinese ancestry and political dissidents. The Soviet Union sent about 9,300 JWs to Siberian gulags in 1951 and the religion was also banned in Australia. Witnesses suffered widespread persecution and mob violence in those countries. Witnesses in Japan were imprisoned and tortured.

In addition to these large-scale persecutions, the Witnesses' military refusal has resulted in their jailing, assaults and bannings in Armenia, Australia, Benin, Bulgaria, Canada, China, Cuba, Eritrea, France and its protectorates, Georgia, East Germany, Greece, Japan, India, Malawi, Mozambique, New Zealand, the Philippines, Romania, Russia, Singapore, Spain, South Africa, the Soviet Union, Turkmenistan, the United States, Vietnam, and many Islamic states based on JW refusal to salute national flags, stand for national anthems, or perform military service.

South Korea, in particular, has no provision in law for conscientious objection and relentlessly persecutes Witness COs. Jehovah's Witnesses' Kingdom Hall was founded in South Korea more than 100 years ago and currently comprises 99.962 Ministers in 1,331 congregations.

Since 1953, when US and other foreign militaries went home, South Korea has relentlessly imprisoned more than 19,000 Jehovah's Witness conscientious objectors to military service for a total of 36,000 years, or about 18 months each. The UN Human Rights Committee (CCPR) has ruled five times, most recently on January 14, 2015, that Korea is in violation of the International Covenant on Civil and Political Rights to which it is a treaty partner and which guarantees conscientious objection to military service as a fundamental human right. There are 393 JW COs in prison as of April 2017.

On April 20, 2017, the Supreme Court of the Russian Federation declared Jehovah's Witnessea an "extremist or terrorist organisation" and ordered their dissolution. Russian government immediately moved to confiscate the church's national headquarters in St. Petersburg, and all 395 local congregations, enormously profitable for the state.

All church activity, prayer groups, Bible study, and all public meetings by some 170,000 Russian Witnesses is now illegal. Police have already halted Jehovah's Witness religious services.

The JW New World Bible has been banned along with other Witness literature, all financial transactions have been blocked, and any sharing of JW religious beliefs in now a criminal act. Dozens of individual Witnesses have already been charged as "extremists" and trials are ongoing. Some of these have been charged with the import of "extremist literature" for religious tracts from overseas. At least some banned material, not of JW origin, was planted by police in raids on Kingdom Halls by military-armed and camouflaged SWAT teams during religious services.

The United Nations Special Rapporteur on the Rights to Freedom of Peaceful Assembly and of Association, Maina Kiai, stated, "the right to freedom of association includes the right to association for religious purposes, and under international law this right can only be restricted in very narrowly-defined circumstances. The fact that people belonging to a majority religion may disagree with a minority group's beliefs or activities – or even be offended by them – is not a legitimate basis for a ban, so long as that group's activities are peaceful."

The Witness ban was also condemned by the UN Special Rapporteurs on Freedom of Expression and Opinion, David Kaye, and on Freedom of Religion and Belief, Ahmed Shaheed. Their statement reads, "This lawsuit is a threat not only to Jehovah's Witnesses, but to individual freedom in general in the Russian Federation, The use of counter-extremism legislation in this way to confine freedom of opinion, including religious belief, expression and association to that which is state-approved is unlawful and dangerous, and signals a dark future for all religious freedom in Russia." They called on Russia to "drop the lawsuit in compliance with their obligations under international human rights law, and to revise the counter-extremism legislation and its implementation to avoid fundamental human rights abuses."

Russian human rights defenders also spoke out against the ban, calling it "Not simply a mistake, but a crime." Maksim Shevchenko, member of the Presidential Council on Human Rights, who described the ban as "unconstitutional, violating the fundamental principles of freedom of conscience." He added: "If it is possible in this way to ban an organisation with hundreds of thousands of members, then it is possible to repress other religious or public opinion groups quite easily. I believe that this is arbitrary, and it is impossible to agree with this arbitrariness. We must protect the rights of Russian citizens who are members of this religious organisation."

It is unclear is what will happen to hundreds young Jehovah's Witness men who seek to undertake alternative civil service rather than military service on grounds of their pacifist religious beliefs.

The Russian Jehovah's Witness organization plans an appeal to the Federation's Administrative Court and, if unsuccessful, to the European Court of Human Rights in Strasbourg.

Jehovah's Witnesses have been added to the Justice Ministry's Federal List of Extremist Organizations, joining 59 banned or liquidated groups, JW texts added to the Federal List of Extremist Material. Individual Witnesses may now be placed on the List of Terrorists and Extremists prohibiting all financial transactions, such as being paid for work, maintaining a personal bank account, or use bank cards, if they defy the ban. Russia, in case you missed the memo or are incapable of learning from history, you've just created 170,000 prisoners of conscience! Good luck with that…

The American Civil Liberties Union found by the end of 1940 that 1,500 Witnesses had been beaten, tarred and feathered, hanged, shot, maimed, and even castrated for their refusal. Even the U.S. Supreme Court ruled against the Witnesses 8-1 in 1940 for failure to salute its flag in schools, though reversing its decision three years later.

There is no group of absolutist conscientious objectors so universally persecuted and prosecuted as Jehovah's Witnesses. In every country that has a draft, there are young Witness men in prison, often serving lengthy and repeated sentences for their refusal.

Historically, JWs were never thought to be pacifists. Traditionally, the sect believes in God's final battle of Armageddon. However, modern Witnesses, in fact, find the Bible says Jehovah will vanquish sinners and mortals will not have to fight. JWs cannot be both Christians and soldiers. Their witness was the largest during World War II. 4,441 JWs served prison sentences for draft refusal in the United States. In all the bloody warfare of the 20th-century, not one single Jehovah's Witness has taken up arms.

"Return your sword to its place, for all those who take the sword will perish by the sword."

- Matthew 22:21.

Consider the Witnesses' witness next time their knock comes to your door or you pass a street corner where a Witness is giving away the JW tracts and Awake! magazine. There are nearly twenty million Witnesses forming 116,000 congregations in 184 countries. Ω

☦☮☦

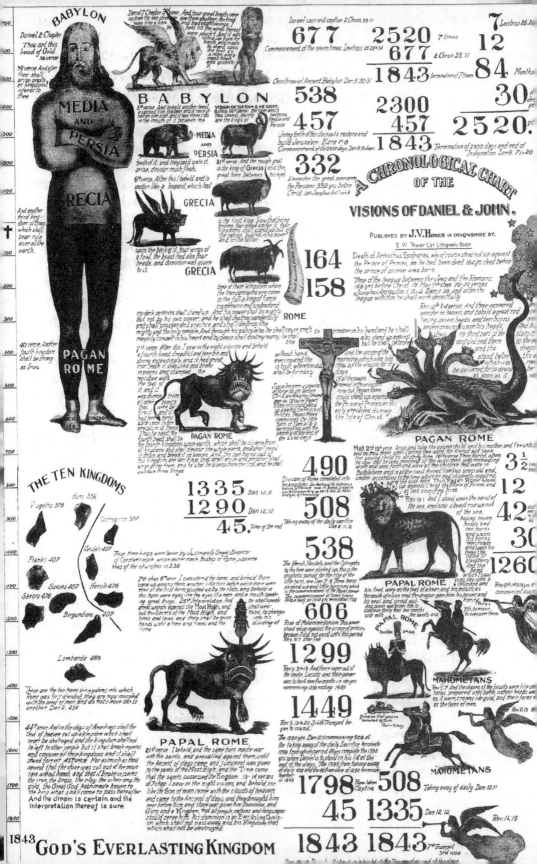

A CHRONOLOGICAL CHART OF THE VISIONS OF DANIEL & JOHN.

PUBLISHED BY J.V. HIMES 14 DEVONSHIRE ST.

E.W. Thayer Co's Lithography Boston

GOD'S EVERLASTING KINGDOM

1843

$\oplus\oplus\oplus$

SHOULD I STAY OR SHOULD I GO?
Conflicted Christians:
The Seventh-Day Adventists

CJ Hinke

B oth Seventh-Day Adventists and Jehovah's Witnesses grew from the Advent religious movement of the early 1800s. In 1833, New York Baptist lay preacher William Miller first stated his belief in the Second Coming of Jesus Christ. Miller's Protestant hypothesis was that Christian time began counting 2,300 day periods beginning in the seventh year of the reign of the Persian king, Artaxerses I, in 457 B.C. with his decree to rebuild Jerusalem leading up to Christ's mathematical return, roughly, between March 1843 and March 1844.

Miller's millennial evangelism quickly became a national movement. Switching calendars and calculations, Millerites resolved to wait. October 22, 1844 resulted in what was named "The Great Disappointment." After this, many Millerites turned to Shakers, founded in England in 1747, who believed Christ had already returned, in female form, in the person of Mother Ann Lee, or "Ann the Word."

COs at Dartmoor Prision.

The Seventh-Day Adventist Church was founded in 1844. American Adventists refused military service in the U.S. Civil War, often purchasing commutations, for $300, until SDAs were recognized as conscientious objectors.

The German church curried favor with its government by allowing its members military service in World War I; some 4,000 who refused to bear arms were expelled from the church. A pacifist reform movement accepting only civilian alternative service schismatized the church following World War I.

Many Adventists were court-martialed and received sentences up to 99 years at hard labor in England during the Great War. SDAs faced similar situations in Canada, Australia, New Zealand, and South Africa. Following World War I, the church reverted solely to acceptance of noncombatant military service, calling their members conscientious "coöperators" rather than "objectors."

The SDA church in Germany compromised pragmatically with the Nazis by accepting conscription and military service to avoid the persecution suffered by, notably, Jehovah's Witnesses and Jews, despite many similarities in beliefs and practices. On the other side of the Atlantic, 12,000 American Adventists served in World War II as noncombatants.

Of particular note was Desmond Doss, an Adventist combat medic, the first conscientious objector ever awarded the Medal of Honor by the US President, one of only three so recognized (the other two were killed in action in Vietnam). The Seventh Day Adventist Church named a school after Doss in his hometown. Georgia and Alabama named highways after him; the U.S. Army named its guesthouse at Walter Reed Army Medical Center in Washington for him. Doss is the subject of three biographies. His story was told in comic books and a 2004 documentary film, *The Conscientious Objector*, and the 2016 Academy Award film, *Hacksaw Ridge*. This is a war story with a difference.

In the 1950s and 1960s, at least 100 Korean SDAs were sent to prison with sentences up to seven years for failure to obey military orders. Two Adventists were executed on the front lines during the Korean War; many more were brutalized and imprisoned.

American SDAs rejected conscientious objection by the 1950s. The director of the SDA General Conference, Carlyle B. Haynes, was quoted in *Time* magazine in 1950: "We despise the term 'conscientious objector' and we despise the philosophy at the back of it ... We are not pacifists, and we believe in force for justice's sake." Strangely, Haynes continued, "But a Seventh-day Adventist cannot take a human life."

Project Whitecoat guinea pigs: Seventh-Day Adventist COs

Adventist objectors were offered participation in Project Whitecoat by the Army Surgeon-General to test nerve gas and other biological weapons. Some 2,200 SDA volunteers joined the project between 1955 and 1973. The Vietnam draft increased SDA participation in the project which tested biological weapons – both for offensive and defensive purposes. Many other Adventists sought CO status with Selective Service. However, the Annual Council in 1969 voted that SDAs should be directed that the historic teaching of the church was non-combatancy.

This deeply divided the church into militant patriots and pacifists, declaring military service to be a matter of individual conscience in 1972. The conference amended the statement on military obligation resolved in 1954 by adding a new conclusion: "This statement is not a rigid position binding church members..." Nevertheless, many Adventists view their church as one of the historic peace churches.

However, the SDA church stopped teaching non-combatancy in its Sabbath Schools, youth programs and its school system. When the Vietnam Draft was suspended in 1973, U.S. military recruiters targeted many racial minorities, including low-income Adventists. Young SDA men began to volunteer for military service with no provision made for non-combatant status. The church began to train a military chaplaincy corps to provide for American Adventist soldiers. "Most young SDA adults are [today] unaware of the strong pacifist thread in the fabric of Adventist history."

Six thousand to eight thousand Adventists were registered as U.S. soldiers in 1991; more than 2,000 fought America's first "Gulf War" in Iraq and Kuwait. More than 56,000 SDA combatants serve militaries worldwide. Adventists seeking non-combatant status remain unrecognized under conscription laws in Switzerland, Israel, Singapore, Thailand, South Korea and Taiwan.

One U.S. Marine was baptized first by an SDA chaplain in 2002 in Dubai and again on shipboard in the Seychelles. He re-enlisted in 2004, discovered conscientious objection and, while his status was pending, refused to take up a weapon during training. Although he volunteered for his area of specialization, clearing landmines, as a noncombatant, a military court-martial found Joel Klimkewicz was only trying to avoid posting to the Iraqi warzone.

Normally, such refusal is a non-judicial matter and is punished by fine and demotion. However, Klimkewicz was sentenced to seven months, reduced to the lowest rank, and denied all benefits, pension, and pay. Following his bad conduct discharge, Klimkewicz joined the Adventist Theological Seminary at Southern Adventist University to study for the ministry. On appeal, Klimkewicz received a general discharge under honorable conditions and restored all benefits.

The refusal of Adventist convert Klimkewicz caused SDA conference president, Jan Paulsen, to reiterate the church's historic position dating from 1867 as unequivocal. "... [T]he bearing of arms, or engaging in war, is a direct violation of the teachings of our Savior and the spirit and letter of the law of God." From the church's official position paper on peace: "In a world filled with hate and struggle, a world of ideological strife and of military conflicts, Seventh-day Adventists desire to be known as peacemakers and work for worldwide justice and peace under Christ as the head of a new humanity." In 2008, the SDA church sponsored a symposium on conscientious objection (with vegetarian food) at its Kingsway College in Oshawa, Canada.

It only took one man to turn his church around and bring back its pacifist roots. In 2013, there are an estimated 18 million SDAs worldwide, the world's 12th most populous religion. with a missionary presence in 200 countries. Imagine the influence such numbers of believers could have united against the world's wars!

In 1863, Church co-founder and "Prophetess" Ellen Gould White (1827-1915) had a vision to counsel a vegetarian diet. The Church has been advocating a health-based vegetarian diet since the late 1860s.

Adventists produce many vegetarian food products and all SDA hospitals and clinics, as well as their 11 medical schools in as many countries, 143 hospitals, and 142 universities provide only vegetarian food under the Adventist Health System established in 1972.

If vegetarianism means non-killing, then surely the same principle can be applied to military service. Not to do so would be a great disappointment.

The Seventh-Day Adventist Reform Movement, active in 132 countries, remain pacifists. Ω

☮ ☮ ☮

NOT Universal Soldiers:
Unitarian Universalist COs

CJ Hinke

U nitarian Universalists are centered in liberal Christian philosophy. However, in practice, Unitarians may be humanists, atheists, agnostics, pantheists, deists, polytheists, Christians, Jews, Baha'i, neopagans, Buddhists and many more.

The American Unitarian Association was founded in 1825, followed by the Universalist Church of America in 1866; both were historically Christian denominations. The present Unitarian Universalist Association, begun in 1961, is a consolidation of the two.

The 800,000 Unitarians have no common creed, scripture, or dogma and are free to celebrate their spirituality as they choose. Early Unitarians rejected the Christian trinity; early Universalists rejected the Christian concept of hell and damnation. "Heaven and hell are states of mind, created by human beings. Hell is created in injustice, violence, tyranny, and war. Heaven is created in compassion, mercy, liberty, and love." UUAs often choose meditation over prayer.

These concepts grew from the doctrines of Socinians in Poland in 1566 with belief in Jesus as a common man with a special relationship with God, spreading to England and Wales. Hounded from Poland due in part to conscientious objection to military service, Socinians were forced into conversion to Roman Catholicism; most migrated to Transylvania where there was a Unitarian monarchy or to Holland.

Denying the trinity was a capital offense under England's 1667 Blasphemy Act. Ministers denying the Nicene Creed were not so charged. An Act of Toleration was promulgated in 1689 for 17 dissenting religious groups but failed to include the Unitarians. A further liberalization law, the Doctrine of the Trinity Act, was passed in 1813 but, by then, many Unitarians had decamped for the New World. In America, the Congregationalists (later called the United Church) schismatized into Trinitarians and Unitarians.

Another of the good works believed in by Unitarians is universal sex education in schools and freedom from abortion laws, as well as freedom of speech, thought, belief, faith, and disposition. UUs' covenant is based on unconditional love. UUs support gay marriage and polyamory. UUs eschew religious ritual rather defining themselves as humanists in support of social justice.

American suffragist, Susan B. Anthony, was both a Quaker and a Unitarian. Many Unitarians were active in the abolition and civil rights movements, and the feminist and gay rights movements. UUs were among the founders of the National Association for the Advancement of Colored People in 1909 and the American Civil Liberties Union in 1920. For whatever it's worth, five U.S. presidents were Unitarians.

UUs support, though do not require, conscientious objection to military service. They have opposed war and conscription since at least 1815. The UU program, Leave My Child Alone, opposes military recruiting at schools and colleges. The National Network Opposing Militarization of Youth advocates against Reserve Officer Training Corps (ROTC) programs on campuses.

In 1967, the UUA resolved that the "Selective Service Act, affirm... the principle of equality of sacrifice" and to broaden the SSA to broaden "the concept of conscientious objection to include those opposed to military service on ethical and moral grounds" and accepting that objection may consist to opposition to a particular war." Notably, the resolution stopped well short of recommending an end to America's War on Vietnam and abolition of the draft.

However, by 1980 a General Resolution of the UUA affirmed that "the settlement of international conflicts by war is inconsistent with our commitments"; "urged that the Selective Service System be abolished and replaced by an all-volunteer force"; and "Opposed the resumption of draft registration and conscription." The 1980 General assembly adopted a resolution which called "upon its societies to establish, support, and encourage educational and counseling programs, so that all men and women may make informed decisions regarding registration for the draft and the option of conscientious objection or non-violent civil disobedience, with particular concern for those forced to consider military service by pressures of economic or racial discrimination."

In 1983, the UUA proposed a National Academy of Peace and Conflict Resolution to the president. The UUA publishes the resource, Conscientious Objectors and the Draft and since 1940 has maintained a Registry of Conscientious Objectors. Ω

☮☮☮

MILITARY SERVICE ACT, 1916

Every man to whom the Act applies will on Thursday. March 2nd, be deemed to have enlisted for the period of the War unless he is excepted or exempt.

Any man who has adequate grounds for applying to a Local Tribunal for a

CERTIFICATE OF EXEMPTION UNDER THIS ACT

Must do so BEFORE

THURSDAY, MARCH 2

Why wait for the Act to apply to you?

Come now and join of your own free will.

You can at once put your claim for exemption from being called up before a Local Tribunal if you wish.

ATTEST NOW

Published by the PARLIAMENTARY AND JOINT LABOUR RECRUITING COMMITTEES, LONDON.　POSTER No. 159.　W. W. 17/47 (9).

☮ ☮ ☮

Mormon COs:
Adhering to the Bible and the Book

CJ Hinke

The Church of Jesus Christ of Latter-Day Saints, known as
Mormons, is another American-bred religion, founded in 1830 by
Joseph Smith. The church's first prophet was 17 when the angel
Moroni appeared to him and directed him to its engraved golden plates
buried beneath a hill in Wayne County, New York.

The book is said to contain the ancient writings of prophets living in
North America from 2200 BC to AD 421 considered to be forbears of
American indigenous peoples. Mormons believe the book as historical record to chronicle God's first teachings to the ancient peoples of the Americas,
having been led there from Jerusalem by God in 600 BC by ship.

The Lamanites burying their arms.

Before leaving for the Americas, the Nephites and Lamanites, as recounted in Mormon's "Book of Alma," warred against each other for centuries. However, when the children of Laman attacked, 2,000 of their enemies were protected by God. Led by Ammon, the Lamanites repented of war, declaring they would never again cause bloodshed, even in self-defense, and buried their swords deep in the ground.

Through the 19th and 20th centuries, latter-day saints believed in obeying government orders and, rejecting the Lamanite doctrine, often served as soldiers. In so doing, they placed temporal obedience above divine guidance.

WWI CO Prisoners at Fort Douglas.

However, Mormons were detached and pacifist during the U.S. Civil War. Although Mormons raised an Army battalion in the Mexican-American War, their participation was nominal and they did not see battle. In the February 1917 issue of *Improvement Era*, LDS leader, Fred L.W. Bennett, first proposed Mormons as conscientious objectors to war. During World War I, a number of U.S. Mormons joined 3,700 CO prisoners at Fort Douglas, outside Salt Lake City, Utah, where LDS was headquartered.

Influential LDS leader and American diplomat J. Reuben Clark supported the 1928 antiwar Kellogg-Briand Pact outlawing war and condemned World War II as "fiendishly inspired slaughter." Conscientious objection was neither encouraged or disparaged by the church and President Truman's proposal for universal military conscription was opposed by the LDS presidency.

There was much support among Mormons for Vietnam draft refusers. One of the most prominent Mormon scholars, Hugh Nibley, a World War II veteran, became increasingly vocal in 1971 in embracing Mormon pacifism and conscientious objection. In 1981, the Mormon presidency voiced its opposition to the nuclear MX missile program to be based in the Utah desert.

However, in general, the nonviolence of the Lamanites was expunged from church teachings and curricula. Legal recognition for Mormon conscientious objection was achieved in the United States in 1981, but exemplary pacifism continues to be a minority opinion among Mormons. Many believe the principled antiwar position of the ancient anti-Nephi Lehis is no longer relevant. This position was codified into Church manuals into the twenty-first century.

Mormons are now free to followed their consciences and refuse to go to war.

More than 150 million copies of the Book of Mormon have been translated into 108 languages. LDS has a membership of over 15 million and 74,000 missionaries. Ω

☮☮☮

PENTECOSTALS & PACIFISM:
Charismatic COs

The Pentecostal Assemblies of God in Christ adopted Quaker principles and found its brethren "opposed to the spilling of blood of any man." The very first Pentecostal to speak in tongues, on New Year's Eve 1901, Agnes Ozman (1870-1937), was a pacifist. In the 1930s, the *Pacifist Handbook* listed the Assemblies as the third largest pacifist denomination. Pentecostal congregations were among the most inclusive, adopting women pastors.

Pentecostalism was embraced by "the disinherited" or disadvantaged Americans looking for salvation and spiritual succor, particular in America's Deep South and other rural areas. This was a new religion for the poor.

From 1906 through the 1950s, Pentecostal men were expected to be conscientious objectors to military service and submit to alternative service in either a civilian or noncombatant role.

Pentecostals did not vote or participate in government. They rejected as much modernity as practical, along with "Hollywood culture" and politics. Pentecostal historian Roger E. Olson described them as "urban Amish." They were a group closed to outsiders, particularly non-Christians and married within their church.

In 1900, Charles Fox Parham (1873-1929), a white evangelical preacher and faith healer, began to teach that speaking in tongues was evidence of baptism by the divine spirit. Parham is considered to be the founder of Pentecostalism, however, the actual Pentecostal movement originated among black revivalists.

William Joseph Seymour (1870-1922), a Negro Holiness preacher, had studied at Parham's Bible school in Houston, Texas, and did much to advance Pentecostalism among freed slaves, sharecroppers, and other poor rural blacks. Himself the son of slaves, he emphasized racial equality and drew in disenfranchisedblacks.

Seymour was the motivating force behind the Azusa Street Revivals in an old Los Angeles African Methodist Episcopal church which lasted, day and night, for three years. Parham was disgusted at Azusa Street's racial mixing, calling the Revivals "Southern darky camp meetings" and whites withdrew from the Revival in 1908 with the exception of those inspired to the multiracial ethic by black Marxist scholar W.E.B. DuBois whose landmark *The Souls*

Azusa Street, Los Angeles 1906.

of Black Folks had been published in 1903. However, many missions modeled themselves after Azusa Street with racially integrated services.

Pentecostalism grew in America by embracing the Pentecost, the Greek name for the Jewish Feast of Weeks during which Jesus baptized his apostles. First known as the Revivalist Movement in Protestant Christianity, Pentecostals emphasize glossolalia and divine healing through laying on of hands.

Believers describe their movement variously as Apostolic or Full Gospel or Foursquare Gospel: Jesus forgives all sins, Jesus baptizes with the Holy Spirit, Jesus practices divine healing, and Jesus is coming again.

Pentecostals are born again through baptism with the fruit of the Spirit. Belief demands continual faith and repentance. Pentecostals believe the spirit dwells within every Christian but all Christians must seek to be filled with Him.

Pentecostal pastor Charles Harrison Mason (1864-1961), another son of freed slaves, encouraged his congregation to register as conscientious objectors following President Woodrow Wilson's declaration of war in April 1917 and the advent of national military conscription. Pastor Mason was detained in Lexington, Mississippi to prevent his lynching by a white mob. The sheriff took him to Jackson where the *Jackson Daily News* blazed, "Lexington Negro Pastor Held Under New U.S. Espionage Law." He was arraigned for 'treason, obstructing the draft, and giving aid and comfort to the enemy' and released on $2,000 bond.

Mason celebrated his freedom with a large baptism in Memphis as an immersion into the way of Jesus' nonviolence. Pentecostal historians

THIS man subjected himself to imprisonment and probably to being shot or hanged

THE prisoner used language tending to discourage men from enlisting in the United States Army

IT is proven and indeed admitted that among his incendiary statements were—

THOU shalt not kill

and

BLESSED are the peacemakers

Amos Yong and Estrelda Y. Alexander found "Mason's theology of nonviolence was based on his experience of violence against the black community, against black manhood in the South."

Like many Pentecostals, he adopted such liberation theology from the Azusa Street Revival in 1907. More than 20 cultures were represented at the Revival, Ethiopians, Chinese, Indians, Mexicans, Portuguese, Spanish, Russians, Norwegians, French, Germans, and Jews. "'Half the elders were women, a fourth African-American and one a ten- year old girl.'"

The baptism of the Pentecost fired the pastor to reject the violence of war and lynch-mobs. Mason's conversion experience was drawn from slave narratives and passage into manhood. The pastor's worship was a celebration of blackness, including "black styles of dress, movement, and color," "roots, guitars, drums, oil, testimonies, healings, and dance" as manifestation of black beauty. Afro-Pentecostals believed the evils of Christ's crucifixion and the black lynching tree grew from the same stock. The Ku Klux Klan, in particular, perverted the Christian cross as its symbol.

Early English evangelist Arthur Booth-Clibborn references Justin Martyr, Tatian, Clement of Alexandria, Tertullian, Cyprian, Origen, Ambrose, Irenaeus, Dio Chrysostom, Jerome, and Cyril to explain Pentecostal pacifism. British Pentecostals Donald Gee and Smith Wigglesworth also opposed participation in war, as did American leaders Charles Parham, Frank Bartleman, former Quaker Ambrose Jessup Tomlinson, Stanley Frodersham, William 'Burt' McCafferty, and Lycurgus Reuben Lynch. In 1915, Bartleman penned eight antiwar articles in the *Weekly Evangel*.

During World War I, 62% of congregations, including the Pentecostal Assemblies of God, Cleveland's Pentecostal Church of God, the Church of God in Christ, Portland's Apostolic Faith, Pentecostal Assemblies of the World, and Azusa Street Revival all declared themselves pacifists. Almost 1,100 Holiness or Pentecostal men in America declared themselves religious conscientious objectors during the drafts of 1917 and 1918, accounting for 5-10% of all COs. Pentecostal periodical the *Evangel* published this categorical declaration: "The Pentecostal people…are uncompromisingly opposed to war."

In Weimar Germany, Pentecostal resisters were court-martialed and shot by firing squad.

Dave Allen, a 26-year-old Pentecostal in Alabama, was beaten and shot to death in 1918 by two police officers in his home in the presence of his wife for being unwilling to serve in the military. J.B. Ellis, the overseer of the Church of God in Cleveland, Tennessee, who had himself served time in jail for refusing to buy war bonds, wrote, "Brother Allen was in the second draft... Knowing that his Bible church opposed war, he felt he could not kill ... We feel he might be classed among the martyrs."

Stafford Silas Winn, elder son of the freed slaves who were founding leaders of the Church of God in Guthrie, Oklahoma, was sentenced to Fort Leavenworth for military detention for his refusal. His younger brother, Edward, followed him.

Alpha Edward Humbard, minister of the Pentecostal Assembly in Pangburn, Arizona registered for the 1917 draft as a religious objector. Humbard gave his reason as "against religion." Elder Humbard was the father of 1950s televangelist Rex Humbard.

The Selective Training and Service Act (the Burke-Wadsworth Act) became the first peacetime military conscription in United States history. Religious objectors were provisioned by application for deferment before their local draft board, usually a panel of old white guys trying to cajole young men into the military. Successful deferment resulted in 1-O status for civilian alternative service and 1-A-O, military noncombatant status. Pentecostal COs were safe.

Angelus Temple Headquarters, 1937.

However, in Canada, a further obstacle to conscientious objection presented itself in World War II when many 16- and 17-year old young men were drafted. One is not considered a full member before one is baptized at age 20, disallowing Pentecostal youth from securing exemption.

In Canada, there were thirteen classical Pentecostal denominations and numerous independent congregations plus believers with the Anglican Church and United Church of Canada. In Canada's 1941 census, 58,000 Canadians considered themselves Pentecostals.

In 1935 and 1936, former Mennonite Brethren in Christ minister, Peterborough, Ontario Pentecostal preacher George A. Chambers, a leader in the Pentecostal Assemblies of Canada, penned the four-part article, "Should Christians Go to War?" However, many Canadian Pentecostals saw the war as a great evangelical opportunity to attract converts.

Although the Reverend James Eustace Purdie, principal of Winnipeg's Western Bible College began to lobby the Pentecostal Assemblies of Canada for assistance in securing ministerial exemption on behalf of his promising students, the military was just as intent on securing clergy as chaplains.

As Pentecostals became more affluent in the 1950s and 60s, they were expected to donate more to world evangelical missions. Parishioners displaying their affluence in conspicuous consumption were often subjected to church discipline.

However, despite official and unofficial pacifist commitments by most Pentecostal denominations, most chose to ignore and refute that part of their heritage. This shift in attitude saw Pentecostal support for U.S. foreign policy.

However, the modern Assemblies of God affirms Pentacostals' right to individual conscience. The United Pentecostal Church International goes even further in its current interpretation of its 1930 *Articles of Faith* and reaffirmed the policy in 1940. While declaring "human government as being of divine ordination" (!), the church is most strongly pacifist, forbidding its congregations to bear arms for the state.

As the Pentecostal movement grew, it divided into more than 700 denominations and many independent churches rather than adhering to a central body. Most affiliate with the Pentecostal World Fellowship with over 279 million members worldwide.

Converts are drawn to the faiths socially progressive and egalitarian message which, in 2016, subscribed to the Black Lives Matter movement. World believers number over 600 million, one-quarter of all Christians

Afro-Pentacostals see their cultural dance and conscientious objection as affirmations of life. Conscience became their counterculture of resistance to white domination and subservience.

21st-century Pentacostalism has strayed dangerously far from its pacifist roots, and is largely forgotten by young congregants. It is just waiting to be proclaimed. Ω

☮☮☮

WORLD WAR II:
The Conscientious Objector
and the Federal Prison System

FEDERAL PRISONS AND THE WAR

Editor's Note: Upon the outbreak of war with the bombing of Pearl Harbor, the United States was faced w i t h huge cutbacks in the domestic budget. It was taken for granted that one of these cutbacks would include the federal prison system, which already housed several thousand conscientious objectors.

In in effort to avert this cutback, the Bureau of Prisons played upon the patriotism of the times in order to win public and governmental support for its operations. Of course, this attitude reflected on the conscientious objectors and, although times were not quite so hard as this article presents it, the sincerity of the prison COs was questioned by the other convicts and the prison administration.

This article was written for a booklet published by *The Atlantian*, the newspaper of the United States Penitentiary at Atlanta, where not so many years before, Gene Debs resided. Ω

The most potent contribution to the war effort being made America's federal prisoners is their fine attitude toward the job to be done.

The day after the blow at Pearl Harbor, a prisoner working in one of the industrial shops put up on the wall a hastily drawn poster on which were the words, "Work Now and Fight Later."

There was a note of genuineness and honesty in this phrase. The prisoner who so perceptively limned the needs of the emergency in these succinct words has unwittingly, perhaps, given officials and prisoners alike a goal and an objective. In the days that followed the Declaration of War, there came a stream of letters from individual prisoners and petitions from groups of prisoners pleading and arguing for the utilization, in the war effort, of the many thousands of prisoners throughout the country. These men wanted to work or fight. Like other American citizens, prisoners everywhere bought War Bonds, contributed to blood banks, donated their earnings to the Red Cross, and worked with unequaled enthusiasm in the institutional industrial plants, knowing that their products were intended for the Army and Navy and other military purposes.

At the heart of this all-out war program is a nation of men and women who are trained to work coöperatively and efficient at the tasks and production which must be done. Like all other American institutions, the prison faced the problem of converting its productive equipment to war needs, of extending its facilities for doubled or tripled production, and of training its manpower for the specific nature of the tasks at hand.

The prisons must, in effect, create efficient manpower where there was, before, only inefficient manpower; they must produce strong new metal from the human scrap piles of the Nation; they must produce war materials from sources that should be productive of little that is good or useful and much that is bad.

In the administration of a prison, security of custody is important, the assessment of penalties fixed by the courts is important, but none of these is sufficiently important unless men are returned to society with the training and readiness to participate in the work to be done. "Gearing Federal Prisons to the War Effort" is intended as a report and record of what the federal prison service is trying to accomplish toward achieving the very objective implied in the title as well as in the slogan which the prisoner hung up in his shop.

A very great deal is being accomplished.

A great amount of production for military use is being achieved in the industrial plants of the federal prisons. Plants are being operated by night and by day. Men who are qualified are being assisted toward induction or enlistment in the military services. Men are being trained to take their places in the production lines of democracy, in the shops and foundries and shipyards of the Nation's war industries. Men are being placed in these vital jobs.

Added to the routine job of rehabilitation is a war program that advances the right of the competent and qualified prisoner to assume his rightful yet privileged role as an American in industry outside of prison, or upon the battlefield; to be one of the hundred and forty million strong working together for a victory that is as certain as the faith and determination which beats the heart of every American.

And the prisoner's objective is as admirable as his patriotism; he hopes to return to society as an ex-soldier rather than as an ex-convict.

☮☮☮

☮☮☮

ENVELOPMENT
Lowell Naeve

The doors behind him suddenly
clicked tight.

He struggled to comprehend the
antæan dimensions of imprisonment,
then rose to his outside window.

Before him lay the highway to
nowhere, and he saw the great
carrion bird for the first time.

It rode atop a beast
and slowly passed him by.

☮☮☮

☮ ☮ ☮

PROSECUTION, TRIALS AND IMPRISONMENT OF CONSCIENTIOUS OBJECTORS

Mulford Q. Sibley (1912-1989) and Philip Jacob

Editor's Note: Mulford Sibley was born on June 14, 1912 in Marston, Missouri and was educated in Oklahoma and Minnesota, where he received his Ph.D. from the University of Minnesota.

He came to the position of conscientious objection after reading Norman Thomas' book, *Is Conscience a Crime?*, and through his study of history. He was classified a conscientious objector during World War II, but failed to pass the physical examination.

Mulford has taught political science at the University of Illinois, the University of Minnesota, where he now teaches, Stanford University, Cornell University, and the State University of New York at both Binghamton and Buffalo. He is a frequent contributor to professional and other journals and is active with the American Civil Liberties Union in defense of conscientious objectors of all persuasions. He considers himself both a Quaker and a socialist.

Philip Jacob was born in 1914 and is a professor of political science at the University of Pennsylvania, currently on a leave of absence as a senior specialist at the Center for Cultural and Technical Interchange between East and West in Honolulu, Hawaii. He teaches international relations and is director of International Studies of Values in Politics.

Mulford has edited The Quiet Battle, a collection of pacifist writings and Philip is the author of *Changing Values in College and Dynamics of International Organization*. Together they have written a very comprehensive guidebook, of which this article provides only a small sampling, *Conscription of Conscience: The American State and the Conscientious Objector 1940-1947*. Although this work has long been out of print, it is well worth the effort to find one in a good library for the serious student of our movement. Ω

The Department of Justice reported 5,516 prosecutions of COs to June 30, 1945. COs thus amounted to 37% of the approximately 16,000 persons convicted of violating the Selective Service Act.

Non-registrants received the greatest publicity. On the first registration day eight Union Theological Seminary students publicly announced their refusal to register and were later sentenced to prison; a relatively large number of pacifists over age fifty refused to register but, with the exception of Julius Eichel, were not prosecuted.

The denial of a IV-D (ministerial exemption) to Jehovah's Witnesses was the explanation for the bulk of failures to report to the army or Civilian Public Service; the denial of IV-E came next; slowdowns, Refusal to Work (RTW), and Absence Without Leave (AWOL) accounted for an increasing percentage of objector prosecutions – 2.9% in 1942, 3.4% in 1943, and 9% in 1944-45.

The most famous trial was that of the Glendora CPS strikers. As will be recalled, they were making an all-out attack on conscription. On May 17, 1946, six were arrested for refusal to transfer or work; a picket line of 30 strikers and sympathizers kept constant vigil at the jail; the men were let out on bail; court hearings were postponed to June, July, September, October, and March; the arrested number increased to 62; nearly the whole camp was on strike and sympathy strikes existed elsewhere; offers of discharge if they returned to work were rejected.

The Department of Justice dropped charges against all but 22; finally on March 24, 1947, came the anti-climax – [Edward] Behre and [John] Atherton, considered the ringleaders, were sentenced to two years and paroled to their parents and the other 20 were sentenced to 10 months, sentence suspended and two year probation decreed.

The trials of objectors were varied. Bail was usually $1,000 to $2,000; the objector could plead "guilty," "not guilty," or "nolo contendere"; most used "nolo contendere" as permitting a statement without a trial.

Judge Welsh, himself a Friend, "felt like Pontius Pilate" in sentencing one CO and expressed "sorrow and deep admiration" in sentencing Kenneth Cuthbertson, opining that the Sermon on the Mount could not yet be followed. Hon. Ralph Jenney of Los Angeles expended his own money to determine the effect of probation on walkouts and finally reluctantly sentenced four AWOL men to road camps.

Some Judges delighted in lecturing objectors on their lack of patriotism. Judge Michael Igoe of Chicago attacked the War Resisters League and shouted at Wispe: "You are a slacker of the worst type." Judge Abruzzo of Brooklyn reviled a CO as a slacker before a courtroom of persons being naturalized. Judge Symes of Colorado wanted a CPS walkout "dragged in front of the German machine guns."

It must be admitted that the judges had a hard time understanding CO positions when Jehovah's Witnesses spoke of Armageddon, members of Mankind United debated the World Conspiracy or a Molokan stated, "the Holy Ghost forbids me to accept anything." At times there was badgering by the district attorney as in the case of Rev. John Marshall, a Negro preacher charged with counseling and aiding evasion, where expressions like the following abound: "But you are the king-fish, aren't you? The high muckity-muck?"

Sentences varied widely; down to 1943 the average in Vermont was 1.1 months while in South Dakota it was 55.7 and the countrywide average of Selective Service violators was 30.6. In the same period violators of the narcotics laws averaged 20.8 months, liquor laws 10.6, postal laws 27.3 and white slave laws 28.3.

Of the 5,516 COs sentenced, four paid a fine only, 218 received probation, the greatest percentage (1,721) were sentenced from two to three years and 64% received over one year. Considerable re-conviction occurred: James Ball refused to register and was sentenced to one year; registered by the jail, he was classified 4-E; refusing to report he was sentenced to five years. Similarly Arnold Satterthwait received one year for refusal to register and later, three years for failing to report for physical examination. There were about 100 of these "cat-and-mouse" cases during the war.

Lodged in county jails before trial, COs had a chance to confirm the Federal Bureau of Prisons' judgment that these were dirty, badly managed, and diffused with graft and corruption (and yet the jails used by the Federal government were the "best" jails). In federal prisons to which all drawing sentences of over one year went, 30 days were spent in Quarantine, with physical and intelligence tests, orientation interviews, and demonstrations of discipline, bed-making and "count." From six a.m. until ten p.m., every minute was scheduled with from two to five "counts" per day.

Physical conditions varied greatly from a maximum custody institution like Lewisburg to a camp like Tucson. Many were surprised by the excellent setting of prisons, scrupulous cleanliness, good food, courtesy, and recreational facilities (the federal system is probably the best in the world), but depressed by walls, loneliness, lack of women and the usual "prison feel."

Since prisons were emphasizing the production of war goods the Bureau tried to assign COs to other tasks – often maintenance of the prison and food supply, as well as teaching. The prison CO met all types of attitudes in fellow prisoners from respect and friendship to antagonism and attack as a "slacker."

COs frequently experienced discipline; how much of this was usual routine for others and how much was brought on by prejudice against COs or their refusal to conform to prison practices is hard to say. Light discipline would involve taking away privileges: movies, recreation, use of the yard, loss of visiting or corresponding rights. Or they might be subjected to punishment like sitting on the "bench" and "monotonous diet."

They might be placed in solitary, in the "dark hole" or transferred to heavier custody institutions.

And there can be no question that some COs were beaten, the cases of Lester Lermond, Larry Gara and others being fairly well proved. Yet in every case director Bennett's report would be: "He was not mistreated." Some COs felt that the prisons were using psychiatry as an additional punitive method against them.

We refer elsewhere to individual conflicts of conscience with prison and non-coöperation carried on, sometimes against prison abuses, sometimes against the system itself. Here we shall consider a sampling of collective "strikes." Opinions as to strikers differed: "abnormal personality," "normal reactions to an abnormal situation," "primarily reformers," "bewildered and frustrated," "over-protected and mother-fixated," or "the most able leaders of the pacifist movement."

In the first Danbury strike 16 COs had been given permission to fast one meal as a "strike against war"; when the warden reneged they refused to work or observe routine and were sentenced to two days in solitary and 30 in cell. Two years later at Danbury, 19 COs went on work strike to protest racial segregation at meals; they were confined to cells, visiting time cut one-half and monotonous diet given. They returned to work when a cafeteria was put in and segregation was no longer required.

In May 1943 at Lewisburg, eight and later 13 COs refused to eat in the "white" dining room while a Negro had to eat elsewhere; weakened and unable to work they were put in the "hole." Later they were kept together in one room and writing privileges were limited. On September 28th five transformed major emphasis to protesting prison censorship and went on hunger strike. Letters to Bennett brought a compromise which admitted the right to take away privileges as punishment but that the prisons would not censor religious and political opinions.

In 1944 a number of strikes were carried on: three strikers in Petersburg against segregation and the war-connected prison industry; a large group in Danbury against the parole system; at Lewisburg against loss of "good time"; in Ashland against segregation. Similar occurrences continued far beyond the surrender of Japan.

One of the most difficult and frustrating problems was securing the release of COs and their restoration to ordinary life. For all types of prisoners serving more than one year, "regular" parole could be requested from the Parole Board at the expiration of 1/3 of the sentence. But the Parole Board engrafted special rules as to COs – that they should not go back to their communities, should work in hospitals, etc., and should get no more pay than an army private.

A "special" parole for Selective Service violators was provided by Presidential Order 8641, by which men would be classified 1-A, 1-A-O or

4-E, as they should have been by their local boards and would then report to the proper camp. About one-third of the regular parole applications were granted (a lesser percentage for JWs). Paroles under 8641 were less satisfactory and less frequent and the best part of it – parole to special-service unit (plan 4) was virtually eliminated. A conditional or "good time" release was also possible but many COs could not sign the release papers for any parole since they were deemed a privilege granted for a pledge of future law observance – clearly not geared to a man who broke the law originally because of conscience.

Three thousand COs remained in prison at Japan's surrender and a year later there were still 2,000. Those released were on parole and without civil rights cancelled by their sentence – wherefore arose the problem of amnesty.

Two points of view were held in pacifist ranks; one emphasizing publicity and amnesty, the other parole and "silent" approaches. Beginning as a request for release of all COs from prison and restoration of civil and political rights, the amnesty struggle broadened into an insistence on amnesty for all violators of the Selective Service Act.

Originated by the Absolutists, the movement formed a Committee of Amnesty in December 1945. On Christmas eve 1945 President Truman issued an "amnesty" proclamation for all ex-prisoners who had served honorably in the army or navy.

The campaign for amnesty moved into high gear: the White House was picketed on October 15, 1945, May 11, October 16, December 22, 1946 and June 22, 1947. Strikes, fasts and publicity were carried on in Danbury, Sandstone, Chillicothe and Lewisburg and some were picketed outside. Roger Axford and Ashton Jones picketed the Department of Justice and camped on its steps after September 20th. The "freedom train" was picketed. Hundreds of church, labor and liberal organizations, labor unionists like Walter Reuther, Mark Starr and John Keller, Congressmen like John Coffee, Harold Hagen and Compton White, papers like the *Saturday Evening Post, Christian Century* and *New York Times*, prominent persons like General Holdridge, Dorothy Canfield Fisher, Pearl Buck, Rexford Guy Tugwell, Harper Sibley, Walter VanKirk, William Phillips, Reinhold Niebuhr, and Harold Ickes were demanding amnesty.

On December 22, 1946 there was a nation-wide amnesty demonstration at Fifth Avenue in New York, Philadelphia and the White House. President Truman's reply on the 23rd was: No general amnesty but appointment of a three man board to recommend executive clemency.

It took the board a year to reach any conclusion. Finally on December 23, 1947 (nine months after the expiration of Selective Service) the President proclaimed an unsatisfactory amnesty: it divided the 15,805 convicted under Selective Service into two categories: "willful violators" (10,000) and religious violators. Generally speaking, the ones pardoned as religious violators were those who asked for and were not given 4-E by their boards. Most walkouts, nonregistrants, etc., as well as JWs were considered unfit for amnesty.

A segment of the public represented by the *New York Times* approved the report but most liberal groups were widely critical on at least five bases: distinction between religious and political objectors, exclusion of JWs, inconsistencies of the board, impropriety of considering past criminal record, misunderstanding of the meaning of amnesty.

Rightly or wrongly, the President's proclamation had penalized indefinitely four-fifths of all Selective Service violators and five-sixths of all COs who had dared appeal Chief Justice Hughes' "higher form of conscience." These men might have to wait, as political offenders did after the first World War, fifteen years for a general amnesty. Until then they could wait and agitate and pray.

The story of conscientious objection, and particularly conscientious objection in prison, would be incomplete without some separate treatment of what came to be known as "absolutism" – a sort of sect within the ranks of pacifists and conscientious objectors who carried breach of law or CPS and prison regulations for conscience reasons to its ultimate. Typical are the stories of Corbett Bishop – prophetic absolutist, Don DeVault – vocational absolutist, Stanley Murphy and Louis Taylor – absolutists *celebres* who fasted for 82 days, and Bent Andresen – absolutist of the atomic age.

Corbett Bishop, a retail book seller, was inducted at Petapsco in March 1942. Three months later denied a furlough to wind up his business, he started his first 44 day fast. After recuperating in a hospital Corbett was transferred to West Campton; at mealtime he would read from the Bible and diatribes against Selective Service and AFSC for maintaining payless slave labor.

On February 11, 1943 Corbett began a 21 day fast in sympathy for Gandhi's current campaign. On June 19th with Myron Marks he issued a statement charging AFSC and NSBRO with conspiracy to maintain slave labor camps and conducted an 18 day fast. AFSC tried to have him released as psychopathic. Selective Service refused. Moved to Mancos and Germfask he resumed his dinner quotations, left on furlough and never returned.

On arrest and in prison Corbett refused to coöperate, eat, stand up or dress himself. Allowed to go free pending decision, he traveled the country speaking for absolutism and against conscription and did not return for sentencing. Picked up and sentenced to four years, his attitude to officers and court was, "I am here – in body only." He had to be carried everywhere and forcefully fed. Corbett was getting weaker and a parole was granted him July 13 to the Morris Mitchell coöperative farm in Georgia; he had signed no papers, did not consider himself bound by regulations and traveled the country preaching absolutism.

On September 1 Corbett was picked up at the home of Ashton Jones (another absolutist) in Ohio and returned to prison. Once more he started fasting and non-coöperation. After 193 days of non-coöperation and tube feeding, he was paroled to his home. Corbett fasted a total of 426 days, considered himself a prophet to denounce all conscription. And this, most agreed, he achieved without any belligerency or bearing of ill will.

Don DeVault, like some others, based absolutism on his call to a particular task and ignored a system which refused to permit this work. He was a chemist, deferred until 1942 for teaching and research. Refused a 4-E and given 1-A-O Don failed to report and was sent to prison. Paroled to the government camp at Mancos and later Germfask, he spent the day digging ditches but gave all his nights to chemical research on penicillin while subjected to annoyances of "lights out," moving his equipment, etc. When he could not get permission to go on with research full time he broke with the system, refused to report for work and kept at his research.

Sentenced to three and a half years in prison, Don was there finally assigned to chemical work until finally discharged in 1946.

Stanley Murphy and Louis Taylor became the center of one of the most controversial phases of conscientious objection. Highly respected by project superintendent, director and fellow campers, they walked out of Big Flats on the second anniversary of Selective Service. Sentenced to two and a half years, they entered Danbury prison and the same day began a "fast unto death" against conscription. From the 17th day on they were tube-fed. They broke their fast on the 82nd day after Selective Service promised liberalized paroles and significant work.

The Bureau of Prisons claimed they agreed to take parole to charitable institutions with $2.50 per month wages. The men insisted they did not understand the terms. On June 13, they were transferred to the Prison Medical Center in Springfield, Missouri, allegedly in view of their physical condition and threat to further fast. They did not fast but refused to work or coöperate.

Murphy's mother went to Springfield and sent back alarming reports of brutality, padded and strip cells (at first denied by Bennett, director of prisons, and then admitted). Bennett chose Austin MacCormick, an authority on prisons, Charles Palmer, AFSC prison visitor and M.R. King, medical director of the Bureau, to investigate. In separate reports all agreed that the strip cell was a "mistake."

King and Palmer discounted allegations of beating; MacCormick's most detailed report accepted them. In the meantime Murphy smuggled out a letter to his mother giving details of beatings and removal of Taylor to the "beating" part of the hospital.

The warden was replaced, Murphy got his vegetarian diet, and Taylor reported no further brutality. In February 1944 Taylor smuggled out a *habeas corpus* petition of an inmate, Lono Hammonds, which documented a number of brutalities and perhaps one death due to beating.

The *New York World-Telegram* gave this wide publicity and Norman Thomas demanded that Attorney General Biddle conduct an impartial investigation. Bennett and Kolb from the Bureau, and Judge Moore, and newspaperman John Bell, (four of the five appointed investigators), thought charges of brutality had not been substantiated though there were some cases of mistreatment and strip cells. They came to this conclusion by refusing to believe inmate testimony. Newspaperman Julius Klein, the fifth investigator, believed brutality did exist, urged investigation under oath and placed most weight on statements of Catholic and Protestant chaplains and the psychophysiological investigator at the prison.

Murphy unsuccessfully sued for damages and a writ of habeas corpus. Out of all the charges and counter-charges we must conclude: Murphy and Taylor suffered mistreatment; the prison administration seemed amazingly ignorant of conditions; these COs' action aroused the public and the Bureau to awareness of brutality just as other COs were doing in mental hospitals.

Bent Andresen's absolutism was shocked into existence by the first atomic bomb. He had once before gone "out of bounds" to attend an Easter sunrise service but other than this he had been a "good" camper and guinea pig. For two days after the Hiroshima bomb Bent meditated and then walked out of camp for the purpose of "awakening America to what she has done." As he left camp and all along the way as he hitch-hiked back to New York to surrender himself to the District Attorney he distributed statements and propagandized against atomic warfare.

Taken back to the west coast for trial, Bent broadened his opposition to the whole Selective Service System and confinement of COs. He began a fast, was tube-fed and sentenced to two years in Springfield. Offered various paroles with conditions, he turned them down and finally was paroled without his approving any conditions, though he found in his trunk an 8641 parole with conditions which he continued to disregard as he spoke on street corners for the War Resisters League.

A young man of very gentle temperament Bent was symbolic of those who saw in extreme non-coöperation the only effective resistance to the increasingly immoral claims of the State in an atomic era.

Meet Jerry Nelson, a tough
private eye, who knew what
to feed a public enemy

25c

LET THEM EAT BULLETS

HOWARD SCHOENFELD

☮ ☮ ☮

THE DANBURY STORY

Howard Schoenfeld (1915-2004)

Howard
Schoenfeld

Editor's Note: Howard Schoenfeld refused to register under the Selective Service Act of 1940 prior to the entry of the U. S. in World War II. He was one of a group of pacifists who challenged the constitutionality of the peacetime draft. However, the case died in court when it was no longer peacetime.

Sentenced by a Judge of the Federal District Court in New York City to 18 months in prison, he was sent to the Federal Correctional Institution outside Danbury, Connecticut, where during his imprisonment, one of the most radical strikes against war occurred.

A writer of fiction, articles, and poetry, Howard has contributed to numerous anthologies and periodicals, the latter including literary, music, political, science fiction, mystery and men's magazines. His novel, *Let Them Eat Bullets,* a spoof of the hard-boiled detective story, written so it could be taken either straight or as a parody, went into three printings, each in excess of 200,000 copies and was widely published outside the U.S. with total publication figures approximating a million copies.

The versatility of his writing took on an amusing aspect recently when his work appeared with that of Emerson, Thoreau, Gandhi, Garrison, Freud, Einstein, et.al., in The Pacifist Conscience as one of the "classic writings on alternatives to violent conflict from ancient times to the present" while simultaneously *The Saint Magazine* published his hard-boiled crime thriller, "Dealer in Death."

He's also done TV work, adapted a play by the French writer, Boris Vian, and worked on "Recall," one of Vian's short stories published by Penguin Books in *French Writing Today.*

Currently, he's at work on a new novel of his own. Ω

The Warden adjusted his glasses.

"Men," he said, "This is my last appeal to you. Your group is conspiring to buck the authority of the bureau of prisons. If you persist in your foolhardy conspiracy not only your lives, but the lives of the 600 other men in this institution will be adversely affected.

So will the lives of the thousands that will follow thorn. If you won't think of yourselves, think of them. Do you want them to be punished for your actions?"

The Warden paused. His future in the prison system was bound up in his ability to meet such situations as this, and he was doing his best to reason with us. He was a man of about fifty, with a clean cut, intelligent face.

His position was both delicate and difficult. If word of our impending strike reached the public, there would, undoubtedly, be a terrific reaction to it, and he was certain to be made the scapegoat. On the other hand, if word failed to reach the public he would probably be accused of suppressing the information, and meanwhile his authority within the Prison seemed sure to be undermined.

The Warden was a man with a comparatively advanced outlook. There were adequate recreational facilities in his prison, smoking was permitted in the mess hall, movies were shown once a week, inmates were allowed to put on shows, the yard period was long, the institution's Softball team was given ample time to practice, and the prison generally was run along what are considered liberal lines.

The Warden was a good natured man with a sense of humor and a keen feeling of sympathy for the underdog. Ironically, he requested the prison bureau to send us to his prison; and, to be perfectly honest, the worst we suffered at his hands was solitary confinement, whereas wardens at other prisons allowed guards to beat and torture inmates of our type.

The Warden was a sports enthusiast of the first order. No broadcast of a fight or an important game passed without the inmates hearing it. He had been known to rouse the whole prison after lights out to show a new fight film, even going so far as to let the men in solitary out to see it. And no inmate was happier than he over the fact that the prison Softball team was undefeated in a really excellent league, and was scheduled to play the other undefeated team, a group of college men, in a few weeks, for the championship of that area.

The prison team's high standing was due to the good pitching of a convict in our group of strikers, and it was this, coupled with the Warden's love of sports, that was partially responsible for the extraordinary event which occurred in the prison later.

The Warden was a liberal with a position of authority in an evil system. On the whole he attempted to use his authority to alleviate the evil. However, the reforms instituted by the Warden seemed to us to be of a piddling nature when placed alongside the general horror of everyday prison life, though we weren't striking against the prison system at that time. Many of us had clashed with the system and would continue to do so, but on this occasion our strike was of a more fundamental nature.

Inescapably, the Warden was forced to oppose us, and uphold his authority; and, with it, the authority of the evil system that gave him his power. For a kind man, which he seemed to me to be, it was a tragic situation.

A good impulse prompted him to ask the prison bureau to send us to his prison. His fate was to discover us unmanageable.

The Warden continued to speak.

"If you carry through with this strike, not only will your lives be affected, but liberalism itself may be wiped out in the prison bureau. All of you know how hard some of us in the bureau have struggled to better the lot of the inmate. We've made progress lately, and we expect to make more, but the forces against us are powerful, and the balance delicate. A strike at this time may upset the balance and throw the prison bureau backwards to the conditions of 20 years ago. None of you men want that."

"But we aren't striking against the prison bureau," someone said.

"It doesn't make any difference why you're striking. The question is can any group in a federal prison call a strike at any time. The issue here is whether your group of 20 or 30 men has the authority in this prison or whether the people of the United States through the Federal Bureau of Prisons and the Warden have it."

The Warden was good-humored and even friendly despite the forcefulness of his words.

"I want to be fair to you men," he said. "In many ways the circumstances behind this strike are unusual, and therefore I'm willing to make concessions. For example, I might allow your group to cease work on the designated day and turn the chapel over to you, provided you give your word not to ask the rest of the inmate body to join you. You'll have to make it clear, however, that you're not protesting against the prison bureau and that the nature of the services is religious, rather than a strike."

The fairness of this proposal struck me at once and I was genuinely sorry we couldn't agree with the Warden on it. Unfortunately, any arrangement other than a strike would have destroyed the meaning and effect of our protest.

"Any inmate who wants to join us has been invited to do so," a convict said.

The Warden shook his head.

"Impossible. Supposing everybody joins you. Who will man the hospitals and take care of the sick? Who will take care of the kitchen and other chores?"

"We'll leave skeleton crews on duty," another convict said. "None of the other inmates are going to join us, anyway," someone else said.

Others chipped in with similar comments.

The Warden raised his hand for silence.

"I've made my offer," he said. "It's up to you to decide whether you'll take it or not. If not, you'll have to take the consequences." We decided to take the consequences.

The other inmates, though they failed to join the strike, kept us informed and/or misinformed via the grapevine of the Prison Bureau's moves the following day.

The Bureau, thoroughly aroused, acted swiftly.

Apparently fearing a general strike of riot proportions, carloads of Department of Justice men, armed with machine guns and tear gas, were unloaded at the prison gates, according to the grapevine. Other Department of Justice men, it seemed, were released in the prison disguised as inmates. Guards, on their own hook, and probably without official knowledge, went their rounds letting the inmates know they'd be safe in starting fights with any in our group of conscientious objectors, if they wanted to do so. Our case as pacifists would be less clear in the public eye if we fought back, thereby making it possible for the Bureau to get tougher with us.

Early in the afternoon stool pigeons began circulating among the men in an effort to bring inmate pressure to bear on us. The prison would be punished as a whole if the strike took place, they explained. Smoking, letter writing, and visiting privileges would be withdrawn from all. Other punitive measures would be taken.

The six or seven hundred bootleggers, counterfeiters, embezzlers, smugglers, pimps, white slavers, con men, dope peddlers, robbers, murderers, and what have you, comprising the so-called criminal population of the prison, stood to lose considerably by our strike; yet not one of them put the slightest pressure on us to change our stand.

During the few months we had been in prison the inmates had grown to love and respect us – as we had them. They were a patient, forbearing body, daily putting up with the most depressing kind of living.

Furthermore, in our group of absolutists, were many spiritually developed men of almost saintly stature. Even the judges who sentenced them recognized it. One judge, after hearing the Union Theological Seminary students in our group, wept and apologized as he passed sentence on them. Another judge, sentencing Arle Brooks, after reviewing his life of service to others, remarked that he felt like Pontius Pilate.

These men and the others seemed to me to be the first truly religious men I had ever met. Under their influence many an inmate, who had never known kindness or even decent treatment before, discovered his own spiritual potential.

The guards and prison officials were also aware of the unusual situation in the prison, and more than one commented on it. There was less swearing, fighting and sex talk; more studying, discussion, and quiet reappraisement. A general restoration of self respect seemed to be taking place among the men.

Our strike was one in which they had no apparent stake; yet they were as zealous of our welfare as if they had been blood relatives.

By late afternoon the prison was in a state of nervous apprehension. When the supper whistle blew that evening the men poured out of their cell blocks and surged across the prison yard toward the mess hall, carrying us along with them. Midway, they came to a sudden halt.

The Warden was standing on a small box in the center of the yard. Guards quickly rounded the men up and herded them into a bunched mass in front of him. Other convicts continued to pour out into the mob. I moved toward the rear and two guards detached themselves and moved in behind me. Other guards stationed themselves wherever there were conscientious objectors. The men stirred restlessly, anxious to get to their suppers. Night was falling and a high wind was whipping through the yard.

The Warden began to speak.

As everyone knew, he said, a general strike was being called next morning by a small group of inmates. The nature of this strike as he saw it did not concern the rest of the inmates and he expressed the belief that they wouldn't join us.

The patriotism of the group calling the strike, though we were not yet at war, was of a questionable nature, he pointed out. We had deliberately disobeyed the law of the land and that was why we were in prison.

Everybody was against war, including himself, and he had gone along with us as long as he could, offering to allow us the use of the chapel for prayer and meditation on the designated day, but we had rejected the offer, preferring to flout the authority of the prison bureau and the government.

The selfishness of our course was apparent. A strike in the prison at this time might prove disastrous. The Bureau was more liberal than at any time in its history. He dwelt on the gains that had been made recently and emphasized the benefits accruing to the inmates. Our strike would be a blow to those gains, giving the reactionary opposition an opportunity to criticize, and halt them, possibly destroy them altogether. The inmates, he said, would see the wisdom of steering clear of our strike, and the selfishness of it. He expressed his confidence in the men and his expectation that they would support him in whatever action he took. He paused for applause.

Silence met him.

Hastily, he continued his speech. He emphasized again the gains that had been made in the bureau, the threat to them, the selfishness of our group of men. We had so little consideration for the inmates we were going to deprive them of their food, if we had our way, by calling the kitchen help out on strike. We were going to deprive the hospital of help, leaving the sick and dying to shift for themselves. The Warden was interrupted by a clear, but respectful voice, "That's not quite true, Warden."

The speaker was Arle Brooks, a minister of the Disciples of Christ, known among the men for his meek character and spiritual humility.

The Warden focussed his attention on Arle.

"Seize that man," he said, pointing at him.

Guards quickly surrounded Arle, locking their arms together around him.

The inmates, knowing Arle's character, broke into spontaneous laughter at the unnecessary precaution. The laughter died instantly as the Warden ordered Arle taken way and thrown into solitary.

A wave of angry muttering swept through the crowd.

The Warden demanded silence and went on with his speech. The muttering continued ominously. The Warden quickly ended his speech, got off his box, and staying close to his guards disappeared into one of the buildings. Guards shoved the men across the yard toward the mess hall. The muttering continued.

After supper we circulated among the men as much as possible, attempting to quiet them. By lights out, the prison was somewhat calm. I was quartered in an inside steel wire enclosed space, called a medium custody dormitory by the prison officials. The floors were concrete and the small area was enclosed by concrete walls. In it were eight or nine crowded rows of steel cots on which the men slept. Between the steel wire and the back wall was a small walk along which the guards made their nightly rounds. In the dead of night I was aroused by a guard carrying a flashlight. He shook me awake.

"Get your clothes and follow me."

I picked my way through the mass of sleeping men and followed him into an adjoining room where I was allowed to dress. Speech was forbidden. After a long wait a guard came down the cat walk leading two other conscientious objectors. We followed them silently down the corridor through the maze of the prison. I had no idea what was store for us, but knowing the prison bureau, I had no doubt that it was going to be unpleasant. We emerged in front of a large waiting room. Inside were the other men of our group, sitting silently. We went in and took our places with them. I lit a cigarette. A guard took it from me. The clock on the wall ticked.

A Lieutenant of guards entered and checked our names against the list be was carrying. He disappeared down the corridor, suddenly; and, as suddenly, reappeared. He read a name.

"David Dellinger."

Dave arose and followed him. David was a divinity student whose first act in prison had been against the segregation of Negroes. Walking into the mess hall, he he had deliberately stepped out of the white men's line and sat at a Negro table. The mess hall is the most heavily guarded spot in a prison and the simple action took extreme courage. His punishment was swift and ruthless; yet afterwards, he had consistently opposed the Bureau's racist policy along with the rest of us. Outside, he had done settlement work in slums, while still attending Theological Seminary.

Previously, he held an English exchange scholarship which, in the religious world, parallels the Rhodes Scholarship. He failed to return.

We waited. The guards watched. The silence was heavy, broken only by the ticking of the clock. The sound of footsteps, coming from the distant end of the corridor, reached us. The Lieutenant arrived at the door, entered, and looked at his list.

"Sturge Steinert," he said.

Steinert arose and followed him. We listened as the echo of dual footsteps receded in the corridor and faded out. Steinert had been a student at Temple University; the American Legion had awarded him a scholarship for winning an essay contest on Americanism, a scholarship which, I believe, was withdrawn when he carried his pacifist ideals into practice. He also failed to return.

The Lieutenant entered and read another name.

"Gordon Goley."

Goley was a religious man who had renounced all things material, and devoted his full time to a study of the Bible. Independently, through prayer and meditation, he had attained a spiritual stature as yet unachieved by most western religionists. His unaffected simplicity and truly holy character were a source of inspiring strength, and his mere presence in any group was a powerful agent for good. In the ancient meaning of the term, he was, and is, the only living holy man in the United States.

He, too, failed to return.

The Lieutenant called for us, one by one. The wait, for those of us who were not at the top of the list, seemed interminable. I became extremely nervous. I looked around the room at the men waiting with me.

They were the finest people I had ever known. Gathered up from everywhere they seemed to me to embody the imprisoned conscience of America. Each could have obtained his release from prison almost immediately by registering in the draft, and nearly all, being ministers and divinity students, would have been automatically exempted from service. The rest, for one reason or another, would also have been also have been free at that time. Each in his own way had led an exemplary life, and I was proud to be associated with them.

Eventually, the Lieutenant entered and called my name. I arose and followed him. Walking down the corridor, I remember being amused by the situation, and for the moment, enjoying the sensation of participating in a comic opera. The reality of waiting Lord High Executioner destroyed the brief pleasantry.

At the end of the corridor I was frisked before being led through the steel barred door that opened into a section of the prison devoted to administration offices. The Lieutenant opened the door to the Warden's office, and motioned to enter.

If before I had had the sensation of being an actor in a comic opera, the sensation now on entering the Warden's office, was that of stepping into an Arabian nights adventure.

For months we had seen nothing in the way of furniture or decoration except steel cots, metal chairs, and concrete walls. The Warden's office, by contrast, seemed luxurious. Furnished with thick rugs, modern furniture, invitingly deep chairs, and an abundance of wall pictures, the comparative splendor of the room momentarily dazzled me.

Incongruously, the Warden completed the picture. Apparently having left a social function to return to the prison, he was still wearing full dress evening clothes, the coat of which he had discarded in favor of a smoking jacket. He was sitting at his desk, a volume of poetry in one hand, while, with the other, he tuned a station in on his desk radio. The luxury of his office coupled with his, for a prison, bizarre dress had the effect of sharply emphasizing the differences in positions.

The Warden invited me to be seated and, to my astonishment asked me had I read Walt Whitman's Leaves of Grass, which he had in his hand. His manner was friendly and disarming though he continued to manipulate the dial of the radio nervously throughout the interview. He expressed his regret that he hadn't had the opportunity to discuss my viewpoint with me previously and stated his hope that when I was released we could meet on more social terms over a glass of beer. I returned the polite sentiment. He went on to show his interest in my reasons for joining in the present strike, and I showed him a copy of a note I had given earlier to the Captain of guards, stating my motives. He read the short note, which, as I remember it, went something like this:

"As an expression of solidarity with the student peace strike outside, the majority of the people cf the United States, and countless millions throughout the world, I intend to refuse to work April 23, 1941. I am not striking against the U.S. government or the Bureau of Prisons, but against war, which I believe to be the greatest evil known to man."

The Warden brought the interview to a close a few minutes later and called the Lieutenant of guards who led me away, and threw me into solitary confinement.

A friendly guard explained to me later that a dictaphone was concealed in the Warden's office, connected with his radio, and that transcripts of his interviews with each of us were made and sent to Washington. What the purpose was, I cannot imagine.

Solitary confinement was referred to as 'constructive meditation' by the prison authorities. It differed in no way, insofar as I know from solitary confinement anywhere.

My cell measured five of my paces long and two wide. The walls and floor were bare concrete. The door was metal with a small glass square built in it. Guards spied in on me from time to time. Owing to our number, a new cell block, not ordinarily used for solitary purposes had to be opened up, and the advantage was that light seeped in to us through glass apertures. Strict silence was maintained, although I soon discovered I could get a response from George Houser, who was in the next cell by pounding on the wall.

The first day dragged uneventfully, the second monotonously, the third worse. I paced my cell for hours on end, throwing myself on my cot exhausted, and losing myself in daydreams. Insatiable sexual desires overwhelmed me, and I lost count of the days in the interminable silence, which was broken only by the dull voice of the guard during count. I began to look forward to mealtimes when an inmate, prevented from talking to me by the presence of a guard, deposited a tray inside the cell. One evening I found a cigarette and match taped neatly on the underside of the tray. Delighted, I smoked it to the end, burning my fingers, becoming dizzy and nauseated on the smoke.

The days passed. I made up songs and listened to the words in my head. I wrote mental essays, novels, plays and short stories. I scratched my growing beard and braided my hair to while away the time. I reviewed my life, picking out the incidents I liked best and dwelling on them endlessly. I thought about god and prayed. I pounded the wall and paced the cell. One day I began screaming mad parodies of patriotic music at the top of my lungs, and brought a guard scurrying down the corridor to my cell. I told him I'd been bit by a patriot and had caught patriotic fever. He grinned at me and told me to shut up. I fell on my cot and laughed at my own joke.

More than anything I longed to hear a voice, not dully counting but saying something with feeling in it – speech, a polite conversation, a political discussion, or even a poetry recitation.

I got my wish on the calmest and quietest day of all, a Sunday when not a sound of any kind was audible in the cell block. Unexpectedly Ernest Kurkjian, an ascetic of Armenian descent, began to sing the Latin version of "Ave Maria." The holy music sounded incredibly beautiful after the awful days of silence, and it seemed to me I was hearing, really hearing and feeling, the human voice in its true splendor for the first time. The saintliness and purity of angels seemed to me to be in Kurkjian's song and something profound and hitherto untouched inside me, went out and mingled with it.

The song ended, and down the corridor, Bill Lovell began to intone the Lord's prayer. The other Christians joined in and recited it, and Al Herling, Stan Rappaport, and myself joined together and recited an ancient Hebrew prayer.

It was a good day.

Weeks passed.

One day a guard entered the cell block, walked down the corridor to Don Benedict's cell. Benedict, like most of the pacifists in our Group was a fine athlete. Outside, his physical prowess was a legend in amateur athletic circles, and, in particular, he excelled as a softball pitcher. Big muscled, strong and agile, his speed ball was so swift only one man in the prison could catch him. The prison team, built around his pitching, was tied for for first place in its league, and his ability to hold the opposition scoreless had placed it there. The inmates, probably for the first time in the history of prison ball, were solidly behind their team, which originally entered the league expecting to serve as a scrub practice team for the other amateurs in that area.

The Warden, a sports lover, was delighted with the unusual situation, and it did not surprise us to hear the guard offer Benedict his freedom if he would pitch the Championship play-off games which were scheduled for that day. Benedict pointed out he was in no condition to pitch after his long confinement and wasn't sure he could make it. The guard explained he would be given time to limber up and mentioned how disappointed the inmates would be if the championship were lost. Benedict thereupon said he would do it. He added, however, only on condition that all the men in solitary, including the inmates not in the pacifist group, were released. The guard said he would speak to the Warden about it, and we heard him trudge down the corridor.

We waited in silence till he came back. The Warden would not agree to Benedict's terms, but he offered a compromise. He would release all the conscientious objectors for the game, and Benedict permanently. Benedict refused. The guard disappeared, returning shortly thereafter with another offer. The Warden would release everybody for the game, and Benedict permanently. Benedict refused. The guard disappeared.

Fully an hour passed before the Captain of guards entered and released us. The prison team had lost the first game of the series, and the Warden, unable to endure further losses, had agreed to Benedict's terms.

About a half hour later a Lieutenant of guards entered and told Benedict the men were warming up for the first game. The inmates, he said, were aware of his refusal to pitch, and were resentful towards him and the rest of us. He then said he thought he could prevail on the Warden to release all the conscientious objectors permanently, and the other men in solitary for the game, if Benedict would do it. Benedict refused.

Grinning hugely, we left our cells, and laughing at each other's pasty complexions, bearded faces, and unkempt hair, hurried out into the prison yard. A wave of applause went through the inmate stands as Benedict rushed down the field and began warming up.

Benedict, in true Frank Merriwell fashion, summoned his strength after the long weeks of demoralized living, and, in a superhuman and prodigious performance, pitched batter after batter out, enabling the prison team to rally and score, and win the series.

Word of the remarkable feat reached the neighboring cities through the sports pages of their newspapers, and later, when Benedict was released, over 20,000 people paid fancy admission prices to see him in action at a benefit game.

Morale broke down completely in the prison after the games, when we were rounded up, including Benedict, and thrown back into solitary. The guard on duty was so disgusted he did not even bother to lock our cells.

The next day at noon the Warden reversed his stand and released us. The midday whistle had blown and the men were already in the mess hall, eating. We straggled across the empty yard, basking in the sun, enjoying our freedom. A spontaneous wave of applause broke out among the men as the first of our group entered the hall. Surging across the hall the wave became a crescendo. Six hundred pairs of hands joined in and the crescendo became pandemonium. Guards ran up and down the aisles; they were ignored. The pandemonium increased when Benedict entered the hall, maintaining itself at an incredible pitch. A volcano of thunderous and deafening applause burst out when Arle Brooks entered, but when the convicts who had been solitary came in, the men in the mess hall literally went wild, beating their metal cups on the tables, and stamping their feet.

We stood in the center of the hall, astounded at the demonstration. It became clear to me that although they were applauding Benedict, Brooks, and all of us who had been in solitary, they were doing something more. A mass catharsis of human misery was taking place before our eyes. Some of the men were weeping, others were laughing like madmen.

☮☮☮

Racists beating Freedom Rider, Jim Peck, Birmingham, 1961.

☮ ☮ ☮

ENDING JIMCROW:
Two Wars Later

Jim Peck (1914-1993)

Editor's Note: James Peck was born on December 14, 1914 and was still a teenager when he made the decision that, if war came, he would rather choose jail than the army. He had reached that decision through his own reading and through a pacifist friend, Wayne Andrews. The summer after his graduation from high school, he and another friend, Bob Preyer, wrote an anti-war leaflet at their own expense and distributed it to friendly stationery stores.

At that time, Jim knew of no organization that shared his belief. Then, in the late 1930s, he found the War Resisters League, which he joined and has worked with ever since. In 1948, he began as a half-time volunteer, using the other half of his time to work with the Congress of Racial Equality, where for some years he was editor of the CORElator. In 1965 he became the full-time WRL volunteer staff member that he is now and does a massive job with the WRL's literature distribution.

Jim entered prison in November 1942 for refusing induction as a conscientious objector and an atheist. He spent three years in the federal prison at Danbury, Connecticut, and was instrumental in the several strikes led by conscientious objectors in prison during World War II.

Since his release, he has been very active in both the peace and civil rights movements and has written three books about his activities for social change: *We Who Would Not Kill*, concerning his prison experiences; *Freedom Ride*, on the non-violent movement for desegregation in the American South; and *Underdogs versus Upperdogs*, an autobiography.

He was one of those who, in 1958, sailed the "Golden Rule" toward the United States nuclear bomb testing zone in the Pacific Ocean, a protest for which he spent 60 days in an Hawaiian jail In 1961, Jim joined the first Freedom Ride in Birmingham, Alabama, where he was beaten nearly to death by a white mob.

Since his start in federal prison, Jim Peck has been arrested thirty-two times and has walked hundreds of picket line miles. In his *Liberation* article of March 1966 titled, "Thirty Years on the Picket Line," he wrote, "I might be considered eligible for retirement, but I do not plan to retire until I die." Ω

From the spring of 1946, a year after I had completed a three-year prison sentence as a conscientious objector, until mid-1965, when the Congress of Racial Equality abandoned its basic principles of nonviolence and interracialism, I was active in CORE'S Direct Action Projects. I was the only individual who participated in both the first CORE freedom ride in 1947, the Journey of Reconciliation, and the Freedom Rides of 1961. On the 1961 Freedom Ride, I was severely beaten by a segregationist mob in Birmingham, Alabama, and required 53 stitches in my head.

But the first CORE-type project in which I participated took place inside Federal prison at Danbury, Connecticut. On August 11, 1943, 18 war objectors went on strike to end segregation in the prison messhall. Although the prison is located North of the Mason-Dixon line, blacks were required to sit at separate tables. After considerable deliberation and endless discussions, we had decided that segregated eating facilities constituted the major injustice at Danbury.

Striking inside prison meant confinement in solitary, as a punishment, and we all knew it. However, we were prepared for the consequences. When we were denied reading matter in our cells, despite promises to the contrary, we decided to start a hunger strike. We recently had read how anti-Fascist prisoners in Italy had conducted a successful hunger strike-on this issue and we realized that twenty-four hours daily in a 5 x 8 foot cell without books might break the strike's morale. It took three days of fasting to make the administration capitulate and deliver books and magazines to our cells.

After the hunger strike we settled into a routine. As the days and weeks slowly passed, we became more accustomed to being locked in cells all day. There were five daily breaks: the three meals brought to our cells on tin trays, a 40-minute yard period, and mail deliveries. Even smaller things like showers and the distribution of clean clothes were welcome. We spent most of our days reading, writing letters and walking back and forth in our cells.

I used to play chess with Dave Wieck, who was in an adjoining cell. We drew boards on paper and made cardboard chessmen. Then we would yell our moves through the connecting ventilator.

Between the bottom of the cell doors and the concrete floor was a three-quarter inch space. These openings enabled us to conduct strategy meetings and hold bull sessions by lying on the floor with our mouths at the slot. Since the concrete was cold, we used to spread our blankets. The slots also proved handy for passing around newspapers, magazines and notes. Any business we wanted to keep secret had to be transacted by notes, for when we talked under the doors, we never knew whether a prison guard was eavesdropping at the end of the hall.

Toward the end of the first six weeks of striking, some of us were discouraged. Our protest had received no publicity on the outside and the warden had made no move toward abandoning the jimcrow policy. Several thought it might be good strategy to call off the strike temporarily, return to the general prison population, reorganize and strike again in greater numbers. After much discussion and several test votes, we agreed unanimously to continue the strike and try again for outside publicity through friends and relatives.

Shortly afterward, the publicity began to break. Our new press agent was Ruth MacAdam, the fiancée of one of the strikers. She formed a strike auxiliary among friends and relatives of the strikers. Then she went to Harlem and persuaded Congressman Adam Clayton Powell to organize a special committee in support of the strike. Further, she saw to it that the black and the liberal press got news stories.

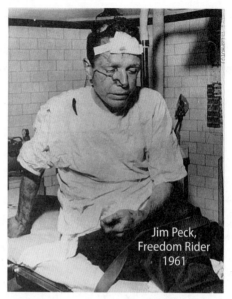

Jim Peck,
Freedom Rider
1961

At Danbury we eagerly awaited the evening mail. Each day there was a bit more news. The story of our strike had appeared in another paper. Every evening after supper we used to get down on the floor to exchange news under the doors.

Six weeks passed before we saw the first sign of a possible settlement. The increasing publicity apparently softened the warden to the point where he accepted the offer of Edward and Agnes Wieck, parents of my chess opponent and longtime militants in the labor movement, to serve as mediators. The immediate result of the first conference was better living conditions. Yard period was increased and our cell doors were opened from 11 a.m. to 7 p.m. As we doped out the prospects, the improved conditions were possibly a prelude to a settlement offering some concessions to our demand. However, none of us were prepared for what happened on the morning of December 23. Our cells were unexpectedly unlocked and we were summoned to the recreation room. At the head of the table sat the warden. He told us to sit down.

Then he said, casually, "I just came to tell you boys that starting February 1, the inmates may sit anywhere they please in the messhall. Are there any questions you would like to ask?"

It was a long moment before we understood that we had won a total victory. Somebody asked whether the new policy would apply to all three meals. The warden said it would. As soon as he left, we ratified the settlement by a unanimous vote In the briefest meeting of the strike. Then we drafted a note to the warden declaring the 135-day strike at an end.

Danbury thus became the first federal prison to abolish segregated seating. However, the warden never admitted that we had won the strike. He told visitors that our action had nothing to do with the policy change.

In fact, he said, he would have acted sooner if the strike had not tied his hands. He felt obligated to perpetuate the system's myth that the prisoner is always wrong, even when the prisoner is on the side of justice.

Several weeks after I was released from Danbury, in April 1965, I learned that in the federal prisons at Ashland, Kentucky and Milan, Michigan, conscientious objectors had struck against racial discrimination, just as we had in Danbury.

I decided that a support committee should be formed outside like the one which Ruth MacAdam had organized in Harlem in support of the Danbury strike. A group of ex-prison war objectors met at the home of the Wiecks and the outcome was the Committee to End Jimcrow in Federal Prisons.

The committee's first action was to picket the 1945 convention of the American Prison Association in New York. The Ashland and Milan strikes, like the Danbury strike, accomplished their limited air in the same manner as on a much larger scale the lunch counter sitins did in the south 10 years later. Segregated eating facilities became a relic of the past in federal prisons as they did on the outside, in the south, in the early 1960s.

The technique for effecting the change was the same: nonviolent direct action.

In retrospect, our successful strike against messhall segregation stands out as the most meaningful action during my three years of imprisonment.

However, I took part In several other protest actions both individual and collective. On one occasion I did ten days in solitary for refusing, on my paint-gang job, to paint red-white-and-blue victory garden signs. I maintained that this war propaganda assignment was contrary to the beliefs for which I was imprisoned: that if I had wanted to do this type of work, I could have gotten a job with the Office of War Information.

As for collective action, the most effective was the "Scrap the Scrapple" campaign. Scrapple at Danbury was a doughy mass of cornmeal, fat and other remnants. Including a few hairs. One evening after a scrapple supper, one of the prisoners remarked: "Next time they put out that goddamn scrapple, everybody should refuse to eat it." The idea caught on and throughout the prison a boycott campaign got under way. In cell houses and dormitories, both the war objectors and other prisoners were busily promoting the "Scrap The Scrapple" drive.

When scrapple next appeared on the menu, the slogan was shouted openly all over the yard. At supper that night all but about 30 of the 600 prisoners passed up the scrapple. We did not see it again for eight months. Probably assuming that all had been forgotten, the steward tried scrapple again. The prisoners' response was the same, and the dish never came back. Adopting the same attitude as with the anti-segregation strike, the warden explained to one prisoner that the boycott had nothing to do with the removal of scrapple from the menu – he had intended to eliminate it for some time.

Next to the anti-segregation strike, my most worthwhile action during my prison years, I feel, was to volunteer as a guinea pig for a yellow jaundice (infectious hepatitis) research experiment conducted by the National Research Council. There were eight volunteers – five of them war objectors. Four of us, including myself, who contracted the disease, were put in a separate ward in the prison hospital. At first we had fever and chills and our urine turned the color of bock beer. Then we entered the most disagreeable stage, resembling a bad hangover. Food was injected intravenously. Every few days the doctor in charge came to the prison to get specimens of urine, bowel movements, blood and sputum.

All eight of us realized that the sickness would be at least unpleasant if not dangerous. The doctor had explained that one's liver is eaten away and is rebuilt only during recuperation. However, we were each willing to take the risk – for selfish reasons, unselfish reasons or a mixture of both. Volunteering for such an experiment improved considerably a prisoner's chances of getting parole. This was not involved in my case since I was getting out within a couple of months.

I viewed it as an opportunity to do a small part in helping discover a cure for a disease which, according to the doctor, plagued people in many parts of the world, particularly in the Near East. I realized that my role as a guinea pig was a minute one, but I thought it worthwhile.

This research was to assume added significance to me nine years later, when jaundice resulting from radiation caused the world's first hydrogen bomb fatality. I refer to the death of Aikichi Kuboyama, a radio operator aboard a Japanese fishing boat which was sprayed with ash from the U.S. H-bomb test on March 1, 1954.

Aside from what I did in prison during those three years, I want to emphasize that for me, being in prison was not a "waste of time." Today in the course of draft counseling for the War Resisters League, I am asked by many young men: "Would you do it all over again?" My answer is yes.

In retrospect, my position of choosing prison rather than the Army seems as valid as it did back in 1942. In fact, Hiroshima and Nagasaki have made it more valid. Outlawing war becomes more urgent in an era in which nuclear weapons could mean total destruction.

And to me, the most effective way for an individual to start outlawing war is simply to refuse to take part in it. Eventually, the mass murder which war is, must be recognized as a crime just as individual murder in peacetime is today.

☮☮☮

☮ ☮ ☮

1969 – I'VE CHANGED MY MIND

Lowell Naeve (1917-2014)

Editor's Note: Lowell Naeve was born on May 8, 1917 in Bronson, Iowa. In 1940 he refused to register for the draft and was involuntarily registered by officials. He refused to coöperate with the conscription process, and served four years, four months, most of it in the federal prison at Danbury, Connecticut.

Lowell is the author of two excellent works on his own experiences in prison, *A Field of Broken Stones*, published in 1950, illustrated by the author, and a fine book of line drawings, *The Phantasies of a Prisoner*, published in 1958. Two of these line drawings were chosen as among the best graphic art in the United States and were included in an exhibition which toured European and South American capitals and was organized by the US government!

He is also a very proficient filmmaker and editor. Lowell made a film of the first student protest at a confrontation in Washington D.C. The film was used by peace groups and television networks in Germany, Norway, France and Japan.

Every mid-August a three-day film festival takes place on the Naeve farm in North Hatley, Québec, eighty miles east of Montréal. A short story relating his encounter with the F.B.I. while making the student protest film was included in the peace anthology, *Changeover*, edited by his wife, Virginia. Lowell also made the anti-war film, "The Inventor," several years ago, which enjoys a wide U.S. distribution.

Since his release from prison in 1946 he has built with his own hands, three houses, in Florida, Vermont, and the Naeves' present home in Canada. Lowell and Virginia have four children: Adrienne 26, Gavin 21, Serena 14, and Brandon 12.

This last summer, Lowell directed a children's art workshop and camp and has opened an art gallery in their barn. He is now editing a film for Dr. Rodney Jurkin who heads an experimental project involving Negro and Puerto Rican teenaged boys. The boys are building their own summer camp in Vermont.

Lowell Naeve has changed his mind about prison as he feels today's wars bear little resemblance to World War II. "Prison is a senseless waste of the human potential for change and to the wonders of two people finding their way together." Ω

I am basically glad to see you working away at a task that needs to be done ... but the approach some of you use – the attitudes – seem out of date. To me ... they appear at times to run contrary to what is in fact taking place already, let alone what appears to be store for us on the horizon.

For instance, the very conscientious – somewhat religious – young ones write me an occasional letter. They have read *A Field of Broken Stones*. They are, it seems, very definitely relating what may happen to them to conditions of the World War II experiences some of us had! To me, our World War II experiences bear almost no relevance to the situation of 1968. It seems to me that if we forget World War II and take a simple, straightforward look at the present and the future, we will come up with entirely new answers.

If we stopped to think, I am convinced that very few of us would voluntarily walk into jail as we did in 1940-45.

I think Canada is one new answer and seems reasonably relevant, but somehow when we get into other areas, we come to the relatively secure position of going to prison. I say secure because, basically, prison is a very fixed terminal and it is safe in that in the past it has been nearly excessively respectable and while in prison, one's sincerity was unreproachable – or nearly so.

But now I think one can question its effectiveness. I believe that not only the individual's effectiveness, but peace demonstrations as we have known them in the past few years bear little relevance to meaningful peace, but serve instead imperialist goals.

The U.S. wants *that kind of peace* so they can further penetrate foreign markets, further control raw materials, and foreign politics.

I think the pacifist movement faces a tragic dilemma. They have basically helped with this imperial process. For a pacifist, I see no way out but a half-way station position of which Canada is one. And before I leave the subject of Canada, I believe that, at present, moving to Canada causes more unsettled thought and interaction than going to jail. This has *definitely* been our experience.

For one of our family to go to prison, I believe would have surprised few and caused little new thinking...but the fact that we thought it was so bad that we left...and that, we appeared to consider Canada a better country than the U.S.A., was a literal shock to our neighbors. My relatives, particularly, could hardly stomach the latter thought! Two rather comprehensive cross-country trips in the U.S. to visit my relatives and some friends convinced me that some of them were in a near speechless boil, which I consider in many cases is just a prelude to new thoughts and some possible later reflection.

We have never had so many visitors from people in the States – and the discussions in our house have multiplied as a result of our "moving out of the situation."

We are now in mid-winter. This last weekend we have had three groups come to talk about the questions we are discussing here and a good deal more. One group, three draft-age men from Boston, have been here three or four times! The second group, three Berkeley student graduates, have settled in a house three miles from here. The third group of three new immigrants from Pakistan, are also interested in these same questions. And in the summer is when people really come! In all seriousness – if we wanted to get out of the action, we would do better by moving back to the States.

I am not suggesting that to move to Canada is the only alternative. There are, I believe, several other alternatives available in the States – of a nonviolent sort – but I don't expect them to develop significantly because going to jail or coming to Canada is a far easier out.

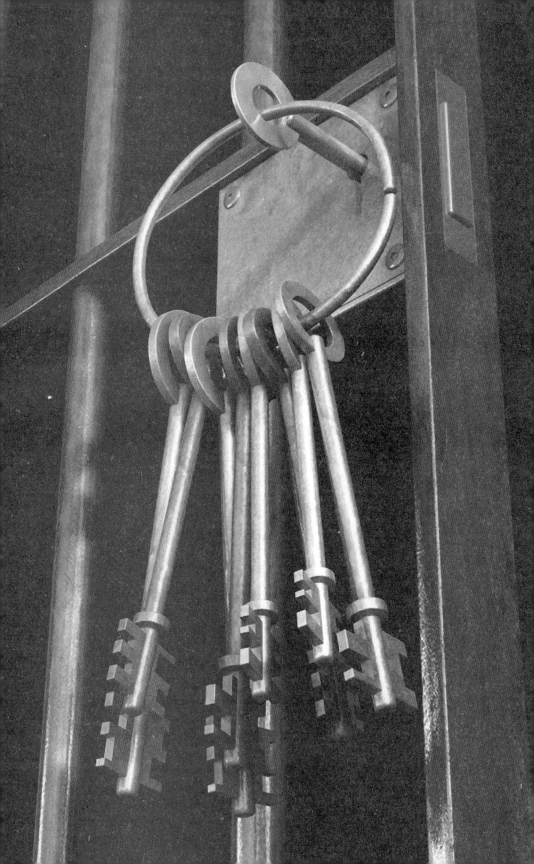

☮ ☮ ☮

I Don't Close Jail Doors

Wally Nelson (1909-2002)

Editor's Note: Wallace Nelson was born in Althiemes, Arkansas on March 27, 1909. He believed in the principle that all men are brothers early in his life and his minister father often observed, "We must love everybody – even the white man!"

Wally was also strongly influenced by Christian teachings and the Sermon on the Mount, as well as the Methodist Youth group who were anti-war by declaration, and with whom he worked and associated. He participated in the first student strike against war in 1934, held at the University of Chicago. Wally pledged, with others, "I will not support my country in a war of aggression."

The next year, he was one of 500 Methodist youths who pledged, "Because war is anti-social and anti-Christian, I will not support my country in war." However, Wally registered under the 1940 Act as a CO and finally was classified as a conscientious objector – a term he now dislikes because of its implication of privilege. Subsequently, he was drafted and sent to Civilian Public Service Camp #23 near Coshocton, Ohio.

Only a year and four days later, he and six others walked out of the camp. Several months later, they were tried and found absent without leave from C.P.S. Each received a five-year sentence.

Since his release in September 1946, Wally participated the following spring in the Journey of Reconciliation, the first freedom ride in the South, sponsored by the Fellowship of Reconciliation and the Congress of Racial Equality. He was arrested on the last day of the Journey, but spent only a few weeks in a county jail in Virginia.

Later on in the year, he began organizing the first CORE chapter in Cincinnati. In the early 1950s, Wally became the first full-time field secretary for CORE. During those years, he directed three summer workshops in Washington, D.C., using nonviolent direct action in attempts to break down racial discrimination in the city.

Wally and his wife, Juanita, stopped paying federal income taxes in 1948 because the major percentage of each tax dollar is expropriated for war or "defense" purposes. They lived in community with Ernest and Marion Bromley and their children for six years between 1950 and 1956. Ernest and Marion now edit The Peacemaker, tri-weekly newsletter devoted to direct action against war. Wally and Ernest, along with others, helped to found Peacemakers in 1948, with the idea of refusal to coöperate with conscription, war, and withholding of war tax-es. For the last ten years, Wally has helped plan and acted as coordinator of the annual Peacemaker Orientation Program in Nonviolence.

He is currently on the board of Operation Freedom and was one of its founders and for livelihood is the Northeastern manufacturing representative for the Antioch Bookplate Company. Ω

Wally's release from prison, with Juanita

One day as I was talking to fellow inmates in the Cuyahoga County Jail in Cleveland, Ohio, the chief deputy appeared, escorting a group of college students. As I looked at their frightened and curious faces I couldn't help turning the clock back nearly two years. I saw myself among them. As a sociology student at Ohio Wesleyan, I took a course called, "An Introduction to Criminology." During the semester the class visited several of the penal institutions of the state. Now, on the inside looking out, I was struck by the thought of how unfortunate such visits were. Not only were they demeaning to the inmates (rather like animals in cages), they gave the wrong impressions to the visitors. The inmates weren't people, weren't hu-man; they were criminals, prisoners, less than human beings. In writing later to my ex-professor I suggested that such visits be stopped.

Along with five cohorts, I was serving a five-year sentence for leav-ing Civilian Public Service Camp (alternative service for COs during "World War II") without permission. I was one of two who remained in Cuyahoga County Jail for seventeen months while the case was being ap-pealed. When the appeal was ruled against us, we followed the others to the federal prison at Milan, Michigan.

The 17 months in the county jail seemed to pass pretty fast, primarily, I think, because of our activities. On the third day there, the four whites were removed to a section of the jail for white male prisoners, the two blacks to a separate area. This move came as a bit of a surprise since new male prisoners were housed together for the first night or two. And so Joe Guinn and I began at once working to "erase the color line" in the jail, a continuing struggle for almost the entire 33 months I was confined.

For the first six or seven months Joe and I were a bit successful in organizing food boycotts as protest against color separation in the cell block where we were housed. Committees were set up to wait upon certain of the jail officials, including the sheriff and the chaplains. In the Protestant services black male inmates were seated in one section while the whites were placed in another; there was no such separation in the Catholic masses.

However, the six pacifists sat together in both services. Church attendance provided the only opportunity to see each other. Another reason for sitting together, aside from the moral issue, was to enable Joe and me to receive contraband from our buddies, two of whom worked in the kitchen. While prayers were being offered, our friends would take from their shirts sandwiches, pies, fruits and other goodies with which they came laden and quickly passed them on to us. We stored these in our shirts. Services over, they would return to the cell block pounds lighter. Joe and I would return to our friends loaded with "manna from heaven." All the guys in the cell block joined in the feasts.

Those fellows who attended religious services had an additional reward – a chance to glance at the female inmates. The women were ushered in last and seated in the rear of the chapel. For hours after each service the hot lines (utility pipe holes in the thick cement floors) were kept hot with verbal and written messages between men and women, usually housed on different floors. Having the women in the same building helped greatly in breaking the awful monotony of doing time in a county jail.

The day we were transferred to Milan was the second time I had seen out of doors for 17 months. We arrived at Milan too late for supper. The next morning we ran head on into color discrimination. We were denied breakfast when we refused to eat at a table reserved for blacks. We did not eat for three days. This was not a fast nor a hunger strike. It was a case of simply being unable to eat. I doubt that I could eat in a hogsty. Nor can I eat under conditions as noxious and degrading as what was then called jimcrow. We began eating after we wore lodged in individual cells, termed administrative segregation. From this point on to my release I was classified a noncoöperator.

Several months later I was transferred to Danbury via the Ohio Reformatory (what euphemisms! reformatory, correctional institution) and the federal pen at Lewisburg. The overnight at Lewisburg is still vivid in my mind because I barely missed being beaten. One of the two guards assigned to get transient inmates bedded down became irate when I refused to close the door of the cell in which I was placed. When he and his buddy appeared before the cell door demanding to know why I refused to close it (every door in the cell block had to be closed individually before the master switch could be thrown). I replied, "I don't close jail doors." He became so enraged that he had to be restrained from punching me. I was grateful for the intervention.

I will certainly not lock myself up and, once locked up, I will take as much control of my actions as is physically possible.

Upon arrival at Danbury I was carried directly to the second floor of Hartford House where the noncoöperators were kept. Noncoöperator classification usually meant bypassing the entrance ceremonies into a new penal institution, and such things as quarantine, physical exams, and filling out forms.

In terms of the anti-war movement of those years, Upper Hartford was certainly where part of the action was; this was quite definitely the case at Danbury itself. The fellows housed in Upper Hartford were more than war objectors or pacifists: they loved freedom. Theirs was a continuous struggle expressing their need for and their refusal to accept less than their personal freedom. So the months in Upper Hartford were scarcely dull. There were religionists to atheists. Politically, there were both Marxists and non-Marxists, but all left of center. The discussions were often lively and stimulating.

Much time was spent in planning and carrying out various types of actions. There was the time when a group of us sat outside the warden's office from early evening until about ten the next morning protesting the treatment of a fellow inmate in population by the guards.

From Upper Hartford meal boycotts were planned, letters of protest were written to various prison and government officials. The climax of this type of activity was reached when we were successful in getting about half the entire inmate population to boycott a chicken dinner prepared to subvert our efforts. This demonstration ended with a march around the compound, singing "Solidarity Forever." At the same time nearly a hundred peacenik friends, mostly from New York City, were demonstrating outside.

It wasn't until late April 1946 that I came to realize my complicity in the brutal and immoral acts being committed against my person. If it was immoral for the government to imprison my body, wasn't it also immoral for me to assist the abductors by assuming the responsibility of keeping my body alive? The answer "Yes!" came to me loud and clear. Furthermore, I seriously questioned the right of one man to judge another and condemn him to prison.

Accordingly, on April 30, 1946 I wrote to Tom Clark, the Attorney-General, "I vigorously deny any man or group of men, least of all those who run the prison system, the right to take over my entire being and to do with it as they please." After pointing out that they had cheated and lied so as to take "undue advantage," I declared, "No more do I desire to fight for better conditions in prison for myself."

In closing I announced that "I shall refuse to eat again until released." I haven't eaten in prison since. I have been jailed seven times since and I am still inclined to view jails as unfit places to eat in. I suspect they're bad for the digestive system.

There were two of us on this 1946 hunger strike. Tom Parks from the Bronx started three days before I did. The strike lasted 117 days for Parks, 114 days for me – when we were both released. The last 87 days we were force-fed. We were hospitalized for most of the time. Our days were spent reading, submitting to one force-feeding a day and keeping constant watch on how our fellow inmates were treated. More than once we threatened noncoöperation with the feeding to win concessions for ourselves and the other inmates.

One of these incidents involved Parks. He had been denied visits with his mother because he refused to shave his beard. His mother was able to make these visits once a month, on the first Sunday. For two months she had been turned away. Even under this pressure Parks refused to bow to this senseless demand. His beard certainly wasn't harmful to anyone. As the third month approached, Tom revealed to me his plan to take action should he once again be denied a visit with his mother. He would noncoöperate with the feeding.

I highly approved and so readily announced that I would act similarly. We knew this united front would be much more effective in moving the prison authorities than would his acting alone.

I sent a note to Warden Alexander (now head of the Federal Bureau of Prisons) in an attempt to circumvent our having to pull out our most potent tactic. He stopped by to see me and we talked for about thirty minutes. I scored him for having such a rule as the shaving requirement, stupid on the face of it. In order to run prisons you must have rules, he argued. Though of course, if everyone were like you and Parks, there wouldn't be anything to worry about.

I reminded him that we were all prisoners, felons, jailbirds, emphasizing that we did not want special treatment. He took his leave after we reminded him that the coöperation with the forced feeding would be discontinued should the visit be denied. This was the day before the planned visit.

Mrs. Parks arrived in the late morning of the next day as Tom and I talked together in the cell where he was kept. A guard appeared with Mrs. Parks. As I was about to leave, and before Tom could greet his mother with a kiss, I heard him roar at the guard, "And what do you think you're doing?" As the guard sat in the empty chair at the end of the bed, he replied, "I am going to supervise this visit." Parks sat up in bed and, pointing a finger at the guard, answered, "Not in here!" Both men held to their positions. Finally the guard ushered Mrs. Parks out. As they went out we called, "Tell the warden to send up a bunch of hacks when mealtime comes because we won't be staying still for the feeding."

I soon returned to the cell where I slept. In a few minutes the captain of the guards appeared, wearing a scared and worried look. He wanted to explain to me their position. Did we want special privileges? Of course we didn't. But Nelson, you can't really mean that you expect us to have unsupervised visits in private for all the inmates? he pleaded. He assured me that he felt that people like Tom and me were all right.

While we talked, he produced a note from the warden addressed to me. The warden seldom worked on Sundays, and this was the answer he had promised me the day before. Alexander was skilled in using language that could have more than one interpretation. I don't remember this note verbatim, but its essence simply indicated that there could be a visit, supervised, with the door open and the guard stationed outside walking back and forth so as to pass the door every now and then.

This began to sound all right, depending on how much the door was open. The door of the cell was full open. I pulled it half closed and then asked if the captain considered it open. With a short hesitation, he agreed that it was. I continued pulling the door closed, stopping to see whether he still considered it open. Finally I stopped when the door was within about two inches of being completely closed. The captain strongly objected, saying that it wasn't open.

I pointed out that the door was still open, but only slightly ajar.

As long as the door wasn't completely closed, it was open, I insisted. The captain feared that the warden wouldn't accept this interpretation. It was my belief that the warden had used such language so as to make it possible for the captain to make a decision which was acceptable to Parks and me. This I told the captain, pointing out that he had worked long enough with the warden to realize this.

By this time the captain was sweating. The warden was away and couldn't be reached. In desperation we consulted a dictionary on the meaning of the term 'ajar'. When I found the word I gave the dictionary to the captain. He paled as he read 'ajar – a door slightly open'. Then he said, "Well, that's one man's opinion." I agreed. Then he said he could never win with me.

I ended the conversation by warning him that should Mrs. Parks be sent away without being able to visit her son, we would not coöperate with the feeding anymore. I went over to Tom, still waiting for his mother to be allowed to return, to tell him about the captain's visit.

In a few minutes the first guard reappeared ushering Mrs. Parks. As I left the guard opened the door and started walking out into the hall. I walked back and pulled the door almost shut. To the guard's amazement and confusion, I stood between him and the door shaking my head. He ran downstairs to check with a superior. He returned mumbling something about "Oh, hell." After a round or two, passing the door where Tom and his mother were, he disappeared.

Our visits from that time on were in unsupervized rooms with doors closed.

Being in prison need not be a loss of time. It can be viewed as a continuation of life, as society in miniature. In many respects, the problems are similar, i.e., the practice of racism. Before my imprisonment in 1942, I had been engaged in actively combating discrimination against Negroes and other minorities. The struggle was continued in county jail and federal prison.

Some of the nonviolent tactics learned on the outside were quite helpful on the "inside."

On one occasion the associate warden at Milan opined, "Wally, you are trying to get us to do here what they don't do on the outside." I agreed, but went on to point out that I was on the inside. If he would release me, I would leave immediately and turn my energies to trying to erase the "color line" on the outside. My point here is that whether in or out, one addresses himself to the problem of one's environment. This, I suspect, might be one good answer to the question as to where one might prove to be more effective.

As can be seen, I started out in 1943 doing my first prison bit believing in prison and the prison system, but as a reformer. I left jail at the end of nearly three years feeling that the prison system should be abolished.

It is barbaric, one of the most brutal, violent, coercive forces in society. It would seem to me that the nonviolent theorist and actor must seek methods more human in dealing with problems of malbehavior.

☮☮☮

THE
Conscientious Objector

Re-entered as second class matter Nov. 10, 1941, at the Post Office at New York, N. Y., under the Act of March 3, 1879.

Vol. VII—No. 8   New York, August, 1945   300   Price Ten Cents

War Teaches Lesson of Disobedience, Writer Asserts

By Alex Comfort
(Reprinted from NOW)

The war is not over, but we can see the end of it. Millions of citizens everywhere are looking for a reprieve. Many of them will get it. Secret diplomacy is concocting the peace—we shall subscribe to it and be put back in our boxes. Intelligent people debate whether we shall occupy Germany for five, fifty or five hundred years. The intellectuals of the Allies seem to have been so far taken in by their own propaganda that they look at Germans shyly and are half relieved to find that they have no tails or horns. The most fantastic aspect about the impending peace will be the speed with which the nonsense which it is a moral duty to believe in wartime will

be forgotten: its consequences, the material commitments undertaken under the influence of the same nonsense, will not be so easy to escape.

Few people can remember what it was like to be sane, to live in a world where one could not earn a decoration for butchering a few thousand civilians, where a good many national heroes would have qualified for the gallows and the mental hospital and where a single news bulletin of the present time would have produced nation-wide nausea and vomiting.

This War Not Unique

This war has not been unique. Its lesson is identical with the lesson of every previous war. The record of it is the record of the incredible, somnambulant heroism

(Continued on page 6)

Bishop Free After 142-Day Fast

Demobilization is Deferred

Buchenwald Yields 300 CO Survivors, Document Shows

Clark's Action Is Taken After Extended Delay

Favorable Vote Is Expected On Winstead Bill

Measure Would Eliminate Present Plan in Favor Of Army System

By Max Pawl

WASHINGTON—The House Military Affairs Committee last month favorably reported out an amended Winstead Bill which would eliminate the present point system for demobilizing Civilian Public Service (CPS) men in favor of one identical with that of the army, severely curtailing CPS discharges. Proponents of the measure, led by Representative Arthur Winstead of Mississippi, believe the bill will be placed on the unanimous consent calendar for an early favorable vote in the House.

Meanwhile, Selective Service deferred initiation of the point discharge system pending disposition of the legislation.

Under the Winstead Bill—the first measure solely concerned with COs—points for wives are eliminated, number of children eligible limited to three, and 85 points made necessary for discharge, making it impossible for a CO to be released on points since the highest possible score which an assignee can achieve under the army system is 84. It was observed that even if the minimum were lowered, few COs would be eligible.

The Bill is not applicable to regular physical or other discharges, nor to those for reasons of hardship or overage, but, if passed, would virtually eliminate the

(Continued on page 6)

A Nice Thing

"Editing a newspaper is a nice thing. If we publish jokes, people say we are rattlebrained. If we don't, we are fossils. If we publish original matter, they say we don't give them enough selection. If we give them enough selections, they say we are too lazy to write. If we remain at the office, we ought to be out looking for news items. If we go out, then we are not attending to business."
—*Kansas Herald*, quoted in Acumen

By Worldover Press

LONDON—Approximately 300 German religious objectors to Nazism and war were found to have survived under the horrors of Buchenwald and 28 more in Belsen, two of Germany's most notorious concentration camps, according to a belated report in the British weekly, Peace News.

The report, hitherto unpublished in the United States, was based on a radio broadcast by Hr. Bjorn Hallstrom, London editor of the Swedish daily, *Svenska Morgonbladet*, following his discovery of a document in the Buchenwald camp shortly after liberation. Facts based on the same document were also released through the International Bible Students Association (whose members are Jehovah's Witnesses in the U. S. and Britain).

Some of the religious survivors, according to the document, were arrested and imprisoned as early as 1934, shortly after Hitler's rise to power. The greatest wave of arrests began in 1936, and by 1937, the number of objectors, most of them Jehovah's Witnesses, had reached 270. The highest figure of 450 was reached late in 1938, according to the document. (Dr. Emil Maurer, district chairman of the Socialist Party in pre-

war Vienna, who went to Buchenwald in September, 1938, asserted in The Tribune (London) that out of 6,000 inmates then in the camp, about 1,200 were religious pacifists of the J. W. sect.)

"Once," Hr. Hallstrom said, "they were going to compel the Bible Students to do military service. If they refused they were to be shot as conscientious objectors. Two SS companies marched up ready to fire. The prisoners calmly faced the rifles. They refused unanimously to fight for the State which had taken from them the freedom of worship. The rifles were lowered and instead of being shot there was a further deterioration of food and new ill-treatment." Some of the religious prisoners were later executed, Hr. Hallstrom added.

SS Men Turn CO!

In addition to Bible Students, Hr.

(Continued on page 5)

Absolutist Accepts Parole Without Signing Papers; Goes to Georgia

By Purnell Benson
Special to The C.O.

NEW YORK —— ... the Church of Christ, won his freedom from the federal penitentiary here last month, climaxing a 142-day period of refusal to eat or lift a finger to help the state conscript him.

He had been kept alive by force-feeding of liquids, and it was uncertain how much longer he would have survived. Following his release, he went to the Cooperative Community at Macedonia, Georgia, to recuperate.

Bishop accepted parole without signing any papers or making any promises. He intends to exercise complete freedom. His release was finally effected through favorable action taken by Attorney General Tom Clark after months of delay.

During his three years and three months in CPS detention camps, jails and prisons, Bishop came, through his words and actions, to be a living symbol of freedom.

Inducted into CPS at Patapsco, Maryland, on 10-day notice, he sought a deferment or an emergency furlough to settle his bookstore affairs in West New York, N. J. On June 26, 1942, he began to fast, drinking water only, until the government either paid him for loss of property, gave him maintenance and a "fair salary for acceptable work," or else released him altogether. He told his conscriptors: "To me the present choice is worse than death."

For three weeks Bishop continued to work in the kitchen. Then he was listed as sick, but was not confined to bed. Two weeks later Selective Service issued

(Continued on page 6)

CO Wins Reparole

Robert Currier, objector whose parole was revoked in May because he married without waiting for the consent of the U. S. Parole Board, was released from the federal penitentiary at Danbury, Conn., last month on a reparole, which expires in May, 1946. His original parole would have terminated in September, this year.

Draft Referendum, Conscription Abolition Sought by Legislators

Would Submit Question of Compulsory Training to People for Vote

WASHINGTON—A joint resolution providing for a national referendum on the question of universal peacetime conscription was introduced in the Senate last month by Senator Hugh Butler (Rep., Neb.).

In offering the measure, Sen. Butler said he realized it would have the effect of delaying action on legislation now under consideration by Congressional committees, but added that he thought it was "generally agreed that Congress will not act on these proposals this year, anyway." He said the referendum would clear up many doubts in the minds of Senators concerning the

(Continued on page 8)

House Member Proposes Nations Drop Policy of Military Service

WASHINGTON—World-wide abolition of compulsory military service was called for last month by Representative Joseph W. Martin, Jr., minority leader of the House. He proposed that while an international agreement to that end was being sought, action be withheld on the pending American universal training program.

Mr. Martin's resolution urged President Truman, James F. Byrnes, Secretary of State, and Edward H. Stettinius, Jr., "to work increasingly for an immediate international agreement whereby compulsory military service shall be wholly eliminated from the policies and

(Continued on page 8)

☮☮☮

THE STORY OF
CORBETT BISHOP

Ernest Bromley (1912-1997)

Editor's Note: Ernest Bromley graduated from Boston University with a Bachelor of Science degree in 1939 and began study for the ministry at the Duke School of Religion (now Duke University Divinity School) in Durham, North Carolina, in the fall of that year; after a year and a half, he left the school to be pastor of a church in the North Carolina Methodist Conference.

A year later Pearl Harbor was bombed. After Pearl Harbor, Ernest stated again his intentions not to support war, even though the U.S. might be a part of it. After the declaration of war, every automobile using the highways in the U.S. was required by law to have a "defense tax stamp" on its windshield. These could be purchased at any post office for $2.09 and were valid from January 31, 1942, until the end of the federal fiscal year on June 30 of the next year. Then another $5.00 stamp would have to be purchased.

Ernest, of course, did not buy one and was intercepted by county police, working with the FBI. He was arrested and on October 5 pleaded not guilty to the charge and accepted no lawyer.

He was convicted and given a $25.00 fine on each of the two counts. Upon his refusal to pay, Ernest was given the mandatory 60 days (30 days on each count) and served it in the Wake County Jail in Raleigh.

In September 1943, after he had lost his church, Ernest went to New York as Youth Secretary of the Fellowship of Reconciliation where he met his wife, Marion. He was appointed to this capacity by the North Carolina Methodist Conference, but during the year his appointment was rescinded, and he continued on at Union Theological Seminary, graduating in 1945.

He returned to North Carolina and held two pastorates before publishing his "Termination of Active Ministry" because of the complicity of the Methodist Church in the defense effort. Ernie has refused to pay taxes for war, with several interruptions, since 1942.

In the spring of 1948, he and Marion helped to found Peacemakers, a group of absolutists whose special concern was the nonpayment of war taxes. They have three children, one of whom, Dan, is presently serving a three-year sentence for refusal to register for the draft at the Federal Youth Center at Ashland, Kentucky.

They publish The Peacemaker, a fine journal of notes and comment, every three weeks, from their Gano, Ohio, farmhouse just outside Cincinnati. Ω

Corbett Bishop is dead. He was killed on the night of May 17, 1961, in his house in Hamilton, Alabama by an 18-year-old youth who said later he had gone to the residence to commit robbery and had procured $42.00 from the wallet of the victim. The youth, who had been drinking, stole a car and wrecked it near Bishop's house late at night. He went and woke Bishop who treated his scratched ankle with antiseptic. He then shot Bishop in the hip, followed him and broke his neck with the rifle butt.

One of Corbett's sisters, Mrs. M.J. Shotts, writes "We are all still in a state of confusion. We just can't seem to pull ourselves together. It was a horrible death for anyone to have to die."

Newspaper clippings which she sent give in detail the youth's story and describe in brief Corbett's life. Stating he was 55 years old and a native of Hamilton, one clipping continues, "Corbett Bishop was a graduate of Auburn and held a master of arts degree from the University of Wisconsin. When World War II started, he was operating a bookstore in New Jersey. Believing that all war was wrong, Bishop joined the ranks of the conscientious objectors, where he was known as an absolutist. He fasted a total of 828 days, 144 days in one stretch, as a means of expressing his passive form of resistance to any phase of war. He was force-fed in order to prevent his starving to death.

"He made many talks on the evils of war and violence.

"Bishop case back to Hamilton after the government released him in 1946. It was in Marion County that he stayed except for intermittent trips to Chicago and New York City. He sold books for a living and his collection of books filled the four buildings of his home to the ceilings. He had books on practically every subject known to man. Bishop called his home 'Paradise Ridge'.

"A striking figure with his piercing eyes and white beard, Bishop walked the five miles from his home to Hamilton almost every day."

I saw Corbett for the last time in Chicago on a snowy February day just as Maurice McCrackin and I were leaving the office of the American Friends Service Committee to begin the trip home from our support of Sis Robinson who had just been imprisoned there for nonpayment of taxes.

Corbett was planning to leave Chicago soon for permanent residence in Alabama where he had been shipping books.

The three of us went to a restaurant, talked about Sis Robinson's situation, reminisced some, and left after an hour or so. But I remember now that he mentioned he had become concerned about the thievery that had been going on at his little place in Hamilton which he had occasionally been visiting, and to which he was gradually sending all the books he possessed. "They are young fellows," he said. "They break windows, and take things."

After going to Alabama he was particularly anxious to keep up with news of people through The Peacemaker, and occasionally wrote letters which we published.

Corbett is remembered as one of the best known COs who were in prison during World War II. A vocal opponent of alternative service, he eventually left civilian public service, was arrested, and put in prison. He did not coöperate with either the arrest or the imprisonment. Because of this he became a highly controversial figure in pacifist circles.

I remember Corbett's exit from CPS in 1944. He came to New York City and to the apartment on West 24th Street where my sister Eleanor and I and three others were living. Eleanor had known him in CPS where she had been camp nurse. He talked with a number of us about his impending arrest and imprisonment. "I'm not sure what I want to do," he said, "but I don't want to coöperate with the system which punishes people for refusing to kill in war." This was a new idea.

When he was arrested a short time later, he had pretty well made up his mind to give no assistance. The FBI carried him. Into court he was carried. He talked whenever he felt he had something to say, but he paid no obeisance to officials or institutions which were "carrying out their duties." He went where they took him, he sat where they set him, he lay where they laid him.

But he never got up, never lay down, he never walked. He responded to no external orders while in this situation; he responded only to the internal ones.

Corbett was in prison. But he tried not to feel a part of the prison, either its physical confinement or its system. When they spoke of "your bed," or "your cell," or "your window," he would remind the speaker of the bed, the cell, the window. "For," he would say, "they are not mine. I can claim no such ownership, nor would I."

Days and weeks went by. He did not move about or change his posture at any time. But he would always talk to whoever came around. Guards and the warden himself began to spend quite a bit of time in conversation with him. He had something neither they nor most pacifists understood, and they wanted to find out more. An avid reader and collector of rare books, he had stored up in his memory much on which he could now draw. He was jolly, witty, and profound. Some pacifists who obtained permission to visit him came away amazed.

I do not remember just how many days went by before the warden put him in an automobile and drove him a considerable distance and deposited him at a lonely crossroads, but it seems to me now that it was well over one hundred. He came again to New York City and to our apartment which had also been the hospitality headquarters for two of his sisters who had come from Alabama to meet with the Absolutists in New York City. The Absolutists, a group headed by Julius and Esther Eichel, were working for the release of Corbett.

I had not been opposed to the idea of complete noncoöperation when Corbett had first talked with me some months before about it, but I hadn't favored it much either. I did not, immediately, understand it, and had wondered if anyone could actually proceed consistently and thoroughly in this. It was obvious, however, even before he was ejected from the prison, that he had made the position wholly understandable and that there was a technical completeness in what he did.

But what I was now seeing for the first time was how he had been able to accomplish this. I noticed he referred to "the body." They took the body there, they did this or that to the body. Just as if he were outside his body observing what they did to it! "They had the body on a cart-like contraption," he said, "wheeling it into a room. The wheels of the cart struck against the high threshold and stopped suddenly. But the body didn't."

Thoreau had said of his night in prison, "It was a great waste of brick and mortar" and "I did not for a moment feel confined." Corbett, leaving his imprisoned body where they put it and not worrying about it at all, was able to have his mind completely free to take him anywhere he wanted to go and do anything he wanted to do. And he did these things without losing sense of what is often referred to as "reality."

It wasn't long before the Department of Justice again arrested Corbett and he was on his way back to the custody of the Bureau of Prisons which had only recently effected the departure of its most uncoöperative prisoner. The warden at Milan prison went to Wally Nelson, also one of the CO noncoöperators, and said, "What have I done that they are sending Corbett back?"

Corbett, unperturbed, took up where he had left off a few weeks before. After several months he was once more deposited outside the prison somewhere, and was never picked up again. To other COs in Milan it was abundantly clear that no prisoner stood higher in the respect of the warden than Corbett Bishop.

To many pacifists through the years, he has become a symbol of complete noncoöperation. He has become sort of a legendary figure about whom even people who have never met him tell fascinating stories.

Corbett Bishop had insight. He had courage. He did what he felt led of the spirit to do. He was a magnificent pioneer.

☮☮☮

☮☮☮

Two Years In Upper Hartford Cell House, Danbury Federal Prison

Lowell Naeve

To me the prison feels like a place way up high, with sheer perpendicular cliffs descending on all sides. I imagine that no greenery grows for miles around the place, that the surrounding countryside is nothing but a field of huge, jagged, broken boulders very difficult to pass through. I imagine if I were out among the boulders I'd find those closest to the cliffs to be the sharpest and largest. Out a few miles from the prison, I'd expect to find smaller boulders and stones. Then as I got further away, the stones would become smaller and smaller, smoother. If I were out among the stones the further I got away from the prison the easier the travel would be.

If I could get to one of the prison's outside windows, and look out, I imagine I would be able to see the greenery begin just beyond the field of broken stones. It would be barely visible, all around, just on the horizon!

☮☮☮

CONSCIENTIOUS OBJECTORS IN THE 1950s:
A Study in Repression

The Selective Service Act of 1948, Multiple Prosecutions, Nonpayment of War Taxes, and the Smith Act Victims

The Conscientious Objector
Karl Shapiro

The gates clanged and they walked you into jail
More tense than felons but relieved to find
The hostile world shut out, the flags that dripped
From every mother's windowpane, obscene
The bloodlust sweating from the public heart,
The dog authority slavering at your throat.
A sense of quiet, of pulling down the blind
Possessed you. Punishment you felt was clean.

The decks, the catwalks, and the narrow light
Composed a ship. This was a mutinous crew
Troubling the captains for plain decencies,
A Mayflower brim with pilgrims headed out
To establish new theocracies to west,
A Noah's ark coasting the topmost seas
Ten miles above the sodomites and fish.
These inmates loved the only living doves.

Like all men hunted from the world you made
A good community, voyaging the storm
To no safe Plymouth or green Ararat;
Trouble or calm, the men with Bibles prayed,
The gaunt politicals construed our hate.
The opposite of all armies, you were best
Opposing uniformity and yourselves;
Prison and personality were your fate.

You suffered not so physically but knew
Maltreatment, hunger, ennui of the mind.
Well might the soldier kissing the hot beach
Erupting in his face damn all your kind.
Yet you who saved neither yourselves nor us
Are equally with those who shed the blood
The heroes of our cause. Your conscience is
What we come back to in the armistice.

☮ ☮ ☮

LETTERS FROM THE FOUR DOTY BROTHERS

Joel, Orin, Paul and Sid Doty

Editor's Note: The Doty family of Bruno, Minnesota, had a long record of conscientious objection to war. The head of that family, William N. Doty, served a little more than two years in a military prison during World War I. He based his position on both religion and politics, although he belonged to no church.

Joel was 24 before Federal agents came to arrest him and his brothers for refusal to register for the draft in 1950. Although he was liable under the Selective Service Act of 1940, he did not register and was not prosecuted. Orin, Paul, and Sid were between 23 and 21 when their arrest came under the 1948 law.

Sentenced on April 6, 1951, Joel received two years and his brothers eighteen months to be served at the Medical Center for Federal Prisoners in Springfield, Missouri.

Upon their arrival there, Orin, Paul, and Sid refused to work in "payless slave labor" on June 5 and their brother Joel on June 14. They spent time in solitary at Springfield and then were transferred to segregation where protests were lodged with the government because of their treatment.

The brothers were transferred to Ashland because of a nationwide protest to James V. Bennett, director of the Bureau of Prisons, who had discovered "no evidence of mistreatment" in their case.

Only shortly after a year had passed from the time of their release, they were ordered to report for induction into the armed forces in Duluth. The four brothers, Joel, Orin, Paul, and Sid did not appear for this "slave labor," either, and were once again arrested and on March 5, 1954, were sentenced to two years for failure to report for induction. Imprisoned in the Federal Correctional Institution at Texarkana, Texas, they were released on parole in late 1955. Ω

September 1, 1951

Mr. J. Howard McGrath
Attorney General
Washington, D.C.
In Re: "American Freedom and Human Rights"

Dear Sir:

Recently you stated in a speech to the National Catholic Education Association, as follows: "American freedom and human rights are mutually dependent. Either without the other will collapse." May I ask just what do you mean by "American freedom and human rights?"

Many of the laws that a rubber stamp Congress have been enacting recently are so confusing that even the judges of our Supreme Court are unable to agree as to their validity or constitutionality, for in a recent decision they were split four to four, and one of them even remarked, "This is justice turned upside down."

Do you expect honest, intelligent God-fearing people to respect our high court when they are indicted by one of their own members? And this is the same court that decided the validity of Prussian military conscription which is so sweetly labeled "Selective Service."

I cannot help but question the validity of military conscription or any form of "slavery and involuntary servitude." For under our Constitution and in conformance with God's Laws, the Members of Congress, the President and Judges of the Supreme Court have no jurisdiction over any man's conscience or spiritual beliefs, for the fact that no man or woman has to answer to any man or public official in the Judgment Day, but we all must give an account of our lives to our Creator and His Son Christ who is the Supreme Judge of the universe.

I am convinced beyond all reasonable doubt that the prosecution and imprisonment of all war objectors in these United States, or anywhere within its jurisdiction, is in violent conflict with both American and Christian jurisprudence. And it is in these circumstances that I respectfully request the immediate release of all conscientious objectors to the evils of war and military conscription, including my four sons, Joel, Orin, Paul, and Sid Doty, who are now imprisoned at Ashland, Kentucky, recently transferred from Springfield, Missouri.

Judge Donovan's remarks about my sons not being "baptized" was contrary to Constitutional prohibitions against a religious test.

It was also rather ironic in view of the fact that Christ was not baptized until He reached the age of 30 years, and then he was not baptized by an Army Chaplain or a hypocritical Pharisee, but by John, one of God's greatest prophets. Also the fact that Hitler was "baptized" and a member in good standing of a well-recognized religious creed, and it cost the American taxpayers three hundred billion dollars and one million casualties to overcome Hitler and his military conscription, granted him by a rubber-stamp Reichstag-congress. Without military conscription, there could be no "Police State" dictatorship established in any Nation on earth.

Under our Federal Constitution, which is "the supreme law of the land," any man or woman has the God-given unalienable right to "worship God in spirit and in truth," as Jesus Christ so stated, or worship Baal and his military stooges like many of these war criminals who were only recently executed in Germany and Japan, even though they had been "baptized" in some religious creed.

Our God and Creator has granted us our religious freedom when He said, "Choose ye this day whom ye will serve, God or Baal." It is my understanding that God created us all free moral agents to choose for ourselves whether we wish to serve him or the forces of evil – Satan and his religious, political and commercial stooges, all of them Anti-Christ. "Know ye not, that to whom ye yield yourselves servants to obey, his servants ye are to whom ye obey; whether of sin unto death, or of obedience unto righteousness?" Romans 6:16.

Instead of you requesting congress for additional thought control laws "to cover the oath-taker's status and beliefs" past, present, and future, camouflaged as a "loyalty oath," you should enforce the oath taken by all public officials to "preserve, support, and defend the constitution," which is the best loyalty oath extant. Violators of this "constitutional oath of office" could be prosecuted for perjury.

The "Early Christians" were people who had learned the gospel of Christ and were conscientious objectors to war, and the pagan Rome politicians rounded them up and placed them in the arena where they could be torn to bits by wild beasts and made human torches of them by tying them to the torture stakes and saturating them with inflammable oil and burning them to death. "A terrible crime," we say.

Today, we as a nation are doing exactly the same thing to millions of helpless men, women and children in Korea, who are being torn to bits by beastly bombs and burned alive by napalm gasoline jelly bombs and causing thousands of our own youths to be murdered yet we have the audacity, the gall, to call ourselves Christians.

If we could sum up all the crimes committed, including murder by the prisoners now serving time in Alcatraz, "The Rock," their total crimes would fade into insignificance compared to the enormity of our crime now being committed in Korea and against the Korean people who were created by the same God that created us.

There are millions of honest citizens in these United States, and the whole world, that are fully aware of this terrible crime and among them are thousands of conscientious objectors to war who refuse to be made a party to said crime by refusing to be drafted into the armed forces, and they not only have a constitutional right to refuse, but they all have a God-given unalienable right to refuse to be made *particeps criminis* to this wholesale murder of innocent human souls which is even worse than wicked Herod's slaughter of innocent babes in his dragnet to get the child Christ.

Of the many thousand war objectors that have been imprisoned in both the second world war and this third world war that we are now in, only a few war objectors have been pardoned, after they had served their prison terms which is like granting a pardon after a man has been executed, yet several criminal politicians have been pardoned or granted executive clemency which places us, as a nation, on the level with the mob that cried: "Free unto us Barabbas, the murderer, but crucify Jesus, the innocent man."

Who are the real criminals? The conscientious objectors to war, or the advocates of rearmament and military conscription which only leads to more war and thereby produces more real war criminals? Honest people know the answer to these questions.

It is not only a crime against society but a crime against our Creator to arrest law-abiding young men and imprison them, and if they refuse to be slaves in a slave labor camp they are caged in like wild beasts in solitary confinement and their only "crime" is that of refusing to be made a party to the war crimes of the war criminals. "By their works ye shall know them."

Again, I request that you, as a public servant, order the immediate release of all war objectors.

I am an American Citizen of Mayflower lineage.

Respectfully submitted,
Wm. N. Doty

May 31, 1951

Dear Mom and Dad,

Well, I haven't much to write but I will continue to write at least once, sometime during each week as long as I have such a privilege, but you know what can happen to privileges.

We are well and getting along so don't ever worry about us here, I am working every day, six days per week, on the farm. I have been working and thinking and I have formed some definite conclusions. A man can do a lot of thinking here. That's one freedom they can't take.

I would like to be home now, but don't expect me home soon, not even in October. Don't work too hard and raise a large garden as we may not be home for a while.

The weather is still nice here, but it's starting to get a little warm.

I am getting plenty of fresh air and sunshine so I manage to stay in good health.

This is all the news for now but maybe I'll have more in the near future.

So long for now.

Your son,
Orin
3864-P.C.

May 31, 1951

One must be spiritually strong in order to succeed in times like these. I do not ask, nor expect, any mercy from my captors. If my captivity is meant to weaken my spirit I can assure you that it is having just the opposite effect. This rule can be applied to all political prisoners.

Don't worry if we can't always write as writing is only a privilege.

Orin
3864-F.C

June 5, 1951

Well, I have some news to report since writing my last letter. Orin, Paul, and Sid went to the "hole" today for refusing to work. I have given it considerable thought also but so far as yet I see no constructive meaning for it. I realize that by working I am aiding to some extent the "system" which sent me here but on the other hand I don't work too hard and to keep busy is also good for body and mind. However I may change my mind at any time on this problem. I am not afraid of not making parole or losing "good time" as the principle of that is to more or less keep a man "in line," etc. I suppose they will be there for an indefinite period of time or until they change their mind.

It is hard to accomplish anything while locked up here, and so far we have received good treatment.

Well, that is about all the news for now so will close with love. Write often if you have the time as the letters seem to be few and far between.

Love,
Joel
3865-P.C.

June 12, 1951

Dear Mom and Dad,
I didn't write last week, but I'll write now. I received Dad's last two letters dated May 30th and June 4th with clippings enclosed.

Well, as far as I know, we are all getting along as well as can be expected. We are getting plenty of good plain food, but I miss the milk, eggs, butter and meat we get at home. Nevertheless I think I have gained weight since I have been here. I only weighed 136 lbs. when I first arrived here.

I hope everything is going well at home. I imagine it is quite hard for Dad to work around the house and away on the job, too. You'll just have to do the best you can for now and don't worry about anything as worry is never the determining factor in solving any problem.

I'll try to make the best use of my time while I am here. If I have any difficulties I'll try to solve them as constructively as possible.

So long for now.

Your son,
Orin
3864-P.C.

June 15, 1951

Dear Mom and Dad,

I received Dad's two letters one dated June 7th and the other dated June 10th.

Well, June the 4th, Orin, Paul, and I quit working and June 5th, we were put in "isolation" after continuing to refuse work. We were kept in "Isolation" for one week and then transferred to "Segregation." I believe we shall remain here for the duration. In "Isolation" and "Segregation" we get plenty to eat and shave and shower twice a week. The room is about 7' by 12', stool and sink with cool water. We sleep on a mattress on the floor. We have two sheets, a pillow and two blankets. Each room also has a large window, with so many bars and screens it gives a person a headache to try to look out any length of time.

I heard that Joel came in yesterday. He got tired of working against himself, too, I think.

Now don't raise too much in that garden as two don't eat as much as six.

I seem like I'm busy all the time here, first I read and before I know it, it's time to eat again. Time by moment flies away.

Well, that's all for now.

Your Son,
Sid
3866-P.C.

June 16, 1951

Dear Dad and Mom,

I received your special delivery letter of June 11th on the 14th. I wrote you two letters since then, one on the 14th and one on the 15th, but I got then back today for the following reasons of which I will quote: "discussing institutional set up and procedure" and "Please do not mention names and activities of other inmates." The other "inmates" are your sons too, but in order to obey the "rules" I will refrain from mentioning their names anymore. I'll also have to refrain from mentioning anything that happens here; therefore, do not expect very much information from me.

If I may, I would like to give you the following information: I am getting along as well as can be expected and I still get three meals per day.

I acquired my present status June 4th when I "refused to work." I assume that it is meant as a form of "discipline."

It should be noted that COs, by the nature of their understanding of the teachings of Christ, do not harbor any hatred or bitterness toward their enemies. To do so would be in conflict with Christ's teachings which they are attempting to follow by their "works."

I still remember the statement made by the judge: "Your father accomplished nothing by serving time in prison in World War I." I don't know exactly what he was attempting to imply by such a statement. I would like to ask this question, though: What do the "War Lords" and their "political stooges" consider accomplished by their sentencing of COs to prison? Or do they commit these acts without reason? I might go even further and ask: What do they consider accomplished by placing COs in solitary confinement? One can plainly see that the only apparent answer they have, to the Christ-like approach to life, is imprisonment, etc.

In "refusing to work" I feel that I am exercising my constitutional right. I also realize that our "invisible super-government" has very little regard for the U.S. Constitution, except when they attempt to use it as an instrument of propaganda, but I will still show my respect for it.

So long for now and don't worry about anything.

Your Son,
Orin
3864-P.C.

July 10, 1951

Dear Dad,

I received your letter, dated July 10th, yesterday. It was mailed from Virginia. The copies of the two letters and the leaflet about fraudulent money systems were enclosed.

I was especially interested in Dr. Richard's letter because understand "parole" and "good time" are an insult to anyone who was convicted because of high principles. I told the high officials here, when I refused to work, that I could not be concerned with "good time." It seems very inconsistent and illogical to me, for one to sacrifice his personal physical freedom because of his high principles, and then try to regain meager bits of that freedom by submitting after imprisonment.

I want you to know that I am never in the least bit discouraged, because I am unable to compromise, nor am I fearful of the outcome.

So long for now.

Your son, Orin
3864-P.C.

July 22, 1951

Dear Mom,

I have just had my exercise for the day. It consists of sweeping out and mopping up my room.

I guess you could say that I am "enjoying" the great "security" that Gen. Eisenhower spoke of a couple of years ago in a speech before Congress.

Well, there isn't too much to write about from here. Everything is the same. The only thing I miss is fresh air and sunshine, plus a little exercise. They offer "exercise" here that consists of being taken out of your small cell and led down the hall to a larger room, (the room is bare except for a long table and a couple of benches), where one has the honor of playing with a tennis ball for approximately 30 minutes per day. You are left alone to "enjoy" this privilege of playing ball by yourself. I assume that this is supposed to have a psychological effect on a person. However, it does strike me as child's play and I do not indulge in this fascinating sport.

The other day I was reading an article in the Reader's Digest, on the opportunities in Canada. The country is thinly populated and there is a boom going on up there in the oil fields, iron mining, and railroading. Also the Canadian enjoys a certain freedom which no longer exists in this country. Maybe upon my release from this institution, I should like to go up there and be able to live like a human being for a change.

Well, that's about all for now so will close with love from all of us here.

Your Son,
Joel
3865-P.C.

☮☮☮

☮ ☮ ☮

A Second Time Around

Arlo Tatum (1923-2014)

(*Editor's Note.* Arlo Tatum was born in Perth City, Iowa on February 21, 1923, brought into the world by an osteopath. His birthright membership in the Religious Society of Friends is recorded in West Branch, Iowa.

Arlo consciously became a conscientious objector at the age of 14 when he wrote a dramatic poem about seeing a clothesline pole from his bedroom window which looked like a cross, to him a symbol of conscription. When he was 18, he was participating in a Quaker workcamp in Mexico when the Selective Service law was changed, reducing the age of registration from 19 to 18. He did not want to be considered a draft dodger, so Arlo returned to the U.S. to find counsel in his own position of nonregistration at the American Friends Service Committee in Philadelphia. They spent three days trying to convince him to register.

He left sick at heart and went to see Dr. Evan Thomas in New York, at that time chair of the War Resisters League. He was the one person Arlo knew who had not coöperated with conscription, so Arlo explained he was not planning to register, but did not know how to go about it. Evan said, "Young man, I advise you to register." Arlo turned from his desk, walked to the door and was beginning to cry. Evan called after him, "Well, are you going to register?"

Arlo spun around and said, "No." Evan called to him and said, "Then we had better discuss it." Eventually, Arlo wrote the U.S. Attorney-General saying he would not register.

Arlo was arrested by a neighbor who lived in the same apartment house as his parents in Fort Dodge, Iowa. The federal marshal and his wife played bridge with Arlo's parents, and Arlo was a friend of their son, a boy the same age. The Marshal came to the door that morning, a great bulky man who filled the door. When Arlo's mother opened it, tears came to the Marshal's eyes and he finally managed to say, "I've come to take Arlo." Arlo's mother called him. The Marshal was given coffee and assured he was only doing his duty and Arlo was taken to the county jail in Humboldt, Iowa.

Twelve of Arlo's relatives managed to post bond by putting their property up for it. Arlo was released pending sentence after entering a guilty plea and was sent to the Federal Correctional Institution in Sandstone, Minnesota, where he served out his two-year sentence.

Arlo's arrest and sentence was in 1941 and 1942, when President Truman contrived the State of National Emergency in connection with the Berlin Airlift and – with the help of future President Lyndon Johnson – managed to get the draft law re-enacted in 1948. Registration was required up to age 26 and Arlo was 25 at that time. As events happened, Arlo was on a singing tour in Canada and was strongly urged (and was tempted) to stay. He was also tempted to fill out the forms and register, because by that time, he would have been 26 and nothing more would have been required of him.

But Arlo Tatum was unable to talk himself into coöperating even to that extent and so was arrested while on a concert tour for a faculty of the University of Minnesota. Again Arlo was sentenced, this time at the Medical Center for Federal Prisoners in Springfield, Missouri.

The only men liable to multiple prosecutions were those who fell into this age group. Several hundred were eventually sent to prison for the second time, their first sentence under the 1940 draft law and the second under the 1948 Act. In at least one instance, a third prosecution was reported! Today, only one draft resister, Peter Kiger, of the War Resisters League in New York, who served one year in Springfield for refusal of induction under the 1948 Act, has been prosecuted a second time and sentenced to three months for burning a draft card under the 1967 law. Many others who have served prison terms have been reclassified 1-A under Selective Service.

Arlo is presently Executive Secretary of the Central Committee for Conscientious Objectors in Philadelphia, where this editor worked under him as a draft counsellor and editor of CCCO's 18th edition of the Handbook for Conscientious Objectors. Arlo also co-authored a book, Guide to the Draft in 1969 with Joseph Tuchinsky of the Midwest Committee for Draft Counselling.

Arlo married his wife, Polly, when he served as General Secretary of the War Resisters' International in England. They have two strikingly lovely daughters.Ω)

T he government's offer was to go into what would be called a forced labor camp in the Soviet Union and to pay $35.00 a month for the privilege. This was called Civilian Public Service and, if you were put into one of the camps run by the Mennonites, Quakers or Brethren and didn't pay, someone else paid for you. In fact, many a Meeting was obliged to devote its entire income to keeping alternative servicemen in the camps, although later the government set up a few camps at which there was no cost.

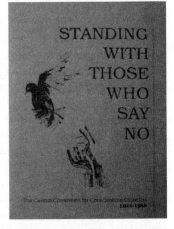

When I entered the prison at Sandstone, I was immediately impressed by the large number of very kindly prisoners who wanted to be my protectors. I had requested assignment to the library which I received; I guess that also made the assignment unusual.

A few weeks later, however, I was transferred to a job as denture maker for the prison dentist. He was a very lazy man and rather brutal, so I also ended up doing most of the teeth cleaning. I didn't clean teeth as well as he might have done, and it was a bloody mess. One of the reasons I was glad to get out of the prison was that it rather embarrassed me to meet my smiling clients in the exercise yard, all with ill-fitting teeth.

My approach to prison was to get the maximum benefit out of it and perhaps this was a selfish approach. I felt that it was an unusual opportunity to be with social discards as a peer, and I knew the really dangerous criminals were more likely to be elective office than in prison. These men in prison were, of course, unsuccessful criminals. Too many of them seemed to never have had anyone to really listen to their problems, and I spent a great deal of time as a listening post. I was also instrumental in getting one man who was too good to be a prison guard to resign.

I like to feel that a few men did not return to prison because of my presence there. I started a glee club; I organized inmate shows for the two Christmases I was in and, in fact, was granted parole in order to spend the second Christmas at home. The date was advanced but I was unable to accept it because I had accepted the obligation of producing the show. I added the innovation of doing a second performance for the guards, their wives and children. I did this partly to show the prisoners that guards had wives and children and partly to assure myself that they did.

I shall always have a secret suspicion that I was more valuable to my immediate community when I was in prison than I have been since. I think that my objection to noncoöperation in prison is that it separates one from other prisoners and removes from one the only opportunity that he will have to associate as an equal with such men.

Sandstone was closed at the time I was sentenced for the second time so I was sent to the Medical Center for Federal Prisoners in Springfield, Missouri. There I was assigned to work on the farm, pick-axing manure to be put on carts and taken to different places where it would stand until it was taken to be used as fertilizer the following spring. This struck me as made work and, although there was no conscious decision involved, I decided that I didn't care to do it. I submitted my resignation, giving two weeks notice. I was called to the Associate Warden's office, which, in Springfield, is not on the compound.

The associate Warden is often a disciplinarian and runs the institution while the Warden is out making liberal speeches at the Kiwanis Club and Rotary. He waved the paper upon which I had submitted my resignation in my face and asked me what it was. I told him it was a resignation. He asked if I didn't know where I was and I assured him I realized I was in the

Medical Center for Federal Prisoners. "Then you know you can't resign." I explained patiently to him that this was obviously untrue because I had just done so and asked whether he was incorrect in thinking that for an unskilled job I should have given more than two weeks notice. He ended up holding me before his classification committee.

After threats of being placed in segregation, which I had anticipated, I was given a different assignment as diet clerk for a civilian dietician. The dietician was a woman named Miss Carnes who had one stiff leg and was less than five feet tall. After I had worked with her for several weeks, she announced to me that she had resigned because she felt I could fulfill her job as she had wanted to quit for some time and had stayed on only under pressure. I then became dietician, relying upon one diet book produced in 1928 and another produced in 1934. I was constantly afraid I would kill someone, but it never happened. I was in a difficult position because I had civilian cooks working under me. The situation infuriated them and caused a certain amount of suspicion on the part of the other prisoners. I worked very hard and am quite convinced that those on special diets had better food during the time I was there than they had before or have had since. On the other hand, I realized I was saving the government quite a bit of money and this rather distressed me.

I can't remember now whether I failed to make parole or whether it can so near my release date that I rejected it. I rather suspect the latter. In any event, I was released after 13 months of my year and a half sentence. Upon reflection, I would say that going to prison when you are younger and going to prison once is more than half as easy as going to prison twice. But if it is necessary for me to go to prison again, I shall do so, knowing that it will again be an interesting and challenging experience; one which everyone – particularly judges – should undergo until we are civilized enough to get rid of prisons. Although I do not advocate that men refuse to coöperate with the draft, I do urge that they follow their own consciences. And I object strongly to those who talk about "wasting time" in prison. There are men who waste their time in a university, or in a job, and well as in a prison.

I feel that had I not accepted the consequences of my total rejection of conscription, I would not now be visible in the peace movement. it is a part of me and my position, an expression of myself, just as is my present work for ending the draft and helping those who find it a problem in the meantime. A prison experience can be debilitating or it can be a stimulant to work for the elimination of the law which is sending men to prison unnecessarily.

Toward the end of World War II, an Amnesty Committee was set up. One of its leading figures was Albon Man, Jr., and it demanded amnesty for all those who refused Selective Service during the war. While no amnesty was granted, the pressure did bring about the establishment of a Presidential Pardon Board which theoretically went through the file of every man who violated the draft law and eventually granted pardons to about 1,000 men.

I was one of those pardoned. None of these men applied for pardons, but a good many of the remainder have applied for them since that time. There had been earlier instances of amnesty – such as after the Civil War and even after the First World War – but there was none forthcoming at the end of World War II. I know of no instance in which a draft violator who applied for a Presidential pardon being refused. I dealt with a number of men who wanted pardons during the Goldwater-Johnson campaign in 1964. These were men who had not previously voted and felt it important to vote for the peace candidate, Johnson. We all know how that turned out.

I think that amnesty becomes a political possibility if and when the draft ends or becomes substantially altered. I would like to see pressure for amnesty when the law is changed. If the administration is not of the same political party that brought about the escalation of the war in Vietnam, it is possible that a substantial number of criminal convictions might be expunged. This approach, however, is not a radical one, because a good deal of the amnesty work contains the suggestion that the vote is a means to really change society.

THE CONSCIENTIOUS OBJECTOR IN THE 1960s:
Direct Action for a Warless World

Omaha Action; *The Golden Rule* and *Everyman I, II, and III*; Polaris Action; and the Draft.

☮ ☮ ☮

THE NONVIOLENT REVOLUTION AND THE AMERICAN PEACE MOVEMENT

Karl Meyer

Editor's Note: Karl Meyer was born in 1937 in Wisconsin and was raised in Vermont by parents who communicated to him their own peaceful ways and an interest in Gandhi. He registered as a conscientious objector at the age of eighteen, and then went to jail for the first time with Ammon Hennacy and Dorothy Day of the Catholic Worker movement for refusing to take shelter during New York State's compulsory civil defense drills. Since then, Karl has been to jail a dozen times.

Four years after he registered, in 1959, Karl tore up his draft cards and returned them to his local draft board, refusing any further collaboration with Selective Service. He was declared delinquent and ordered to report for induction as a 1-A. He naturally refused to report.

Several months later, Karl took part in Omaha Action in Nebraska, led by the Committee for Nonviolent Action, which was destined to develop as the pioneer in direct action. Omaha Action was directed against an Atlas missile installation. Karl and eight others served sentences of six months for trespassing on a federal installation. His time was served at Springfield, Missouri, and Allenwood, Pennsylvania. During his imprisonment, he was reclassified 4-F by his draft board. He returned the new cards and has not heard from them since.

In 1961, he walked to Moscow with the San Francisco to Moscow Walk for Peace, organized by Bradford Lyttle of the CNVA. In 1966, he was thrown out of South Vietnam with A.J. Muste and four others for demonstrating against the war outside the U.S. Embassy in Saigon, and has also refused to pay all federal income taxes since 1960.

Peace walkers in Moscow, 1961.

Karl's most recent imprisonment (40 days) was the result of having expressed a message of peace to Dean Rusk at the 1967 convention of the Lions International. He is presently out on appeal bond for speaking against the war at a Chicago street corner forum.

Twelve years and ten convictions later he expects to resist the prison system at every level, and says that all revolutionaries have suffered imprisonment or death in the search for freedom. "Such is the price of reverence for life." Ω

Douglas County
Jail Omaha, Nebraska
July 1959

I-Words and Facts

In Bread and Wine
Ignazio Silone says
that the peasants of Italy
did not submit
to the propaganda
of Mussolini.
They submitted
to the fact of his power.
And they would not respond
to the counter-propaganda
of the Revolutionists,
but they might respond
to revolutionary facts.

Peter Maurin said
that a leader has only
to shout a word.
Silone says
that the leader had only
to present a fact.
Peter Maurin said
that discipline
was Mussolini's word.
Silone says
that discipline
was Mussolini's fact.

I believe
that the liberals,
and the students,
and the intellectuals of America
do not submit
to the propaganda of the military.
I believe
that they do submit
to the fact
that the nation
is committed to war
overwhelmingly.

And I believe
that they will not respond
to the counter-propaganda
of the pacifist movement,
but they might respond
to the fact
of a nonviolent revolution
against war.

II-The One Man Revolution and The Nonviolent Revolution
In order to have a revolution,
it is necessary, first of all,
to begin.
The nonviolent revolution begins
with a one man revolution
and a two man revolution
and a three man revolution.
But not every one man revolution
is the beginning
of a two man revolution
and a three man revolution.
If the one man revolution
aims to be a beginning and
an end,
that is what it will be.
But if the one man revolution
asks to be not an end
but only a beginning,
that is what it may be.
Yet in either case
the one man revolution
is, at least, a fact.

III-The Pacifist Movement and The Nonviolent Revolution
The American pacifist movement
is in four phases.

The first phase is
peace education,
as exemplified by
The American Friends Service Committee.

The second phase is
public witness,
as exemplified by
Peacemaker projects.

The third phase is
the nonviolent direct
part time and summer revolution,
as exemplified by
CNVA projects,
like Omaha Action,
manned mainly by
summer supporters and sunshine radicals
on leave of absence
from the first phase
and the second phase.

The fourth phase is
the nonviolent revolution,

as exemplified by
nobody.

IV-Bourgeois Pacifism and The Nonviolent Revolution
American pacifists have
little sense
of personal responsibility
for the poor
or for each other,
and therefore they have
little sense
of personal responsibility
for creating
the reality of peace.

American pacifism is
a bourgeois pacifism.
Bourgeois pacifism is
a verbal phenomenon.
Its habitat is
the atmosphere of outer
suburbia
and the college campus.

 William James said
that voluntary poverty might be
a moral equivalent of war.
Bourgeois pacifism has
no moral equivalent of war,
except in the sky,
bye and bye.
Bourgeois pacifism offers itself
on the altar
of nonviolent resistance
to aggression,
but not until
a future that,
thinks the Supreme Being,
will not happen along
very soon.
Bourgeois pacifism does not offer itself
on the altar
of nonviolent divestment
of wealth,
or the altar
of nonviolent resistance
to war,
today.

The nonviolent revolution
lives
in poverty.
Its habitat is prison,
Therefore its habitat is
locked and barred
against the entry
of bourgeois pacifism.

Therefore the nonviolent
revolution is
locked out
of the war society,
(I was going to say
that bourgeois pacifism is
the scab of the war society
in the nonviolent strike
against war,
but I am not sure
that that is accurate,
in every case.)

V-Unity and The Nonviolent Revolution
The nonviolent revolution is
a union.
The bond of union is love.
The characteristic of love is
solidarity and mutual aid.
The function of the union is
to go on strike against war.
The union makes absolutist pacifism
a common action,
the action of a body.
Common action makes the pacifist stand
a political reality.
The political reality is revolutionary.
The revolutionary reality is
the overthrow
of the United States army
by love.
The political reality is
a spiritual reality.
The spiritual reality is
the reality of peace.

VI-Hard Words and Hard Facts
These have been hard words.
I am sorry.
I should give you
hard facts.
When Jesus spoke hard words,
some went away
and walked with him no longer.
When he gave them
a hard fact
he made a revolution.
Since then we have
no right to speak hard words.
Since then we have only
an obligation to live hard facts.

Cassius Spurns Service Oath; Faces 5 Yrs. in Pen, 10G Fine

Houston, Tex., April 28 (Special)—Cassius Clay, proclaiming himself 10% boxer and 90% Black Muslim minister, today refused to take the oath of induction into the U.S. Army and walked out of the Houston Induction Center under threat of a five-year prison sentence.

The N. Y. State Athletic Commission and the World Boxing Assn. promptly stripped Clay of his world heavyweight title.

The government immediately started plans for criminal action, although a U. S. attorney said it could take as long as two years before Clay's case can be fought out in the courts.

Clay showed up at the induction center shortly before 9 A.M. with his assistant trainer, Drew (Bundini) Brown and a personal photographer, Howard Bingham. The 25-year-old popoff king went through the formalities.

WHEN AN OFFICER asked Clay at roll call what name he wanted to use, the champion replied: "I am Muhammed Ali."

Clay then went through approximately four hours of physical and mental examinations, in addition to filling out forms.

When it came time for him to step forward with about 30 others for the oath administered upon induction, Clay was motionless.

HE IMMEDIATELY was led to another room, where it was explained that failure to take the step could result in a penalty of five years in prison, a $10,000 fine, or both.

Clay then returned to the induction room and the opportunity to take the oath again was presented to him. When he refused this time, Clay was asked to sign a statement that he refused induction into the Armed Forces.

"MUHAMMED ALI has just refused to be inducted into the U. S. Armed Forces," said a subsequent statement by Lt. Col. J. D. McKee, commandant of the induction center.

"Notification of his refusal is being made to the U. S. Attorney, the state director of the Selective Service System, and the local selective service board for whatever action deemed to be appropriate," the statement continued.

Another spokesman said: "Mr. Ali met all the requirements for induction."

Following his refusal, the champion, nattily dressed in a blue suit, strode before TV cameras. A newsman asked him how he had been treated.

"Respectable," he answered unsmilingly.

CLAY REFUSED to comment further. Instead, he passed out a four-page statement, neatly typewritten and bearing the signature, "Muhammed Ali."

Clay personally handed out the statement. As he did, he suspiciously asked certain members of the group: "Who are you?" If the identification suited him, Clay handed the newsman a copy. Clay then walked out of the gray, four-story building.

THE STATEMENT, for the most part, was a repetition of Clay's harangue explaining his resistance to the draft. The statement also had anticipated the loss of his title.

"Regardless of the difference in my outlook," Clay's statement said, "I insist upon my rights to pursue my livelihood in accordance with the same rights granted to other men and women who have disagreed with the policies of whatever administration was in power at the time.

"I AM LOOKING forward to immediately continuing my profession," Clay continued. "As to the threat voiced by certain elements to strip me of my title, this is merely a continuation of the same artificially-induced prejudice and discrimination.

"I have the world heavyweight title, not because it was 'given' to me, not because of my race or religion, but because I won it in the ring through my boxing ability," the statement added. "Those who want to 'take' it and hold a series of auction-type bouts not only do me a disservice, but actually disgrace themselves. I am certain that the sports fans and fair-minded people throughout America would never accept such a 'title-holder.'"

FELLOW INDUCTEES said after the examination that Clay had been jovial and cooperative. Once, he shadow-boxed for them and demonstrated his "Ali Shuffle."

Richard Budrow, 26, of Philadelphia, said he had asked Clay whom he thought would succeed him as champion.

"Oh, they'll pick up some dodo or junior champion," Budrow quoted Clay.

WHILE CLAY WAS having his exam, a disorganized group of about 50 anti-war pickets marched and chanted outside the center.

Seven demonstrators made their way into the building and up to the third floor where the exams were being conducted. An officer grabbed two anti-war signs from the women who were carrying them. One woman was identified as Pat LaMariana of Plattsburgh, N.Y.

Government men repeated their

forecast about the length of time it will take to prosecute Clay.

"IT WILL TAKE us 30 to 60 days to prepare charges," said U.S. attorney Morton Susman. "This matter could drag in the courts for months and perhaps as much as two years. Meanwhile, Clay can keep on preaching and fighting."

Clay cannot be stopped from preaching, of course, but it is believed virtually impossible he can line up a bout in any state. Should he choose to box overseas, it is doubtful any TV network would carry the bout.

CLAY'S ATTORNEYS, Hayden Covington and Quinnan Hodges, said they would appeal last Thursday's court ruling which refused to grant Clay a temporary injunction against induction.

The attorneys also said they plan to file a new suit today in federal district court here, asking for an injunction to keep U.S. attorneys and draft board officials from formally reporting the champ as a delinquent inductee.

Close Call

Cassius Clay's famed mouth is closed as he enters Induction Center yesterday.

(UPI Telephoto)

Clay's Crown Up for Grabs; N.Y. Planning Eliminations

By Larry Fox

Within an hour of Cassius Clay's refusal to accept military service, the heavyweight champion yesterday was stripped of his title by both the World Boxing Assn. and the New York State Athletic Commission and plans were set in motion to fill vacancy through an elimination tournament.

Before the ink was dry on New York commissioner Edwin B. Dooley's statement, Madison Square Garden volunteered to help with the matchmaking and promotion of the tournament.

THERE WAS A TOUCH of sadness in the announcement of WBA president Bob Evans, who lives in Clay's birthplace of Louisville, Ky.

"Muhammed Ali has defied the laws of the United States regarding selective service," Evans said. "I've known him since he was a young amateur and was proud of his achievements through his professional career. But his action today leaves me no alternative. . . . He should have acknowledged the superiority of the nation's laws and gone into the military service. He chose not to, so the WBA feels it should not protect the champion's crown for him."

Evans said the WBA, in collaboration with boxing authorities around the world, would start work "immediately" to designate a new champion.

DOOLEY SAID Clay's "refusal to enter the service is ... detrimental to the best interests of boxing."

Dooley said New York also would start work on an elimination tournament and would seek the cooperation of other bodies.

Dooley named eight candidates for the elimination bouts—Ernie Terrell, Floyd Patterson, Karl Mildenberger, Joe Frazier, George Chuvalo, Jimmy Ellis, Oscar Bonavena and Thad Spencer. Two others ignored by the New York commission are Zora Folley, Clay's last victim, and Manuel Ramos of Mexico.

HARRY MARKSON, the Garden's managing director for boxing, said his organization would like to make some of the elimination bouts, but pleaded not to be bound by pairings "pulled out of a hat or determined solely by the fighter's rankings."

He suggested matchmakers be allowed to use their promotional

British Agree

London, April 28 (AP) — Europe and Britain will almost certainly follow the lead of the N.Y. Athletic Commission and the WBA in stripping Cassius Clay of the heavyweight crown, a British official said today. J. Onslow Fane, president of the British Board of Boxing Control and vice president of the European Boxing Union, said the world title will be declared vacant and an elimination tournament started to find a successor.

experience to line up "s[...] fights" and that "this way [...] best qualified heavyweight [...] emerge on top."

Markson said the Garden w[...] go "right to work to make [...] meaningful fights" among heavyweight contenders.

SOME ATTRACTIVE pair[...] might be Chuvalo against Fra[...] Frazier against Patterson or [...] terson against Bonavena. In [...] dition to Terrell, who still is q[...] tionable because of his eye in[...] Clay has beaten Chuvalo, Pat[...] son and Mildenberger. Among [...] contenders, Terrell has bea[...] Chuvalo, Frazier beat Bonav[...] and Patterson beat Chuvalo.

California, which like N[...] York does not subscribe to t[...] WBA, said it probably would [...] along with the ban on Clay. H[...] ever, Texas, a WBA state w[...] Clay has claimed as his "ho[...] said it would wait before p[...] ably joining the crowd.

Liston KOs Rush In 1:58 of Sixth

Stockholm, Sweden, April [...] (UPI) — Former world hea[...] weight champ Sonny Liston re[...] tered Elmer Rush of San F[...] cisco to the canvas eight ti[...] tonight before knocking him [...] in 1:58 of the sixth round. L[...] who weighed 223 to 216 for R[...] started slowly.

Liston twice decked the [...] in the fourth and fifth rou[...] Liston knocked Rush down tw[...] for eight-counts with punche[...] the chest, sent him to the c[...] again with two short righ[...] finally finished him with a [...] uppercut in the sixth.

A Good Joe

Joe Louis was the heavyweight boxing champion during World War II. He entered the Army when called in 1942 and his title was saved for him until he returned in 1946. It was the accepted procedure to freeze all titles when the champion entered the service.

Louis did box some exhibitions during the war but his first real fight wasn't until June of 1946 when he defended against Billy Conn, who also had been in the Army. Their rematch drew almost $2 million with the first $100 top.

⊕ ☮ ⊕

PEACE –
WHAT (SOME) MUSLIMS WANT
MUHAMMAD ALI:
"Float like a butterfly, sting like a bee"

CJ Hinke

The Nation of Islam was founded in Detroit in 1930 with influence from the defunct Moorish Science Temple Movement, itself thought to draw on Masonic roots. NOI's founder used more than 50 aliases. He called himself "The Prophet" and may genuinely have been born in Mecca, Saudi Arabia in 1873. In any case, he disappeared four years later, allegedly over a ritual murder involving human sacrifice.

NOI was ruled by the self-styled "Messenger of Allah", Elijah Muhammad until his death in 1975, establishing temples, banks, businesses, real estate holdings, charter schools, and a university. By that year, NOI had more than a million adherents, 76 mosques and $85 million.

In May 1942, Black Muslim leaders were arrested for sedition in Washington and Milwaukee. In July, 12 black leaders were arrested in Kansas City. In September, five black leaders were arrested for sedition in New York. That same month, federal agents arrested 85 African-Americans in Chicago, including 65 from NOI.

Three men and nine women were charged with sedition; the rest were charged with draft "evasion." Their number included Elijah Muhammad and his son as well as leaders of Muslim and black nationalist organizations. More arrests of black leaders followed. October saw a New Orleans arrest, followed by two more in East St. Louis, followed by seven in Newark.

During a one day trial on October 5, 1942, 38 Black Muslims pleaded guilty to draft charges and were sentenced to three years in prison.

The charges against the leaders of black communities across the United States outspokenly opposed to World War II included violations of the Espionage Act of 1917 and the Selective Service and Training Act of 1940. The beliefs of these sects are wildly variegated but appeared to be more anti-American than merely pro-Japanese. However, Japanese representatives had been ingratiating themselves in American black communities since the 1920s. At least some blacks saw Japanese as a messianic race who would lead black men out of bondage.

Muhammad was charged with eight separate counts of sedition at the intervention of FBI director, J. Edgar Hoover, for instructing his followers not to register for the draft or serve in the armed forces. At least one news articles reports Muhammad wearing "desert robes" into court. Muhammad established the Nation's first prison "temple" from 1942 to 1946 in the federal penitentiary in Milan, Michigan. He and his son served four years for refusing to register with Selective Service, despite the fact Muhammad was 45 years old at his arrest and not required to register.

Hoover's goal was to imprison all black nationalist leaders in order to see their populist empowerment fail without strong leadership. In all, some 125 black Americans were arrested for resisting the draft or sedition during World War II.

After Muhammad's death, his son was replaced as leader by an internal coup, succeeded by Louis Farrakhan in 1981 up to the present. Black Muslims have been schismatized many times in various power struggles, none of them conclusive.

Frequently accused of racism and anti-Semitism, the Nation teaches that brown, yellow, red, and white people originate from an original black race. Whites are not permitted to join NOI. Black Muslims have been encouraged by Farrakhan to study Scientology since 2010.

The Nation of Islam attracted many black converts in prisons, including Malcolm X, then Detroit Red, in 1948. Malcolm was found "mentally unfit for military service" after telling his draft board he wanted to be sent to the South to "organize them nigger soldiers…[to] steal us some guns and kill us [some] crackers." Malcolm also expressed to President Truman his opposition to the Korean War. and declared himself a communist. Malcolm, by then El-Hajj Malik El-Shabazz, broke with NOI in 1964 and was assassinated by three Newark, New Jersey Black Muslims in 1965. Accusations often blame the Nation's leadership for Malcolm's murder.

Music and boxing were some of the few professions in which young blacks were permitted to rise. Cassius Marcellus Clay, Jr., named after a 19th-century white Kentucky abolitionist, won the U.S. a gold medal as a light heavyweight boxer in the 1960 Summer Olympics in Rome at age 22. In 1963, the young boxer became world heavyweight boxing champion. Clay had joined the Nation of Islam after meeting Malcolm X in 1961. Malcolm soon became Clay's spiritual and political mentor. Malcolm X taught him the life-changing lesson that Muslims felt no fear.

Clay subsequently renounced his "slave name" and was given the NOI name Cassius X. He was then renamed Muhammad Ali by NOI leader Elijah Muhammad himself. However, Ali never became a hate monger and spoke frequently in both public and private about religious freedom, racial justice, and living life according to one's principles.

Muhammad Ali's biggest fight, however, was outside the boxing ring. Ali's draft board classified him 1-Y, "qualified for military service only in the event of war or national emergency," after he failed the U.S. Armed Forces Qualification Test, an intelligence test, in 1964 due to poor writing, spelling, and math skills. Testing resulted in the rejection of many potential cannon fodder. South Carolina congressman L. Mendel Rivers resulted favored lowering its standards: "Korea taught us one thing if it has taught us anything. You don't need a Ph.D. degree to fight those Chinks."

The Secretary of War created Project 100,000 in 1966 to resolve these inequities. 100,000 men who had failed the qualifying test were enlisted every year for four years. Half of the 400,000 men were sent to Vietnam. 40% were black and their combat deaths were twice those of other soldiers. Worse yet, the project was cast as part of Johnson's War on Poverty and Great Society initiatives. If you want equality, you have to die first!

The FBI began surveillance of Ali in early 1964 after observing him meeting with Malcolm X. In 1966 FBI director J. Edgar Hoover took advantage of the Army's recalibration of eligibility standards which did not require retesting. Hoover made sure Ali was reclassified 1-A, fearing his influence on young blacks. Ali's fame and influence on young men made him dangerous to the warmakers.

All Ali's communications were illegally monitored by the National Security Agency, including his conversations with civil rights leader Dr. Martin Luther King, U.S. senators, and journalists who criticized the war, along with other black and antiwar activists.

According to the *New York Times*, Ali is said to have inspired civil rights leader Dr. Martin Luther King, Jr. to voice his own opposition to the U.S. War on Vietnam.

Ali stated at the time: "War is against the teachings of the Holy Qur'an. I'm not trying to dodge the draft. We are not supposed to take part in no wars unless declared by Allah or The Messenger. We don't take part in Christian wars or wars of any unbelievers." Ali stated, "I got nothin' against them Vietcong...No Vietcong ever called me a nigger."

However, Ali was denied status as a conscientious objector. The Selective Service hearing officer hearing Ali's petition, a retired judge, was inclined to grant him CO status but was overruled by an all-white draft board. In 1967 in Houston, Texas, he refused three times to step forward at his scheduled induction, even after being threatened with arrest.

In a 2006 *New York Times* article: "The government offered Ali the same opportunity given to Joe Louis in World War II. He could fight exhibitions for the troops and keep his title without seeing a battlefield. But Ali refused, saying, "I'd be just as guilty as the ones doing the killing."

After his arrest, he was stripped of his title by the World Boxing Association, his U.S. passport was revoked along with his boxing licenses in every state. Ali was sentenced to five years in prison and a $10,000 fine, the maximum penalties for draft "evasion" by an all-white jury which deliberated its verdict for only 21 minutes.

Ali's appeals took four years which also kept him out of the boxing ring. During this period, he spoke frequently against the Vietnam War at colleges across the U.S. and Muslim gatherings advocating African American pride and racial justice.

In 1971, the U.S. Supreme Court overturned his conviction in a unanimous decision based on the fact he was denied the due process of law as guaranteed in the U.S. Constitution. Ali's draft board gave no trial to his convictions as a conscientious objector. The Court, in its deliberations, found the ministers of the Nation of Islam to have the same protections as COs as did the Jehovah's Witnesses.

Following his boxing career, Muhammad Ali received numerous accolades for his stand. In 1987, Ali was chosen by the California Bicentennial Commission as its exemplar of the U.S. Constitution and Bill of Rights and was the chosen the 1997 recipient of the Arthur Ashe Courage Award.

In 2005, he was presented the Presidential Citizens Medal and the Presidential Medal of Freedom even as President Bush denied Ali's petition to grant a posthumous pardon to Jack Johnson, the first black American heavyweight boxing champion; Johnson was convicted in 1913 and jailed for having a romantic relationship with a white woman.

In Germany the same year, Ali was awarded the Otto Hahn Peace Medal by the United Nations Association. In 2007, he was awarded an honorary doctorate of humanities by Princeton University and a star on Hollywood's Walk of Fame. His war refusal was the subject of a 2013 documentary, *The Trials of Muhammad Ali*.

Ali spoke out frequently, saying "No, I am not going 10,000 miles to help murder, kill, and burn other people to simply help continue the domination of white slavemasters over dark people the world over. This is the day and age when such evil injustice must come to an end...Why should they ask me to put on a uniform and go ten thousand miles from home and drop bombs and bullets on brown people in Vietnam while so-called Negro people in Louisville are treated like dogs and denied simple human rights? ...My enemy is the white people, not the Vietcong...

"You're my opposer when I want freedom. You're my opposer when I want justice. You're my opposer when I want equality. You won't even stand up for me in America because of my religious beliefs, and you want me to go somewhere and fight, when you won't even stand up for my religious beliefs at home...They're all afraid of me because I speak the truth that can set men free."

Ali also spoke out at an antiwar rally of around 20,000 in Los Angeles in 1967 on stage with Dr. Benjamin Spock: "Anything designed for peace and to stop the killing, I'm for 100 percent. I'm not a leader. I'm not here to advise you. But I encourage you to express yourself."

Muhammad Ali lit the Olympic torch in the 1996 Olympics in Atlanta.

This seems the right moment to mention the resistance of black Chicago jazz musician Sun Ra. Born Herman Poole Blount, Sun Ra often speculated he was the love-child of Elijah Poole who later became known as the Prophet Elijah Muhammad.

In any case, Sun Ra received a military induction notice in 1942. He declared himself a conscientious objector and was eventually approved for Civilian Public Service. However, he never showed up at CPS in Pennsylvania and was subsequently arrested in Alabama.

Sun Ra debated the draft with his judge and told him, if drafted, he would turn his weapons on the first high-ranking officer he met. The judge stated, "I've never seen a nigger like you." Sun Ra replied, "No, and you never will again."

Camp psychiatrists described him as "psychopathic" but also, "a well-educated colored intellectual." After CPS in Pennsylvania, doing forestry by day and playing piano at night, he was declared 4-F and returned to Chicago. His philosophy drew on the Kabbalah, Rosicrucianism, channeling, numerology, Freemasonry, black nationalism, and Afrofuturism; his life-long career was punctuated by space travel leading him to found the Association of Autonomous Astronauts. Sun Ra is certainly 'far-out'!

Although draft resistance appears never to have been adopted as an official position of the Nation of Islam, countless young blacks found the courage to refuse the draft because of the courage of Muhammad Ali. He lost everything but still followed his conscience. He really lived his nickname: "The Greatest." Nelson Mandela said that what Ali was willing to lose in order to oppose the war was what defined him.

The Nation of Islam has grown the largest prison ministry in the world's largest prison population since 1984 and, of course, blacks form the largest segment of the U.S. prisoners. NOI finds fertile ground in America's most disenfranchised preaching black pride. Black Muslims have taken over prison conversions from Christian sects. In prison, you take what you can get and only 0.2% of U.S. prisoners identify themselves as atheists.

NOI leader Louis Farrakhan sees prisons "being used as a new form of slavery" and promotes the release of all black inmates to form a new African colony. Black Muslims also seek converts at predominantly black colleges and universities, though blacks are far less populous there than in American prisons.

The Muslim population of the United States has grown to an estimated 2.6 million by 2010 through birth, immigration, and conversion. Although Islam was nominally suppressed on U.S. plantations, at least 15-30% of black African slaves sold prior to the Civil War were Muslims and 50%, some 200,000, were captured from regions where Islam was the dominant religion. 64% of Muslim converts in the U.S. are black. NOI now counts one of every 15 American-born blacks as Muslim.

There are some 15,000 Muslim soldiers currently serving the U.S. military machine. In 2013, there are no opportunities for stalled lives in America's failed inner cities.

The Nation can certainly make no claims to pacifism of any sort. NOI once considered boxing among all "filthy sports" but then openly supported organized violence in the form of professional boxing…for money…in order to capitalize on the "sport's" celebrities, notably Muhammad Ali. Nevertheless, Black Muslims logically saw the U.S. War on Vietnam as a white man's war on people of color much the same as the oppression of poor ghetto blacks in the United States. Ω

☮ ☮ ☮

LETTERS FROM JAIL

Julian Beck (1925-1985)

Editor's Note: Julian Beck, founder of the Living Theatre, is currently traveling with the Theater in Europe. These letters are written from Julian to pacifist activist photogrqapher, Karl Bissinger. Ω

Jan. 28, 1985

DEAR KARL,
Thoughts on the theatre from jail. Remember that our two greatest successes, "The Connection" and "The Brig," came out of our jail experience. Judith's and mine. Judith dedicated the production of "The Connection" to "Thelma Gadsden, dead of an overdose of heroin ... and to all other junkies, dead and alive, in the Women's House of Detention."

She had known Thelma in jail, we both met many addicts there and had come to respect them as individuals. In jail you get very close to your companions in a way that you don't "on the street." There is a candor, an honesty, that prevails in the talk; and the close living breeds understanding and affection. In doing "The Connection" we wanted to show these people not as degenerates, but as individuals worthy of our respect, such as we had felt when we had come to know them.

When you leave jail you don't leave altogether. Anyone who has ever been in is in some ways forever tied to it through a bond of sympathy coupled with the hope that some day everyone will be free. Jail gives you new ideas about freedom. We felt compelled to do "The Connection" not only because of our great admiration for Jack Gelber's accomplishments but also because we were still somehow bound to jail and the junkies there and hoped, naively, that a play might help set them free.

The connection between "The Brig" and our jail experience is obvious. When we did "The Brig" we wanted to bring to the production all of the facts, without faking, as we knew them. That, for instance, is why we made the play so loud. Jail is loud and we wanted the audience to feel the affliction of the noise, the reverberation of sound in steel and concrete buildings. Audiences complained, but we insisted on keeping the sound level, because that's the way it is. And, again, by showing facts, we hoped, in our usual naive way, that the theater might bring freedom, at least from the abuses of authoritarian discipline.

It is interesting that in here my chief thoughts about everything, theater and life, revolve around the concepts of freedom and honesty. And when I dream of a theater of the future I dream of a theater that will be honest and free. Now my chief criticism of the contemporary theater is that it is neither honest nor free.

Honesty. I'm not even talking about truth; that's less accessible; the truth is so holy, so related to abstract values. I think, that it would be asking too much to ask for that. I am, however, asking for the simple presentation of things as they are; and I ask this of actors, directors, designers, and producers. Just give us a chance to see what things are really like, then maybe the theatre can lead to real understanding.

But the theater, like life today, is so drenched in attitudes and phony concepts; it labors, like life, under the weight of so much propaganda from advertising, newspapers, public agencies like the F.B.I. and the Narcotics Bureau. Senatorial committees, campaign speeches, and classroom information molded by the morals of school hoards that we hardly know any longer bow to think honestly.

I am not putting down imagination or fantasy or symbolism. The imagination of the poet is not dishonest; it is the real factual statement of his imagining. I do not put down what masquerades as imagination: when writers are only dishing out pre-conceived notions of what's supposed to be imaginative.

I think if we will look at the world as it really is we will find that even what is most ugly has within it the sparks of life, and is therefore moving and worthy of our attention. And I think we go to the theater to glimpse those sparks. That's why we get so excited with anticipation before we go to the theater. It's because we're looking for light in a very dark world.

As I write this I am sitting in a very ugly room in this jail but I find it, strangely, more beautiful than most of the settings I've seen in the past year on the stages of London, Paris, Berlin and New York. Because stage designers are more concerned with dramatic effects, sentimental lighting, tricks and imitation of both art and life themselves. Life is very dramatic, you don't have to fancy it up. Art does not simply dispose of charm, which seems to be the constant effort of contemporary stage design.

Life in jail is very real. No one has to fake. I hear real speech all the time, and how I wish I could hear more of this kind of speech in the theater. Actors don't have to speak better than people. Nothing is better than people. We have to get rid of the idea that elocution constitutes good speech; I think elocution and the throaty way even our best actors often speak is related to some kind of respect for royalty. 1965. We ought to be beyond that.

I want actors to stop posing. I'm talking to Method actors, too, to stop trying to create effects and break through into the representation of honest life. It would be thrilling to hear Shakespeare spoken honestly, and Brecht. I think it would be startling. We might be so moved that we might begin to respect ourselves, and, instead of accepting substitutes for life in the theater and "on the street," we might find that what is real surpasses all our foolish notions.

Faithfully,

JULIAN.

January 30, 1965

DEAR KARL,

I got so hung up on honesty in the last letter that I left out freedom, a common fault. Am I overwhelming you with polemic? I'm guilty of that all the time, but jail makes you want to rail and yell. I often think that if the people on the street would realize how the world we live in is a prison, they'd do more yelling and railing, too. The sad, perhaps tragic, thing is that people do not realize they're not free. How thoroughly we have lulled ourselves with our pride into our brand of limited liberty.

There's liberty here, too, within the rules of the institution. There are books, lectures, classes, movies, television, though the programming is table d'hote, pretty good food, air, trees, clean clothes, cleanliness in fact almost to the point of sterilization, much as modern American life upholds cleanliness so much that we have become enslaved to the process of keeping clean. But here we know we're not free.

Outside, people delude themselves because they don't see the bars. I dream of a theater that is free. What do I mean by that? To begin with, let us recognize the fact that everyone is not free to go to the theater, it costs too much. And then there are the production costs that are so great that even the plays many people might want to do they are not free to do. But the public is also guilty. We applaud too easily expensive productions, which leads me to believe that we are enchained by the notion that only wealth can give us something worth major attention. In the theater we aren't free to speak freely about sex, or politics, nor are we a free enough thinking public to permit the theatre to criticize all but our obvious frailties without becoming irate.

Nor are we free to fail. That's the great fear. We are so much the slaves of the success-pattern idea, that we regard failure as killing. And it is often psychologically killing. Directors and actors aren't free to work in this so-called free society of ours. You have to plot, scheme, deceive, and dissemble to get a job. Or spend months, or even years, of your life waiting for the opportunity to work. And when, finally, you do work, you are not free to act, you have to be realistic the way, let us say, so much sculpture is realistic. No pubic hair. And when finally you do work, the pressures of time and money are so severe that you are rarely free to see your work through to completion.

What remedy do I suggest? I guess I am recommending complete social restructure. Just changing a few conditions in the theatre won't help. That's an illusion. How? No answer. But if enough people start thinking about the state of things we're in, we might find a solution, an action, together.

Faithfully,

JULIAN

Jan. 31, 1965

DEAR KARL,

Will try to make this letter less gloomy than the others. Fortunately you know me as, at least, occasionally cheerful. A fellow inmate remarked, "You know, there are two kinds of guys in jail, the guys that are hip and the nondescripts." "How do I classify?" I asked. "You! Why man," he replied, "you're entertainment."

Entertainment. My high-priest act tends to cover the fact that I'm an ardent admirer of entertainment, of the theater of music and dance. I think even the Hasidim regarded the delights of the flesh, and their cultivation, as ways of celebrating the lavish world created by God. But I think entertainment loses its purity and joy when it tries to put itself over as an art and becomes arty.

Genet adores popular songs because of the lush words they put in the mouths of common men who otherwise might never utter such phrases as "I adore you." Bring on dancing girls, pretty boys, music, color. Swing. But too often the true spirit is destroyed by the falsehood of artistic pleasure.

Repertory. Its chief virtue is that it provides a chance for artists to work together on many plays over an extended period of time, and therefore there is the chance to develop as men working communally. Repertory theaters will fail when they keep working competitively and will succeed, at least in their work, as they develop communally and as the public develops its admiration for art made by unified groups us opposed to that of lone star individuals only.

The Theater of Cruelty. The only prediction I venture: More and more will he seen and heard of and about this kind of theater, named by a Frenchman, Antonin Artaud, who envisaged a theater which did not numb us with ideas for the intellect, but stirred us to feeling by stirring up pain. We are a feelingless people (consider all the suffering we permit in this world as we go about our business); and if we could at least feel pain, we might turn towards becoming men again instead of turning more and more into callous automata.

Black Theater. The theater is a mirror of the world. In the West, especially in the United States, the more it avoids the presence and problems and world of the Negro, the more distorted it is. More black writers and actors are only part of the problem; the other part is that the whites, who control most theater, if they want to see the truth, will find ways of bringing black into the theater. And to do that we must learn to communicate, black and white, each learning about what goes on in the other's heads and lives. We don't know now. That's part of the work. Love is the measure of the degree of communication. When I love someone I want to be with them.

I look forward to being with you soon.

Faithfully,
JULIAN

☮☮☮

Life at 'Camp Cupcake'

Inmates: 1,055 women

Opened: 1927

Daily schedule: Lights on 6 am, out 11:30 pm

Jobs: plumbers, painters, groundskeepers for 12¢ to 40¢ an hour

Telephone: about 10 minutes/day, outgoing only

Visiting: weekends & holidays only

Recreation: basketball, volleyball, softball, track, library

SOURCE: BUREAU OF PRISONS

☮☮☮

EXPERIENCES AT ALDERSON

Marjorie Swann (1921-2014)

Editor's Note: Marjorie Swann is 48 years old and has four children, ranging in age from 11 to 23. She attended Northwestern University and majored in modern languages and has worked for Antioch College, the American Friends Service Committee, and the Council for Equal Job Opportunity.

She was a charter member of the first local committee of the Congress of Racial Equality in Chicago in 1940 and has long been active in the civil rights and peace movements. Marjorie is now a member of several pacifist organizations and has been a founder, coordinator, and staff member of the New England Committee for Nonviolent Action since its inception. Her work for New England CNVA includes organizing and coordinating nonviolent direct action projects, planning and conducting training programs in nonviolent direction and education, speaking, writing, and editing Direct Action, the bulletin of New England CNVA.

Marjorie was the United States Coordinator for the World Peace Study Mission of 25 survivors of the atomic bombings of Hiroshima and Nagasaki in 1964. These 25 made a world tour with 15 interpreters from the International Christian University In Tokyo and spent seven weeks in the U.S., visiting over 100 cities and towns. In fact, according to Eric Schlosser, only 1.38% of the uranium in Hiroshima's "Little Boy" a-bomb actually fissioned, the rest way blown away. The fission of 0.7 grams of uranium, less than the weight of a banknote, instantly killed 100,000 people and destroyed the city.

Marjorie Swann has been arrested several times for her peace and civil rights work, and has served the resultant jail sentences. This is the first time she has written extensively about her six-month federal prison sentence at the Federal Reformatory for Women at Alderson, West Virginia in 1959 and 1960. Marj was arrested for trespassing on an Intercontinental Ballistic Missile Base near Omaha, Nebraska in 1959, an demonstration coordinated by Omaha Action. Ω

"**D**on't become too close friends with anybody. Do your own time, not anyone else's." That's the very first thing I was told as I entered the Federal Reformatory for Women at Alderson, West Virginia, back in August, 1959. That advice was constantly repeated.

But what stupid advice. No reasonably normal human being can survive in an emotional vacuum, and emotional feelings and needs are heightened and intensified in prison. There is an unspoken grapevine, circulating tension. I remember when one distraught young prisoner screamed all night and broke the glass window in her room, then slashed her wrists. The tension spread through the whole prison. The same thing happened when another woman became very ill during the night (a large number of us were in the Orientation Building at that time, and officers and guards only check into the building – into any building, as a matter of fact – once every two or three hours). She called and called for help, and other prisoners began calling and shouting, beating on their locked doors with their fists – all to no avail until morning. I was told later by an officer that she had been taken to the prison hospital that morning with acute appendicitis. Rumors were repeatedly passed around that pregnant women had their babies alone in their rooms during the night. I never verified any of these stories. And when a prisoner escaped – never for long because the city women were afraid of the mountains and wild animals – the suspense hung in a cloud over the whole prison.

The loneliest time in prison is around Christmas. The tension begins to mount several weeks before, and prison officials try to offset it by planning all the usual Christmas observances such as choir sings, church services, contests for decorating cottages and lawns, a special Christmas dinner, etc. But these gestures are a travesty of the true meaning and spirit of Christmas for women who have spent or anticipate spending years behind bars, who may be thousands of miles away from home, some of whom never have any visitors or letters, who can't really give anything even if they wanted to, but only receive what is doled out to them. The Christmas I was there, I received, as do most pacifist and resistance prisoners, hundreds of Christmas cards. I was very conscious of the barrier between myself and other prisoners, so I gave many away, asked for help in setting up an exhibit of the most interesting cards, such as those from foreign countries, and tried in every way to indicate that these were not for me alone.

That Christmas, so I was told by one of my fellow prisoners who worked in the administrative offices in the supplies department, many extra weapons, including tear gas, were being shipped to Alderson in anticipation of a rumored riot.

But women prisoners never seem to be able to organize themselves for any concerted effort, whether it be a riot, or a protest against prison regulations, or even simple requests for better movies and more handicraft lessons. Though for the most part fully as intelligent and sensitive as any cross section of suburban American women, female prisoners are highly individualistic and very rebellious toward any leadership or coöperative effort. I suppose that's one reason they are there in the first place – because their individualistic desires and impulses put them outside "normal" society, and also outside organized rebellion against "normal" society.

While I was at Alderson, I tried to encourage a number of women to channel their rebellion and their energies and skills, when they got out, into protest actions in civil rights or peace activity. Many indicated interest, but whether they actually followed through is doubtful. And of course the administration did not like these suggestions coming from me, because prisons expect and prefer to deal with the fractured body of prisoners who submit sullenly to authority, and then on release go back to the same environments and occupations, only to start the whole cycle over again. (The warden told me when I was at Alderson that about 80% of federal prisoners were recidivists.)

In addition to tension and recalcitrance among prisoners, there is of course the frustrated need for normal human affection and sexual activity. So there is a good deal of homosexuality, overt and subdued, which the administrators openly deplore and try to prevent, but at the same time turn their backs and close their eyes, because they know it cannot really be prevented. As far as I was aware, there was little if any actual sexual attack, such as we hear about in men's prisons.

But there were plenty of overtures, much flirtation, a good deal of natural affection, and of course open sexual alliances among some women. Whenever an overture was made to me, I talked about my husband and children; no one ever seemed to resent this, partly because many of the prisoners had children of their own about whom they spoke longingly. I did allow myself affectionate gestures toward some especially lonely women, particularly the younger girls who many times needed a "mother substitute." And several times I had frank talks with other prisoners about sexual needs, and the relation between sex and love.

Perhaps one of the most obvious things about prison – it becomes more obvious after one is released – is the total lack of responsibility and opportunity for decisions and choices afforded to prisoners. Alderson is more rigid than many of the men's federal prisons, because as my parole officer said, "We get all women prisoners here, and all kinds. So we make the rules for the 10% you can't trust, and the rest of you are stuck with them."

There was never more than 10 or 15 minutes at a time that I was not aware of an officer or guard checking on us; never a simple decision I made on my own – how much hay to unbundle for the dairy cattle, for instance. I worked in the dairy, which I had chosen – actually insisted on, and the administration evidently feared crossing me in that choice because they did not know when I would commence to noncoöperate altogether.

That was probably the last real choice I made; no, I made one other. I refused to be a driver for the dairy, because it meant I had to supervise and keep track of other prisoners for the five minutes driving time between the dairy and the main buildings.

At any rate, when I got out of prison, I found the simplest decisions immensely complex. Walk into a supermarket, and try to pick out what foods to buy, what menus to plan for my family. What should I do with my time today? How deal with two-and-a-half-year old Scottie's needs and whims? Should seven-year-old Carol come home from the family she had been staying with and the excellent school she had been attending, or should she remain until the end of the year?

How much harder it must be for women who have been in prison for years, instead of six months, to start in again immediately taking care of children who do not remember their mothers, to budget a tiny amount of money from a job – perhaps to hunt for a job – with the stigma of prison sentences hanging over them. No wonder some women seem almost to prefer staying in prison, where everything is taken care of for them.

I was fortunate: I had a loving, supportive family to come home to, a nice home, friends and neighbors who were admiring and helpful, enough money in our family budget to cover our needs. So many women prisoners are resigned to going back to their same old environment, their same old associations, the same frustrations. Very few of them had any hope of staying off drugs once they got out, they felt helpless and hopeless. Only one woman I knew (and I knew, at least slightly, several hundred of the over 800 prison population while I was there), insisted that she was absolutely not going back on drugs. I often wonder how she made out on that pledge to herself.

At Alderson, in 1959 and 1960, the warden was a middle-aged spinster whose motto was, "Keep them busy; then they will be too tired to get into trouble." This was her stated policy. She did not believe in psychiatric therapy, individual or group; she allowed with reluctance the existence of an Alcoholics Anonymous group; she felt that any prisoner who said she was ill was malingering.

In a certain sense she was right; there was so much psychosomatic illness in the prison that no one could tell what stemmed from physical causes and what from psychological frustrations and needs. The two doctors, very pleasant and concerned young men who were assigned to the prison by the Public Health Service to repay their government scholarships received while in medical school, recognized the problem and often insisted that women should be put on "light duty" and even bed rest. They were in a constant fight with the warden about their leniency and pampering of the "girls" (all women in prison, any prison or jail, are "girls," even if they're 70 years old).

So in prison, as in the armed services and in many bureaucracies and even commercial businesses, everyone learns to goldbrick. It's not even an organized slowdown; it's just an individual response to the lack of freedom, to the frustration, to the authoritarian environment, to the whole stupidity of prison.

I tried a little different type of slowdown when I was in orientation. (I was there for six weeks, an unusually long period, because so many new women had come in just ahead of me and had to be processed.) Since the obvious purpose of orientation was to break one's spirit and will – for instance, dusting and polishing a particular section of a hallway floor seven or eight times a day, over and over again – I decided to exert a little spirit in the other direction. When I was assigned to a job, such as cleaning the orientation officers' office, I did such a thorough, deliberate job each and every morning that it was hours before the good ladies could make use of their office. If I was assigned to sweep the sidewalks in front of the building, I would meticulously sweep away every particle of dirt and every tiny leaf, thereby tying up one officer's attention for a long time, because of course no one in orientation could be outdoors without an officer to guard her. I'm not sure it was nonviolent, but it was enjoyable to throw a monkey wrench into the smooth, docile workings of the prison system in that way.

When I was finally assigned to the dairy, however (after dire warnings about how "we put all the tough girls, including the homosexuals, out there so they can work off some of their steam"), I found I really enjoyed the work – and my companions. I suspect this was partly because I was closer to nature, away from the enclosure of the main prison, working with animals, immersed in the beauty of the changing seasons of the West Virginia mountains. I often said, "If it only were not for the place I am in and the reason I'm here, I could be content for a long time."

I got into good physical shape, too, pitching hay and manure, wheel-barrowing heavy loads of fodder, feeding baby calves, carrying 100-pound bags of grain and heavy bales of hay. One thing I refused to do, and was never forced to, was to climb up in the silo. I have a fear of heights. There were so many women eager to go up there (to sneak a forbidden smoke or engage in some sexual play), that the officers did not force those of us who were fearful to go up. We had reasonably good food at the dairy "cottage," perhaps better than soma of the other cottages. (Alderson is laid out on a two-quadrangle plan, with brick buildings euphemistically called cottages, holding from 30 to 50 women each.)

There was always plenty of milk; there were excellent baked goods and usually dessert at least once a day, because the prison authorities thought such goodies helped keep down dissension and unrest. Meat was much more plentiful at Alderson than in any city or county jail I have ever been in, and there was often a fresh salad. There were always plenty of beans to fill up on; and when I learned that most women did not like the

Cheddar cheese ("rat cheese," they called it) and I was given permission to eat as much as I wanted, my protein needs were amply taken care of. One interesting sidelight was that all sugar, spices, raisins, vanilla, lemon extract, and other flavorings were kept locked up. This was because of the use to which these items were put – obviously to make moonshine. There was an occasional raid to try to discover hidden stills, but they usually were not found, especially at the dairy where there were innumerable hiding places.

I have spoken of the officers (administrators and guards) at the prison in mostly derogatory terms. Actually, the "line officers" – the local women for whom a job at Alderson meant more money and more prestige than any other job in this depressed area of West Virginia – were mostly very kindly, often motherly women, many of whom took a genuine interest in the "girls" under their care. They frequently talked with us as equals, discussing all manner of subjects, including their own personal and family lives; and a number of them pitched in and worked as hard as we did.

Most of the administrators were different, however. They were career women in the prison service; many of them were unmarried; some were rumored to have homosexual relations with other officers or prisoners. They were for the most part rigid, and certainly not of the "rehabilitation" school of penal thought. I remember an encounter with one of the parole officers in particular (not my own, who considered herself a liberal and frequently would spend a couple of hours in discussion with me).

This particular lady was probably the oldest officer in the prison in terms of seniority. She had been there since the beginning of Alderson. Alderson was built during the wave of prison reform led by many liberal women in the late twenties and early thirties, and the first warden had helped plan the prison architecturally and had set policy from the beginning. According to a book she had written (somewhat through rose-colored glasses, no doubt), she had helped pioneer the "classification" system now supposedly used in all federal prisons and in some state institutions. According to this reform theory, the individual prisoner was to receive certain achievement and ability tests during the orientation period, and given certain information about the opportunities available in the prison for formal education and vocational training. Then at the end of the orientation period, the prisoner was to sit down as an equal with the classification board – made up of several officers, the chaplain, and perhaps the staff doctor and together they would work out a rehabilitation program individually tailored to suit the needs and capabilities of the woman. At almost any time, the prisoner could come back to the Classification Board and request a change in job or educational courses.

Furthermore, the first warden had written, each cottage had a steering committee composed of inmates, who made decisions and judgments regarding the conduct of the women living in the cottage and an all-prison inmate council which was composed of representatives from each cottage. Relations with the outside community were favored, and culminated each year in a kind of international festival, where both inmates and residents of the greater community joined together In presenting exhibits, entertainment, folk dancing, etc. None of that remained at Alderson in 1960.

I asked this venerable parole officer what had happened to that approach, so different from the one now in use, where a prisoner was led in to the Classification Board like a lamb going to slaughter, told what job she was to have, and warned in stern tones about the behavior expected of her – and almost always, with myself as an exception as far as I could discover, the prisoner did not get the job she most wanted, or perhaps even her second or third choice, but whatever the authorities thought "good" for her. The parole officer replied, "Oh, that was a lot of nonsense, and I saw that it was done away with as soon as I could."

Chaplains in federal prisons are paid by the Bureau of Prisons, and are part and parcel of the administration. Therefore, they are not trusted at all by most prisoners, and they tend to acquiesce in decisions by administrative officers, confining their activities to conducting church services and superficial counseling. The chaplains at Alderson were very nice men, kindly and concerned, but seemingly unable or unwilling to put up any struggle for prisoners' rights or needs. I understand there are exceptions to the general pattern, and at least one chaplain currently at a men's federal prison, is doing a really excellent job.

The physical facilities at Alderson are somewhat unique for federal prisons, as I have suggested. The "cottages" contain dormitories for three, four, or perhaps six women, but many women at the prison have their own rooms, furnished with a comfortable bed, a dresser, desk, sometimes an arm chair, curtains, linens and bedspread. Of course the doors are frequently locked – from the outside – and the windows are covered with "safety screen." There are comfortable lounges, attractive dining rooms, adequate bathrooms with showers and tubs. At the dairy cottage, we were allowed to have a TV because we did such heavy physical labor; the "honor" cottage was the only other one furnished with TV at that time, although I understand that has changed now.

At the time I was in the institution, the educational and vocational programs were deplorable. The education director must have been a teacher who couldn't make it in the outside world, and she had little concept of what was needed or what could be done to help women with their formal education or with handicrafts. One of the things I really looked forward to was learning to weave, but when I asked to do so, I was abruptly informed that no one could do so unless they had been in the prison for six months. This was true of almost all such activities, so my recreation was limited to

TV, playing cards, reading and writing, and movies – usually lousy ones. The best teachers seemed to be inmates, but not nearly enough of them were allowed to share their skills. Some of the native Indian women did beautiful leather work, but few others were allowed to learn.

The library was also deplorable. Most of the books were ancient cops-and-robbers stories or westerns. There were a few good classics, which I managed to ferret out. When I discovered the book about Alderson written by the first warden and began to pass it around and inspire other prisoners to ask for it, it was quickly removed from the shelves. I was allowed to receive a few books sent in by publishers, and was required to leave these with the library when I was released. Thus the library acquired *Flowers of Hiroshima*, one or two of Erich Fromm's works, and several others. However, when two book club selections were sent to me, Warren Miller's *Cool World* and Norman Mailer's *Reflections of Myself*, the education director, with much clucking, rejected them, saying, "Why, these would be a terrible influence on the girls here!" I laughed and asked her where she thought most of the "girls" came from, pointing out that the language and content of the books was probably mild compared to the experiences of many of the prisoners.

No luck, though, the books were held for me until I was released, because I refused to take them and keep them "strictly to myself."

News from Suzanne Williams indicates some things have changed at Alderson. Correspondence restrictions apparently have been loosened, and Suzi says each inmate is (at least theoretically) allowed one telephone call a month, something unheard of in my day. Inmates are allowed to receive and wear their own clothing in the prison, something also unheard of except for personal shoes in case of foot problems. The education department seems to have improved; Suzi is already taking typing and shorthand courses, and speaks of other activities. The warden has changed, and the present one is reputed by some prisoners who know her to be quite liberal and understanding. The Bureau of Prisons administration and Director have changed also, probably to a more liberal approach.

But prison is still prison, and I remember women at Alderson saying they preferred to be in a tough city or county jail where they knew what the score was.

Alderson resembled the iron fist in the velvet glove. One quickly learns in jail or prison to expect nothing, to count on nothing; then if anything good or enjoyable happens, it is a pleasant surprise, a bonus, so to speak. Although I knew this, I forgot it temporarily and so had my most traumatic experience while I was in Alderson.

My husband was coming to visit, our first sight of each other in about four months, and brought our youngest daughter, Carol, who was missing her mother most intensely. The drive took longer than expected, and Bob and Carol did not arrive until about an hour before lunch. Bob had been assured by telephone that, they could visit with me all morning and afternoon, with the exception of the lunch hour. (Suzi tells us visitors may now eat with prisoners in the cafeteria, the latter in itself an innovation.) As Bob and Carol left at lunch time, they were assured they could come back in an hour.

An hour and a half went by; still I received no call to the visiting room. Two hours, three hours; finally I was informed close to dinner time that they had not been permitted to resume the visit. Bob had argued in vain; I was heartbroken; Carol was sick all the long drive home.

I could only assume it was a deliberately punitive measure, perhaps because of some of the protests I had made about silly regulations, perhaps because someone just thought my spirit was not sufficiently broken.

Despite all I have said about prison, my experience at Alderson was one for which I have always been glad, and would not avoid had I to do it over again.

For one thing, I learned anew what I had already known: that people in prison are human beings with the same feelings, needs, desires, joys and sorrows as all other human beings. I learned that prisoners are acutely aware of the fact that they are imprisoned for very minor "crimes" compared to the giant crimes being practiced every day by big businessmen, by the military, by smoother-operating "big shot" criminals. For instance, there was the very young woman who was serving several years for forging a check for $45.00 in order to buy food for her baby (her story was verified by an officer). She said, "I know bankers and others who get away with $45,000.00 of other people's money, and they never go to jail for it." The majority of women, who were drug addicts, cursed the big-time dealers and pushers (who seldom go to prison) and followed closely the methods of dealing with drug addiction in Great Britain, clipping newspaper and magazine articles on the subject and passing them around.

I learned that most federal women prisoners are quite intelligent, that their intelligence has been misdirected into channels which are destructive to themselves and to others – often, of course, for very obvious social or economic reasons. I certainly learned that black people, Indians, and poor people are the ones who go to prison, while white, wealthier people for the most part don't get caught or don't get put in prison.

During my imprisonment I had the warm encouragement of my family and friends, and the welcomes when I got out were most moving. My first day home, a beautiful bouquet of flowers was delivered to our door, with a note, "To add to your homecoming." It was from one of my husband's sub-contractors, an electrician originally from Poland who had spent time in both Nazi and Communist concentration camps. Contrary to our experiences with other such refugees, this man was most sympathetic to my action, discussing our beliefs for hours with my husband.

The flowers were his way of expressing agreement and empathy. Bob had many similar discussions with workmen, suppliers, and clients during the six months I was gone, and he and the children received all kinds of assistance from friends, neighbors, and complete strangers. Despite their apprehensions, our two barely teen-aged girls not only were not subject to jeers and ridicule in school, but instead received several comments such as, "Gee, your mom must be real brave."

It is good to know the reality of prison before one goes, but there is no need to fear the experience or to let it scar one's life. For the "prisoner of conscience," prison can be a positive experience which adds depth to one's commitment to brotherhood and peace.

☮ ☮ ☮

PRISON AND ME

Arthur Harvey

Editor's Note: Arthur Harvey was born in 1932 in Ridgewood, New Jersey and became active in the peace movement through the New England Committee for Nonviolent Action. He was a participant in Polaris Action in Groton and New London, Connecticut, as well as Omaha Action at an ICBM base near Omaha, Nebraska.

Art and several others were sentenced to six months plus a $500.00 fine (which, in several cases, the government is still trying to collect from the pacifists). The law provides that unless a fine is committed, one may serve only an additional 30 days, no matter how large the fine, on a federal rap and be free of any obligation to pay; in several of these cases, that provision has been disregarded and the government is still trying to collect. He served out this sentence first in the Douglas County Jail and then in the Federal Correctional Institution at Sandstone, Minnesota.

Arthur Harvey presently operates Greenleaf Books, a concern for the distribution of Gandhian publications. Each autumn and winter, he is manager of the pacifist-renowned Greenleaf Harvesters which picks apples in the beautiful New England countryside surrounding the area of Canterbury, New Hampshire and rakes blueberries around Hartford, Maine. Art has nots filed tax returns or paid Federal taxes since 1959. Ω

In 1950, when I registered for the draft, I was entirely too conceited and anti-social to dream of risking prison for any cause or idea beyond myself. Also, of course, my strong opinions on some matters merely concealed my lack of experience and commitment. A few years later I applied for a 1-0, or religious objector status from Selective Service. It was denied on the ground that my basis was personal and philosophical, not religious – a verdict which I did not appeal since it seemed true enough. Later I was happy to be classified 4-F. But whatever comfort I derived from considering myself a man of principle and a pacifist was challenged when I discovered that others had gone to prison for rejecting the privileged sanctuaries of deferments or alternative service.

So I found myself past the age of 26, with little danger of being inducted, sharing a point of view that normally leads young men to prison. Perhaps that was the most important reason (although I did not recognize it at the time) for my act of "courting prison" along with a dozen other pacifists at the entrance to a missile base near Omaha in 1959. Most of us were sentenced to six months plus a $500 fine for "illegal re-entry of a military reservation."

I spent a few days in Douglas County Jail – where cockroaches grow two inches long – learning to relish a breakfast of one stale roll. I never went so far as to drink the cup of black coffee.

Federal marshals, I noticed, try to exhibit a tough manner, as when they chained Karl Meyer and led him away from the missile base. But after a while, even marshals begin to act with some politeness, as when Marshal Raab took me without even handcuffs, in his car to the Federal Correctional Institution at Sandstone, Minnesota. All the same, one of the nastiest shocks was my awakening to the fact that officials and guards, in cold blood, whether politely or otherwise, systematically lock people in cages and keep them there so as to stimulate suffering.

Sandstone prison had recently been re-opened and was being filled with men transferred from more crowded prisons – men considered relatively adjusted and unlikely to want to escape. The warden was eager to set up the various occupational, recreational and educational programs which are thought to keep the inmates quiet and obedient – and, theoretically, on the road to rehabilitation. So I suggested myself for the job of librarian, to organize and circulate 3,000 books that were gathering dust in cartons (from the shut-down prison camp at Mill Point, West Virginia).

My suggestion was approved, and I spent many overtime hours happily locked up alone in one whole wing of the prison, repairing and cataloguing books. I improvised a simple catalogue system which was replaced by the Dewey system after I left, since the prison was more interested in standardization than efficiency.

The warden, a liberal, readily approved my request for $1,000 to purchase new books. Theoretically, they were selected by an "education director"; but in reality, the man who came to visit the prison with that title merely approved the list I submitted, after removing two or three books related to race or sex. I had drawn up the list of recommended new books with the help of Ammon Hennacy, a friend who followed me to prison by the same route a few weeks later.

I like to cite the library experience to refute the old saw about losing one's social effectiveness behind bars. In view of the intensive use given to serious books by a good many inmates, I don't believe I would have been any more socially influential as a "free" man during those months – not to mention my increased ability to communicate with people afterwards and my reduced terror of prison and hence increased freedom of action.

I have been pleased to hear of pacifists who have been at Sandstone more recently and been surprised at the quality of the library.

Eventually, order was imposed on the library and I was given forms to fill out, indicating the titles of books borrowed by each inmate. I was told the information might help the Parole Board evaluate a prisoner's attitude; and of course some prisoners borrowed books without reading them simply to impress the board. I refused to submit the information – in fact, I destroyed the records as the books were returned – as an intrusion of privacy.

After refusing a direct command by a lieutenant, I was taken to the captain, presumably for punishment. But he was a sophisticated fellow, and probably recalled that I had stated in my original job interview that there were limits to what I would do to help run the prison system. He simply said I could not return to the library under the circumstances, and asked what other job I would like.

I said some outdoor physical work would be a good preparation for my release in a few weeks. The captain agreed and I was assigned to clearing brush. Ironically, my little act of noncoöperation led to a loosening of classification. In the library I had been restricted to the prison compound (medium security). Clearing brush was outside the walls under a sleepy guard (minimum security).

I had some bad moments, including one time a prisoner tried to get me to submit sexually while threatening to attack me with a screwdriver. But I did not get angry or upset, and held him off without any offensive remarks until he stopped. Also, of course, there was the torment of separation from friends and activities vital to one's balance of mind. But life goes on, and you find substitutes. After my release from prison I returned my

draft card to the local board and continued my refusal to pay Federal tax or file a return. No punitive action has yet resulted. I have continued my literary interest by publishing pacifist works and distributing the writings of Gandhi.

From August until May I organize and direct a variety of agricultural labor crews in New Hampshire. Several members of Greenleaf Harvesters have gone to prison, and I believe that the self-confidence and comradeship these men have developed in this work has contributed to their ability and strength to maintain a firm pacifist stand.

Though the difficulties of prison are great and unusual, I do not see that they are harmful or unfitted to the pacifist who claims to embody an idea and a way of resolving conflict superior to violence. It seems a dozen times better for a young pacifist to endure the rigors and pain of prison, serving as best he can under the circumstances, than to devote years of "civilian service" to some job the government orders him to do for the national "health, safety and interest."

By doing alternative service he allows the government to tuck him conveniently away – a symbol of obedience who offers no useful example to the multitudes of young men who do not want to kill yet are not qualified for 1-0 status. Their only real alternatives are the army or jail. Pacifists who accept the 1-0 compromise to avoid prison, may be saying by example that the multitudes should accept military service to avoid prison.

☮ ☮ ☮

1970s PRISONERS:
From Witness to Resistance

☮ ☮ ☮

How I Was Carried to a Cell in a Wheelchair and Evicted from Prison in a Laundrycart, With Some Observations Made in the Intervening Period

John J. Phillips

Editor's Note: John Phillips was born on June 6, 1943 at Lynn, Massachusetts. He became an objector to war on "religious, moral, political, æsthetic, and internal (can't stomach it)" grounds.

Since his release from federal prison in 1967, he has coordinated the Prisoners' Information and Support Service (P.I.S.S.), which disseminates information about life in prison. He feels that the basic aim is the education of draft resistors and society as a whole to the point where they realize that there are prisons with identifying labels throughout our culture: schools, factories, armies, and to point out that all prisons are inside the mind.

John believes in noncoöperation with the prison system because as the average age of the federal prisoner is constantly lowered (now more than one half are between the ages of 17 and 28) and more politically sophisticated men are put in prison – men who are not ashamed of their actions and cannot be bought off – there is a good potential for political and social movement within the prison environment.

After he had refused induction on September 19, 1966 in Boston, his sentence was cut to 18 months, which he served, minus four months good time, at the Federal Reformatory at Petersburg, Virginia, and the Federal Prison Camp at Allenwood, Pennsylvania.

Phillips again refused to submit to induction on October 4, 1968. The chairman of his local draft board asked him if he knew the possible consequences of his noncompliance. "Yes, I do," he replied. Ω

On September 19th, 1964, in Federal District Court at Boston, Massachusetts, I was sentenced to three years imprisonment for my refusal to be inducted into service in the armed forces of the United

States. When the sentence was pronounced, I stood up in the courtroom and announced that I could not in good conscience coöperate with my own imprisonment for what I considered to be an act of righteous disobedience to illegitimate authority.

"I believe that my act was morally right, your Honor, and I must resist this injustice. Forgive me for this." I sat down and refused to move. "Young man," pleaded the judge, "surely you don't want to be manacled and dragged from this courtroom?" "If that is necessary, sir, then I accept this consequence." But the marshals were gentle as they lifted me from my chair and into a wheelchair, and, (having ordered the courtroom and corridor cleared), rolled me to a cell elsewhere in the building. Once deposited in the cell, I began coöperating, for my symbolic protest had been achieved.

I had passed the point of no return. Prior to the sentencing, it had been possible to entertain the thought that I could somehow find a way to avoid imprisonment. My ignorance of prisons had instilled in me a horror of what I might encounter behind the locked doors, a dread that had grown so intense in the last weeks that I had become virtually paralyzed emotionally For the first time in my life I considered even suicide to be a valid option, though in retrospect, I question whether I was capable of going through with this.

Yet somehow I had summoned up enough gumption to see my courtroom drama through, half in wavering confidence, half in that attitude of stubborn recklessness and resignation that characterizes most action-centered individuals in moments of crisis: an attitude aptly summed up in the phrase, "What the hell!"

And on the morning of the 19th of September I had cast myself into hell, for all I knew. The familiar symbols, the dependable items that structure one's everyday experience and constitute security, were swiftly disappearing for me, and my pulse was rapid as I awaited transfer to the institution that would be my abode for the next three years. But almost immediately I found reassurance in the mood of the people around me.

I spent the first night of my incarceration at the Norfolk House of Correction in Dedham, Massachusetts. There I was kept in a cell apart from the inmate population, except during the brief period necessary for processing. Yet I did have contact with one prisoner, a middle-aged man who gave me a pile of magazines to read and confided, in a soft voice so that only I could hear, "For what it's worth, I think you people are doing the right thing."

In the middle of the night, I was aroused by the noise of a new prisoner admitted to my cell; he had been convicted of bank robbery, and was my "traveling companion" when we departed from Dedham in the morning. This man had been incarcerated at the Lewisburg Penitentiary for a considerable period prior to his latest violation, and he took some time to describe to me the conditions and structure of the prison. We both anticipated that I would be sent to Lewisburg, so I listened eagerly to his advice; we got along well as cellmates, and I gained appreciable confidence from this exposure.

But when the federal marshals came to escort me from Dedham in the morning, I learned that I was not to go to Lewisburg, but rather to the Federal Reformatory at Petersburg, Virginia. My new acquaintance travelled with us as far as New York, where he was transferred to a prison bus bound for Lewisburg, Pennsylvania.

The two marshals drove me as far as Baltimore, Maryland that second day. The marshals, who were stationed in the Boston district, were jovial sorts who engaged with me in conversation as we rode. They were open to my views, and did not seek to bully me with contemptuous accusations or the catechism of the established order. They expressed their opinion that "I would have been better off in the military service, where a clerical position of some sort would surely have been open to me."

Many other employees of the Bureau of Prisons later used this same logic to try to convince me that I had acted foolishly. Yet this was clearly a different attitude from the contemptuous traitor-branding types; it left open the possibility of the give-and-take so vital to genuine communication, regardless of the differences in our value orientation and our politics.

I stayed overnight at the Baltimore City Jail. In the short time between my arrival and assignment of accommodations in a cell block deep within the lower intestines of this institution, I was able to mix with many of the prisoners in the receiving area. I was in good humor and delighted to find that the other young men were not only tolerant of my "offense" but in many cases openly sympathetic.

In particular, I discovered that I easily attained rapport with the young blacks; I was beginning to understand the depth of grievance that they had with the government that had subjected them to violence and deprivation for so long. The fact that I had defied the same authority by refusing to obey its orders provided the basis for acceptance.

Finally, on the following day, the marshals retrieved me and drove me the rest of the way to Petersburg. My first impression of the prison was that of a large camp, in some respects not unlike a college campus. But I soon took full notice of the multiple fences that ringed the area and were topped with barbed wire. The four huge guntowers standing watch over the camp, were they there to protect us from invading forces, like the garrison of an old fort? The old khaki uniforms of some inmates at work in the open.

I was puzzled at the sight of numerous low buildings that I afterward learned were dormitories for the inmates in which different levels of "security" were maintained to correspond to each inmate's assigned "custody." Except for new arrivals, who required orientation and processing, and exceptional prisoners who required special treatment or supervision, the population at the prison was divided into categories of minimum, medium, and close custody.

Minimum custody prisoners were allowed certain privileges that were prohibited to the other "castes" and individuals in close custody had the hardest lot. I use the word 'caste' because there was very little mobility between these categories, and it seemed to me that the very structure of the prison inhibited mobility, except in the final weeks of incarceration when that structure became more flexible.

For about a week, I was assigned to a cell in the "Cellhouse," and lived under conditions of confinement which I had associated with county jails. The other fellows in my cell block were all new admissions, and we soon got to know each other well as we underwent the processing together. We were of diverse backgrounds, but the common conditions and anticipations drew us together in a strange community. If I had wished to avoid a confrontation on the matter of my particular offense, however, it would have been impossible. The obvious question was, "What are you in for?" Again, I was fortunate in that these young men were curious rather than blindly hostile, that they shared to some extent an attitude of suspicion toward authority, and that they were much too concerned with their own prospects in prison to devote much attention to me.

Yet I recognized that the nature of my offense provided them with a convenient target for aggressions that were generated and kept alive by the frustration and anxiety of the essentially hostile environment. This was brought home to me when I found myself the focus of a mock trial, a sociodrama complete with lawyers for the prosecution and defense, judge and jury, marshals and court clerk and witnesses. I was charged with having destroyed my draft card. I sought to divert the threatening trend of this exercise by injecting humor into the dialogue whenever I had the opportunity to speak (as the defendant). I acted the fool, the bungler who had intended to light a cigarette but had somehow accidentally ignited his draft card. This approach was abruptly challenged by the shrewd "prosecuting attorney," who had observed that I am not a smoker; to demonstrate my perjury, he insisted that I smoke a cigarette before the court. But I was equal to the challenge, and as I slowly exhaled the fumes, I knew that I had routed the immediate danger.

Even so, the "jury" at last brought in a guilty verdict, and I was penalized by several sharp blows upon my chest. I was sore but not seriously hurt, and I was very grateful that my cell-block fellows had found this way to express their hostility; for in the aftermath of this incident, I found that I was more easily accepted into their number.

At the end of the orientation period, I was moved into a medium security dormitory to await classification and work assignment. I was given temporary sanitation chores during the day; in the evening, I could "escape" into the world of television or plug in my earphones to one of the available radio stations; usually, I preferred to read or to write letters. There were no cells in the dormitory; instead, large numbers of bunk beds were set up in rows along the walls and through the center of the building, with no dividing panels between them. Privacy was at a premium; the toilet and shower room were usually in use by several inmates at a time. In this dormitory, the television set was in a room apart from the sleeping area. In others this was not the case, and in all the dormitories one suffered from an overdose of noise.

There was fierce competition among the inmates for status, in particular for physical superiority. Many prisoners were drawn into weight-lifting for this reason. A fight offered the inmates a chance to show off their prowess, so with little excuse a fight would erupt. Target individuals, or, in the case of the Jehovah's Witnesses, target groups, absorbed a good deal of verbal abuse and sometimes bodily harm. Of course, the familiar racial conflict situations existed and were intensified by the unique prison environment.

Although I felt the hostility and shared the tension at the prison, and although I mixed freely with various segments of the population, I was able to avoid abuse for the most part. From the start, I held a position of advantage. Because the administrators recognized that I had been comparatively better educated than the other inmates, I was assigned to clerical work and encouraged to become involved with the inmate newspaper, discussion groups, and other activities. The administrators seemed also to be considerably permissive with me, to make special allowances for my deviation from the highly codified behavioral regulations.

I learned quickly that most inmates were concerned with "doing their own time" – that is, with avoiding entanglements and interactions that would make the imprisonment oppressive or perhaps extend it. By "keeping your cool," not meddling, not trying go impose one's own value-system on others, not becoming offensive, one avoided becoming a target, unless the antagonist was completely unreasonable. Through the prison newspaper, I had hoped to develop a basis for better understanding among inmates; but I soon realized that very few inmates actually took the trouble to read what was printed, with the exception of the joke columns and the movie schedule.

I found that I enjoyed using the medium of humor to get the message through. For example, I am sure that pointed jokes printed at the expense of the conscientious objectors helped in a small way to transform the attitudes of the remaining prisoners toward them from hostility to amusement, and thus provided a new level for communication. At the same time, it was probably healthy for the "persecuted element" to feel the brunt of humor and perhaps to have a hearty chuckle at themselves.

In addition to the confined condition at the camp, at least two other factors w»re responsible for the tense and hostile atmosphere that prevailed at Petersburg. One was the narrowly defined nature of the inmate population.

The inmates at Petersburg Reformatory numbered about 560. Of that number, approximately eighty per cent were serving sentences for interstate transportation of stolen property, usually automobiles. There was a small but growing band of Jehovah's Witnesses imprisoned for refusal to coöperate with the Selective Service program, and there were two other draft refusers who, as I, could be roughly characterized as "philosophical" objectors with varying degrees of religious or political involvement. Most of the prisoners were in the narrow age range of between 18 and 21 years of age; at 23, I was an exception.

The other major factor was the oppressive management of the institution, in particular on the level of custodial supervision. Many of the custodial guards were rookies who treated the inmates with contempt and refused to allow them any credit as responsible beings capable of making simple decisions for themselves and of regulating their own behavior.

Not only did this result in truncation of the inmates' potential for self-development, but it created bad feeling toward the guards. Occasionally the hatred aroused would express itself in a fight between an inmate and a guard, but more often it would be redirected toward the other prisoners.

Curiously enough, difficult as the prison situation became at times, I was more obviously affected by changes in my family situation at home. A good letter boosted my spirits and self-confidence immeasurably, and when I received bad news I reacted with severe depression. The prison routine, after all, was dependable, if tedious and stultifying; one could adjust to that. Letters, and to some extent also newspapers and television, brought home the point that one was involuntarily separated from the people and the things he loved.

Sometime after the fourth month of my imprisonment, a letter from home made me acutely aware that my family was in the process of disintegration, due in part to the involuntary separation caused by my imprisonment. In my state of emotional depression, the prison routine was severely oppressive, and I had to find some outlet for the pain and frustration. I had always wondered under what circumstances I would cease to coöperate with the prison system, and I found the option attractive to me at that point. I made no attempt to conceal the fact that I was acting in response to an emotional need only vaguely related to the restrictions of the prison; but neither did I attempt to disguise my convictions that prisons are essentially value-destructive and dehumanizing. I wrote a statement in which I incorporated both of these considerations, and left it for my supervisor at work to discover. I then walked to the "control center" of the administration building, and informed the guard on duty that I was refusing to work.

At the guard's instruction, I went without escort to the Cellhouse and turned myself in to be held in "administrative segregation" to await the trial board that would decide how I should be handled. I did not have very long to wait before I was called out to speak with the captain, the Supervisor of Education, and other members of the staff. By this time, they had become familiar with the statement I had left, and they indicated that they were impressed by the courteous manner in which I had gone on strike. They also expressed sympathy for my family problem, but advised me that I was acting in a self-destructive way that would benefit no one. When they saw that I could not be persuaded to return to work, I was ordered placed into a control cell (the prison's closest punishment to solitary confinement).

As it turned out, there were two varieties of control cells. One was in a regular cell block, where the bunk beds had been replaced with thin mattresses, but where one had the advantages and disadvantages of the company of a good number of other inmates. In addition to verbal contact, one was able (and obligated) to pass items like cigarettes from cell to cell. The meals were a much smaller version of what was served in the central cafeteria, without milk or fruit juices or dessert.

The condition was a tolerable one, because I slept easily for most of the day to substitute for my usual activity, and because I had no conflict with my cellmate. After staying for two days and nights in the first control cell, I was ordered by the guard in attendance to shave, whereupon I refused.

It had occurred to me at that moment that I had not yet completely broken with the prison routine. Had I agreed to shave, I would have given recognition to the authority of the prison administration. I was also curious to see the officer's response to my refusal. For a moment, I became concerned about the reaction of my cellmate to this turn of events but his response was to emulate my act of refusal, and we shared a moment of conspirators' delight until the guard returned to deal with us. He sought to persuade us that we were "merely being stubborn" and that we were placing him in a difficult situation.

When it became clear that we had decided to stand firm, he unlocked our cell and transferred us to the legendary area of the prison that had acquired the epithet of "The Hole." In "The Hole," in the basement of the Cellhouse, conditions were slightly different from the other control cells.

The chambers were separated from each other, so that we could not pass items from cell to cell by hand; and each one was intended to hold a single prisoner.

The toilets could be flushed only from the outside of the cell, at the prisoner's request and the guard's convenience or whim. Also, there were huge doors that could be closed and locked just outside of the bars, if a prisoner were the noisy or violent sort. While I was confined in "The Hole," I never once saw a guard make use of those doors. Eventually, by order from Washington, they were removed from the cells altogether. I found happily that when I tired of conversation with the other prisoners in "The Hole," and wished to rest in silence, I could isolate myself by closing the door. When I did this, my cell became very dark and I slept easily.

My experience in this type of confinement was far from unhappy. I knew that so long as I remained in that condition, I was continuing, and even renewing, my defiance of the prison authorities. Furthermore, I had not known such privacy since the beginning of my incarceration. At once, I cast off my prison garb and jumped gleefully in celebration of what I viewed as a new-found freedom.

The days in "The Hole" passed rapidly. Other inmates were deposited and released from the neighboring cells; my obstinacy in refusing to shave kept my credit good in this strange hotel, and soon the guards became amused by my playful attitude. They began to refer to me as "the naked White Muslim Santa Claus": Muslim because, like the adherents of Elijah Muhammad, I refrained from eating pork; Santa Claus because of my beard. But after about two weeks, I was ready for a change of scenery. And when the morning officer asked, as he had on previous days, if I had decided to shave, I agreed to do so.

However, I was unwilling to return to work. I was therefore transferred upstairs to what the inmates know as "Deadlock," but is euphemistically titled the "Treatment Unit." Here one is confined to a cell, either alone or with another inmate. Unlike the control cells, one is served a "full tray" at mealtimes, including fruit juices, milk, and dessert. One has commissary privileges, if he has money on account and wishes to purchase candy, cigarettes, or various other items not otherwise provided by the institution; one has access to writing materials throughout the day, and he may receive newspapers through the mail. At first glance, then, the prisoner held in "Deadlock" has many more advantages than in the control cells. But I soon was disillusioned.

I was placed in a cell with another inmate, a fellow who at first struck me as a friendly and harmless type with whom I would have little difficulty. His interests were obviously different from my own: he was eager to talk to me about automobiles and nothing else. His loquaciousness was a little annoying, but I was confident that I would be able to accommodate myself to that. Even after four days in the cell together, when I had a chance to leave the cell and visit the prison psychiatrist (with whom I had had occasional chats to relieve the dull monotony of the prison), I could report only that my cellmate and I were on good terms and that no special problems had arisen.

However, almost immediately following my return to the cell, I began to notice abrupt changes in my cellmate's disposition. Soon afterward, I began to feel besieged in that tiny cell by some kind of unpredictable and dangerous animal who represented a threat in terms of my physical well-being and my mental health as well. Because I had been totally unprepared psychologically for the metamorphosis that was taking place before my eyes, I felt panic. I found it necessary to retreat to my own (upper) bunk, with the excuse that I desired to read a book. As soon he sensed why I had done so, he understood the fear that he had instilled, and like an animal of prey, he pursued me and refused to allow me the sanctuary of my own bunk.

I found that my ability to converse – what I counted on in emergencies to mitigate the wrath of an opponent – had soon become almost totally frozen by the terror that had seized me. There was no escape; even in sleep. When he permitted me to sleep, my fantasies began to express the same terror that I knew all day. I dared not ask the aid of the guards. Apart from the usual reluctance on the part of inmates to rely on officers (part of the prison etiquette), I was convinced of collusion on their part. (Later, when I diagnosed this feeling as a part of my general paranoiac reaction to the unexpected aggression, I was informed by some members of the prison staff, in confidence, that they shared my suspicion.)

For brief periods of time, I found that my cellmate's attention could be diverted to working crossword puzzles or to listening to the passages that I read aloud from the few books I possessed. But as the days passed, even these tactics failed. There were also moments in which he seemed to return to the talkative-but-harmless attitude of the first few days, but these moments were harder to come by in time.

He had assumed the role of a crusader trying to "make a man out of me" or destroying my masculinity altogether and rendering me a completely submissive ("female") plaything. For these were the only two categories in which he could place someone. As a "draft-dodger" he identified me with the submissive, weakling image. My refusal to work, and later, my refusal to shave, did not seem consistent with that image, and his conclusion was that I was confused as to my own identity. He tried to force me to fit into one or the other of his categories.

To become a "man" apparently required that I be willing to fight; and he sought continually to provoke a violent response from me. At such moments, when I felt myself battered both physically and emotionally, I drew what strength I could from my faith in the nonviolent response to aggressive behavior.

But there were times when this proved insufficient, when I lost all confidence and cried out to Whomever might be listening to witness my struggle and renew my strength. "How dare you call God's name," my antagonist would challenge, "you who are so far from God!" And it almost seemed that we had suddenly been transported from that cell, and that I was facing some Divine Agent to account for having abandoned my faith except in moments of crisis.

He wanted me to see him in that sort of role; he began to claim that he had the power to manipulate my mind, that he could turn me into anything he desired. He enjoyed forcing me to serve as his handmaiden; to roll cigarettes for him, to be continually busy cleaning up the cell. In the final days of the ordeal, his aggression began to take a sexual turn, but fortunately my reprieve came before a confrontation was necessary to prevent my sexual integrity from being violated.

While I was enduring the days in "Deadlock," I desperately sought for a way to be released from the cell. I was hesitant to give over my resistance by returning to work, for it seemed to me that I had been placed in such a difficult situation for exactly the purpose of breaking my resistance; thus I regarded the experience not only as a personal challenge to overcome violence and reason with love, but as a test that would determine how the prison authorities would deal with recalcitrant types in the future. So instead, my thoughts went beyond the prison situation to the broader question of my relationship to the Selective Service System. I began to think that I might hope to be granted parole and therefore, release) almost immediately if I compromised my original stand of noncoöperation with conscription and announced that I was now willing to accept a position of civilian alternative service.

The need for immediate release from my present difficulties, added to the heightened awareness of the needs of my husbandless wife and fatherless son, and led me to consider a reversal of my former stance to be morally imperative. Human logic told me that such an unexpected turn could not reasonably be attributed by the prison staff solely to their experiment in coercion, as could a reversal merely of my refusal to work.

(When I had recovered from this period of desperation, I regained my former moral perspective and realized that my desire to be out of the cell had been the principal motive for my "change of heart." I did not consider any decision reached under such strain to have any real validity, but viewed it rather as an aberration.)

At the same time I was pursuing that avenue to release by writing to the judge who had sentenced me, I considered forms of direct action to assure my transfer from the cell. My first idea was to refuse again to shave, thus making it necessary for the guard on duty to remove me to a control cell in "The Hole" again. But I found that my cellmate violently opposed any such move on my part; he sensed that I was defying the regulations only to escape from his influence, and even a self-justified act of defiance against authority was in his eyes beyond the proper limits of the submissive type of person. I looked in vain for another opportunity to leave the cell – for example, another visit with the psychiatrist – with the idea in mind that once I had left the cellblock, I would refuse to coöperate with my return. Finally, the pressure became so great that I believed I would have to resort to violence in dealing with my cell partner if I did not accept the alternative of returning to work.

I had little hope that violence would be of any benefit to either of us, apart from necessitating our separation by the guards (or would they have continued to ignore us?). I also felt deeply that if I then resorted to violence I could no longer in good faith insist on nonviolence as a viable alternative to armies or police units. I therefore decided to return to work, and sent a note to the associate warden indicating I would do so. After a few days of painful delay, I was released from the "Deadlock" area. I had been in the cell for a full two weeks. (Again, in retrospect, I think that the strain of the situation of continuous confrontation with violence had begun to influence my logical analysis to the point where I generalized a specific conflict situation unjustifiably. Gandhi would perhaps have advised me to resort to violent means as an alternative to the submission or avoidance of conflict, in the absence of a viable nonviolent option; yet, in any case, the specific conflict here depicted is essentially different from the larger problems of armies and police.)

Apparently, the administrators were satisfied that I had come to my senses and given over any thought of rebellion. They not only reassigned me to my former clerk's position, but allowed me to return to the minimum custody classification I had before the strike. Although I returned easily to the routine of the prison, the thought that I had succumbed to bullying and had "sold out" under pressure continued to bother me. The other inmates helped to persuade me that I had made the only realistic decision, however, and three more months passed without any significant incident.

In April, a small number of us – there were by that time seven "philosophical" objectors in the camp who had refused to be inducted into the armed forces, and several other inmates who were openly sympathetic to our positions – began to be excited by the prospect of the forthcoming Mobilization demonstrations that were to occur in New York and San Francisco.

Many of us would have participated, either with organizations or as individuals, if we were "on the outside." The possibility of staging a demonstration of some sort within the prison, to indicate "solidarity" with the events beyond our reach, was considered, but not very seriously. By this time most of us had resigned ourselves to "doing our time" quietly; in addition, the pressures of conformity in the institution had acted to strengthen our individualistic impulses, so that the idea of being associated with a mass movement was not popular. Yet a week before the scheduled Mobilization activities, two other draft refusers and I found ourselves in "The Hole" again.

This time there had been no emotional "hang-up" to which I could refer as the overt motivation for my strike. The usual antipathy toward the prison system was certainly a factor, but the decision to rebel at that particular moment was largely impulsive and spontaneous. We three came to view our refusal to work as an æsthetic act, a playful, joyful move in contrast to a serious, goal-oriented protest. Instead of making pompous, self-righteous statements about the rationale for our refusal to work, we simply declared a holiday and did not report to our assigned details.

At last a custodial officer ordered us to go to the warden's office, where we were confronted by the warden himself, the associate warden, the captain and two of his lieutenants. These men were bewildered by our attitude, which was certainly "unreasonable" in their view; they tried to evoke from us an indication of the "real" motivation for our action: Were any of us having problems with the other inmates or with the officers? Was there a specific gripe? Or, perhaps, were we acting to protest the prison system?

We patiently explained that we looked upon our action as a creative expression of value in itself, that had no such political motive. The captain, at one point, lost all patience with us: "Impulses, eh? If I followed my impulses, I'd give you a good beating." He raised his fist; I had never seen him lose his composure before. Charlie, one of my companions, later told me that he was tempted at this point to challenge the captain to find a job where he could give free expression to his "impulses." At last, the encounter was over and we were delivered to adjoining cells in "The Hole."

After a week of this confinement, Gary (a politically-oriented young black with whom I had first become acquainted in civil-rights activity, who was not averse to working with white pacifists when "they were the only ones doing something meaningful to end this war") decided to return to work and was promptly released. Charlie accepted a transfer to the other section of control cells, where he stayed for another week before returning to work.

Because of my earlier bad experience with cell transfers, I was determined to stay in "The Hole" this time. At first, a mere verbal refusal to leave the cell was enough to ensure my staying; but to provide against the possibility of forcible eviction, I decided to refuse to shave and to wear no clothing. In the event that the guards might decide to carry out the transfer in spite of these gestures, I resolved to refuse to move in the manner of "going limp" when they came to fetch me.

I tried to keep myself psychologically alert for a change of tactics on the part of the guards, and this made the days in "The Hole" seem longer and less comfortable than they would ordinarily have been. But after the first week, I relaxed considerably as my confidence returned. The morning officer was amused by my attitude, and this fact enabled us to communicate outside of the categories of "guard" and "prisoner." At one point, he confided to me that he had "more friends among the inmates than among the other guards."

I began to receive bigger helpings of food at mealtime, and certain items that had previously been omitted from the meals in "The Hole" began to appear: hard-boiled eggs, fresh fruit and fruit juice, butter on pancakes and toast, and milk. I no longer had to beg daily for my ration of toilet paper, but was given a roll of my own; the guard teasingly referred to me as "a permanent resident" of "The Hole."

The guard even allowed me once to leave my cell for a visit to the psychiatrist, provided that I would wear a pair of coveralls; he did not insist on my shaving. As I moved along the corridors of the Cellhouse I came into contact with at least a score of other inmates who were awaiting treatment in the hospital unit. By this time, my beard was very much in evidence, and my appearance startled them.

One fellow asked me, "Why don't you like freedom?" I smiled broadly, winked, and proclaimed that in many ways, I was much freer than he. Some of the others present nodded understandingly. Later I discovered that this incident had become widely publicized among the inmates in the dormitories, and that I had attained a measure of respect for my defiance of the administration.

At suppertime one evening, I was informed by the officer on duty that a visitor was waiting to see me in the trial board room across the hall. I expected to have a new confrontation with a member of the staff, but instead I was amazed to find an Ivy-league type shuffling through various documents as I entered the room.

At once I recognized that he was a special agent of the F.B.I., but I could not understand why I had been summoned to see him. I was amazed anew when he informed me that he had come to the prison to hear my testimony on behalf of a young friend who had recently applied for conscientious objector classification. Apparently, the government considered me to be a valid character reference for him. At one point in our conversation, the investigator began to realize the absurdity of this situation: "I understand that you've had some problems with the draft yourself...," he said. The experience was so incongruous with the deprived condition to which I was returned that I was unable to sleep following this interview; instead

I danced about the cell alternately repeating portions of the dialogue and laughing until several hours later.

Altogether, I spent 19 days in "The Hole" the second time. I had at first intended to return to work after two weeks, I began to wonder whether I might remain there until the termination of my sentence. But on the eighteenth day I received a telegram from my wife, indicating she would be at the institution on the following day to visit me.

I had previously tried to discourage her from visiting, because I knew how upsetting the experience of an isolated visit could be for all parties concerned. I was, however, completely captivated by her telegram, and decided to suspend my noncoöperation in order to see her. The next morning, as I was escorted to the admissions area to shave and have my hair cut and to receive fresh clothing, I was greeted with what amounted to almost a triumphal reception by the inmates working there.

As I left the Cellhouse and walked toward the visiting area in the administration building, I was accosted by the warden and informed that the staff had decided to transfer me and my two fellow rebels to the Federal Prison Camp at Allenwood, Pennsylvania to avoid further problems.

Apparently, our little rebellion had succeeded to a greater extent than we had expected. I think that the staff had realized that we could no longer be intimidated by the threat of violence or deprivation into tolerating the anti-human structure of the prison routine and regulations. They saw us now as a threat to the stability of their control over the rest of the population, and only by transfer could they remove that threat.

I found my wife in surprisingly good health and humor. It was a good visit, and I was surprised later that I did not experience a new depression as a result of the separation then.

For the few days that I remained at Petersburg awaiting transfer, there were no new incidents. The prison bus that transported us to Pennsylvania looked something like a sightseeing bus from the outside, except that where it should have been labelled "Sightseeing" it read, "Department of Justice, Bureau of Prisons." In a way, it all fit in; the officers at federal institutions wore uniforms that made them appear to be bus drivers, or perhaps more appropriately, zoo-keepers. The bus was a traveling menagerie, with its live exhibits carefully caged and secured with manacles inside.

As we passed through Arlington, Virginia, we came close to the Pentagon; it was May 12th, and I noted happily that some of my friends would later on the same day be at that very location to confront the leaders of the war machine with their plea for peace, in the climax of a Walk for Peace that had traversed 450 miles from Boston. So the government had made it possible for me to add my witness, briefly, to that event.

We were delivered to the Federal Penitentiary at Lewisburg, to be held for about a week before removal to the Allenwood Camp. The Camp has a skeleton staff of its own for administration, but it is run as a subsidiary unit to Lewisburg; therefore, all our processing was done at "The Wall," as inmates referred to the big prison. I didn't see much of Lewisburg during the week that I was detained there, but many differences were readily in evidence from the Petersburg Reformatory.

Most obvious were the differences in the inmates and the guards. The inmates were generally older, and there was a wide age range; many had been incarcerated for more serious crimes, and consequently were serving comparatively longer sentences. I found no difficulty in mixing with the population. The officers seemed to be much more professional in their demeanor: polished, inflexible, automatonic; one knew precisely what his limits were in dealing with them, they didn't put themselves in vulnerable positions as had the "amateurs" at Petersburg.

Following my transfer to Allenwood Prison Camp, I was assigned to work in the Education Department, proctoring aptitude and achievement tests to which new arrivals were submitted. I was encouraged to teach also, and soon began classes in algebra and geometry. Nearly half of the prisoners at the Camp were conscientious objectors; many of the remaining prisoners were older men who had committed white-collar offenses.

There was little tension among the prisoners, although it was disappointing to discover that there were some serious personality clashes among the COs. There were few guards, compared to Petersburg and Lewisburg, and most of them were kindly, older men whose only concern was to maintain the quiet regularity of the Camp. In this peaceful setting, content with daily walks along a mile stretch of road permitted to us, I passed an undisturbed six months. Only the impact of the thought of my release brought an abrupt end to my reverie.

On November 1, 1967, eight days before my scheduled release from custody at the Allenwood prison camp, I submitted a letter to the warden at Lewisburg in which I demanded the unconditional simultaneous release with me of all other political prisoners, and the simultaneous parole of all so-called "criminal" offenders. I stated that if the prison authorities were either unwilling or unable to fulfill my request, then I desired to be kept in custody, and would resist an attempt to evict me from prison.

In making these demands, I was deliberately trying to upset the "standard operating procedure" which dictated that each prisoner was in a kind of "time-slot," scheduled to be ejected, fully packaged in his newly-issued civilian clothing, handed a bus ticket and thirty bucks, and left off at the bus depot, pointed homeward with a standard wave of "Hope we don't see you again."

It struck me that the whole process of release was a dehumanizing process, reducing people to mere numbers that could be shuffled about at the whim of the authorities. In defying the order to leave prison, I was challenging that process and asserting myself as an individual. Furthermore, my thoughts went to my buddies – some of whom had been in prison longer than I had, though they had committed the same act. How could I accept a scheme of "justice" in which I would be released and they would remain behind? Not until after I was back "on the streets" did I realize that there was yet another meaning to what I had done after all – I hadn't been released to freedom, but merely to ANOTHER KIND OF PRISON. One that is taken for granted by the people doing "life sentences" in the dungeons of the "outside world," one where freedom to live as one chooses is just as rare as the freedom I sometimes knew "behind the walls."

On November 2, I was summoned to the office of the camp superintendent, where I was confronted by him and by the caseworker at the camp. Not only did these men appear to take seriously my request to remain at the prison, but they seemed to consider the idea of releasing all the prisoners as a reasonable one; either they were good actors or I had greatly misjudged them.

In any case, it was plain that they would not allow the others to go ("could not" in their administrative capacity, for they had limited authority). They were just as reluctant to allow me to forfeit my four months "good time" to delay my release until January.

It was plain that they wanted to avoid trouble, and I presented them with an embarrassing choice. The caseworker sought to persuade me that the right way to go about the business of staying in prison would be for me to accept release and then go out and commit a new offense. I argued that my refusal to obey the order to leave constituted a violation of the prison regulations, for which I could be punished by having to forfeit my "good days," which were, after all, conditional upon my compliance with the rules of the prison game. But neither man was willing to accept the argument they weren't sure how to handle the situation, since it hadn't been described in the manual of regulations. So the matter remained unsettled at that point.

Another six days went by. I refused to sign a receipt slip for the civilian clothing I was issued, on the grounds that I didn't anticipate leaving and saw no need to sign for clothing I would not need. On Wednesday, November 8, I was again summoned – I assumed, for another confrontation – to the superintendent's office. But this time, before I had a chance to let my fellow prisoners know what was happening, I was whisked away in the superintendent's sedan to the Lewisburg penitentiary, where I was ushered into the office of the Associate Warden.

I learned from the Associate Warden that the prison administrators (the top men at Lewisburg were also in charge of the prison camp) had decided definitely to evict me – bodily, if necessary – from the prison on the following morning. When the matter of civilian clothing was raised, I indicated that I saw no reason to change clothes since I did not intend to coöperate with my release; the A.W. became impatient, and insisted that I would be released, in any case, and that his guards would change my clothes if I remained stubborn.

"Surely you wouldn't want me to put my men to the embarrassing task of dressing you," he said. (Prison personnel are uptight about naked human bodies...institutions don't allow for anything but uniforms.) Later, I decided to get dressed myself in order not to unnecessarily antagonize the guards. I wanted to confront the administration, not its hirelings, with the challenge. "What will you do when we leave you off at the bus depot?" he pursued. I replied that I had been giving the matter considerable thought, and that I might decide to walk back to the prison to demand readmittance. He told me I could be charged with "trespassing on government property" for that; I only smiled.

I was placed in a segregated cell at the penitentiary overnight. I slept well there, and was aroused at slightly after 4 a.m, by one of the guards. (The "eviction" was timed so as not to arouse the curiosity of other prisoners, who were asleep throughout the episode.)

The guard escorted me downstairs to the "dressout area," and seemed a little surprised when I voluntarily put on my civilian garb. But then, as he got ready to leave, I indicated that I would coöperate no further. Another guard and he rolled a huge canvas laundry cart – on casters, with a wire frame – over to where I had taken a seat.

"Are you going to get in?" I was asked. That was ridiculous, plainly, and I refused. The men lifted me, very gently, and placed me inside the cart. Then they pushed the cart into an elevator, where another guard took charge of it, and I was brought up to the main floor. When we were out of the elevator, the guards rolled the cart down the main corridor of the  prison; there were a number of guards standing at attention all along the corridor, apparently summoned for special duty at that early hour.

Finally, we were outside the building. They bumped the cart down the entrance steps and wheeled me out under the central guntower. As we came to the tower, one of my escorts shouted up to the man controlling the gate, "Believe it or not, this is a RELEASE!" Another guard continued to mumble, "My mother would never believe this."

Instead of the "standard operating procedure," I was lifted into a waiting sedan, and I learned that a U.S. Marshal and one of the Associate Warden's secretaries would drive me all the way from the prison in

Pennsylvania to the court building in Boston, Massachusetts, where I had been sentenced fourteen months before.

I was amazed that they would go to such lengths to prevent further difficulty. Perhaps they thought I would go to the press with my story and bring reporters with me when I returned to the prison to demand that I be let in. Typically, prison officials are overly sensitive to publicity; people aren't supposed to set eyes on the prisons, and who could anticipate the public reaction to my stunt?

Ordinarily, my release would have taken place at about 10 a.m. and I would have had to endure waiting for bus transfers, etc. As it was, the early release and a direct auto ride to Boston meant that I was home by noon. The conversation in the car as we drove was an interesting one. "I thought you people didn't fight!" the marshal protested. "What do you mean?" I asked, bewildered. "Well, what do you call what you just did back at the prison?" I understood, and was glad he got the point. As he left me off at the Federal Court in Boston, he reminded me to send a postcard when I decided to straighten out my life; I suggested that he do the same, and we parted.

☮☮☮

☮ ☮ ☮

A PRISON JOURNEY

F. Paul Salstrom

Editor's Note: Paul Salstrom was born in Rockford, Illinois on August 16, 1940. He became a conscientious objector at the age of 19 and developed strong feelings toward humanity.

He was sentenced to three years by the Federal District Court in Rock Island, Illinois, under the 1948 Act. He served two years and two weeks, the bulk of this at the Medical Center for Federal Prisoners in Springfield, Missouri, before being released on good time or "mandatory release." He was out only three months, from July to October 1964, when he was rearrested for returning East to work with the New England Committee for Nonviolent Action and given his "entire good time to serve – eight and two-thirds months at the Federal Correctional Institution in Danbury, Connecticut.

After prison, Paul took LSD for the first time to unwind and relax with excellent results. He has stayed in the peace movement but now considers that he is more involved in a constructive program for himself in writing and poetry.

Prison is "just another place to live, when necessary" for Paul Salstrom. Ω

Beyond finding prison at times enjoyable and at times frustrating, its essential effect upon me came in contributing to a toughening-up process. The future of America looks grim of late. I tend to evaluate political activity therefore by its contribution to preparing us for constructive response. And in my case, jail did contribute – it gave substance to my Gandhian and pacifist partisanship.

My personal commitment to pacifism, before *and* after prison, has been humanist rather than religious and more than philosophic. But commitment isn't enough. My overall evaluation of those few years in prison is that they put politics into manageable perspective in my own life, suggesting concrete steps toward coping with what seems to me the key present opportunity offered by Gandhian (political) nonviolence: namely, the opportunity to tackle some problems of U.N.-type peacekeeping without encountering the contradictions which today invalidate military methods. Facing prison was a significant aspect of preparing myself for future engagement in nonviolent peacekeeping – a strategic activity which may play a key role in building a viable peace and freedom movement. Thanks to prison I grew familiar with what nonviolence will come down to in concrete situations.

Now, nonviolence is at best a value, not a goal. As was the case in India's independence movement, in America's black freedom movement a person for whom "nonviolence" is an end rather than just a means toward other ends both feels and looks out of place. In fact, it's perhaps *because* freedom riders and sit-inners have held quite different goals – such as social justice or integration or, more recently, black power, but not the value of nonviolence *per se*.

They've learned something we peaceniks haven't grasped yet: nonviolent action isn't very effective in changing attitudes unless it is met head-on by violence. Jail-going constitutes one form of confrontation, but apparently it is not quite direct enough a confrontation to change American society.

To change America's foreign relations, just as to change her race relations, a body of opinion needs nonviolent action more dynamic than jail-going to spearhead it, but never forget that the actionists in turn need a sympathetic body of opinion to spearhead.

Let's think back two years. As of April, 1967 large scale anti-draft action had been organized all over the country by ghetto groups, by We Won't Go groups, by pacifists, and others.

All was combustible tinder for some creative and constructive disorder. Creative disorder was a change instead of meek and orderly regimentation.

But where was the spark to set this off? Merely speaking, writing, banding together, merely mailing back draft cards, refusing induction and spending a year, or three, in the clink – all these had been going on for 19 years against the 1946 [*sic* – 1948] draft law.

Personally, I had expended the prior six years on them. A quantitative step-up of the same activities could not and did not strike the new spark. For action to be effective, it had to be a bold and unpredictable initiative, able to unmask the opposition by drawing out into better view its assumptions, its violence and its pathology.

Gandhians call this moral *jiu-jitsu* – the fundamentally (for Gandhi) friendly use of an opponent's energy to throw him off balance – to throw him *open* to examination by himself and everyone else.

In the course of six years of anti-draft work, I had seen only one bright spark ignited by the four draft card card burners at South Boston Courthouse in the spring of 1966. There the pattern of developments, partly by accident, followed by lessons James Bevel and others had painfully learned in Birmingham and masterfully applied in Selma. There in

South Boston we relearned the discomfiting fact that nonviolence tends to work well only if applied (with guts) in the face of a dangerous situation and only if witnessed by many observers.

Police brutality helps this unveiling of reality, of course, and police protection obscures it. Let's face facts: police protection of "free speech," since it is extended only selectively, when appearances count, means police complicity in a lie.

There is apparently only one way to truly grapple with and defeat a matrix of violence: head-on nonviolent confrontation. This was the background behind the historic emergence of The Resistance. When 175 young men burned their cards at Sheep Meadow in April of 1967, we knew that the isolated, hopeful sparks of earlier days had not been struck in vain – we knew that America's youth had a new fire.

The 1948 Universal Military Training and Service Act offers "alternative service" to religiously-oriented pacifists – and, in practice, to some who are non-religious. In April of 1961, because of opposition to conscription in any form, I personally became a non-coöperator, a draft refuser.

Also, I did so because it seems to me to have been a mistake for most earlier pacifists to largely ignore the problem of peacekeeping. My rejection of "alternative service" as well as military service doesn't imply that I consider service on behalf of social development to be irrelevant. On the contrary, social development work (whether conscripted or voluntary, as the case may be) can obviously help to *shrink* the international problems of our own and other countries.

But imagine the potential represented by the many thousands of young men currently serving their two-year civilian work "in the national interest" – if they now were to begin rejecting conscription. Who better than experienced constructive workers could take on the challenge of creating pilot programs for local civilian defense and for nonviolent peacekeeping?

Why did I choose prison in preference to "alternative service"? Because I think nonviolent action could be a peacekeeping technique superior to military methods. By choosing prison, I emphasized my dissent about how this country should be defended. For it's to *defend* the country, essentially, not merely to serve it any which way, that young men are in demand.

A few years behind bars didn't dampen my intention to help make peacekeeping a solidly reliable rather than an illusionary possibility.

It is for psychological reasons that I'm assuming acts of civil disobedience, and even the experience of being imprisoned, will be necessary before most COs are likely to feel motivated toward building major defense and reconciliation experiments around nonviolent action.

Why did I choose prison? To express a choice, yes, but also to prepare to implement it: to toughen up, mind and body. When it was finally time to begin serving the three-year sentence, I fasted and non-coöperated for fifteen days. Now, always for me learning about life seems to mean learning the hard way. In the case of jail-resistance, the lesson wasn't quite what I expected, apparently I had somewhat misapprehended what it means to be tough.

What is strength? Many different things, depending. But strength is never non-social, never de-humanized: all strength is grounded in love.

So I learned the hard way that my original point of view about jail was in need of humanization. When that humanization began coming (first from outside), I began changing, and a seed was planted that is now developing into an idea called Pen-pals for Prisoners, many years later.

The first influence was a letter from Jules Rabin, a writer and film-maker: "I wish you well, Paul, on your ordeal, and hope you can find a way to let your time in jail do well by you. I worry when you say you are going to hate every minute in jail. Don't be intransigent, Paul, for intransigency's own sake.

"Unless you are going to be a perfectionist, and take no responsibility whatsoever for any requirement of your body, you will be caught up in the universe of compromise – which is in fact where we almost all live our lives, and which it is incumbent for everyone to live in who doesn't have perfect conviction. We draw lines, and you know this well, at various points between ourselves and our ultimate ideology.

"Be wise, and determine from your own heart what are the appropriate points for you to draw the lines. Don't make this determination on the basis of some principle outside yourself. Such external principles are the domain, often, of heartless logicians and geometers.

"Life is soft and unknowing, often, like a plant. Speak to yourself, and yield where you must. Your impulse to yield may be a betrayal; but it may instead be an opening to such a further course of wisdom as the abstract geometry of principled morality could not reveal to you."

Thus spoke Jules Rabin, to good effect. Two years passed for me at the federal prison system's Medical Center in Springfield, Missouri – beginning with summer, 1962. Incidentally, that was the first summer in seven years I'd spent separated from mountains and ropes. Eyeing the walls made my hands itch.

Prison is the kind of place that makes one restless, the kind of place I'd never previously lingered long – worse than college or any of the successive jobs I'd hastened to quit in former years. But I nevertheless did eventually settle down securing an assignment out-of-doors to gardening and began collecting first-hand reports of brutalities perpetrated by guards, corresponding heavily with mysterious girls, and closely observing human behavior behind walls.

Life behind bars tends to be oppressive, notwithstanding the "paternalistic benevolence" of the federal prison system. To begin a severe sentence alone is one of the steepest challenges our society imposes; to endure it alone, sane or insane, is one of the most painful. And most embittering...

Every convict in this country probably knows the three time-honored homilies for doing easy time: (1) walk slowly, (2) drink plenty of water, (3) do your own time (not your buddies' as well). With the help of fasting one day a week I mastered the first two, but the third still eludes me. And inevitably, when the week comes for release, the empathy with friends doing long, hard time builds up to overwhelming sadness.

In July of 1964, after those interesting two years (during which parole was twice denied), I received a "Mandatory Release" due to automatically earning good-time – in spite of refusal to abide by the "conditions" of that release. After two months of prison writings, I violated the "conditions" by returning from the midwest to New England and making preparations for an anti-draft caravan. I was re-arrested and served nine months of revoked good-time at the Federal Correctional Institution at Danbury, Connecticut, receiving an unconditional release in June of 1965.

Thus empathy with luckless friends doing long, hard time had to be endured again.

During that second nine months of imprisonment at Danbury, I had again begun with a 15-day fast.

Later my assigned work was silk-screening and commercial art. As at the Medical Center, I ignored rules from above with which I did not agree, although not without some compromises, trying to support personal rights as well as personal responsibilities.

Since in the outside world, I don't take issue with the *right* of others to gamble, for instance, or to brew apple-jack, stash marijuana, be homosexual, or even sabotage the government – behind walls I likewise respected such rights.

Perhaps I should ask you, the reader, to pause and consider how you view extreme permissiveness on my part regarding the rights of others – their right to break social rules and suffer the consequences? Was I going too far in allowing rot-gut apple-jack to ferment in my back cabinets or marijuana to be stashed there?

My own feeling then and since has been that one's best impulses are impulses on the side of freedom. *Anyone's* freedom. I can't help but wonder what my own fate would have been had I not followed my strongest impulses – to quit jobs right and left, to test endurance on mountains, to turn in my draft card and join peace walks.

But the point is that none of this would have contributed much to my personal strength or growth without respect from others; rarely respect for the decisions I made, frankly, but always for my *right to choose and take the consequences.*

Therefore today as an ex-con my self-respect and happiness seem to be above the American norm. Of such "currency" as happiness is one's true standard of living, not of money. My standard on living, *in terms of living,* is in fact so high that my financial income has nonchalantly gravitated to the lowest level in America, where it will happily remain.

Incarceration can often involve for an inmate a destructive and unnecessary emotional pain, essentially consisting of lack of meaningful communication and relationship. Curiously, the shared un-free status of fellow inmates apparently does not open up meaningful communication between them on a human level.

Meanwhile, without at least some intimate relationship with another human being, something near the core of a person's personality can wither, leaving him capable of "criminal acts" which would previously have been out of the question.

This is an absolute withering in the lives of relatively few prisoners, but to a sadly damaging extent it seems to happen to virtually all.

Jules Rabin had written that impulses can lead to the unfolding of a "further course," and mine did. On five or six occasions when some fellow convict was in desperate need of morale-boosting – of a feminine contact in the world outside, in my empathetic interpretation – I violated the prison rules which forbade correspondence between strangers.

I would smuggle out a letter to some girl I knew, suggesting she befriend as a pen-pal the friend inside. None of the girls ever declined, and the effects always seemed to transcend mere morale-boosting. Sometimes the extent of influence, easily measurable in the fellows' self-improvement endeavors, such as, for instance, night school, vocational training, weight-lifting, reading, would be astounding – all the result of one or two letter exchanges a month (hesitant and bashful both ways, needless to add).

Alienation is likely to be the experience you first encounter if you go to prison. I had the good fortune to go behind bars on behalf of something I think worthwhile – draft refusal, pacifism. But I didn't thereby avoid encountering alienation. Likewise, alienation will probably be the initial feeling encountered if one corresponds with a prisoner.

But the alienation which permeates such a relationship by mail, with or without visits, is a passing stage, because inevitably it becomes *shared.* There is no point hoping to skirt the discomfort of alienation; its reality had best be faced. The only position from which real communication can begin is the position in which people honestly find themselves: that position today tends to be alienation, jail or no jail.

I'm convinced that the Pen-pals for Prisoners service will be a vital aid in the struggle which a prisoner must wage to retain free feelings and authentic experiences. This I learned while still a prisoner myself and long before the idea of an organized pen-pal service arose.

If administrative approval can be gained for the free working of a pen-pal service – whether channelled through prison chaplains, through case-workers, or through committees of actual prisoners – there would be a groundswell of response from men who find themselves doing hard time.

Allow me to explicitly make clear that the pen-pal service is to function on behalf of all prisoners, no matter what they are in jail for. Actually COs would rarely need so impersonal a method of making outside friends; but just the opposite would apply to heroin salesman, armed robbers, and juvenile delinquents.

The idea's central merit is the power of personal communication to relieve suffering through undergirding self-help, an approach which should appeal to anyone aware that suffering cannot be redemptive when it is not voluntarily chosen.

For someone doing enough time behind bars, it's of course possible to correspond voluminously as well as to suffer voluminously. Bob Stroud, the "Birdman of Alcatraz" was such an individual. During the year and a half we knew each other at the Medical Center for Federal Prisoners (ending with his death in November of 1963), Mr. Stroud often spoke of the many personal events which kept his spirit alive during forty-three years in solitary at Leavenworth and Alcatraz ("The Rock" in San Francisco Bay).

Thinking back over those events, I can't remember a single case not involving the aid of outsiders, and thus dependent upon correspondence.

As an unfree man, Bob Stroud's suffering was emphatically not redemptive, but he managed to do fifty-three hard years without losing his capacity for constructive initiative.

My opinion has come to be that true rehabilitation must be self-rehabilitation: that is, to help another person means to make possible self-help. In Bob Stroud's last days, so far as either of us knew, there was as yet no prison system in the U.S. which did not censor mail.

After the initiation of his diseased-bird analysis business in Leavenworth in the 1920s, Stroud for decades had sent all important correspondence secretly between the laminations of his bird boxes (a fact never discovered by the Federal Bureau of Prisons, but there's no point in concealing it now).

During the early campaigns for his release, Stroud authored the public petitions personally and smuggled them out that way for printing. Who of us in the outside world could justifiably condemn such forms of rule breaking?

If Bob Stroud had never made peace with the prison system, perhaps I, too, might (albeit grudgingly) have decided to "leave well enough alone." But the last thing I heard from his lips in November 1963 was that from 1909 on he had fought the injustices of the prison system every step of the way, and would never stop fighting until the day he died.

Then on the night of November 20-21, Stroud was up twice, due to a heart attack, attempting to exercise his right to communicate with the doctor on duty. It was common knowledge among the inmates in the building that, the desk officer in charge refused this right to Stroud. Since medical heart stimulation was thus denied to Stroud which the doctor thought might have pulled him through, it is reasonable to say that this arbitrary decision by the desk officer assured the Birdman's death.

At 6 A.M. our mutual friend Morton Sobell called him for breakfast, shook him and even felt for him pulse before looking him in the face and noticing his open eyes.

Let there be no misunderstanding in regard to my motivations. Allow me to state explicitly that I oppose the entire practice of imprisonment – and hope that the Pen-pals for Prisoners service will give convicts a more effective wedge than they now have to *beat the system* – to sustain the sensations and the spirit of freedom rather than to finally emerge from their incarceration as broken men.

☮☮☮

☮ ☮ ☮

WHAT WILL IT BE LIKE WHEN YOU GET OUT?

Darryl Skrabak

Editor's Note: Darryl Skrabak was born on March 18, 1941 in Long Beach, California. He was educated in San Francisco public schools and then attended Oregon State College, the University of California at Berkeley, and California Polytechnic Institute at San Luis Obispo, majoring in mechanical engineering and journalism.

Darryl was sentenced in March 1966 to two years for failure to report for induction, which he served in the Federal Correctional Institution at Lompoc, California. Lompoc is presently where most West Coast draft violators serve.

His charge was incorrect, although it was not disputed legally; Darryl did report for induction but refused the oath. Initially desiring status as a conscientious objector, he refused to file Form 150 after some consideration.

He was released from Lompoc in August 1967 to the Federal Community Center, a liberally (for prison) oriented halfway house which few draft violators qualify for or accept. Community centers provide reorientation to the outside and no prisoner serves more than 30 days there.

After prison, Darryl was appointed prison visitor for the West Coast Office of the Central Committee for Conscientious Objectors at Lompoc, in coöperation with the Resistance.

He is presently at work on a new film in rural southern California. Ω

So you've signed up to do your time for Resistance, and now you're in prison. And you want to know: What will it be like when you get out.

It will be better than being in!

A flip answer, that. Also, deliberately evasive. Why? Because each man does his own time, and he comes out his own way. To offer a pat answer, therefore, would be a fraud. The answer depends on the man. And this is especially true of men who go to prison for Selective Service violations. Those I know and others I have met in print are all people whom I would hesitate to categorize.

Having said that, I will go on and try to make an answer anyway.

First of all, release from prison may not mean release without strings. Release may be under terms of parole or supervised probation, which involve a number of restrictions. Life is lived under the supervision of a local federal parole officer. He wants you to get a regular job, tell him how much you're making and what you're spending it on. He has monthly reports he wants you to fill out.

He wants to know where you're living, and with whom. He has a certain interest in the company you keep and what you do and where you go: Don't associate with former criminals. Don't break any laws. Don't buy a car, get a driver's license or get married without my approval. Don't travel outside a certain area without asking me first. Don't, or you'll be violated and back in prison without a trial.

All that sounds terrible. But it can be livable. I've talked with some draft refusers who got along quite well on parole. They report the parole officer's principal request is often not to cause him any concern, as he's got other people on his caseload who he's really worried about.

Should you be released on parole, a great amount of the question is answered. You'll have to go back to a certain community and live in a somewhat prescribed place and manner and get a job. You'll be plugged in.

There's a good chance, unfortunately, that you'll not be released on parole. A good chance, because the current practice of the U.S. Board of Parole in Washington is to deny parole to draft violators.

This means most of your sentence must be served in prison, rather than on the streets.

Let's suppose you're released with time off for good behavior, and there's no parole officer to bother you. Now you're in a position similar to the man who's just graduated from college. You've been in one place for a long time and you've had to put off or leave off things you like doing. You've been thinking about a million things you wanted to do, you've made a thousand schemes with your friends, all for the time when you'd get out. Now you're out. What happens?

You go back normal. Your people are there. The places you knew before are still there, mostly, almost like you knew them. You look up your old friends. Some of them are gone. The ones you find look at you like some madman hero stranger. New people look you up, and they regard you the same way.

You know you'll never be quite the same again.

You'll want to get next to a good woman, and let's hope there's one waiting for you or let's hope you can find one quick.

If you're like many draft resisters, you won't have much money. You'll have to get a job. The Resistance and its allied groups, if they are strong in your area, may help you find work. It's better, however, to count on finding your own job.

Your record will deny you some employment. My experience has been that lower-level and trades-level jobs will be open to you. Jobs on what I will call the middle level may be difficult to acquire. For example, my record has prevented me from employment as a newspaper reporter and an apprentice draftsman, both fields in which I have college background. But I have no trouble finding work as a motorcycle mechanic if jobs are available for which I can qualify.

If you've got a Ph.D., you'll have no problems for work. You're on the upper level where talent counts and it's scarce.

The trouble with this job business is that it may remind you of the joint. Seeing people working to a schedule, conforming in dozens of ways to outside forces, being made to do these things yourself, is very likely to repel you. Too often, you will see, people carry their prisons with them.

In some states, like California, you'll be able to vote, if that's a concern. I voted in the last elections in San Francisco.

This, then, is part of the answer to what it will be like when you get out. The remaining parts I urge you to find in yourself, because there is the only source. When you arrive at the point where you must answer the question yourself, I am sure you will not shirk it.

It will be better than being in.

☮ ☮ ☮

THE SCENE AT SPRINGFIELD

Michael Vogler

Editor's Note: Michael Vogler was born on November 23, 1945 in Little Rock, Arkansas. He spent 1959 to 1964 in a Catholic seminary after completing high school and one year of college.

Mike filed for CO classification at Christmas 1966 with Local Board #60 in Little Rock and received his 1-0 on March 16, 1967 after a hearing with the board. His position was "opposition to war as a means of realizing human brotherhood and community, or of furthering human relationships in a qualitative way."

He returned his registration and classification cards on January 15, 1968 and subsequently refused to report for alternative service work. It was then only a matter of a few short months before he was sentenced to three years in prison, where he is now. From the time of his arrest, he refused bail because of its discrimination against the poor, would not plead before a man who claimed the right to judge his fellow man, and would not take a lawyer to speak on his behalf. Michael Vogler stood very tall before the court and nodded when the sentence was handed down.

Now he writes from the Medical Center for Federal Prisoners in Springfield, Missouri, "My attitudes today are by and large negative, but more than that I am not ready to say. My present perspective is drastically limited and would rather wait until release before making some evaluation." Ω

Rise around 5:00-6:00 for breakfast; 7:35 to work; 10:35 to lunch; 11:00 watch T.V. show "Jeopardy"; 12:00 back to work; 3:30 count and mail call; 4:00 supper. After supper we are free until 10:00 P.M. (In the yard until 8:00.) Most of this time is spent playing softball, bridge and watching T.V. if anything decent is on.

My job is secretary to the Parole Clerk. There does not seem to be much work, and mostly I read and write letters; on weekends, there is no mail, or work, or anything, so they really seem to stretch out endlessly.

The institution here is technically a Medical Center for Federal Prisoners. Most of the clientele are hospital patients, both psychiatric and medical. I am in the prison camp which is attached to the medical center. People in the camp are, supposedly, normal – at least we need no extraordinary medical or psychiatric care.

Haven't thought too much about parole lately. (This is sort of funny since I work for the Parole Clerk.) Actually the whole problem of coöperation is one I think about almost constantly. It is impossible not to think about it. And the others here, in similar positions to mine, worry too. All I can say is that at present I have chosen to do what I have to do to get out. Perhaps not a very admirable decision, but under the circumstances I, personally, do not feel able to do anything else. How this would affect parole I can't say. But it is very likely that I would not be granted parole even if I applied for it. The last parole board denied 80% of the applications.

(There is a sheet of rules and regulations put out by the director of the prison, Dr. P.J. Ciccone, concerning correspondence and visiting. The first thing mentioned regarding this is that prisoners will be permitted to receive letters only from persons on their approved list of correspondents. Letters received from persons not on the approved list are normally returned to sender. Visits are intended for members of a man's immediate family. Close friends, if on one's correspondence list, may visit if there are no close relatives to visit. Any other person must have written permission in advance. Persons not cleared as to eligibility prior to arrival will normally not be admitted. Visiting room is open every day from 8:30 to 10:30 A.M. and 1:00 to 3:00 P.M. Groups of not more than three visitors at a time.)

☮ ☮ ☮

To Stand Where
One Must Stand...

Robert Gilliam

(*Editor's Note.* Robert Gilliam was born on March 28, 1945 in Moline, Illinois and brought up in Winona, Minnesota. In the summer of 1964 between his sophomore and junior years at college, he worked at the Catholic Worker House of Hospitality on the Bowery in New York, ministering to and caring for the poor.

When he returned to Winona, he applied for conscientious objector status. Bob at this point was aware of the alternative of complete noncoöperation with the draft but waited until he had "suffered and muddled" through high school before making his decision.

Bob spent the summer of 1965 working in voter registration with the Mississippi Freedom Democratic Party in Meridian, Mississippi and spent 13 days in jail in Jackson because of demonstrations. In 1966, he received a B.A. from St. Mary's College in Winona and spent much of that summer traveling, discussing and deciding the extent of his plan for noncoöperation.

Late that summer, he returned his draft cards and joined the staff of the Catholic Worker. In November, Bob refused a pre-induction physical examination and in December refused induction. In June 1967, he was arrested while visiting at home, waited until July for arraignment, plead guilty and was sentenced by Judge Earl Larson to two years imprisonment on August 14, 1967.

After spending 15 days in the Minneapolis County Jail, he was transferred to the Federal Correctional Institution at Sandstone and served ten months until his release on "expiration with good time" on March 3, 1969. Nine days after his release, Bob Gilliam returned his new draft cards to his local board.

He writes, "I am still in a state of shock. I was released the day before yesterday. Life feels very strange but very good."

This is a wonderfully eloquent collection of prison letters to Jennie Orvino, a Catholic Worker, now on the staff of the Milwaukee 14 Defense Committee supporting 14 Catholics who destroyed 20,000 draft files in Milwaukee, Wisconsin in 1968. In addition to being the skillful editor of these letters, Jennie is also a lifelong poet and is working on a book about the 14, Delivered into Resistance. Ω)

August 26, 1967: (County Jail, Minneapolis): I am almost looking forward to the time at Sandstone. It gives one a valuable perspective on society, will give me time to study and will be a chance for the first time in my life to get a good solid grounding in news and current events...

I got a visit tonight from the American Civil Liberties Union. The guy wants to make a test case on non-coöperation out of mine. The argument would be that my religious freedom is being limited. He admits the chances of winning are small but feels a test case should be argued. He was sympathetic and persuasive. It would mean changing the plea and dragging through the courts, it would mean being free for a year or two and then doing the two years.

I am going to say no but I am upset. I cannot give him any clear, intelligent, theoretical answer (though the personal dislocation of our life and plans is enough). I feel it.

I hear Davy [Miller] saying when being tried for refusing induction, legal arguments are as "a clanging brass or a tinkling cymbal." Though I would like to see it done, I feel clearly that it's not for me. I know that I could not put my heart into such a fight.

September 9, 1967: (Sandstone F.C.I.): My impressions of Sandstone are very mixed. Physically it is quite comfortable. There is a pleasant yard in the middle. At any rate, the prison surrounds a nice "compound" of grass and flowers.

The library is small but has some happy surprises – I have read Fromm's *Sane Society* and Frankl's *Man's Search for Meaning* and *Huckleberry Finn* so far and have some Goodman and Kierkegaard out. There are movies every week – the caliber of State theater [in Winona, Minnesota, Bob's hometown] six months late – which aren't too good but take up some time. The food is not bad at all.

This is not a prison but a "correctional institution," you see. Its aim is to develop a goal-oriented program suited to the needs of each inmate in order that he may be rehabilitated. I have not been able to determine what this means in my case. I think eventually they would admit I am not being rehabilitated – all fall down and worship – but detained, imprisoned, punished.

The facade of liberality here takes the edge off rebellion, confuses the issue. I felt in a way more comfortable in the county jail because relationships were clear there. There could be no doubts when the doors clanged shut on that ugly cell. No matter how you dress it up, prison is slavery.

I had, a few days ago, some serious thoughts about not coöperating – to force clarity. It certainly is a clear and honorable position. When one first realizes how they "bribe" you with all these "privileges" (especially mail and visits), the gut response, mine anyway, is rebellion. (Indicative of our society that rebellion is a dirty word.) But I don't think I will.

Not sure I have the resources, hope the time can be in some way meaningful, there are friends to be made here, and because I feel it can be borne without much of a price. I hope anyway that I will only rarely have to be here, that I can live with thoughts, books, in your letters, with all our holy and beautiful friends. The state only imprisons the body – can only imprison the body.

September 14, 1967: I have been a little depressed lately, more than usual, about the war. It is such a pervasive cancer. Danny O'Laughlin (a cousin) dead and Mike (Bob's stepbrother) on his way over there. How many innocents, Vietnamese and American, will they sacrifice on the altar of this madness? The whole thing is almost beyond discussion, it seems.

If one can't see that the war is vile and rotten, how can anyone tell them? Opinion seems so permanently, hopelessly polarized. The hawks hawking, the liberals liberalling, and the radicals crying, shouting, giving up and some burning themselves. Still to be a person you have to visibly and clearly oppose it.

I amuse the two other noncoöperaters I have gotten to know. They say they just want to see me in four months to see if any of my insanity, cheer and happy sarcasm are left. They both say prison has pretty much sucked out their vitals.

One guy said, toughest of all is to adjust yourself to the fact that you just have to chalk the time up as a total loss. He feels that nothing really can be salvaged and that all his energy goes to just keeping himself together. I still hope. I have more resources – not of myself, but I have you, the Catholic Worker, the family, the "community" and the exciting prospects of future. Despite all this I still have my twinges of irrepressible joy!

The "thing" here seems so permanent, so impenetrable. Criminals are not romantic. They mirror the society – sick, mentally-deficient, greedy, violent – often anyway. Conversation is consistently low or at best trivial. My grossness is of a different kind entirely. There are, don't get me wrong, some really fine people here. Thoreau's line about "quiet desperation" comes to mind.

So many who grew up and live in a loveless world...things bad on so many fronts simultaneously – social, economic, political, educational, moral – and yet a man can only address himself to a few on one front. Perhaps community is relevant here. We as community with different gifts, different vocations, could be so much more effective...

One last thought that has been plaguing me lately. This is not morbid but serious. I wonder how ready I am to accept death, it is essential to nonviolence. It is not a question of anti-vitality, because love and respect for life are essential to non-violence. The *satyagrahi* must believe that to die for the truth bears fruit. Gandhi knew, or had good reason to suspect, that he was going to be killed and still he refused bodyguards and held his regular prayer meeting. I know that I value my life excessively. One cannot take his own life too seriously and still be really a *satyagrahi*.

October 2, 1967: I made a long visit to the chapel the other day in an attempt to pray. Something came. Old, deep, primarily, I think, aesthetic response. The room was dark with one light on a simple tabernacle, lamp, and Book, soft light filtered through the rich green stained glass at my feet. Quiet and really, gut-level peaceful. It's too dark to read the Bible, though, alas.

I endure this small – and really it is small compared to the sacrifices of the men in Vietnam – sacrifice in the hope of drawing people's attention to the war, to the question of war and our complicity in it, to the innocent people who are dying and to the simple unmistakeable words of Jesus, whom we all claim to dig so much. I am grateful for people worrying about me and the violation of my conscience but I am more concerned that according to their own lights and position people do something about stopping this stinking war – that they vote, write, speak, read, march, vigil, and break the law if necessary (and it is).

October 17, 1967: I remember when I used to fear "losing my faith." I was afraid of the doubt, darkness, and of the terrible task to decide from scratch what you believe. Realize now this simple fact – when you strip away all the learned doctrines you "believe" and look at yourself naked and ask what can't be taken away, what is part of me, what truths do I live by (believe) then you know what your faith is. Then you can begin to reinterpret the religious myths and metaphors, to make them your own in a new and more meaningful way. I think I am at the beginning of all this.

October 24, 1967: Can I send you the fruit of some recent reflection?

I have been thinking about "something" that the people I most admire seem to have in common – a prophetic quality, a sense of vocation, seriousness. (Remember what Peguy described as *un homme serieux*.)

They are people who have grasped – or more rightly have been grasped by – two or three essential truths with a kind of lightning clarity. They become in a sense almost fanatical. They do not see other truths with any unusual clarity and tend instead to see other truths in relation to their personal vision. They have a kind of unscholarly and outwardly unjustifiable certainty of their own rightness. They do not blindly refuse to consider the intelligent arguments against them but they are beyond these arguments. For them, their truth is so clear and certain that it demands not only verbal proclamation but possesses them with an urgency to give it living form in action, in their own lives.

They are compelled to witness and strive to discover a form of life that embodies clearly, even starkly, and speaks to even the simplest man, truth they have seen... Aesthetics being at a rather low ebb here, "Garrison's Gorillas" trounced the Beatles in this evening's votings. T.V. infighting and strategy is one of the big things here.

November 8, 1967: Deep melancholy tonight. It was alternately bright and gloomy today. Now it is cloudy with an almost warm and delightfully fresh-smelling breeze. Calm is hard to come by today.

The dorm was quiet only in brief snatches and I just couldn't concentrate... I think tomorrow or one of these days is Dorothy's [Day's] birthday. She is 70...

How does one communicate an idea like nonviolence to a world which cannot believe, much less understand, action from principle? The only answer, and it may be pretty feeble, is to be. To be an unmistakeable sign and embodiment of what you believe. If men cannot understand words perhaps the patient mode: passionate and uncompromising struggle to live the truth may bear some fruit.

December 12, 1967: Perhaps the only positive and relevant lesson here (in Thoreau) also taught by Gandhi, is that those who oppose the State radically and basically (as any pacifist must) and do not coöperate with it in doing what they believe to be evil, must also, as far as possible, remove themselves from the benefits the state offers – which, most basically, I think, means embracing voluntary poverty...

I have in general been bothered by the quote "Render unto Cæsar," etc. One thing is that the "saying" (and I think it would not be called "authentic") does not constitute the basis for a Christian theory of the state. It is too fragile to bear that kind of emphasis. Also you have to remember that it is a kind of trick by Jesus – a way to slip out of a dilemma and put his questioners on the defensive.

One interpretation I have read says that the incident refers not to taxes in general but a special tribute tax to Rome and that the objection of the Pharisees was also due in part to the fact that the coin bore Cæsar's image and therefore there is the suggestion of idolatry. Jesus shames them because they quietly use the coins in daily business dealings all the rest of the year... (from Gunther Bornkamm's *Jesus of Nazareth*)...emphasis on the second half of the sentence, and the need for personal determination of what is God's.

December 26, 1967: You might like this line of Dan's [Berrigan's] on Jesus' parable-speaking: "The purpose of His speech: to create imaginative men, capable of imagining the real world." He also says "to stand where one must stand, to plant the landmarks by which the unborn will be able to walk."

January 10, 1968: A small reflection: Part of the suffering and anguish of embracing nonviolence is the result of the fact that nonviolence is in its infancy as a tool for social change, that is, as an alternative to violence it remains largely unexplored. I refuse to believe that pacifism is simplistic and foolish, because ultimately the question of war must be reduced to its personal moral limits: Will I kill?

The perception of the futility of violence and the fact that it cannot be a means to the transformation of the world, along with the refusal to kill, are the foundations of pacifism. To be a pacifist means to 1) be a center of new values to demonstrate and incarnate or perhaps more modestly, to point to), to be a sign of that spirit (or as George Fox says, "that life and power that take away the occasion of all wars"); 2) to serve and build, to be a constructive and reconciling force; 3) to develop, explore, and experiment with nonviolence as a technique (as well as the above suggests a way of life).

One aspect of the fantastic wisdom of the Catholic Worker is the balance that it offers in this regard.

January 19, 1968: One of the terrible problems about the future is that you can't do everything. Choosing means eliminating. This becomes especially difficult now when I am removed, inactive.

Involved in action, the question doesn't really arise, there is the sense of a great deal to do, of things undone and yet the demands and satisfactions of what you are doing seem sufficient. To decide one must first know himself – where am I strong, where weak, what can I do best? Know the times – every season has its work – and to be aware of the possibilities – the variety of historical responses, what others are doing today.

Thursday it was warm and there was early fog. Until about two the woods out the west windows were white, every twig and branch sheathed in ice. It was very beautiful.

January 30, 1968: I'll start cold. The parole board denied me. I got word in the mail yesterday. It was hardly unexpected and I had thought I had completely set myself to accept it. Still there was some disappointment. As many reasons as there are for not wanting parole it is impossible not to want to get out a few months earlier. If I get extra good days – I am applying for them – I will get out in February 1969, otherwise it will be March. 13 or 14 months to go.

February 3, 1968: Sandstone is such a violent world. The earth is so incredibly violent. Did you hear about the Maryknollers in Guatemala? Again the question of violence. It is a question weighing so heavily on so many dear people today. Me too.

I go through a million lines and the answer in my heart, my head, and my bones is always the same – nonviolence. I have been reading the *Liberation* double issue on A.J. Muste. All of me says yes. Still there is the frightening failure of words, I can't answer, no power to persuade.

The suffering of the people seems so unbearable, so interminable sometimes. When will the earth be born? Scalding tears frequently fill my eyes just reading the news. I worry – am I a fanatic? A purist? Do I set my "conscience" above liberation?

No, I don't. I believe this way is right. Still there is a danger. I must be more flexible, more genuinely tolerant. Other good men have different lights. It is a sign of my lack of maturity that I feel defensive and alienated from those who have chosen a different way.

It is clear in A.J. – he worked with everybody, respecting them and trusting them, loving them as men, as comrades, and never forgetting for a moment his way, revolutionary pacifism. He was a giant. I really love him. February 11 he is dead a year. Do I make any sense?

February 6, 1968: I got a [*Catholic*] *Worker* yesterday. What a light in the darkness! I have only read "Chrystie Street" so far but that was beautiful. The *Worker* is many things, but the foundation, the beginning, the roots, are Chrystie Street.

There is a phrase of Peter's [Maurin's] that has been on my mind much lately. It throws light on many things. Peter talks about "the gentle personalism of traditional Christianity."

To hope to see things rightly I know that I must stand firmly in that ground. That is why poverty and the works of mercy are so essential and any movement that is cut off from them is constantly subject to the cancer of ideological self-righteousness and gives way to rantings.

February 18, 1968: At its worst, this place makes of a man a living corpse, a sort of zombie. There is also the possibility here, as with me, of becoming cerebral. What is impossible is any bodily delight, vitality. As I said before, it is the deadly barrenness that is the deepest fact.

Reading Scripture, though parts are extraordinarily powerful, much is irrelevant and much just plain not true. I am certain that if forced to choose between Gandhi and St. Paul, I would choose Gandhi without hesitation. Gandhi is more revelatory for me. The same is true of Buber, Silone, Camus.

Buber says: "The mighty revelations to which the religious appeal are like in being with the quiet relegations that are to be found everywhere and at all times. The mighty revelations which stand at the beginning of great communities and at the turning point of an age are nothing but eternal revelations."

I suppose this is all really nothing, objectively. But for one who has been a "believing" Catholic to admit this is difficult. The crucial problem, I think, then is this: what is your principle of verification? If you accept the traditional idea of revelation then once you have decided, with the magisterium, on the correct interpretation of Scripture, you know the truth.

This is comforting, secure. One is protected from rationalism and skepticism, and I remember the very real fear they have held for me. The only principle I can assert is personal, the gut reaction, that which is verified in every cell, those truths of abandonment of which I know clearly would be the abandonment of my very self, my own lights. This is the only test that works. I do not mean to imply it is simple. It is rational, but much more than that. Though it is historical, conditioned, still, I experience it as somehow absolute, revelatory. Ultimately I really trust these lights, trust my deepest self, or that which reveals (is revealed) in my deepest self.

March 19, 1968: I am tired tonight and deep down dry. Prison is a hard, illusion-shattering place – that is, one can't long maintain too many illusions because they simply don't sustain. Sustenance is subsistence here. The only real, clear feeling tonight is a hard, hot, quiet, jagged nugget of longing in my stomach – the longing to be with you, to touch you, to know again that infallible "language." To be out of the desert and back again in life's green.

March 27, 1968: Monday I moved to my new dormitory. Quiet, almost morgue-like. It is a thousand times better to work during the day and I am almost ecstatic. It was getting to the point upstairs where I could squeeze out, between the inevitable distractions, at most two hours of quiet per full day. Tuesday it was gorgeous, perhaps 60 degrees – and I blew (was positively snakey) the whole day talking sitting in the sun. At the risk of being deceived by Siberian weather I would say Spring has actually broken through. I think I can see the beginnings of buds on the trees.

I have been getting very involved with the Afro-American group here. I think it could be a very good thing. They have me writing letters, inviting speakers, helping with the educational program and working as associate editor of the bi-weekly newsletter.

April 2, 1968: I wasn't planning on it, because of my low nausea threshold, but because I didn't feel like doing anything else, I watched LBJ Sunday night. I am really happy I did now, of course. I didn't believe he really said it. It really shocked me and I felt that I had personally been delivered some very good news. I couldn't be too analytical because I was just too goosey happy.

The thought that kept running through my mind was: the end of the war is in sight, this is the beginning of the last chapter. What a wonderful thought! I even started liking LBJ. I hope he is a very happy rancher and a grandfather many times.

May 16, 1968: When I think of Phil and the gang [Phil Maloney and family, of the Catholic Worker in New York], presently studying in Toronto, Basil and all the other people in Winona [K.B. O'Leary, a Christian Brother from St. Mary's College in Winona, Minnesota], I just sort of feel like a marshmallow. A big, huggy, indiscriminately lovey, four-beers-under-his-belt marshmallow.

LIFE is bigger, more obstinate, better and just all around prevails – than death. I had a small but important vision I've had sometimes before but often forget. I saw how fragile, dear, shy, mysterious, impenetrable and unrepeatable we all are, how much more than in all of our studied meanness

June 9, 1968: About Catonsville. [Nine Catholics, including the fathers Berrigan, napalm Selective Service files as an act of protest in Catonsville, Maryland.]

I remember something Staughton Lynd said at a Fellowship of Reconciliation meeting. He said we should have faith in those acts which are proportionate (commensurate, he said) with our deepest anguish over the war, our sense of sin, faith that those acts will be redemptive and powerful.

The act does speak to me, it is immensely powerful – for me. I don't know how it can be seen as "an offensive sort of prank" (*National Catholic Reporter* editorial). The editorial faults them for wrongly attributing a "conscious malevolence" to the American ruling class. Obviously, this is irrelevant, because once you admit things are as they say, it is really not too important how conscious the criminals are or what their motives are.

Rosemary Reuther (in a letter in the June 5th *NCR*) is wrong to assume that they feel those who are not with them are "against them and God." They are much mere modest, I would think. Perhaps these – *NCR*, *Commonweal*, Reuther – expect too much from an act.

I suspect the nine people know and are learning the limits of their action. Perhaps we do not know too much about suffering. We reel at a prison term for friends but barely flinch over the incredible suffering the Vietnamese bear. The act points at this, as well as much else.

Though I am confused about this these days, what Reuther says seems to rule out, and I and they can't, is nonviolent revolution. This act may be later seen as an early light in a continuum. The editorial says but really does not believe what they say about the flames in the darkness. The actors are willing to take a little chance. The Spirit breaks in clumsily, but it breaks in.

☮ ☮ ☮

STOCKADE LIFE

Mike Wittels

Editor's Note: Michael S. Wittels was born on November 4, 1939 in Philadelphia, and except for his Army experience at Fort Knox and, subsequently, the Fort Knox stockade, has lived nowhere else.

Mike feels that he would noncoöperate from the start if he had to begin over in the army and not submit a claim for discharge as a conscientious objector as he did. He does not feel that noncoöperation in the stockade is effective as a tactic, but must be supported with one's convictions. He does not, for instance, feel that one should undertake a fast unless one is prepared to carry that fast unto death. The lines for coöperation and non-coöperation have to be constantly drawn as one learns and grows.

Mike Wittels presently lives in Philadelphia with his wife, Barbara, and is a military counselor for the Central Committee for Conscientious Objectors. Ω

I was sworn into the United States Army Reserve on April 21, 1963. I joined because I wanted to avoid the draft. (Just made it, too, my draft notice arrived two days later.) I was, at the time, pretty unconcerned with the meaning of military force. All I knew was that I wanted as little as possible to do with the army. I didn't have enough nerve to fake my way into a 4-F, but I sure thought about it. So for me the reserves seemed the easiest way out. At any rate, I went on active duty in August 1963 and was awakened pretty rudely: the army was nothing but organized barbarism. I wanted out but was the shy type who was afraid to make trouble. I did, however, vow to myself and a couple of buddies that if war ever came I would leave the country rather than fight.

Apparently, my feelings did not show: I was made a squad leader and after basic training was sent to Fort Polk, Louisiana, for training as a heavy weapons infantryman. I was mustered out in February 1964 according to schedule and returned to Philadelphia and resumed attending reserve meetings with a quartermaster group. I kept quiet, internally and externally, until sometime in the spring of 1965 when the Vietnam conflict began to get a good deal of coverage in the press.

I decided then that unless someone could convince me of the merit of that war, I would refuse to go if the unit were called to active duty. I was simply going to go to the company commander and tell him my position but, because I had no idea of the legal intricacies involved, or even if he would listen to me, I decided to talk it over with someone on the Friends Peace Committee, who had been leafletting in the city recently.

At the time I did not consider myself a pacifist and thought that the CO position was reserved for the "hard-line" Quakers, Brethren, Mennonites, and such. But the CO position was presented to me and I spent a few very intensive months of soul-searching, reading, and so on.

On August 27, 1965 I submitted a proper application for discharge from the USAR on grounds of conscientious objection. For four months I questioned various officials but could not get even an indication of whether my application had reached the proper headquarters.

On January 5, 1966 I submitted my resignation. There is no such thing as a resignation for an enlisted man, of course, but I hoped to stir up a little action. In May, more or less as expected, I received word that my discharge would not be granted and that I would be "expected to return to meetings." But I had made it quite clear that I would not do this and didn't.

Thus I was ordered to report to Fort Knox, Kentucky, on August 21, 1966 to receive 45 days of active duty training. Trying to get the order rescinded and my discharge effected, I wrote to many officials involved. No dice. The last letter I wrote during that period was to the company commander of the unit to which I was to report. I told him what had happened and what would happen when I got there. I didn't want him to be surprised.

But perhaps my letter was too polite, because when I reported to him (or rather when I introduced myself to him) in civilian clothes, he asked if I didn't realize I could get in serious trouble, and wasn't it stupid, and every man has his convictions – he even admitted he had some of his own – but we have to do what we are told to do, etc., etc. Then he got firmer, but remained polite. (I wonder would he have been less polite had I not been fairly well dressed and disguised as a respectable person.)

Finally, on August 24, still in civilian clothes, I was arrested and taken to the stockade. I had been charged with two specific of violations of Article 90 of the Uniform Code of Military Justice: "1) In that Private E-2 Michael S. Wittels…having received a lawful command…to wear a military uniform, did…willfully disobey the same) and, 2)…having received a lawful command to report for duty…did…willfully disobey the same."

Most of the guards within and without the stockade had not volunteered for their jobs and therefore represented a general cross-section of servicemen. For the most part, however, they were ones who had not done well with their training as military policemen. Some, however, had not been trained as MP's even but had just been assigned to the stockade for unknown reasons. When I first entered the stockade, I had no idea what to expect from the guards. One hears all sorts of stories about stockade guards and brutality. At any rate, I was not made to feel comfortable by the overgrown private who interviewed me when I was brought into the stockade the first night. He kept making menacing grimaces at me.

Nor was I comforted by one SSG Otting who was round and soft from too many years as a desk jockey (of his 18 years in the army, 17 of them had been spent at the stockade) but who had a pair of the coldest, water-blue eyes I had ever seem. He shoved his face up against mine and said, "I don't know how we'll do it, but we'll break you. I'll see to that. We've had your kind in here before."

Since part of my crime was refusing to wear the uniform of a U.S. soldier, I had decided that I would carry this refusal into the stockade. I was probably the only prisoner ever brought directly into the stockade wearing civilian dress.

I had been away from the military atmosphere for awhile, and although my answers to their questions were polite, they were not the customary, yessir, no sir, and yes sergeant, no sergeant. Nor did I bother to stand at attention.

At any rate, I told then I would wear the uniform of a prisoner because I was indeed a prisoner, but I would not wear the uniform of a soldier because I was not a soldier.

What I did not realize then, though, was that the uniform of a prisoner was simply an army fatigue uniform with a white band sewn onto the left arm. When I saw this, I agreed to wear the pants, but I said I would wear the shirt only if the U.S. Army insignia were removed.

They said nothing doing: either I wore the uniform they wanted me to wear or I went to the box. I said nothing doing, too, so my buddy, SSG Otting showed me the box.

He explained to me what it was like and what kind of meals I would get. He opened the doors and let me interview some of the kids being kept in the box. I was struck by their broken looks, but I still refused.

So I was thrown into the box. The box is officially known as Disciplinary Segregation (or "seregation" or "segreation," if you were a career soldier); it is a cell about 6' x 8' x 8', three of the walls and the ceiling are of steel plate, the door is heavy ironwork with two small openings in it; the floor is concrete, and there it a very small light bulb recessed into the ceiling. The bed is a steel slab fastened onto the wall and there is a sink and a commode.

A prisoner has nothing but his trousers and shirt (no underwear, socks, or shoes); the only movable objects allowed in the cell are a roll of toilet paper, a pocket bible, and the stockade rulebook ("your two bibles"). He is served food three times a day. Breakfast consists of about one cupful of dry cereal and a few slices of worthless bread. Lunch is half a head of lettuce, some half-cooked pieces of potato, and some more worthless bread; dinner is about the same, except that cabbage is substituted for the lettuce.

During my first night an old blanket was thrown in, but later I was awakened and told to take a shower. When I returned the blanket was gone. I asked about it and was told that I wouldn't want it because it was an army blanket and had "U.S." on it. Okay.

Then I was called out in front of the "security desk" and told to explain myself. It was about two in the morning, and there were about 20 soldiers standing about. Most of them were turnkeys. The rest were administrative personnel on night duty. I explained as best I could about the terrible-ness and futility of war. I made it clear that I did not think soldiers were mur-derers, that I had tried to be a good soldier for a while, and that most soldiers think that what they're doing is right.

From somewhere came the question, "Sure, war is wrong. But what are we going to do about it? Suppose someone attacks you. Aren't you go-ing to fight back?" I tried to explain about nonviolence. I tried to explain that the important thing is to live a good life and that I did not believe in being a slave. I talked about racial equality and mentioned Martin Luther King's programs in the South.

I gave a brief history of Gandhi and the Independence movements. I answered several questions and apparently was at least interesting, be-cause I talked and answered questions for over an hour. When I was taken back to the box, one of the guards explained that he really didn't want to be in the army, but that he had got a girl pregnant and did not have a job and wanted to be able to take care of the baby. The other guard explained that he did not know very much about conscientious objection, but he said that he realized that what I was doing would help bring peace to the future world and though he could never be a conscientious objector him-self he certainly admired someone who was.

I did not want to stay in the box for my entire sentence because I wanted to get out into the prison population and find out what was going on. After about three days I told the confinement officer that I would re-gard the uniform as representing the fact that I was in the custody of the army, but that was all.

I offered to remain in the box my allotted time. (I thought that it was 14 days but later I found out that it was indefinite.) At any rate, I found that most of the guards were rather neutral toward me. I tried to treat them as human beings, which they were, and struck up some friendships with them. One of the most hated keys, a young loudmouth with a very large and obvious sense of insecurity continued to revile me for about two months until he found out that I was from his home state and could draw. He asked me to draw him a picture of a deer. And became sweet as all get-out. I agreed to draw him his deer, but never got around to it as he was shipped to a different post.

One of the men who gave me the most trouble the first few days was a young buck sergeant. He looked like Hollywood's version of the handsome young SS officer. He even had the sneer and the German accent. He pushed and shoved me a few times the first night, but I managed to hide my loathing of him and remain pretty cool.

He said that I should be put to death. He said that he had two young sons, and if one of them turned out to be a CO, he would kill him. I pretty much avoided him, though after the first few days he acted pleasantly enough toward me; he even excused me one time when my boots were not shined and merely said that I should try to do better.

The real surprise came, though, when one morning after roll-call he stopped by the solitary cell that I had been put in at that point and told me, "The night you came in here, I wanted to kill you. I was just waiting for you to ball your fist so that I would have an excuse to jump on you, but I went home and told my wife about you. Now, she is German too and has red hair and quite a temper, but, well, we decided you weren't a fanatic and you certainly weren't an idiot, and we decided live and let live.

"I don't agree with what you're doing. Why, if you had your way, I'd be out of a job. But I have to say that I admire you for sticking up for what you think is right. Good luck." I didn't see him again and learned later that he had been transferred to another post.

I could cite other instances, none as dramatic, but they seem to point out that if a man sticks to his beliefs he will gain at least the respect of others, and if he remains civil and not too fanatical, he may very well create a general tolerance for his sort of belief.

After my second release from the stockade, I stayed at a company awaiting a discharge on grounds of unsuitability which never came through. Bunking next to me was a clerk in the traffic section of the MPs. One day he began to tell me of his experiences as a prisoner guard. I asked a lot of questions and did not let on for awhile that I had been in the stockade.

When I told him, he got very interested and said that he felt pretty much the same way I did, but he didn't have the guts, etc. Anyway, this was pretty much the story of being a PG that I got from him. "We were constantly lectured that we were to shoot at any prisoner who tried to escape – and not into the air. We were told that we would be court-martialed if we failed to stop an escaping prisoner. I prayed every day that no one would try to escape. I did not know what I would do if one tried.

"One day I went to the commanding officer of the PGs and asked to be transferred. He said no dice and gave me a lecture and reminded me that I would be court-martialed. I acted very tough with the prisoners so that they would not guess I was scared and so that they would not try to run."

(His story rings true, and one day I had to go over to the administrative offices of the stockade, I spotted a note on the desk of the provost sergeant. It said that a group of PGs had been overheard in the barracks saying that they would not try to stop an escaping prisoner, and that various procedures would be considered to remedy their reluctance...)

One MP I met had been temporarily assigned to the stockade. He came over and began talking to me one day while I was in solitary. He said that he was on his second enlistment but was trying to get out. This war in Vietnam is a bunch of bullshit. Fighting for democracy, hah! What is democracy. We don't even have it in this country. He added that on his first enlistment he was in some other branch of the army and that the MPs were the worst of them all – brutal and sadistic. Why, the way they treat these guys in here Is just going to make them run away from the army and I don't blame them.

I was tried by Special Court-Martial on September 9, and received the maximum penalty under that type of court-martial, six months confinement at hard labor, forfeiture of two-thirds monthly pay, and reduction to lowest enlisted grade. Obviously, I did not mind the reduction in grade, nor did the fine bother me, since I had not accepted any pay in over a year.

The trial was pretty much of a kangaroo court, as are all Special and Summary Courts-Martial. The five officers on the court-martial board (Usually seven, but the defense counsel had eliminated one when he admitted he would be prejudiced in a case concerning a CO. Another was removed preemptorily.) were polite, asked very few questions, and were obviously not terribly concerned even though my case was a bit different than the hundreds of AWOL cases they had to sit through.

Counsel was an energetic young first lieutenant who had been a member of the California bar in civilian life, and who had told me that he was indeed in favor of U.S. presence in Vietnam. But I trusted him because he seemed genuinely concerned with the rights of GIs. We both knew that the outcome would be a maximum sentence and he worked hard in court. The trial counsel (prosecuting attorney) hardly said a thing.

A few days after my trial I was called, along with a dozen other men, to the visitors' room. The confinement officer, Captain Minton, was there, and he told us that we were all going to be made "Minimum Security." MS, he said, was a very fine thing to be since with that status, you could go outside the gates of the stockade accompanied by an an armed supervisor and wouldn't have "that goddamn shotgun sticking in your back." Dramatist that he was, he raised his hand in a gesture and asked, "Is there anybody here who doesn't want MS?"

I raised my hand and said that I didn't want it. He asked me why and I told him and the other prisoners that I didn't want it because it was a step "back to duty" and I wasn't going back to duty. Furthermore, I would not sign the required statement that I would act in a military manner at all times and do all sorts of other ridiculous things.

We were all told to go back to our cells. But I was, within a few minutes, taken to a solitary cell. It was known as Administrative Segregation, and, as Minton told the Provost Marshal the next day, I had been put there so I would not "contaminate the other prisoners." I stayed there for six and a half weeks.

Captain Minton came around every day and asked whether I had any problems – and whether I was willing to become a soldier. My reply to both questions was negative. At one point he asked me, "Wittels, how long are you going to stay on this CO kick?" and I replied that it wasn't a kick, but as far as the army was concerned, I'd stay on it until I was discharged, and as far as I was concerned – for the rest of my life.

He looked me square in the eye and said, "We'll see about that." I replied, "Yes, sir, we'll see." As soon as he left I broke out in a cold sweat because I feared this issue could degenerate into a contest of wills and we'd get away from the point. I can be awfully stubborn sometimes, and I knew he could. But a few days later he had me brought into his office and he asked if I wanted to paint while I was in my cell; he said that he knew from my letters that I was an artist, and this was not a command and I should only do it if I wanted to and he would see that I had everything I needed. I suspected that he had something up his sleeve, but I decided to accept anyway and get all I could out of it.

About a week later he staged an elaborate "interview at which three J.W. COs and myself were present. It became clear that he really wanted me to sign the MS agreement. His purpose for having the J.W.s there was to embarrass me – they could accept MS, why couldn't you.

After he dismissed the other three prisoners, he tried everything from threats to saying that his reasons for wanting me to sign the MS were purely humanitarian. He claimed that he just wanted me t be able to go outside and paint landscapes if I wanted to; he vowed that I would not have to go on any work details.

After over an hour of bickering, I agreed to sign an MS agreement that said "I will obey all stockade rules" instead of the more objectionable, "I will behave in a military manner at all times." Actually, I found the total MS agreement objectionable, but I wanted to see if he'd be true to his word.

He was. And until my first release I was allowed to go out and paint and sketch all by myself. I often went back into the woods and could easily have kept on going and no one would have been the wiser for several hours. Perhaps he wanted me to attempt an escape. Perhaps he just wanted the pictures I was painting.

Each prisoner is scheduled to appear before a "clemency board" at some point before completion of half his sentence. My hearing lasted a good deal longer than the usual ten or fifteen minutes given to simple AWOL cases and the officers were not polite.

Rather than a clemency board, it seemed more interested in giving a prisoner the third degree treatment. (They gave me all sorts of invective: "You ought to be shot and sent over there!" "Are you a Communist?" "No." "Well, you sure act like one. You're sure helping them out.")

Their recommendation – which is always followed – was that I not be given clemency but held to my minimum release date (full sentence minus five days per month) and sent "back to duty," so that I would have a chance to repeat my offense and be given a longer sentence.

This is, of course, what happened. But there is an interesting aside. Before a prisoner is released from the stockade he must "process out" by taking around with him a mimeographed form which must be signed by a cadreman at each section.

One of the last sections is the Mail and Personal Property Room. Behind the clerk here I spotted the happy-go-lucky second lieutenant with whom I had become slightly friendly. He called out, "Hey, Wittels, how soon ya comin' back?" I said I didn't know; I didn't know where they were going to try to send me or anything. He persisted, "Well, can't you give me some kind of idea – 72 hours, 24 hours?" "Oh, 72 hours, I guess." "Okay." "So long."

The final step of the out-processing is supposed to be a short interview with the confinement officer or his executive officer. This usually consists of the officer merely initialing the form and sending the prisoner on his way.

Two other prisoners were being released along with me this February 6, 1967, and their forms were initialed by the XO but I was told to wait for the confinement officer. It was not until after lunch that Minton called me into his office. The first thing I noticed was that SSG Otting was also in the office. Minton asked me how soon I thought I'd be back in the stockade. I replied, "Immediately."

We both laughed because it was considered common knowledge that if I were not discharged I would continue to refuse to perform military service. Otting didn't laugh, though; he just stared at me. Then Minton gave me a little lecture about how things would be pretty rough on me if I came back to the stockade a second time, isn't that right, Sgt. Otting? Yessir! And didn't I think I should think it over. I doubted that he thought his lecture would have any effect on me. Perhaps he was just trying to impress the sergeant.

I was told to wait for my company commander – a new one, whom I had never seen before. When he appeared I saw that he was pretty much a green kid, a first lieutenant, a few years younger than I. Minton, about ten years older, and a foot taller, and a captain, called the kid into his office and talked to him for what seemed to me to be about twenty minutes (though in later testimony he claimed it was only two or three minutes and all they discussed was that I was getting a lot of mail).

When Lt. Cahoo came out of the office, he told me to come along with him. We got into a jeep and the driver took us the mile or so back to the company. I was taken into the lieutenant's office.

Without showing any sign that he expected me to salute or stand at attention, he asked me if I were going to continue to refuse to perform military duty. I said that I would. He did not seem surprised and offered little argument.

He then read from my court-martial record the identical orders that his predecessor had given me, despite the fact that one of the orders was to don a military uniform and I was standing in front of him wearing the prison uniform minus the white armband (which had been pulled off as I left the stockade) – which just happened to be an acceptable fatigue uniform.

While he was having the charges drawn up I borrowed a dime from the company clerk and made a long-distance phone call to my girlfriend (now my wife). Then I was taken back to the stockade and reconfined within twenty minutes of my release. As I was standing in the in-processing room, who should walk up but Captain Mlnton.

He acted very surprised and bellowed, "What's he doing back here? Make him a max – double armbands – and put him up on the hill chopping wood." But I didn't get sent up on the hill that afternoon because the clerks wanted to get me processed back in. When I went to the Mail and Property window, the lieutenant was still there. He shouted to me, "Well, I see the captain won the pool; he guessed two hours."

The next day I was taken handcuffed under armed guard to the legal section, a few miles from the stockade. Upstairs I met with Cpt. Goldstein, who had been my counsel for the court-martial. He told me that though he was now trial counsel, he would stay out of my case and that he would like to help me.

I was introduced to another officer who was to be my new defense counsel (but it didn't turn out that way) and the two of them said that they would like to see me get out of the army but that there wasn't too much I could hope for so I better decide whether I would like to stay in the Fort Knox stockade or go to the disciplinary barracks at Fort Leavenworth, Kansas.

I said I'd rather do neither and that I would like this thing to get into a civilian court and that I wanted civilian counsel. I asked him to call

Arlo Tatum at the Central Committee for Conscientious Objectors in Philadelphia and find out about getting the case into federal court. Arlo said that, yes, it should get into court and that help from the ACLU should be brought in.

This seemed to worry Goldstein a bit. Although I have no doubt that he was sincere in his expressed desire to help me, neither do I doubt that he would get into hot water if he allowed this to get outside the military. All through the case the army had shown little regard for due process.

He then asked me if I would be willing to make a deal: plead guilty at a Special Court-Martial and in turn receive a discharge on grounds of unsuitability within ten days. I was a bit wary and said that 1 would still like to talk to a civilian lawyer. Goldstein assured me that there was a 99.9% guarantee of my receiving the discharge if I accepted the deal. He said that he would have to call Col. Curtis, the post Adjutant-General.

I was taken downstairs and locked in a wire cage. About an hour and a half later I was taken back upstairs and told that it was all set, I would be called in two days to sign the necessary papers.

Two mornings later I was called out to be taken over to the legal section, but at the last minute the order was cancelled. That afternoon, however, I was taken there and Goldstein told me there was a problem – that a high officer was pressing for a General Court-Martial for me, from which I could get five years at hard labor, etc.

CCCO had arranged for an ACLU attorney from Louisville to interview me. Although he made it clear that he did not at all agree with my convictions, he impressed me as capable and conscientious and I agreed to retain him.

Meanwhile, the army had started an Article 32 investigation to determine whether there was enough evidence to warrant a GCM. One of the events in this investigation as the Article 32 hearing, which is similar to a civilian magistrate's court. Acting as magistrate was an affable bulldog sort of old armored captain, not too bright (he had trouble pronouncing my first name, Michael).

The ACLU man, Edward Post, and my military counsel, a Cpt. Ross, were present. Two witnesses, Lt. Cahoo and his first sergeant, Gilberto Cordova, were scheduled to testify. The lieutenant was first. Post gave him a rough time and he was obviously unnerved by the whole thing. At any rate, it became clear to me pretty quickly, that someone, somewhere, was not playing by the rules – the army's rules – and that someone was trying to do a whole bunch of covering up.

When the sergeant testified, it would have been clear to a schoolchild that something was amiss, (e.g., to Post's question concerning how customary it was for a company commander to escort a released prisoner back to his assignment, Cahoo answered that it was the custom and that just a few weeks ago when one of his men was released after serving a bad check rap that man had been personally escorted by the company commander.

The first sergeant, however, not aware of his commander's testimony, who said that in his entire career – of 23 years – he had never known such a thing to happen in a company to which he was assigned. It hadn't really been necessary to question the sergeant, however, because the testimony that released me ran something like this.

Post: And what time was Wittels to report to his duty station?

Cahoo: I told him that he was to report at ohsevenhundred hours the next morning, sir.

Post: And where was Pvt. Wittels at seven o'clock the next morning?

Cahoo: He was in the stockade, sir!

Post: Well, then, how did you expect him to report to his station? Did you think he could just walk out of the stockade?

So I was released the following morning. Under military law a man is not considered to have disobeyed an order if he merely states his intention to disobey.

Mr. Post had done a lot of work and had found out that a second application for discharge (which was instituted through outside channels and which was handled by the army in such a surreptitious manner that I didn't even know I was making it until I got a letter from my girl – somehow delayed in the mail for over 30 days, on January 20th, saying that her Congressman had gotten a letter from the Post Commander, Major General Surles, saying that I was being assisted in the preparation of a second application for discharge as a CO, but that is another story) was being processed in Washington.

He suggested that I play along, since I was to be assigned to minimal non-combatant duties at the company, until word of my discharge was received. Both the company commander and the first sergeant stayed clear of me and I received even less harassment than the average soldier in that company (which was very loose, anyway).

I stayed at the company for about three weeks and then was hustled off the base without a discharge, without leave papers, without anything to show that was no longer supposed to be there. A few weeks after I got home I received a call from the civilian administrator at the reserve unit; he told me that a meeting was scheduled for that evening and asked me if I'd be there.

I told him I couldn't make it as I had a dinner to go to, but that even if I didn't I wouldn't attend that or any other reserve meeting. He seemed apologetic and said that it was just his job to tell me I was supposed to come to meetings.

Two days after my marriage on July 16, I received in the mail a General Discharge under Honorable Conditions. Accompanying the certificate was a set of orders that stated the reason for the discharge was conscientious objection. As far as I knew, it was one of the very few discharges in over a year grant-ed by the military officially for those reasons; usually they got around the issue by discharging a CO as unsuitable or undesirable. I am not impressed by the discharge; I consider myself both unsuitable and undesirable soldier material.

The Fort Knox stockade was designed to hold about 250 men. When I entered it in August 1966, there were 280 prisoners and when I left to-ward the end of February 1967, the population had pushed over the 500 mark. The main building is T-shaped, one-storey structure of concrete. It is surrounded by a cyclone fence topped with barbed wire. The top of the building is strewn with concertina wire.

The east and west wings are occupied by prisoners and are identical in layout, each containing six one-man cells, five 24-man cells, and one 12-man cell. Because of the overcrowding, more often than not the 24-man cells have closer to 35 prisoners in them, sometimes more. One single cell in each wing is used as a barber shop. The barber is an inmate and does not need to have any tonsorial training; there is only one style: one quarter inch of growth on the head, no facial hair showing at any time. The pris-oners shave themselves with "safety" razors.

Occasionally a single cell will have two men in it. Also, because of the swollen population, the yard, which was originally intended for physical recreation, now contains six 12-man tents. The eight cells in the security section used as boxes had, in the early part of 1967, two men in each. They were built to hold one man, and that not very comfortably. In ad-dition, there is a somewhat separated row of three large two-man cells. These were originally intended to house imprisoned officers, but are usu-ally used for DS and SQ purposes.

At the end of that row of cells is a small dispensary. There is also a cafeteria which holds about 200 men at a time (approximately three min-utes was allotted to each meal) and a chapel which holds about 100 men if some of them are standing. What was originally a visitors room and library was usually used as a cell or a room for the stockade band practice.

With perhaps a handful of exceptions, no prisoner was held in the stockade for over six months at a stretch. Those facing longer sentences were shipped to Leavenworth within a few months of their courts-martial.

During my stay of 183 days, I saw one prisoner come and go four times, the last time leaving with his much-desired discharge. Many had been inside more than twice and a countless number more than once. Doubtless the majority of those imprisoned twice would return for a third or fourth time unless they were discharged or shipped to some distant post (at which they would also probably land up in the stockade).

Over 92% of the prisoners were either being detained on an AWOL charge or were serving time on an AWOL conviction. There was a saying, "Once an AWOL, always an AWOL."

A BLACK MARK FOR THE SQUAD

The other prisoners were in for theft, passing bad checks, assault, or being drunk on duty. Most of those accused of auto theft had taken vehicles in attempts to get away from the army as quickly as possible.

The general turnover was 400 a month, according to the social worker I talked to. Most of the prisoners were under 21. Enlistees outnumbered draftees by about two to one (there are about three enlistments for every man drafted).

Many of the enlistees had joined the army to get away from bad home situations, but few found life in the army any more cheering. A surprising number were married; many of these had gone home on leave and decided to stay – until the MPs or the FBI caught up with them. Lengths of AWOL ranged from a few hours to, in a few cases, a number of years.

Many of the prisoners had decided early in their army careers that they did not like the army and left within a few weeks of their initiation. One guy I became friendly with had spent less than 20 minutes on active duty; he managed to get off the train going to the reception station. A quiet sort of anarchist, he had originally refused induction, but when told that this would bring an automatic five years in prison, agreed to submit.

After he jumped off the train, he travelled around the country for a number of months until a friend convinced him that if he turned himself in he would get an automatic unsuitability discharge. But such was not the case. While inside the stockade he rapidly became a model prisoner and convinced the authorities he wanted to go "back to duty."

He was given a six-month sentence suspended (which is usually the case with first offenders) and sent back to duty. But he was gone from the army within a matter of days. This time, I am sure, for good.

Others, not as shrewd, but just as determined, usually got caught because they ran right home to mother or wife or girlfriend or the old gang – and right into the arms of waiting FBI men.

The percentage of blacks in the stockade was well below the percentage of blacks in the entire army. One reason for this is that at that time there was less "black awareness" and it seemed they enjoyed in the military a greater "equality" than was afforded them in civilian life.

The Vietnam war was a deciding factor in many AWOL cases. There were a few who had strong feelings against the war, but I did not run into any outright Vietnam war objectors.

There were a few men who had received their orders for 'Nam and had failed to show up. Sometimes these men were charged with missing troop movement or avoiding hazardous duty or even with desertion, but more often than not, the charge was reduced to plain old AWOL, especially if they indicated a willingness to go to Vietnam.

There were a few who had come home from V-N on emergency leave and, either for family reasons, or for other reasons, decided not to go back. But a great many more, not violently opposed to the war, just couldn't understand it and didn't see why they should be shipped off to some faraway place to kill guys they never even met.

There were two types of COs in the stockade: those who openly stated they were COs and those whom I called non-objecting COs. Included in the latter group were subconscious COs and those who did not have enough education to know that there was such a thing as a CO.

A nice example of this last type was the farm boy, who, during his first week of both our imprisonments, said to me – without knowing why I was in the stockade – "You know, that chaplain's all wrong. He says we should get back to duty and be good soldiers, but it says in the Bible, 'Thou shalt not kill.'" I knew eight declared COs in the stockade, all with lengthy and interesting stories.

Although overt acts of brutality were relatively rare, the atmosphere in the stockade was one of smoldering brutality. I witnessed a couple of beatings and heard the blows and screams of a few more. Policy, of course, was that no prisoner was to be subjected to physical punishment, however, if a prisoner swung at a guard or other stockade personnel, he was to be restrained with whatever force necessary. Often the guards deemed that so ouch force was necessary that the prisoner landed up in the hospital, the reason for his injuries given as, "Prisoner fell down stairs."

One exception to policy occurred on Christmas eve. Silent night, holy night. The guards were drunk and as they travelled from cell to cell taking roll-call, they took wanton swings at a few prisoners. (I understand that a momentary truce had been called in Vietnam for Christmas.) Fortunately no prisoner swung back. The guard commander on duty that evening was later transferred to the supply room, but that may have been coincidental as one of his henchmen that evening was appointed to take his place as guard commander and this hench-man had not been particularly gentle.

A second kind of brutality was evidenced by such samples as this: A boy cut his wrist on purpose. Whether he was actually attempting suicide or was just playing at it, I don't know. But he was taken to the confinement officer, who said that the boy should be put to scrubbing floors and not be given medical attention. The boy scrubbed for a few minutes, blood falling on the floor as as quickly as he could wipe it up. Then he slashed his other wrist. For this he was put In the box.

There was about one attempted – or feigned attempt at – suicide every week. Usually no immediate medical treatment was given.

A favorite punishment doled out by the confinement officer was scrubbing the concrete floor. Scrubbing was done with hands and knees on the floor, no squatting or stooping, with turnkeys yelling, and for hours on end. Minton claimed that the record was 27 straight hours of scrubbing. I doubt that. But it is true that the usual stretch is four hours. Is this brutality? Try doing it and find out.

Another sort of brutality was just an inherent evil in an inherently brutal system. It happened three times during my stay. Once it had no physical results, once it was the end of a life but first the boy lay in a hospital for over a month totally paralyzed. He was shot trying to escape. But there is a great deal of doubt that he was trying to escape. At any rate he was shot wantonly.

One story has it that as the boy, under shotgun guard, with a group of five other prisoners, was on the way to a work detail, a civilian army employee shouted to him to remove a rock from the road. The boy rushed out to comply. Another prisoner shouted to the guard, "There he goes. He's trying to escape." The guard fired dead at the prisoner. The guns the guards carry are not loaded with salt or buckshot; they are loaded with 12-gauge shotgun shells crammed full with nine steel slivers.

At twenty feet from the muzzle the prisoner was hit by all of them. Some went clean through him. Was this boy a hardened criminal? – No, he was a slightly built youngster who was serving a 30-day term for failing to go on KP when told. Did he have a motive for escape? No, he had only a matter of days to go until his release. Is he dead? Yes. And what did the stockade chaplain say to the other prisoners at the end of a service for the boy? "This is what happens when you don't live by the rules."

For the most part the guards were not openly prejudiced against COs. The big hate was supposed to be against AWOLs, so the guards acted as though AWOL was the worst thing a man could be, though they didn't believe it.

Most of the AWOLs were in the stockade because they did not like the army and anyone who had told the army, if effect, to go screw itself was their ally.

I spent six months on active duty and a few days more than that locked up in the stockade. It's pretty miserable in the stockade, but remember, they've just got your body. If you're a soldier and don't think you should be, they've got your will and you mind and your conscience. I felt infinitely freer in the stockade and I'm not a martyr nor a masochist nor the sort who gets into trouble.

I think it is better to have a showdown and refuse orders than to go AWOL. It makes the issues clearer.

Once you decide to do it, go through with it and don't turn back no matter what you are threatened with. If you've been in the military more than a few weeks, you've already realized that 99% of their threats are hot air. If you haven't realized this, you're not sharp enough to get through the stockade, so forget it.

It's best to be as friendly as you are naturally. Phony friendliness will backfire, but if you treat the guards and others with as much respect as you can muster, you'll be surprised how many secretly sympathize with you – even a few officers (they're human, too). But don't expect anyone to be tolerant.

I also found it best not to complain or ask special favors. The army would rather have a CO change his position than keep him locked up for a long time. If they spot your weaknesses you can be sure they'll use them as levers to win you back.

☮☮☮

☮ ☮ ☮

THE NEW ABSOLUTIST

Suzanne Williams

Editor's Note: Suzanne Williams was born on November 4, 1943 in Evanston, Illinois. On September 11, 1968, she was arrested for "damage to government property" and defended herself before the Federal District Court in Boston. She was sentenced to six months to six years indeterminate under the Youth Corrections Act for pouring black paint over the files of Selective Service System Local Board #30 in the Customs House in Boston. Suzi acted with poet/activist Francis Thomas (Assunta) Femia, a former Catholic brother.

Frank was already under a four-year sentence for refusal of induction after returning his draft cards and received one year for this action to run concurrently. After a motion for reduction of sentence by Suzi, her sentence was reduced to one year "flat time."

Both Suzi and Frank had been very active with the New England Committee for Nonviolent Action. Suzi had been arrested several times before for civil disobedience actions and had maintained a position of total noncoöperation with the police, the courts, and the jails, including a total food and water fast until her release.

"Because we are pacifists, and because we believe that war is wrong, we have attempted to interpose ourselves between young men and the conscription which sends them to their deaths. Black is the color of death, and black is the color of the paint we poured on the files…We follow the example of the Boston Tea Party by engaging in 'creative vandalism'. We also take this action in solidarity with others who have received heavy sentences for similar actions. Conscience cannot be intimidated."

Frank began to serve his sentence at the Petersburg, Virginia reformatory, but was recently transferred to work in the Education Department of the Federal Youth Center at Ashland, Kentucky. Suzi's sentence began in the Federal Reformatory for women in Alderson, West Virginia in honor status. And it will not end there.

Even though Suzanne Williams is being held in maximum security now, she would have been released on July 12, 1969 upon expiration with good time. Her sentence will last a good deal longer because she would not bend to imprisonment.

The following are a descriptive series of letters from prison to her mother, Jean. Ω

I feel somewhat lost here, not knowing what's going on, but I expect that will wear off after awhile, when I've been here for a few days. Altho this place is big enough that it will take awhile to figure it out.

All in all, it seems to be (so far) a gilded cage. But a prison nonetheless. To sum it up, people don't have too many complaints about Alderson, but everybody is glad to leave when their sentence is over. I'd like to leave right away, but since this is not possible, I don't think I'll have too much trouble doing my time.

But I do hope that I don't have to do all six years. I don't think so.

October 19, 1968: I've been here exactly one week today. Still don't know everything that goes on here, but I am learning fast, both officially and unofficially.

My chances for release look worse and worse the more I find out about the Youth Act. One thing: contrary to what you may have heard, I cannot be released without parole, although they must release me after four years, but still with parole until the end of the six. Or they can take me off parole after I have had satisfactory parole for at least a year after being released from prison.

But I won't summarize or make any conclusions from the various things that I have found out until I meet the November Parole Board and talk to them about my situation. They are supposed to come here on November 4th of all days. Some birthday present!

Another thing – I wrote to Judge Garrity, and told him exactly what his sentence means in practical terms and outlined the situation. I want him to be aware of how the Bureau of Prisons and the Board of Parole apply a Youth Act sentence. I didn't ask him to change it or any such thing – that is up to him. But at least he has a clear picture of the situation.

"Lectures" (on various aspects of the place and programs) began today for me. Also I have been examined by a dentist. Next comes the dreaded physical exam by the medical people. Also today I got a piece of paper which is officially called my "Commitment and Diagnostic Summary" and unofficially called my "time sheet."

It lists my mandatory release date as October 13, 1972, and my sentence expiration, (my "flat time"), as October 13, 1974. If you do the math involved, you will notice that my sentence runs from the day that I was sentenced, October 14, and not from the day I was arrested, September 11. With a zip-six (Youth Act) you don't get time spent in jail before sentencing. So 33 of those days spent at Plymouth are what they call "dead time."

This morning, those of us in orientation got to talk to the guy who heads the Classification and Parole department here, and I asked him about this business of a possible six years (with YCA) when my maximum possible sentence on my charges was four years; was it legal, etc. He said it was – that anybody under 26 can get a zip-what the maximum (even for a misdemeanor!) because this is a commitment to treatment, not to imprisonment.

Actually, there is no difference in how we (Youth Act kids) are treated here as compared to those with other kinds of sentences! We are all doing time in a federal prison. I don't think O'Brien [David O'Brien] will get anywhere with his appeal.

The main reason I am writing this letter (seems pretty gloomy so far, doesn't it? Actually, I am in excellent spirits.) is to wish you a VERY HAPPY BIRTHDAY!!! Although they don't know it here, they are going to have a celebration of your birthday. I expect they'll try to disguise it as a Halloween party or some such ruse, but I will not be fooled! Do have a good birthday.

October 25, 1968: Greetings from the lovely hills of West Virginia. I have been here almost exactly three weeks and I pretty much know the place by now. Have been in "orientation status," but this week I was "classified" and I start my school and job assignments next week. For school, I am taking a number of boring but useful subjects: typing, shorthand, book-keeping and secretarial science. For a job, I have been assigned to work in the office of the Protestant Chaplain, Rev. Jiskoot, who seems very nice, and is both young and modern thinking. So I think the job will be more interesting than many.

In looks this place resembles a college campus more than it does a prison. We live in dormitory-type buildings, called cottages, and have rooms rather than cells. The food is excellent (even OK for vegies!), and we are permitted to wear our own clothes as well as those issued by the institution. We go places around the reservation unescorted, but there is much signing out, signing in, telephoning to check on people, and, of course, much counting. So while it is a high-class prison, Alderson is definitely a prison.

We are grouped by age, and thus I am in one of the youth cottages, YC-1 (even though this past Monday I reached the ripe old age of 20).

I find one of the most annoying things to me is not being trusted in trivial matters by the officers, simply because I am an inmate. Although it's done without malice, it's extremely insulting to have someone go to great lengths to check something you have said, especially in small matters, instead of taking your word for it.

Tuesday I had an unexpected visitor: Special Agent George Patterson of the FBI, asking about the June 17, 1968 women's draft card burning in Washington, D.C. His questions seemed aimed at conspiracy charges, as well as the more obvious one of draft card burning.

I answered his questions and we discussed many other things, such as the draft, nonviolence, human freedom, prisons, etc. He was a very nice guy and we got along quite well. He didn't seem too happy with helping out in a process which will probably result in my getting more time.

Am trying to get permission to write to Frank, even though I don't know for certain where he is.

Mail policy here is more reasonable than at most prisons. I believe I have been getting just about all the letters sent to me regardless of lists. So If anybody wants to write, I'll probably get it.

November 7, 1968: Veterans Day is being celebrated here in a big way, with a steak dinner and other things. It figures. Be joyful and happy when thinking about all the poor devils who have slaughtered each other for political reasons, people they didn't know and had nothing against. At least they could have it be a day of mourning out of respect, but no, there will be a celebration!

Found out today that Frank is at Petersburg (Va.), which is just south of Richmond. Not too far from here. My request to correspond with him is still going thru red tape, but am feeling more hopeful along those lines.

The Catonsville Nine were supposed to be sentenced today, but I don't know how much time they got as this is not the type of news the West Virginia mass media see fit to disseminate.

Have been here three weeks today. On the one hand, seems like I've been here longer but on the other hand, it's been painless and has gone fast. Much faster than time at PCJ [Plymouth County Jail] or other such places.

November 8, 1968: Expect to see you two days from now, but since you will need this form to send a Christmas package, here it is. As you see, the bottom part of the form has to be included with the package.

Also, about that letter you got from Mr. Garrity – at first I planned to send you all the information, reasoning, etc.; but decided finally to send it straight to him, instead, with a note of explanation. I went into a fair amount of detail on a number of matters, and so, maybe now he will understand the whole thing a little better.

But anyway, for your own future information here is (verbatim) what the "Certificate of Parole" says under the section "Conditions of Parole." (Editor's Note. See Question #10 in "Appendix I: Questions and Answers About Federal Prisons." Although the wording is slightly changed for several conditions, the text is still the same. The pledge which the applicant for parole is urged to sign has been changed to allow for arbitrary recommitment or changes by the United States Board of Parole. Ω)

The whole thing presents the question, though, of just who owns me – myself or the U.S. Board of Parole. And this is apparently something I will have to fight mostly alone, since the general consensus seems to be (here and outside, with a few exceptions) that I'm a fool for not telling them what they want to hear, or at least promising to follow parole conditions.

So there are many people pressuring me in that direction. Not that I am likely to change my mind, but it will make my time that much harder. Which is maybe what Mr. Garrity had in mind.

November 20, 1968: Had meant to write sooner, but the effects of your visit were so delightful that they lasted long enough for me to be unaware that quite a few days have passed since then, and I really should write.

The biggest thing in my horizon here since you visited is my application for a job change. When I went to one of the appropriate people about my problem with being useless at work because of two people in a one-person job, he suggested that I ask for a job change. So I did, and yesterday met the "treatment team" about it.

My regular caseworker wasn't there, nor the fellow who had suggested I apply for a job change, and I got denied. This didn't bother me as much as their attitude: I was talked to as if I were a grade-school child. Also it was like talking to a brick wall.

Their minds were made up, so they told me there were no jobs, except those where you had to type 50 words a minute (I type 15 w.a.m). I happen to know that jobs are open, but they didn't want to hear it.

So they made me feel grouchy the rest of the day and more than ever convinced that they don't actually give a damn about us, as long as we don't make trouble or rock the boat while we're here.

I got the distinct feeling that they wanted to hurry up and tell me no so they could get on with the next case. And one feels ganged-up on, with a half dozen or more of them sitting at a table with little old you.

And to top it off, none of them seems to have a sense of humor, which is unforgivable. I think they are trapped people. Anyway, so much for that – griping is over (for awhile, anyway). But I'll pursue this matter.

You know that other political prisoner I was telling you about? Well, I finally met her and she's very nice indeed. You would describe her as a sweet person. We have not had much of a chance to talk, but I imagine we'll become better acquainted over the years.

This is my morning to sleep late, but I couldn't because my roommate was up at the usual time, switching on the bright fluorescent light, banging the drawers and door and worst of all, filling the room with cigarette smoke and hair spray. (Another gripe – good grief, Charlie Brown,

I'd better shut up before I give you the impression I'm miserable, which is untrue..)

Good news: a long letter from Chuck [Matthei], just about to depart Oklahoma for Chicago, where he'll be Thanksgiving, then he'll visit here sometime before Xmas.

November 27, 1968: Got your letter – many thanks. So nice to hear about people getting stuck in snow drifts: we have no snow around here at all, and probably won't until January.

If I remember correctly, this is the old dog's birthday. Tell him he is a sterling hound and to take it easy in his declining years (and not to come up behind people and steal their mittens). And take him on a walk for me – down thru the upper meadow, then cut across the little meadow and go into the woods where the dead tree is. There is an old tractor trail there, which you can more or less follow up into a clearing, where there are vestiges of logging and lots of ground ivy (clubmoss, lycopodia). On the other side of this, the trail continues (vaguely) for a bit more, first a bit of swampy area, and bearing gently but continually to the right. During this last part, the ridge is to the left. When the trail ends, you turn left, and go up the ridge, going along the top of it until you come to the road. There are on top of the ridge various old logging roads (ill-defined), and a property line with trimmed brush and somewhat faded iridescent orange paint markers. The hound and I often took that walk.

It's most lovely and almost like Vermont.

Speaking of Vermont, enclosed please find two parts of an ad for *Vermont Life* calendars, which I clipped from the *New York Times*. Would very much appreciate two of them, one to hang up on my wall, and one to give to my "homie," whom I told you about. She got a letter from her folks in New Hampshire recently, with photos of snowy scenes. If anybody has a camera, photos are allowed to be mailed in and would be much appreciated.

Sounds like you all had a most jolly Thanksgiving. Things here were not so good, but an improvement over last year's situation in D.C.

Finally got to call Erica [Enzer]. We had a most jolly conversation. Have applied for December for one to you, and will get it sometime or other. Applied early, because they will not have any this month from about December 20 on thru to a few days after new year's.

No word yet from Petersburg on Frank – so I wrote them an explicit but extremely polite letter reminding them I would like to know about writing to him.

Am attacking the job change thing from several indirect angles right now, instead of Don Quixote windmill style, which fails because this place has oodles and gobs of "inertia of rest": they are allergic to change, and those who are responsible for such things have the general attitude of, "Don't bother us, kid. Can't you see we're busy?" So I will be well-armed with facts, figures, etc., the next time I present my case, and I will thus be harder to brush off. (Nothing quite as insulting as being lied to in a transparent way – give me credit for a little intelligence.)

My typing varies between 15 and 20 words per minute, except when they want me to do arithmetic on that infernal machine. And speaking of arithmetic, I started bookkeeping today: I hate it already, but expect that I shall learn it. The shorthand comes along fair to middling. Still looks like chicken-scratch, though.

There was was a small matter the other day in which I was actually trusted by an officer! I was so surprised that I didn't believe it at first. When I first got here I was quite irked at not being trusted (still am), and now I am so used to not being trusted, that I am surprised when it happens (which is not often). Such are prisons...

We have been practicing Xmas carols in choir – I alternate between a low alto and a soprano, but this in something my voice does all by itself and over which have no control. (You should hear all the great talent I have when I sing in the bathtub, however.)

December 3, 1968: At last we have snow. Beautiful snow! Am just hoping that it sticks. My opinion of West Virginia weather has gone up considerably, however.

And now it's snowy, I can't go out: I've been sick today (it's now about 9:00 pm) and was half-sick yesterday. I think it's a touch of the Asian flu that's going around the reservation. Or maybe a delayed reaction to some shots (tetanus and typhoid) that I got a number of days ago. Whatever it is, I feel lousy. But time heals all ills, and I have plenty of time. Six years to be exact.

Have decided to hold off on plots for a job change for awhile. Me and my boss had a little chat about a number of things. Also, I want to wait until after I meet the parole board to make any long-range plans. Then I will have a more definite idea of just how long-range I should plan.

Those bunch of phinques at Petersburg wrote back and said they "do not approve correspondence between you and Mr. Femia due to the fact that you are not relatives and there are no extraordinary circumstances that would warrant maintaining a relationship." Made me mad, but I don't suppose I should have expected anything else. I don't suppose it occurred to them that it would make his time easier and make my time easier. But then, none of them have ever done time themselves. Frank and I couldn't possibly corrupt each other as we are both absolutely hopeless cases anyway.

We have a big inspection tomorrow – everybody has been running around like a bunch of idiots cleaning the place, yours truly included.

Although if the truth known, on this particular subject (the immaculateness of the cottage), I "don't feel nothing" as the saying goes.

Somebody "made bush" (an expression meaning "to escape": an abbreviation of "to make bush parole") last night. So far they haven't caught her. Hope they don't.

The mountains are very pretty in the snow. Chuck ought to be here sometime in the next week or two.

December 9, 1968: Today I am a "lock-in" from classes (I have Tuesday afternoon off from work anyway). It isn't that I was feeling lazy, but I was feeling sick. So this morning I went up to sick call, and the officer was even nice enough to call "area patrol" to take me up there, as it was doubtful that I could make it up the hill.

Please send Frank a big beautiful Xmas card, since I can't write to him.

December 10, 1968: Last night I tried to call you but nobody was home. Tonight I was called to make the telephone call, but I was out caroling in town with the choir. As far as I know, there are no more calls this month, so I guess I'll just have to write.

The caroling was great fun – there were about 25 of us (prot. and cath. choirs) along with the chaplain and the two nuns and an m.c.o. who drove the truck that we all piled into the back of – an open truck with a couple of bales of hay to sit on. We drove all around Alderson (about the size of Amherst or a bit smaller) and caroled from the truck. Was much, much fun! just to get off the reservation for an hour was glorious.

Since I've only been locked up about 3½ months, I didn't expect that the outside world would be so strange, but it was! Just to see lots of ordinary things like traffic lights and grocery stores and houses with kitchens and kids and people walking any old way they feel like. And, all kinds of things that you never see here. Kind of like a brief period of cultural shock. It's another world completely, and I guess the feeling I got is probably impossible to explain to someone who has not done time. Anyway, enough of that.

A friend loaned me a copy of Commonweal, which has an article entitled "Guerrilla Christianity" by Paul Velde. It's written for people familiar with various Catholic traditions, thought, liturgy, etc., etc., and thus I have to read it over again several times before I can say what I think of it. It's about the Baltimore, Catonsville and Milwaukee actions and what it means in Christian terms. They seem unaware of the Boston action, possibly because it is a little hard to fit into some of the generalizations they make about the other three.

Unauthorized mail has been cut off. It may be restored, but I get the feeling that a lot of these people don't know the importance of mail when you're locked up, or else, as the saying goes, they don't feel a thing.

This place is often quite ludicrous, ridiculous, amusing, etc., etc. Example: yesterday, at "Christian Living class," it was part of my job to take down everybody's name and cottage number, and then get on the telephone and call in to "control" just who was there from what cottage. Which I did. Today, our officer had to work In the mail room (which is located in YC-12) for an hour, and so she took all of us who were in the cottage (YC-l) with her to YC-12, so she could have us babysat. So yesterday they trusted me to keep track of seven inmates for an hour and one half; while today they wouldn't trust me to keep track of myself for an hour! Hilarious, no? (Also, I was somewhat put out because it's my day off from work, and they woke me up out of a sound sleep to tell me I had to go and be babysat in ten minutes.) Such is life at Uncle Sam's Finishing School for Unrefined Ladies.

Tomorrow night (Xmas eve), we (the choir) will go caroling around the reservation. This will also be fun. Then we'll have a midnight service at which the choir will also be expected to sing (if we have any breath left by then).

December 22, 1968: Tonight the Catholic Choir, Spiritual Choir, and Protestant Choir went caroling around the reservation, ending up at the Warden's house, where we caroled and she had a party for all three choirs. Much fun.

We had a bit of snow yesterday and today, but unless we have more tonight (unlikely: for once it's too cold to snow), the whiteness of our Christmas will be pretty sparse.

Hope you all had a good Christmas. Was really great to talk to you on the phone last night.

The midnight service was pretty good. Also, today I went with a friend to the Mass, which was also not at all bad.

It may be that I can once again hear from a larger number of people than those listed. But of course these things are always subject to various types of fluctuation. We have no rights, only privileges. But you might tell people who have had letters returned to try again, quietly, and there's a chance that I'll receive them. Also: got an issue of *The Peacemaker* today (we get mail on Sundays and holidays: the only real advantage to this place as compared to the free world), but for awhile was not getting it.

Although a zip-six is not altogether a picnic, many have (and have had) a much harder row to hoe. Today we celebrate the birthday of Jesus of Nazareth, one of the great teachers and nonviolent revolutionaries of all time. His struggle was certainly much harder. And although now people mostly worship his name and forget his teachings, I still think that he was the mover of a great deal of good. And there are some who both worship him and practice his teachings, as the Catholic Workers and others of that general belief.

Think DeCourcy [Squire] is going to visit me in January. Don't know when Chuck will show up.

No word from Garrity. But it's o.k. for him to take his time: time is something that I have plenty of.

[*Editor's Note.* On February 8, 1969, Suzanne Williams merely climbed over the fence and started walking. Chuck Matthei was staying with Anne and Theodore Upshure in New York and was told be be prepared for his arrest for failure to report for a physical and for induction in Chicago. That arrest came on February 6th, before Suzi was able to reach him to stand with him in New York.

Suzi left as the guards were occupied with the movie's letting out. Instead of heading for the road, where quick capture would have been certain, she made for the nearest railroad tracks. She kept on walking until she had passed through the small town of Hinton, then changed to the road. Another inmate who had once "hit the bush" warned Suzi not to be seen in Hinton: it's a very small town and strange girls are suspected escapees from Alderson 20 miles away. At Hinton, Suzi was picked up by a newspaper truck driver who, thinking she was a runaway, took her to Beckley, a much larger town. There Suzi borrowed a dime for a collect telephone call and her escape was complete.

She first went to New York to find out about Chuck's situation and then up to New England. She was picked up by the FBI and a state trooper at her brother's home in Vermont on a routine check on February 27th and was held incommunicado in Rutland, Vermont, for that entire week. She was returned to Alderson, where she will be indicted and sentenced in the Southern District of Virginia. The usual penalty for escape is from six to 18 additional months.

Only one other political prisoner, Gary Hicks, walked out of the Allenwood camp and was returned to Lewisburg in solitary and sentenced to 18 months extra time. Gary is a black draft resister and is the only other prisoner in recent times to have taken this action, although other prisoners have been giving the matter serious consideration.

Suzi writes that a little over half of the prisoners at Alderson are black with a considerable number of Spanish-speaking prisoners, and a few American Indians. The only other political prisoner there, though, is a Puerto Rican nationalist who helped shoot up the House of Representatives about 15 years ago, during Harry Truman's presidency. She has has 40 more years to go with little chance of parole.

Now Suzi is being held in maximum security and the only matter that remains to be decided is how much extra time she will have to serve for the crime of freedom. Ω]

Guess what? I'm back in West Virginia. Hope you got the letter I wrote from Albany, New York, where I stayed overnight on the way down. I wrote you a bunch of letters from the jail I was in at Rutland, but they didn't mail any of them.

I guess Xtoph and Penny [Suzi's brother and sister-in-law] must have told you the circumstances of my arrest. The first place I was taken after that was the State Police barracks in Shaftsbury, where I was photographed, fingerprinted, etc. Then I was deposited at the Bennington County Jail for several hours until the marshal came and took me up to the Women's Reformatory in Rutland (that is the only place in Vermont authorized to hold female federal prisoners).

I was there Thursday (February 27th) night and Friday through Tuesday until 3:00 pm or so when I began my trip back here. Tuesday night I was at the Albany County Jail in Albany, and Wednesday night at tho Women's Detention Center in Washington, D.C. I got here yesterday about 4:30.

The Rutland Jail had good food, comfortable bed, etc., but was lousy because I was put in a cell by myself, with the others forbidden to talk to me. This is because I was a "security risk." Albany was almost like a movie stereotype, with bars everywhere, and clanging electronic gates, etc. Poor food, small cells, hard bed. But nicer than Rutland, because there were people to talk to. Wash. D.C. hasn't changed much since I was last there.

The marshal was very nice and also the lady marshal who was along for escort purposes. The marshal used to be a Vermont state trooper, and was at one time assigned to work in the Bennington area, so we had a lot in common.

He remembered that Dad had been involved in county politics, and he told me about how, as a state trooper, he used to chase the Greens and the Moffits all over Shaftsbury. Said they gave the cops more trouble than anyone in Bennington County.

So – talking over the good old days. He did handcuff me all the way down, though. But I guess that's only to be expected with an escape. Anyway, it was a fun trip while it lasted.

Yesterday when I got here, it was just as people from YC-11, my old cottage, were going to dinner, so I was able to wave to them from the gatehouse. Then up to the admissions office, in Davis Hall. There were altogether five of us (from two cars: we had picked up two more people in D.C., and another marshal had come in just before us with two people) who went thru the admissions procedure together.

After that, I was brought upstairs in Davis Hall, and put in seclusion. I don't know how long I'll be up here. Probably I'll find out sometime this week. They told me it was up to the treatment team. But it will be for a long time, I fear. It's very unfancy here. But I guess I can handle it (guess I'll have to – I don't have a choice in the matter!). There is not a lot to do here. As expected, and by design.

I tried to call you on the phone while I was in Rutland, but you were not home the two times they let me try. Maybe I can call you sometime in the next month or so, but right now it looks doubtful that I will be able to.

Enjoy all your snow.

☮☮☮

☮ ☮ ☮

JAIL IS A BUMMER

Jeffrey Segal

Editor's Note: Jeffrey Segal was born in Chicago on June 25, 1941. He is a former national officer of Students for a Democratic Society, based at their national office in Chicago, and has been active in the student movement and, more recently, the radical movement, for a number of years.

Jeff was one of the first S.D.S. people to refuse induction into the armed forces. He is not a pacifist and has a very different approach to jail resistance. He is very definitely considered a political prisoner, and certainly most of the religious objectors are not. Jeff feels that the prisons are potential strongholds for radical organizing.

In May, 1968 he was sentenced to four years by Federal Judge Parsons in Chicago. Jeff Segal has served his time in the Cook County Jail in Chicago and the Medical Center for Federal Prisoners in Springfield, Missouri.

Jeff was transferred to the Alameda County Jail in Oakland, California where he stood trial with Frank Bardake, Terry Cannon, Reese Erlich, Steve Hamilton, Robert Mendel, and Michael Smith on charges of conspiracy to commit a misdemeanor, which is, by government logic, a felony. The charges were brought because of the Oakland Seven's participation in Stop the Draft Week in October, 1967, when they were successful in closing down the Oakland Induction Center on several successive days.

The following is a letter to the S.D.S. National Council explaining just what Jeff Segal thinks about prisons. Ω

Dear Comrades,

I would have enjoyed being with you but, unfortunately, other commitments continue to be overly demanding, and I must remain where I am. Greetings from the bottom of the swamp!

The foremost thing that comes to mind is that jail is a bummer!! I have seen a couple of articles in papers written by dudes who have done time saying that doing time isn't really too bad, that the food is better than college food, etc., which have really pissed a bunch of us off. For people to say that is irresponsible! Both penitentiary and jail time is a very bad scene which, I believe, should be avoided if at all possible.

This doesn't mean not doing things that could mean jail time, but it means trying to do them without getting caught. It also means that when we go to jail it is because of a commitment to build a revolutionary movement, and not just to make our "personal sacrifice" for the cause and then continue a straight middle-class life.

This kind of understanding has been an important tool in the struggle to turn the jail sentence into something more than dead time. What, then, has the time so far been, if not dead time?

Personally, because of the controlled nature of the environment, it has given me a chance to get a much better understanding of what I'm about, how I fit into my physical and social life-flux, what capabilities and limits I have, etc.

This has produced both a much firmer commitment to and a better understanding of the building of a movement to make a revolutionary society. Far from being mellowed by this experience, I have become more intent upon doing what must be done to liberate ourselves and our brothers and sisters. What the time has done is to sear away the fatty elements of bourgeois sentimentality and leave me tougher and more able to deal with some of the difficult tasks we have before us.

Politically, the time has forced me to clarify my own thinking about both strategy and analysis as well as tactics – to think of longer and longer periods of time (building of long-term strategy) instead of just day-to-day and month-to-month happenings. It has led to completion of an ideology.

Ideology, simply, is the development of a set of concepts that provides us with an organized way of viewing the world and our part in the world. A complete ideology gives us the ability to handle most experiences and events; and a reasonable one conforms to objective reality.

The difference between ideology and dogma is that ideology is a tool to be used for the understanding of things (a tool which can and should be modified with the change of living conditions) and dogma are strictures taken on faith into which things are crammed to fit.

I think we must develop an ideology – this means hard intellectual work without being afraid to use complex concepts and intellectual tools. The other side of this process has been the necessity to break down our crazy jargon and politics so that street people can understand what we're about.

I have found this to be very important – because there have been lots of people I have been in contact with who are becoming part of our movement as the result of our ability to rap with them in the language they understand. I purposely haven't dealt with contents of ideology to avoid being embroiled in temporary politics.

Also, there has been the learning of how to work (a) inside an overt police state, and (b) with a non-student population we should be into. Prison is a clear analogy of a police state, with all of a police state's major characteristics, and the experience has been helpful in teaching me how to work in the future American reality. Little else can or should be said in public.

There are in the joints I've been in a lot of fine groovy people who have been my fellow criminals. It has meant the building of a deep inside understanding that a large amount of what society classifies as criminal behavior comes out of the same basic impulses that have made us what we are.

A lot of the guys are people who have rebelled against Plastic Capitalist America, but who did not have access to the channels of "dissent" that we did. We have a lot of potential brothers and sisters in the half-million behind bars and the tens of millions on the street.

Our job is to reach them and turn them on to the ways to struggle that does not just take back a little of what has been stolen from the people, but destroys the system that makes the exploitation and replaces it with a liberated society.

To build a new is to destroy an old,
To struggle and create is the law
of nature and the spirit of life.

Jeff (alias Bugsy) Segal, POW

☮☮☮

Editor's Note: On Thursday, December 15, 1966, sixty-seven peace demonstrators were arrested for allegedly blocking the Whitehall Street entrance of the Military Induction Center in New York City, but, actually, the police arrived earlier to shut the building down with barricades.

The action was planned as a pledge campaign by the Anti-Escalation Committee, an ad hoc committee formed by members of various pacifist groups. The pledge stated that we would commit civil disobedience at the induction center if the war were escalated.

The day before, the Johnson administration had ordered the bombing of Hanoi, and brought more people out to be arrested on a weekday than ever before.

This demonstration led the way for mass civil disobedience and mass arrests. Dorothy Lane expresses the emotions of that time so well… Ω

☮ ☮ ☮

2 MONOLOGUES

Dorothy Lane

Silent night, holy night

All is calm, all is bright

Hark the herald angels sing

Glory to the new born king

Peace on earth

And mercy mild

God and sinners reconciled

Going to lay down my sward and shield

Down by the riverside

Joy to the world

Let every heart prepare him room

Let heaven and nature sing

Let heaven and nature sing

Let heaven and heaven and nature sing

Just like a tree that's standing by the water

We shall not be moved

You are blocking the sidewalk

In violation of the law 722, section 3

We will ask you three times to leave

If you do not clear the sidewalk

You will be placed under arrest

Those who lie down before the arresting officer

Will be charged with resisting arrest

Which is a serious misdemeanor

Do you understand?

Officers, are you ready?

This is the first warning

This is the second warning

This is the third warning

You will now be arrested

Do you refuse to move?

You are under arrest

The truth will make us free

☮ ☮ ☮

☮ ☮ ☮

AUSTRALIA:
Objector In The Guardhouse

Simon Townsend

Editor's Note: Simon Townsend was born in Sydney, New South Wales, on November 27, 1945. He became a pacifist in June 1965 and formed the Sydney Conscientious Objectors' Discussion Group in December of that year. He now also works with the Abolish Conscription Campaign. He is often invited to speak at public and group meetings. He became a controversial figure throughout Australia during tremendous publicity over his mistreatment in an army prison.

Simon's younger brother, Stephen, has recently formed a new absolutist group called The Unconscriptables. Stephen refused to register and now faces two years' gaol for that "crime" under the National Service Act.

After dismissal of two court applications to be exempted as a conscientious objector during 1966, Simon refused a medical order and was fined $32.00 (a dollar per day) in the Special Federal Court in Sydney in January 1967.

He refused to pay the fine and was imprisoned for 32 days (a dollar per day) in the State Penitentiary, a civil gaol, at Long Bay, Sydney. (Fines are now served at the rate of two dollars per day.)

During 1967, Simon made two more unsuccessful applications. In May 1968 he was inducted into the army by force and served 27 days under several forms of military imprisonment while refusing orders. A fifth application was successful and he was released by a magistrate's order.

Simon Townsend is now 22 and a journalist by profession. The first article here appeared in a Sydney political journal, after his civil gaol sentence in 1967. His other two contributions are letters written in an Army guardhouse. The first was smuggled out by his fiancée (now his wife) and published in a newspaper on the morning of his court-martial – causing a furor.

His devious plan to smuggle out the second letter by writing on the insides of envelopes was thwarted; this is its first publication. Ω

I am writing this from a cell in the guardhouse of Bardia Barracks, Ingleburn, NSW.

The cell is eight shoes long by five shoes wide (about 7½ by 4½ feet). It is steel lined and a draught blows through and it is cold.

The thick grey paint on the steel hasn't quite obliterated the etchings of some past prisoners: "Pte. Anderson goes on strike 21-2-63," "I love Christine" and "The Rebels '55."

More recently, in the grey paint, a Private Hartwick has declared, "I hate the army" and "Dusty" has made 20 small strokes and the proclamation, "one day to go." Wishing to leave my mark also I've used the incline edge of a one-cent piece to carve: "Wars will cease when men refuse to fight."

All that scratching filled in a few hours in this lonely, boring hole, but as I survey my handiwork again I wonder vaguely if a soldier was locked up with these eight words for a few days, whether they'd make an impression.

If I didn't believe those words and insist on acting them out, I wouldn't be here now.

Nearly three years ago I decided I was a pacifist – that I believed war was a crime against humanity, that I could not take part any war, or preparation for war and that I should help to remove the causes of war.

A few months later I helped establish the Sydney Conscientious Objectors' Group, which helps intending objectors sort out and clarify their thoughts through weekly discussions.

During 1966, a magistrate and a judge refused to exempt me from compulsory military service because I was not "sincere." I'd managed to "fool" hundreds of other people, but not those learned men of the Bench…

My family (none of whom are pacifists), friends (a tiny minority who are pacifists), many journalist colleagues and lots of acquaintances, including psychologists, academics, politicians, and a few soldiers, had all been "fooled."

Driven by this "insincerity," I openly refused to take a medical examination ordered by the Department of Labor and National Service, and consequently, in early 1967, I spent a month in Long Bay Gaol, Sydney.

I applied again to a magistrate for exemption. He made no judgment on my sincerity, but refused the application on a technicality. I appealed to a judge – who started the case by relating his own war service and telling of his present work for a semi-military organisation – and he declared me, in effect, some kind of giant hoaxer with a martyr complex effect, and a desire to stir up trouble.

During these years the hoax had included chairing weekly meetings of the objectors group, extensive readings both for and against pacifism, speaking publicly and writing about my beliefs and acting as legal representative in court for six other objectors; but what took most time, energy and patience (and probably was most important in the pacifism cause) was the dialogue – when you're a "conchie" everyone wants to know why and most people want to talk it over.

Continuing the "hoax," in February I again refused to take a medical and in March I defied an order to report for military duty. I was charged with these two offences in the Special Federal Court, Sydney, on May 15 and was committed into the custody of an army officer waiting in the court.

I disobeyed his order to accompany him and he called on two Commmonwealth police who escorted me, an arm each, to a car outside. On our way to Eastern Command Personnel Depot, Watson's Bay, the officer told me I was under close arrest.

That night I slept in a room guarded by eight soldiers, two of whom, in rotation, had to stay awake.

On Thursday I had a long chat to the army psychologist and did one of those circle-the-yes-or-no-question-mark tests with questions like "Can you stand as much pain as others?" (I circled the question mark. How the hell would I know how much pain others can stand? From movies? And does "standing pain" mean without wincing, without crying, before fainting?)

The psychologist thought I was pretty stable. My conscientious objection was an administrative matter, he said.

A little later the regimental sergeant major ordered me to draw and sign for army clothes. I refused. He told me the possible consequences of disobeying could be imprisonment and ordered me again to draw the clothes and again I refused.

A summary of evidence was taken by the officer-in-command and I was remanded for court-martial.

On Thursday evening, I was brought, in a cage on the back of a utility truck, to Ingleburn and locked in this cell.

My continual requests that my family be told of my whereabouts were politely to be referred to someone higher up who was always "away" or "busy" or "trying."

I realised I was being kept incommunicado, to avoid any publicity or demonstrations.

I was getting pretty miserable. No one was allowed to converse with me. I had nothing to read but a book of psalms, no pen or paper and I was kept locked up except, for shower time and three short exercise periods a day.

Then late Saturday my younger brother and the girl I'm to marry turned up. My brother had sought help from Gough Whitlam and the member for East Sydney, Len Devine, and eventually the Army Minister. Mr. Lynch had ordered they be allowed to see me.

Suddenly I was allowed book and writing equipment. I'd refused to wear a uniform or army pyjamas and so had been living, day and night, in one suit and underwear; this morning, Sunday, my girlfriend returned with fresh clothes. Except for a flustered officer who took a stick from under his arm to shake it in my face and say, loudly, "You're in the army now, son, and it's "Yes, Sir!" I can't complain about the soldiers I've come in contact with, who have treated me as fairly as possible.

I wish not to dwell on the absence of principles of British justice in the Australian Army, but this taking away a man's privileges before he's convicted seems an incredible infringement.

Personally, I'm resentful that I've been placed in close arrest instead of open arrest (which means I am trusted to stay in the barracks) when I have given every indication that I have no intention of escaping.

I am going to see this out. I have never intended to and I never will obey military orders. The army doesn't want me, of course, but it can't "lose face" by dishonourably discharging me now.

I expect a sentence in Holsworthy Prison and maybe even further courts-martial and sentences.

The hoax goes on.

In Civil Gaol

"Fourteen ninety-three,," the newly migrated warder said with a sigh, as we ended a short discussion of conscription, "I never ever thought that there could be a political prisoner in this country…good luck to you."

"Political prisoner" has overtones of high intrigue and danger, and I'd thought the term "prisoner of conscience" was probably more applicable. My pacifist rejection of any deliberate support of the military is an ethical, humanitarian conviction rather than a consideration of political rights and wrongs. But I was a political prisoner through the decisions of a Liberal Government to join the Vietnam war, to conscript me for it and to punish me under the National Service Act if I didn't co-operate.

"Fourteen ninety-three!" barked the big warder with service ribbons on his coat. "You the joker that chickened out of the army? Y'oughta wake up to yourself..it was good enough for us to fight for you, now you should protect the country." An old lifer told me: "I took a life in a moment of madness and I've lived with the shame for 23 years. They could hang, draw and quarter me before I'd put on a uniform to help kill and destroy." But the young car thief said: I can't see what you've got against the army. I'd volunteer to get out of here. If only I'd taken my uncle's advice and joined up four years ago I wouldn't be here today. I'd have money, security and respect by now…"

So it was a mixed bag of attitudes I met as the gaol's only conscientious objector and the first since World War II. I was an oddity firstly because I was the only prisoner who needn't have been in gaol (I would have been released immediately on payment of the fine, and I refused permission to two anonymous people who came to pay it). And "conchies" are always a curiosity.

No one, warder or prisoner, ever took a poke at me, as some friends had feared would happen, and the occasional abuse was never stronger than the big warder's. I always remained so determinedly pleasant, that what some meant to be an insult session melted into lively discussion.

A gaol is hardly a paradise for conversions to a policy of love thy fellow man, but I believe at the very least I got some men thinking more seriously about questions of peace and war. I talked intently with dozens of prisoners and casually with hundreds, and using them as a representative poll, I gauge overwhelming opposition to conscription. I admit that some of this may be merely anti-authority. But through the (radio station) 2GB news services, weekend newspapers and newsmagazines, the men are quite well-informed on fact and opinion on Vietnam and I'd estimate that more than half are anti-Vietnam.

My job in gaol was pushing a broom and mop, and although I lived in fair comfort and cleanliness, the boredom and separation together with the terrible food that caused me to lose a stone in weight, made it the most miserable month of my life.

HOLSWORTHY

I was transferred here last Wednesday (May 28) after seven days in Holsworthy Military Corrective Establishment, which is several miles from here.

Even military prisons have grapevines and from what I understand there was quite a public controversy after Senator McClelland revealed that I'd been in solitary confinement on bread and water.

After the court-martial sentence of 28 days, I told a senior officer of the prison that while there my attitude and actions would be as if I was a civilian in a civil gaol. I said I would carry out cheerfully and to the best of my ability all the ordinary tasks of prison life, such as cleaning, washing, cooking, serving food, keeping the place clean and tidy, et cetera. I agreed to wear a uniform because in a civil gaol one wears a prescribed uniform.

But, I told him, I would not do anything in a military manner – I would refuse to wear a hat badge, I would refuse to march properly, I would refuse to salute and so on.

The next day I followed this out. Finally, when given a direct order to stand to attention during the evening meal parade, I refused, firmly and politely. Later I refused to lay out my kit. (A kit is all the belongings a prisoner has in his cell and they must be laid out on the mattress in an intricate and exact pattern. I simply stacked it all neatly against one wall.)

The next morning I refused to wear webbing – a small pack on the back and two ammunition pouches at the waist.

I was paraded before the commandant on four charges: three of disobeying lawful commands and a fourth of not having my kit laid out.

I was "awarded" (the commandant's word) two days' "close confinement" and two days' "PD1" rations, the Army way of saying two days' solitary on bread and water.

It had been inevitable of course, but I was somewhat afraid. Would I sink into a deep depression and go dotty? Would I end up doing my block and fling things around? It was imagination, rather than what I was experiencing, as it turned out.

At 9 a.m. on Friday, May 24, I was locked in a cell of "B Block," an oblong building of ten cells, five on each side. It sits on a plot of trimmed lawn and is surrounded by an eight-foot iron fence.

My cell had a concrete floor and ceiling and three blank concrete walls; in the fourth concrete wall was a steel door with a wired-over opening at eye level, and above it, about nine feet from the floor, were two small, barred openings.

The cell contained only a small, uncovered rubber pot holding an inch of water, a plastic flask of water...and me.

In the afternoon a New English Bible was added to my possessions after a visit from a cheery chaplain who left me slightly dispirited because he spent our regulation 20-minutes trying to get me to change my mind.

Then at 4.30 p.m. (I hadn't eaten since 7.30 a.m.) I received the regulation one lb. of bread – 13 slices of fresh white bread and an end crust. While the bread was regulated, I was welcome to as much water as I wanted...

I was dressed in sandshoes, socks, underwear, cotton shirt and trousers and jumper. I'd been chilly all day. but after the sunshine disappeared about 5 p.m., I got really cold.

I was dead-tired by this time because I'd been standing and pacing around most of the day: the floor was too cold to sit or lie on for more than a few minutes and the walls were too cold to lean against for long.

At 7.30 pm I was let out to empty the rubber pot, clean my teeth and go to the toilet. Then I was given my bedding: a rubber ground-sheet, a pillow, one blanket folded thrice to sleep on and three blankets doubled ever to cover me.

I was so tired I wasn't going to be worried even by the light outside, aimed in through one opening.

I was just getting warm and about to drift into sleep, when the door was bashed heavily several times.

The scowling face in the peephole barked: "Come on...up, up!" I jumped up. "Oright," he said. "What's yer report?"

(I'd been told earlier that when checked on by the night guard, I should say "S.U.S. (for serviceman under sentence), 28 days, staff!"

I replied: "Simon Townsend, conscientious objector, sir!"

We repeated this little performance every half hour, another 19 times during the night.

It took 10 minutes each time to rearrange the blankets and get warm, and sleep was never more than dozing and waiting, on edge, for the next knock.

At 6 a.m. I was let out for a shave and hot shower. Back in my cell, I paced around for a while, then had "breakfast" – two slices of bread and a few mouthfuls of water.

That day was pretty much the same banal existence as the previous day. I wasn't interested in reading. I read the New English Bible some years ago. As I have no religious beliefs, it a passages would not have provided comfort. When I put it to its best use at that stage as a barrier between my buttocks and the cold floor – a sergeant threatened to take it from me.

The second night was a repetition of the first. Then I was released at 9 a.m. on the Sunday.

Most of the daylight hours of those 48 hours I spent in thought as I walked or sat or leaned against the door staring out the peephole. The cell had an echo so sometimes I sang a few stirring songs; I was determined not to get too dispirited.

I don't like ordinary white bread in the best situations, and from the 26 pieces I ate only 16. That was my entire solids intake, over the two days from early Friday morning to Sunday lunch. I kept filling my belly with the abundant water, which meant having to constantly add to the rubber pot.

While I came out of this experience without the slightest psychological or physical damage, I don't hesitate to label this treatment as refined torture. Nor, in this State where the lash and leg-irons and other such indignities and cruelties have been done away with, and at this time when reason and tolerance prevail in our civil penal systems, do I hesitate to call it barbaric.

Imagine the damage that three days and nights of cold, hunger, boredom and shattered sleep could do to a 17-year-old serviceman with a personality problem or a big worry.

My two days in "B Block" was calculated to break me, and it failed. Minutes after I was out I was refusing a haircut. I was so convinced that what I was doing was right, that I felt the strength to take as much solitary and bread and water as they wanted to hand out for the rest of the 28-day sentence.

I went on refusing: to shave my sidelevers, to march, to stand attention, to salute, to wear my epaulettes outside my jumper, to learn my army number, to shine shiny brass, and also to call noncommissioned officers "staff" (I addressed all the prison officials as "sir"). I meant, and I trust I appeared, to be polite in all these refusals.

I was, I think, presenting something of a dilemma to the Army. I was obviously going to continue disobeying military procedures; if I were given solitary again it would mean more criticism; and if I were allowed to continue unpunished they would "lose face" publicly and discipline would be "undermined" in the prison.

So I was shifted here. I'm being treated not too unreasonably. While I'm willing to work around the guardhouse, I refuse to work in any other part of the barracks. Consequently I'm locked up most of the day in my tiny cell; but I'm reasonably warm and comfortable and I have plenty of books. This letter has taken three days to write because it had to be done secretly which is difficult. The food is quite good and I get exercise.

The only violence threatened me during my whole "army career" was here when I arrived on Wednesday (May 29). While two soldiers were sorting out my civilian and military belongings, I slipped back into jeans and mohair jumper. A sergeant said that if I didn't change back into "greens," he and several others would do it for me... I pointed out that pulling off my pants constituted a technical indecent assault and I could so charge him under civil law. The idea was dropped and hasn't been mentioned since.

If this is published, my thanks go to my fiancée, family and friends and many others who have given me such encouragement.

I've been warned that contact with the Press while a prisoner could mean another charge. As a young journalist who believes in the reporter's role of getting the facts and making them known, I would almost be proud to be on such a charge.

☮☮☮

THE RESISTANCE TODAY:
Happening now, wherever *you* are

☮☮☮

"Draft Dodger Rag"

Phil Ochs (1965)

I'm just a typical American boy
From a typical American town
I believe in God and Senator Dodd
And keepin' old Castro down

And when it came my time to serve
I knew better dead than red
But when I got to my old draft board
Buddy, this is what I said

Sarge, I'm only eighteen, I got a ruptured spleen
And I always carry a purse
I got eyes like a bat, and my feet are flat
My asthma's getting worse

Consider my career, my sweetheart dear
My poor old invalid aunt
Besides, I ain't no fool, and I'm goin' to school
And I'm workin' in a defense plant

I've got a dislocated disc and a racked up back
I'm allergic to flowers and bugs
And when the bombshell hits, I get epileptic fits
And I'm addicted to a thousand drugs

I got the weakness woes, I can't touch my toes
I can hardly reach my knees
And if the enemy ever came close to me
Well, I'd probably start to sneeze

Sarge, I'm only eighteen, I got a ruptured spleen
And I always carry a purse
I got eyes like a bat, and my feet are flat
My asthma's getting worse

Consider my career, my sweetheart dear
My poor old invalid aunt
Besides, I ain't no fool, I'm a goin' to school
And I'm workin' in a defense plant

I hate Chou En Lai, and I hope he dies
But I think you gotta see
That if someone's gotta go over there
That someone isn't me

So, have a ball, Sarge, watch 'em fall
Yeah, kill me a thousand or so
And if you ever get a war without any gore
Well, I'll be the first to go

Sarge, I'm only eighteen, I got a ruptured spleen
And I always carry a purse
I got eyes like a bat, and my feet are flat
My asthma's getting worse

Consider my career, my sweetheart dear
I got to water my rubber tree plant
Besides, I ain't no fool, I'm a goin' to school
And I'm workin' in a defense plant

Sarge, I'm only eighteen, I got a ruptured spleen
And I always carry a purse
I got eyes like a bat, and my feet are flat
My asthma's getting worse

Consider my career, my sweetheart dear
My poor old invalid aunt
Besides, I ain't no fool, I'm a goin' to school
And I'm workin' in a defense plant

☮☮☮

GIRLS SAY YES

to boys who say NO

Joan Baez and
her sisters,
Pauline Bryan
and
Mimi Fariña

Join The
Draft Resistance

BUDDHISM AND CONSCIENTIOUS OBJECTION TO WAR:

Buddhist Brief to the Court of Human Rights in Support of the Peace Tax Seven

Peter Harvey
University of Sunderland

Editor's note: All Buddhist disciplines must be regarded as historical peace churches. The Buddha's teachings against violence are unequivocal.

THE BUDDHIST STANCE ON VIOLENCE, PEACE AND WAR

- Buddhism is generally seen as associated with non-violence and peace. These are both strongly represented in its value system.

- Though some Buddhist countries have had their fair share of war and conflict, it is difficult to find any plausible 'Buddhist' rationales for violence.

- It can be observed that Buddhism has had a general humanising effect throughout much of Asia. It has tempered the excesses of rulers and martial people, helped large empires (e.g. China) to exist without much internal conflict, and rarely, if at all, incited wars against non-Buddhists.

- Moreover, in the midst of wars, Buddhist monasteries have often been havens of peace.

THE FIRST *UPASIKA* PRECEPT

• A fundamental value of Buddhism, non-violence, is expressed in the first and most important of the *upasika* precept-vows that all lay Buddhists are expected to adhere to.

• This is expressed as an affirmation that: 'I undertake the precept to abstain from onslaught on living beings'.

• The precept is broken if a person intentionally causes death to any sentient being: human, animal, bird, fish or insect. It is broken by a direct act of a person or by a person ordering/requesting someone else to kill a being or do an act that requires a being to be killed.

• This is seen to lead, through the law of karma, to suffering in this and future lives.

COMPASSION

• Related Buddhist values are lovingkindness and compassion. The first involves friendly concern for the welfare and happiness of all beings, including those conventionally seen as 'enemies', and the second involves concern to reduce the sufferings, and the causes of suffering, of beings.

• Compassion is foundational for Mahayana Buddhists such as those who follow the Tibetan tradition. It is held to be the central motivating factor of the path of the *Bodhisattva*. This complements the earlier formulation of the Buddhist path (the Noble Eightfold Path) with an added particular emphasis on concern for others.

BODHISATTVA VOWS

• The *Brahmajala Sutra*, a Mahayana code for lay and monastic followers which became influential in China, holds that those who take the *Bodhisattva* vows should not take any part in war.

• It forbids detention of anyone, the storing of any kind of weapons, or taking part in any armed rebellion. Those who have taken the *Bodhisattva* vows should not be spectators of battles, nor should they kill, make another kill, procure the means of killing, praise killing, approve those who help in killing.

• Its first of ten major precepts states the *Brahmajala Sutra*:
"A disciple of the Buddha shall not himself kill, encourage others to kill, kill by expedient means, praise killing, rejoice at witnessing killing, or kill through incantation or deviant mantras. He must not create the causes, conditions, methods, or karma of killing (italics added), and shall not intentionally kill any living creature."[1]

• In Tibet, the 18 root *Bodhisattva* vows also include ones not to: destroy any place by such means as fire, bombs, or pollution; or encouraging people to abandon their vowed rules of moral conduct (including non-killing).

TANTRIC VOWS

- Tibetan Buddhists also take various Tantric vows, which extend the spirit of the *Bodhisattva* vows. For example the *Kalacakra* tantric vows include one against giving up compassionate kindness for all beings.

CONSCIENTIOUS OBJECTION

- Buddhism sees even defensive violence as less than ideal.

- In line with this approach the *Dhammapada* states:
  "Conquer anger by love, conquer evil by good, conquer the stingy by giving, conquer the liar by truth" (v.223).
  "Though he should conquer a thousand thousand men in the battlefield, yet he, indeed, is the nobler victor who should conquer himself" (v.103).

- There is a sense in which all Buddhist monks and nuns are conscientious objectors to war. This is because intentional killing of a human is an offence which leads to expulsion from the monastic community, in accordance with an ancient rule instituted by the Buddha.

- While non-Buddhists in China sometimes criticised Buddhists for 'shirking military duties', it is difficult to point to any self-conscious movement for 'conscientious objection' to war in the history of Buddhist lands. This is not because the idea is alien to Buddhist values, but because the non-violent principle it is based on is so fundamental to Buddhism.

- Any right-minded Buddhist knows that they should seek to avoid violence and killing. In a context of war, they might be drawn reluctantly into defensive fighting in order to save their country or community: most lay Buddhists have been prepared to break the precept against killing in self-defence, and many have joined in the defence of the community in times of need.

NON-VIOLENT REFLECTIONS ON A VIOLENT WORLD

- There are a number of Buddhist textual passages which reflect on war and punitive violence, seeking to subvert the 'violence is sometimes necessary' of worldly common sense by a dialogue with the non-violent ideal.

- The Buddha himself came from the warrior-noble (*khattiya*) class but clearly implies that conquest leads to tragedy for the defeated, which may lead to hatred and the likelihood of a desire to overcome the conqueror.

- Without justifying defensive violence, it is pointed out that aggression often leads to defensive counter-violence, which can be seen as a karmic result for the aggressor. Such a response happens, whether or not it is justified. Thus aggression is discouraged.

- Kashi Upadhyaya comments that the peace-loving defender is portrayed as only moderately good, falling short of the ideal of complete non-violence.[2]

- Elizabeth Harris, after an investigation of early Buddhist texts, holds:
"That lay people should never initiate violence where there is harmony or use it against the innocent is very clear. That they should not attempt to protect those under their care if the only way of doing so is to use defensive violence is not so clear... The person who feels violence is justified to protect the lives of others has indeed to take the consequences into account. He has to remember that he is risking grave [karmic] consequences for himself in that his action will inevitably bear fruit... Such a person needs to evaluate motives... Yet that person might still judge that the risks are worth facing to prevent a greater evil."[3]

- If violence is then used, it is something that Buddhism may *understand* but not *approve of.*

THE DALAI LAMA AND TIBETANS' PEACEFUL OPPOSITION TO CHINESE OCCUPATION

- In the early twentieth century (1906-08), when the Dalai Lama of that time ordered soldiers to fight threatening Chinese troops, this was seen in a bad light by many Tibetans, as they felt he should not be involved in killing.[4] In fact, at the time, there were hardly any soldiers in Tibet, and the country came to be easy prey for British interference, and then the Chinese Communist takeover.

- The present Dalai Lama (the 14th, born 1935) has set up a government-in-exile in Dharamsala, India. His response to the Chinese is one of patient, but determined, non-violence.

- He sees the action of the Chinese as having reminded the Tibetans about important Buddhist principles such as impermanence, suffering and tolerance. Yet he also has unshakeable confidence in the power of compassion, humanitarianism, non-violence and truth to bring about a restoration of the Tibetans' control of their own country, and more generally in such values benefiting the world through their animation of the 'good heart' of peoples of whatever culture.

- Monks and nuns in Tibet have been very active in demonstrations against the Chinese, and many have been jailed and tortured. Some sections of the Tibetan population feel so frustrated that they have resorted to violence, but the Dalai Lama steadfastly opposes this and reiterates that the principle of non-violence should be followed.

- In 1989, the Dalai Lama was awarded the Nobel Peace Prize. In his acceptance speech, he stressed the need to transform Tibet into a zone of non-violence and peace through demilitarizing it, ending the testing and stockpiling of nuclear weapons there, and protecting the environment by setting up the world's largest natural park.

- He stresses the ideas of human rights and human equality, basing such an emphasis on the idea of the Buddha-nature shared by all.

- He is also deeply influenced by the Bodhi-caryavatara of the seventh century Indian monk Shantideva, with its emphasis that beings are equal in their desire for happiness and dislike of pain, and that the response to provocation should be patience. If Tibetans or others need to act against an aggressor, 'we should react without bad feelings. Deep down, tolerance, compassion and patience must be present'.[5] The Chinese too 'are human beings who struggle to find happiness and deserve our compassion' (Nobel Peace Prize Lecture[6]).

- For the Dalai Lama, the classical Buddhist theme of all being interdependent is especially true today, in a world where international economic, technological and environmental interaction is pervasive.

- He thus stresses that we are 'truly a global family' and by necessity must develop a sense of 'universal responsibility' (Nobel Peace Prize Lecture[7]), and:
    "It is our collective and individual responsibility to protect and nurture the global family, to support its weakest members and to preserve and tend to the natural environment in which we all live."[8]

- In this, responsibility lies not only with leaders and administrators:
    "It lies with each of us individually. Peace, for example, starts within each one of us. When we have inner peace, we can be at peace with those around us. When our community is in a state of peace, it can share that peace with neighbouring communities, and so on" (Nobel Peace Prize Lecture[9]).

- Yet he sees peace as inter-related to other issues, so that:
    "Peace can only last where human rights are respected, where the people are fed, and where individuals and nations are free" (Nobel Peace Prize Lecture[10]).

Modern warfare and its financial support

- Daisaku Ikeda, Japanese leader of the international Soka Gakkai movement holds that:
    "Modern military power must be regarded as very different from the self-defense forces with which man has been familiar throughout the ages. I see no grounds for justifying military power in the world today... I am convinced that examples of warfare conducted for the sake of veritable self-defense are rare."[11]

- In the modern context, taking part in a war is not just a question of being a soldier. Warfare is now often based on expensive, high-tech weapons that require a high level of funding by the parties involved. For states, this will come from tax revenues.

• For a Buddhist, it should be clear that selling arms is 'wrong live-lihood', so that the arms industry is fundamentally immoral. That part of a person's tax payments that go to supporting such an industry, and the death it brings, should certainly make any Buddhist morally uncomfortable.

• The earliest allusion to Buddhist attitude to taxes is in the *Aggañña Sutta*, in a passage which talks of human beings choosing their first king, so as to impose some order on society, in which property, theft and quarrelling had developed.

• It is said that people reflected:

"Suppose we were to appoint a certain being who would show anger where anger was due, censure those who deserved it, and banish those who deserved banishment! And in return, we would grant him a share of the rice."[12]

• This implies the idea of a kind of social contract. Hence when taxes are paid, this is on the implicit assumption that this is to facilitate action in support of an orderly and moral society. To evade taxes for such purposes is wrong, on Buddhist principles – indeed the Upasaka-shila Sutra says it is an offense for a lay Bodhisattva to evade taxes or appropriate public funds[13] – but so would a ruler's misuse of tax revenues.

• Indeed Buddhist texts also advise laypeople to take care of their possessions so that they are not lost by the actions of kings/rulers, thieves, fire, water, or ill-disposed heirs.[14]

• Overall, it is suggested that it is legitimate to pay taxes that support moral social purposes, but that taxes for other purposes are morally questionable.

• In a statement to Buddhist devotees in March 2003, the Dalai Lama has said, on the war in Iraq http://www.tibet.com/NewsRoom/iraq1.htm:

"The Iraq issue is becoming very critical now. War, or the kind of organized fighting is something that came with the development of human civilization. It seems to have become part and parcel of human history or human temperament. At the same time, the world is changing dramatically. We have seen that we cannot solve human problems by fighting. Problems resulting from differences in opinion must be resolved through the gradual process of dialogue. Undoubtedly, wars produce victors and losers; but only temporarily. Victory or defeat resulting from wars cannot be long-lasting. Secondly, our world has become so interdependent that the defeat of one country must impact the rest of the word, or cause all of us to suffer losses either directly or indirectly.

But what can we do? What can we do when big powers have already made up their minds? All we can do is to pray for a gradual end to the tradition of wars. Of course, the militaristic tradition may not end easily. But, let us think of this. If there were blood-shed, people in positions of power, or those who are responsible, will find safe places; they will escape the consequent hardship. They will find safety for themselves, one way or the other. But what about the poor people, the defenseless people, the children, the old and infirm. They are the ones who will have to bear the brunt of devastation. When weapons are fired, the result will be death and destruction. Weapons will not discriminate between the innocent and guilty. A missile, once fired, will show no respect to the inno-cent, poor, defenseless, or those worthy of compassion. Therefore, the real losers will be the poor and defenseless, ones who are com-pletely innocent, and those who lead a hand-to-mouth existence."

• When it comes to the current Iraq war, it is clear that it could not be counted as 'defensive'. Indeed it has added to chaos and death in Iraq and stoked resentment that feeds conflict beyond it.

• On Buddhist grounds, it seems legitimate for an individual not to lend support to it by payment of taxes which in part help it to continue.

1. *The Brahma Net Sutra*: Translated by the Buddhist Text Translation Society in USA: Buddhist Text Translation Society: http://www.purifymind.com/BrahmaNetSutra.htm

2. Upadhyaya, K.N., 1971, *Early Buddhism and the Bhagavad Gita*, Delhi, Motilal Banarsidass, page 537.

3. Harris, E.J., 1994, *Violence and Disruption in Society: A Study of the Early Buddhist Texts*, Wheel booklet no. 392/393, Kandy, Buddhist Publication Society, pages 47-8.

4. Bell, C., 1924, *Tibet Past and Present*, reprinted 1992, Delhi, Asian Educational Services, pages 121, 140.

5. Quoted on Cabezón, J.I., 1996, 'Buddhist Priciples in the Tibetan Liberation Movement', in Queen, C.S. & King, S.B. (eds.), 1996, *Engaged Buddhism: Buddhist Liberation Movements in Asia*, Albany, State University of New York Press, pages 295-320, page 304.

6. Piburn, S., ed. 1990, *The Dalai Lama; A Policy of Kindness: An Anthology of Writings By and About the Dalai Lama*, Ithaca, New York, Snow Lion, page 16.

7. Ibid page 17.

8. Ibid page 114.

9. Ibid page 19.

10. Ibid page 18.

11. Toynbee, A. and Ikeda, D., 1989, *Choose Life: A Dialogue*, Oxford, page 208.

12. Digha Nikaya III. 92: translator: Walshe, M., 1987, *Thus have I Heard: The Long Discourses of the Buddha*, London: Wisdom, page 413.

13. Shih, Heng-ching , translator 1994, *The Sutra on Upasaka Precepts*, Berkeley, Numata Center for Buddhist Translation and Research, Bukkyo Dendo Kyokai, page 82.

14. Anguttara Nikaya IV. 281-5.

☸☮☸

Sulak Sivaraksa

☮ ☮ ☮

THAILAND:
My Declaration On My 18ᵀʰ Birthday

Netiwit Chotiphatpaisal

Editor's note: In Thailand, all young men must register for the draft at age 17 and report to draw lots for military conscription by age 20. One-third are chosen, pulling the red card. Conscripts are subjected to degradation and humiliation, sometimes beatings and torture. As soldiers, they are often used as cannon fodder in the separatist insurgent south of Thailand. In other places, they become the personal servants of military officers who often enrich themselves with conscripts' meagre pay and benefits.

The military is deeply entrenched into ordinary Thais' lives, beginning with soldier-students in primary school. Despite an absence of wars for well over a century, Thailand currently ranks in the top ten countries in military spending by GDP, $6.3 billion or eight per cent of the total state expenditure. The 2014 coup spent lots of tax money on fighter planes, tanks, and submarines.

Thailand has a strong military culture, a cycle of military coups d'etat and repression while generals are in power. The generals rescind the Thai constitution so they may not be prosecuted. Corruption is rife. Military coups only occur in countries with conscription.

Similar to other countries, Thailand's head of state becomes its military commander and the military, in turn, defends the monarchy with heavy-handed repression including arbitrary detention for 'attitude adjustment', civilian trials by courts-martial with no rights to defence counsel or appeals, and enormous sentences for lèse-majesté such as 60 years for six Facebook posts.

Netiwit is the first public draft resister. A student of venerable Thai public intellectual, Sulak Sivaraksa, and part of his Network of Engaged Buddhists, a small number have formed the Thailand Peace Pledge under the slogan: "No Black, No Red – NO DRAFT!"

Privileged young men can escape the draft by bribery and many others do so by fraud. Even within the military, there is growing sentiment for a more tractable, all-volunteer military. Although Thailand is signatory to the major UN conventions on human rights, there is no protection for conscientious objectors, whether absolute pacifists or selective objectors, and no provision for alternative service. "We hope to first secure recognition for CO; next abolish the draft; then eliminate the military itself." Ω

I am a conscientious objector; this means I will not take part in conscription or government required military service in Thailand.

Military rule has dominated Thai society, not only now but also for a long time, and its power increases every year. However the Thai army is a joke for people around the world.

I think it is very important for us, to know that in this time the Thai army have tried to increase their power and brainwash civilians. For example, they banned criticism on TV as reported in the media. They defamed the Thai academics and interrogate the student activists. They controlled the text books to promote nationalism and respect to the army.

We know they want to make Thailand a military state. They have tried before and are trying again now.

Do we want to manage this situation or do we want to bury our heads in the sand like the ostrich?

If you choose the first one then we should join together! This is the time for change.

For me,

We should protest against it and move Thailand or Siam towards democracy and Human Rights, shouldn't we? We should support our young Thai people; support them in rejecting conscription.

In our time conscription is obsolete. Many countries in the world have abolished conscription or have changed the system to voluntary military service.

They have learned that the voluntary system is more efficient. And also it cultivates violence and follow the leader without thinking for themselves; it is a symbol of violence, unreasonable and anti-democratic.

We also know many people don't want to take part in conscription. They can join to The Service Training of Territorial Defence Course for 3 years. Some people, whose families have enough money, can pay under the table. However why can people not have the right to reject this out-of-date system?

Why can we, who support peace and hate war and have the potential for helping society and humanity through non-violent actions, not reject conscription? Don't forget we are citizens of the world. Non-violence can create a better society than wars, can't it?

These are my thoughts since I was 16 year old and now I am 18 years old.

Although I am grounded in Buddhism, I cannot not say I am a Buddhist in a country which is full of violence and violates Human Rights. I should say I am a conscientious man. I want to declare my intention for a peaceful land, in a country that does not allow people to have freedom of speech.

Everyone is a human being; I do not kill anyone.

I will be a 'conscientious objector',

I will not be a soldier in the Thai army or any violent army.

All for Now,
Netiwit Chotiphatphaisal
A Thai student and also an ordinary world citizen.

P.S. If you are interested, I want to persuade you to stop conscription in Thailand by becoming a conscientious objector. We want peace and democracy.

☮☮☮

MILITARY LIES IN OUR SCHOOLS
"Hey, teacher, leave them kids alone!"

CJ Hinke
(with thanks to Scott Harding and Seth Kershner)

In all, there are more than two million US soldiers parsing America's perpetual wars. Military predator drones have invaded our schools, targeting our youngest and most vulnerable citizens. Their purpose is to teach our students to believe that war and violence are normal. They need to fill the ranks, at a quarter-million soldiers per year, with fresh cannon-fodder.

Civil War veterans told inspirational war stories in schools by the turn of the 20th-century. Yet counter-recruitment only started with the Committee on Militarism in Education following World War I to address the direct conflict between military values and educational values.

Military promoters target students with low self-esteem, limited language skills, low grades, and minorities from low-income and single-parent families. This approach results in a misguided shift toward student patriotism and pride in the armed services rather seeing its true nature as a leap from the frying pan of poverty into the military's line of fire. Often, education departments, school boards, school administrators, and guidance counselors collude with military to provide student access and details without regard to personal privacy.

Military recruiters promise students a chance to see the world, never to go to foreign countries to bomb, maim, and kill. An unofficial motto in all three military 'services' is: "Join the Marines. Travel to exotic places, meet interesting people, and kill them."

The purpose of the military, to train killers without remorse, and the risks of soldiering are never mentioned. Honest possibilities of loss of life, permanent disablement and disfigurement, sexual assault, and psychological trauma do not form part of military strategy. Think about it: It's illegal to photograph the flag-draped coffins of dead soldiers.

Instead, recruiters visit a school with flash equipment, customized jeeps, humvees, armored carriers, and even tanks to impress young men and fitted with $9,000 stereo systems. David Cortright calls this a "recruitment racket." What young person could resist this sort of lure?

Young people are trained to respect, obey, and even revere those wearing uniforms but, in fact, students are intentionally told big lies. Military power has become America's national identity. Militarism enforces conformity and distrust of dissent.

10,000 military recruiters have nearly unfettered access to US public schools through the 2001 No Child Left Behind Act. In fact, it is illegal for schools to keep them out. Post 9/11 amendments to this legislation mandate that all high schools provide student information to the Pentagon, putting them on the Joint Advertising, Market Research & Studies (JAMRS) database. Scary, huh?

However, students and parents to have the right o opt-out; choose this option! If a student's name has been inadvertently added to the JAMRS database, with or without parental permission, by school authorities, students and parents may request their information is deleted.

The Pentagon has a budget of $1.4 billion per year just for military recruiting. Often, recruiters visit schools 100 days of a 180-day school year. "Preferred access" to high schools makes these schools *de facto* military recruiting stations in the name of "national security."

Where the military is welcomed into schools, counter-recruiters offering peaceful educational and vocational options are often barred. Yet counter-recruitment is critical activism which can be effective at both the organized and the personal level, in one's community – peace begins at home.

The most important purpose of counter-recruiters is to make peace a real option for students, to reject military culture, teach that a peaceful world is possible, and stop future military conflicts before they start. This is especially vital in countries using military conscription to fill the ranks.

Our kids are not toy soldiers and war is a deadly game in which real people die.

Mostly, the victors rewrite history to their own benefit. Teaching students history and social studies is most often the study of history's wars and the powerful leaders who sent young people to fight in them. It's overtime to turn this view around to teach the accomplishments of peacetime and social justice with a peace curriculum.

In the US, the start of the military lie is often the Armed Services Vocational Aptitude Battery testing begun in 1968. While the ASVAB looks like the genuine article, it has been dumbed down over decades, to allow anyone to pass.

Many school districts use ASVAB testing as a substitute for real career counseling; some even make ASVAB a requisite for high school graduation. Test results are not private unless the schools choose to specifically hold the military to that option before administering the test; few do. College Board testing costs $100; ASVAB is "free."

Military recruiters are trained to call the phones of every student tested and offer to "interpret" the test results for them at a local recruiting center. Administration of ASVAB in secondary schools accounts for 10-15% of all new military enlistments, a figure more remarkable in light of the fact a tiny percentage of students (5%, or 650,000, in 12,000 schools) take the test. Recruiters promise the military's vocational training but cannot be held to it; few military "vocations" have counterparts in the real world (unless one counts, of course, *terrorism*).

The military first invades our elementary schools with deception, then brings their sales pitch to middle and high school careers fairs. Active-duty soldiers are often offered in schools as tutors, test proctors (including ASVAB), and even "lunch buddies," picking out students sitting alone. Can you believe Ronald Reagan's 1982 quip, "What Marines have been for more than 200 years – peacemakers?" WTF!?! The dead don't talk back!

The military is expert at subtle brainwashing, of the public, the media, and our impressionable students and relies heavily on the RAND Corporation's rightwing thinktank for its strategies. The US Army's *Recruiter Journal* calls this "planting the seed" and creating "military awareness," growing an acceptance of military culture. Frankly, there is no greater delusion than nationalism; we're just not better than anybody else.

Recruiters have quotas as do all salesman: two to two-and-a-half new military enlistments every month. These predators hunt, in particular, 17-year old high school boys. Recruiters are taught "total market penetration" and "school ownership." Teachers are offered several days' expenses-paid "educators' workshops" on military bases.

The US military's advertising campaign includes such slogans as "Do something amazing" (Air Force), "Be all you can be" (Army), "Live the extreme (Air Force Reserve), and "It's not a job. It's an adventure" (Navy). The military even preys on unemployed youth: "U.S. Army. We're Still Hiring."

And they were. Big advertising companies were hired for big tax money, $667 million, to come up with these slogans and put a positive spin on mayhem, Grey Advertising (Coca-Cola, NFL), Bates Advertising (Colgate-Palmolive, Viceroy / Raleigh / Kool), BBDO Worldwide (Burger King, Exxon Mobil, Genentech, Pepsi), and Campbell-Ewald (Chevrolet), N.W. Ayer Agency (DeBeers, AT&T, Camels), GSD&M (Wal-Mart, Fannie Mae, United Healthcare), and Weber Shandwick (Anheuser-Busch, Novartis) among them.

The single most famous slogan, selling World War I, is James Montgomery Flagg's 1917 Uncle Sam poster, "I want YOU for the U.S. Army," which has become an American icon. Flagg contributed 46 posters in all to the war effort. Uncle Sam went on to sell World War II. Appropriately, the real "Uncle Sam" (Wilson) was a meat packer who supplied meat to the army during the War of 1812! The army needs a lot of meat.

Some schools and districts even offer Junior ROTC, sometimes on an automatic enrollment or compulsory basis, and often as a substitute for physical education classes. JROTC requires students to wear military uniforms, spend 50% of their time on military drills, and uses "military science" textbooks which are not submitted to competent educators for vetting.

JROTC makes the Boy Scouts look like…Boy Scouts! JROTC often includes weapons training and in-school shooting ranges. JROTC's 3,500 programs, of half a million high school students, emphasize high poverty urban areas identified by the Pentagon in partnership with the US Department of Education, often called the 'poverty draft' or economic conscription. JROTC cadets, of course, have far higher rates of military enlistment.

Schools adopting the JROTC program are required by law to have a minimum of 100 students or 10% of the student body even though it has been shown that instructors often do not have qualifications to teach. Even before JROTC, such military programs as Junior Marines and Cadet Corps target middle schools. Recruiters call our 10- to 14-year olds "pre-prospects," 'volunteering' as Cub Scouts and Boy Scouts troop leaders, and sports coaches while assessing and encouraging their propensity for military enlistment.

Even in elementary schools, the Pentagon budgets $20 million for a program called STARBASE which gets fifth-graders onto military installations to educate them how productive their STEM (science, technology, engineering, and math) skills could be put to use as a "career" in the military. Some 60,000 students per year are made part of STARBASE.

Most legislators, administrators, and educators simply have no idea how deeply entrenched the military is in our schools.

An entire military propaganda machine was created to buy media and movies, depicting our brave boys and the soldier who always gets the girl: "My hero!" War movies are still immensely popular and increasingly graphic, depicting current as well as past and future wars. Even in science fiction, the American hero often is a soldier.

Graphic violence in videogames, television, and film also contribute to young people's disconnect from real-world violence. In fact, the U.S. Army's own shooter game, America's Army, had 17 million downloads in 2004 alone. Attitudes of violence may even start with war toys.

Modern soldiers and police employ video screens to target 'enemies' far away. In the real world, targets don't come back to life for the next level.

The numerous school shootings in the US rely on disaffection in our culture of violence. Does no one notice we're broken?

During America's War on Vietnam, counter-recruitment focused on banning Reserve Officer Training Corps programs from tertiary education. However, ROTC remained in place in many schools and was reinstated on many campuses. ROTC provides the military with nearly 50% of its officer candidates who go from "green to gold" with the program.

Often college and university students are promised payment of all or part tuition in return for an obligation of eight years military service, both active and reserve, after graduation. Terms of duty may be extended under "stop-loss" programs and "re-upped," automatically redeployed to combat zones. Pilot training incurs a 10-year bit. Slogans in the air? "Peace is our profession" and "Death from above."

Can't afford college? There's always ROTC, the devil just wants you to sign right here. The myth of an all-'volunteer' military is exposed by preying on students' economic realities rather than offering genuine opportunities to the disadvantaged.

ROTC training is divided into military units which must practice and drill. ROTC cadets learn such helpful skills as "Airborne, Air Assault, Mountain Warfare, and Security Cooperation." The aim is to create a warrior ethos rather than citizen-soldiers. Do you really want to let soldiers whose unofficial motto is, "Kill 'em all. Let God sort 'em out," loose on your kids?!?

We need informed student and parental consent to programs such as JROTC, legislating student privacy, and barring military recruiters from public schools. Expose recruiters' common fraud and malpractice. No boots on quad!

Counter-recruitment is described by Scott Harding and Seth Kershner "as being *anti-militarist*. Militarism, the cultural trend that normalizes war and a constant state of military mobilization, is both pervasive and hidden in plain sight…" They cite America's 'permanent war economy'. They quote Laura Finley: "Despite the ubiquity of militarism, we are carefully taught not to notice it, acknowledge it, or call it what it is."

They include this quote from Tim Franzen of Atlanta AFSC: "I think that child soldiering is wrong in Nigeria, and it's wrong in the United States too. When we have military recruiters that are sitting at a desk speaking with 14-year olds in our school, that's child soldiering and it's happening in our own back yards… These kids are being filled with lies by folks that basically are taught the same failed techniques as used car salesmen. That's unacceptable."

Although hawks may point out the US no longer has active military conscription, all young men are still required by law to register with Selective Service within five days of their 18th birthdays. However, at least 20 million fail to register, fail to provide relevant details, and fail to update their current address up to age 26, all punishable by five years in prison and a $250,000 fine.

In the more than 100 countries still practicing military conscription, procedures vary. Some countries register young men, and some young women also, automatically, by national identity information at ages 16, 17, 18, or 19. However, others require young men and/or women to register at those ages. This is the first opportunity for resistance or refusal and to engage a support community..

Some countries have universal, mandatory conscription – everyone is drafted. Others employ selective conscription. When lots must be drawn is the second opportunity for refusal.

This is followed by a military physical examination, the third opportunity. Reporting / not reporting for induction is the last chance. After that, well, you're not behind a cow, and resistance inside the military is tougher.

The most important thing military recruiters never tell our students? That they can 'de-enlist' at any time prior to reporting for duty, with no legal or social penalties.

If Americans elect Hillary president, we can expect lots more killing and young women to register, too. Those who do not register face social sanctions such as withholding graduations, diplomas, and degrees as well as ineligibility for student loans or government employment. None have been prosecuted since 1986.

Militarism, the military economy, and military spending is the only issue US politicians should be opposing but never talk about. The infernal engines of the war machine fill the pockets of these fatcats feeding from the public trough at no risk to themselves while creating misery for American families and those in other lands. Stop leaking trillions for killing and all social services become available to everyone.

Careful readers will note the author nowhere uses the term military "service." Signing up for killing does not serve the citizen, his parents, his community, his country, his planet … or anyone else! The war corps is not the Peace Corps! It's just blood sport, pure and simple.

We need to break the vicious cycle of the military's open season on our students. Convincing students not to enlist can saves lives while undermining US designs on military intervention around the globe. Students: "War! Huh! Yeah! What is it good for? Absolutely nothing." Parents: All you'll get from the military is a neatly folded flag.

The military is a deceitful sham. Support our troops? Hell, yes! Bring them home! Celebrate life! Recruit young people for peace not war. Ω

Teaching resources

Tom Albanese, "Dismantling ROTC," Cambridge: University Conversion Project, 1992. https://groups.google.com/forum/#!topic/misc.activism.progressive/w4vZ3WEn6Rw.

Aimée Allison and David Solnit, *Army of None: Strategies to Counter Military Recruitment, End War, and Build a Better World*, New York: Seven Stories, 2007.

Joel Andreas, *Addicted to War: Why the U.S. Can't Kick Militarism, A History of U.S. Wars in Comic Book Format*, Oakland: AK Press, 2002; 3rd revised ed., 2004; 4th revised ed., 2015. Translations in Czech, Danish, Dutch, Finnish, German, Hungarian, Italian, Spanish, both Castilian and Latino, and Thai.

Lara Campbell, Michael Dawson and Catherine Gidney (Editors), *Worth Fighting For: Canada's Tradition of War Resistance from 1812 to the War on Terror*, Toronto: Between the Lines, 2015.

Chapter 6, Cynthia Comacchio, "Challenging Strathcona: The Cadet Training Controversy in English Canada, 1920-1950," pp. 79-91.

Chapter 15, Rose Fine-Meyer, "A Good Teacher is a Revolutionary: Alternative War Perspectives in Toronto Classrooms from the 1960s to the 1990s" pp 201-212.

Paul R. Carr and Brad J. Porfilio, *Educating for Peace in a Time of Permanent War: Are Schools Part of the Solution or the Problem?*, Abingdon: Routledge, 2013.

Paul J. Ciborowski, "Choosing the Military As a Career: A Group Counseling Program that Addresses Issues Not Presented by Recruiters," *School Counselor* Vol. 41, No. 4, March 1, 1994.

Paul J. Ciborowski, "Deciding on a Military Career—The High School Counselor's Role," Chronicle Guidance Publications, *Professional Paper* P92-15, March 1, 1994.

Nakazawa, Keiji, *Barefoot Gen*, 10 volumes, San Francisco: Last Gasp & Project Gen, 2004-2010. Translations in Chinese, Esperanto, German, Norwegian, Swedish, and Finnish.

Pat Elder, *Military Recruitment in the United States*, North Charleston: CreateSpace, 2016.

Owen Everett (Editor), *Sowing Seeds: The Militarisation of Youth and How to Counter It*, London: War Resisters' International, 2013. http://www.wri-irg.org/SowingSeedsOnline.

Rory Fanning, "The Wars in Our Schools: An Ex-Army Ranger Finds a New Mission," TomDispatch, April 7, 2016. http://www.tomdispatch.com/post/176125/tomgram%3A_rory_fanning%2C_talking_to_the_young_in_a_world_that_will_never_truly_be_%22postwar%22/.

Scott Harding and Seth Kershner, *Counter-Recruitment and the Campaign to Demilitarize Public Schools*, New York: Palgrave Macmillan, 2016.

Wally Heinrichs and Rob Macintosh, *The Canadian Peace Educators' Directory*, Calgary: Pembina Institute for Appropriate Development, 1990.

John Hunter, *World Peace and Other 4th-Grade Achievements*, Boston: Eamon Dolan. Mariner, 2013.

Seth Kershner, "STARBASE: The Military's Effort to Indoctrinate Children," *Draft NOtices*, October-December 2015. http://www.comdsd.org/article_archive/ STARBASE.html.

Colman McCarthy, *I'd Rather Teach Peace*, Maryknoll: Orbis, 2008.

Mark Moss, *Manliness and Militarism: Educating Young Boys in Ontario for War*, Don Mills: Oxford, 2001.

New York Civil Liberties Union, *Soldiers of Misfortune: Abusive U.S. Military Recruitment and Failure to Protect Child Soldiers*, New York: NYCLU, 2008.

New York Collective of Radical Educators (NYCoRE), *Camouflaged: Investigating How the U.S. Military Affects You and Your Community*, 2011. http://www.lulu.com/spot-light/nycore.

Connie E. North, *Teaching About Social Justice? Voices from the Front Lines*, Boulder, Paradigm, 2009.

Jody Sokolower, *Teaching About the Wars*, Milwaukee: Rethinking Schools, 2013. http:// www.rethinkingschools.org/ ProdDetails.asp?ID=9781937730475.

Barbara Wein (Editor), *Peace and World Order Studies: A Curriculum Guide*, New York: World Policy Institution, 1984.

James Wood, *Militia Myths: Ideas of the Canadian Citizen Soldier, 1896–1921*, Vancouver: University of British Columbia, 2010.

Cultivating Peace http://www.cultivatingpeace.ca/pematerials/online.html. Peacemakers Trust http://www.peacemakers.ca/education/educationlinks.html.

☮☮☮

AFTERWORD

United States Penitentiary

12 911 NE

SIMPLE FACTS:
The Cost of Killing

CJ Hinke

Proposed conscription bills in England in 1704 and 1707 were found to be unconstitutional, although two acts in the 1750s allowed the impressment of vagrants. In fact, it was not uncommon for naval press gangs to sweep up Quakers for England's wars on Holland and France in this period. In 1757, Quakers were exempted from England's militia service.

The New World was largely settled by those migrants with high conscience. They voted with their feet. Many of these peacemakers refused to appropriate Indian land, keep arms in self-defense, or retreat into armed stockades during hostilities.

In 1658, Francis Barnes, Michael Brooks, Henry Carline, William Cole, Edward Coppedge (who was also 'whipt' by order of the military officers), William Davis, Hugh Drew, Robert Dunn, Susanna Elliot (for her servant's refusal), William Elliott, John Ellis, William Fuller, John Hinchman, Richard Keene, John Knap, Thomas Homewood, Thomas Mears (for the refusal of his son), William Muffitt, William Read, William Stockden, Guy White, and Ishmael Wright in the province of Maryland refused to take up arms and were fined and abused by the sheriff. Quakers and pacifists throughout the colonies exercised "passive" resistance, refusing military training against the Indians.

In 1672, eight Quakers from Flushing in the province of New York, refused to contribute to reparations of a fort against the Indians. In 1673, Rhode Island became the first new province to write conscientious objection into law followed by North Carolina while Quakers in Pennsylvania were America's first tax refusers in opposition to the French and Indian wars. Notably, the statutes provided that COs not "suffer any punishment, fine, distrait, penalty nor imprisonment."

During this period, Quaker conscientious objection was also prevalent in the English West Indian colony of Barbados where refusers were called 'Quaking-dogs'. Some were brutally beaten and others heavily fined in sugar. The situation was much the same in Jamaica, although fines were in cash. In Antigua and Nevis, Quakers were offered civilian service jobs. Dozens of Friends refused to serve in the militias against the Spanish.

In 1703, a 22-year old Friend was gaoled in Dartmouth for refusal to fight the French colonists and their Indian supporters, first for seven months and two days, then again for four months and four days, on a naval vessel. Ill luck accompanied him and another Friend on a journey to England when they were impressed to fight the French, confined, whipped and beaten on shipboard.

In 1704, Quakers in West New Jersey refused to join the militia. And a sympathetic jury refused to convict them. 1712 saw five Quakers from New England Yearly Meeting gaoled for refusal to join a military expedition into Canada. One of the Friends, John Terry, died from his abuse by military officers. In 1748, another Friend was gaoled for six months and fined in Boston for refusing military impressment.

During the French and Indian War, from 1754 to 1763, every 20th man could be drafted into the militia led by a 24-year old Colonel George Washington. Virginia continued to harass Quaker COs, including threat of execution for treason. Seven COs were starved in military guardhouse and then forced-marched with other conscripts. As they would not work, they had no right to "the King's victuals"; as the fare was military, the Quakers would not pay for it. Their eventual sentences, to 500 lashes was never carried out. Following appeals by leading Quakers, G.W. ordered them freed in 1756. He asked of Quakers only that he himself be treated with equal kindness. Four Virginia Mennonites and at least one Baptist fared better, with only fines for their refusal.

One of the earliest laws passed by the Continental Congress was to exempt COs. James Madison inserted a clause into the first draft of the U.S. Constitution included protecting the right of conscience. His proposed Second Amendment read, "The right of the people to keep and bear arms shall not be infringed; a well armed and well regulated being the best security of a free country: but no person religiously scrupulous of bearing arms shall be compelled to render military service in person."

This wording was approved by the House but rejected by the Senate so never was written into the U.S. Constitution. This ensured that conscientious objection was merely a privilege to be granted or withdrawn by the Federal government. The earlier colonies' laws protecting COs were struck down by the new Constitution.

Around 10 to 15 percent of colonists, some 250,000, opposed the American Revolution, both actively and passively. Revolutionary War objectors in general only spent a day or two in prison but one CO in Lancaster, Pennsylvania spent two years in prison and another in North

Carolina suffered a brutal lashing. Although the Constitution contained no provision for military conscription, the Supreme Court did not uphold that power until the dawn of World War I in 1918.

Vietnam draft 'dodgers' were, of course, not the first to flee the U.S. for the safe harbor of Canada. In 1783, 46,000 Tories, or United Empire Loyalists, three per cent of the U.S. population, left New York after the American Revolution to find British refuge in Parrtown, near Saint John in present-day New Brunswick. Many had had their property confiscated by the revolutionaries; they could not vote, sell land, sue debtors, or work as lawyers, doctors, or teachers. In all, 70,000 Loyalists fled the 13 colonies. Benjamin Franklin preferred to call them 'Royalists'.

These British settlers displaced New France in which is now Quebec, receiving 200 acres each. 7,000 remained in Upper Canada, now the Canadian province of Ontario. One fifth of Canadians can trace their ancestry to Loyalists. U.E. is still the only Royal title allowed in Canada, for preserving the unity of the British Empire. They were joined by 2,000 Iroquois, Mohawk, and other pro-British native Americans from the Five Nations, settling in Grand River, the shores of Lake Ontario, and the Bay of Quinte.

At least 8,000 black slaves traveled with the settlers. Many of these slaves were freed – but never equal – or returned to Africa to settle Sierra Leone. 3,500 freed slaves settled New Brunswick and coastal Nova Scotia. England paid the fledgling USA $1,204,960 in reparations for the loss of their slaves.

Two hundred and fifty thousand Loyalists also left the U.S. for other British possessions in the West Indies and Bahamas. Some returned to England. They felt, "Better to live under one tyrant a thousands miles away than a thousands tyrants one mile away."

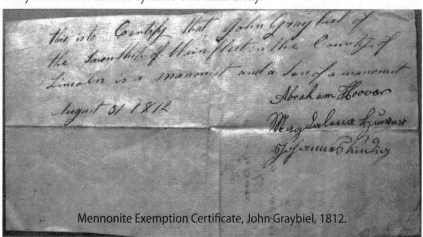

Mennonite Exemption Certificate, John Graybiel, 1812.

These wounds were not healed by the time of the War of 1812-1814. These new Canadians marched to Washington, burned down the White House, and went home. The Canadians won.

In 1807, the fledgeling United States legally abolished the international slave trade. However, domestic slave sales and transport remained perfectly legal. In 1829, Canadian abolitionist William Lloyd Garrison, a fiery speaker and uncompromising advocate for freedom, became co-editor of the Quaker newspaper, *Genius of Universal Emancipation*.

Garrison went on to found the New England Anti-Slavery Society in 1832 and the American Anti-Slavery Society in 1833. He always equated women's rights with opposition to slavery and became an early advocate for universal women's suffrage. When slavery was finally abolished, Garrison became a champion for black suffrage as well.

In 1838, Garrison published his anti-war "Declaration of Sentiments" for a Peace Convention sponsored by the New England Non-Resistance Society. Anti-slavery pacifists compared the evils of war to the evils of enslavement.

This remarkable statement was a gauntlet for non-coöperation in the coming Civil War. It called for mass civil disobedience opposing the military to frustrate government's ability to wage war, including draft and tax refusal for the Civil and later the Mexican-American wars.

Le droit des gens [*The Law of Nations*] by Emmerich de Vattel was published in Switzerland in 1758. The treatise deals with the political philosophy of lawmaking, its theory and practice. The Supreme Court of Pennsylvania upheld the war's draft law, the Enrollment Act of 1863, by relying on *Le droit*, by then a 100-year old book.

The U.S. Secretary of War, James Monroe, had proposed a military draft in 1814 but the prospect horrified the signers of the Hartford Convention who declared Congress had no such power. In fact, the convention proposed a constitutional amendment which was never acted upon.

The Confederacy passed its three year draft law in 1862. In 1863, the Union government enacted the country's first draft law, the Enrollment Act of 1863. These were widely unpopular and divisive laws, leading to fraud in the South and riots in the North.

Both exempted draftees who were able to hire substitute soldiers for a payment of $300. 300,000 men were drafted in the Union but only 260,000 actually showed up and 165,000 failed the entrance standards, leaving only 46,000 to 95,000 draftee soldiers, seven percent of the total called up. There were 800,000 Union volunteers but 74,000 hired substitutes.

In that same year, the Pennsylvania Supreme Court became the only U.S. court ever to exhaustively consider the constitutionality of military conscription. Conscription was found to be unconstitutional three-two and the government enjoined from drafting the appellant. However, only a month later, the term of Pennsylvania's chief justice expired. The federal attorney moved swiftly to have the injunction overturned and the court reversed its decision.

The draft had been unconstitutional for only two months in U.S. history, leaving conscription, in the words of Missouri Congressman Thomas B. Curtis, "one of the most sacred taboos in American political life."

In 1864, the North enacted provisions for conscientious objection to their draft laws by which religious COs would agree to hire a substitute or pay $500 directly. Most pacifists, naturally, refused. Over 500 Union Army soldiers were imprisoned as conscientious objectors after being inducted against their will; no precise figures are available but it is thought many more were in similar difficulties in the Confederacy. The South enacted provision for conscientious objection two years before, in 1862. Still, 12 Southern Quakers were forcibly marched to the Battle of Gettysburg but never took up arms.

Sovereign peoples were not safe from American imperialism anywhere. Hawai'i did not follow the succession rules for European monarchies. Each monarch was elected by a native legislature.

Lili'uokalani became Crown Princess in 1877. Although she had attended Queen Victoria's coronation as queen regant, American businessmen were threatened by her Hawai'ian constitution. In 1893, U.S. Marines and Navy deposed the last monarch of Hawai'i and annexed the territory as a "protectorate" of the United States.

The queen was arrested and sentenced by a military tribunal to five years hard labor in 1895. Lili'uokalani is remembered for her support for Buddhist and Shinto freedom of religion. Hawai'i was made a U.S. (vassal) state in 1959 after being conquered by military force.

8.5 million soldiers and 12.6 million citizens were killed during World War I in only four years: WWI was called "the war to end all wars." However, this slaughter was in vain. WWI codified the causes of war among countries, only serving to set the stage for WWII.

WWI cost the U.S. $20 billion; adjusted to 2013, $263 billion, or 13.6% of America's GDP.

A 1918 U.S. Supreme Court case upheld the first draft law since the Civil War, the Selective Service Act of 1917, by referring to the Pennsylvania decision reached by using de Vattel's *Le droit*. Furthermore, this decision was used to justify the legality of military conscription laws in that year in at least 36 countries! The court found the SSA did not violate the 13th amendment's prohibition of involuntary servitude or the first amendment's protections for freedom of conscience.

Of 2.8 million U.S. soldiers, only 1,300 were exempted as COs and those as noncombatant support for the military, 0.14%, from a total application for status by 64,700 draftees. Only 450 were 'absolutist' war resisters who were then subjected to military courts-martial. They were supported by the American Union Against Militarism. The National Civil Liberties Bureau, (later the present-day ACLU), was founded in 1917 by Roger Nash Baldwin, himself a CO prisoner, specifically to aid CO prisoners and expose brutal military prison conditions and treatment of COs. An additional 4,750 civilians were prosecuted in civilian courts for opposing conscription.

During the 1870s, some 18,000 Mennonites had fled Russia for the United States with government promise of alternative service. However, during WWI, 145 of the court-martialed COs, or 30 percent, were Mennonites. 600 to 800 Mennonites and 1,000 Hutterites moved to Canada to avoid conscription.

17 COs were sentenced to death, 142 to life imprisonment, and 73 to 20, 25, or 30 years. 17 died in such brutal prisons as Fort Jay, Leavenworth, and Alcatraz: 12 religious pacifists, three socialists, and two others whose persuasions are unremembered. At least one absolutist in Georgia was tarred and feathered and died of his injuries; at least one other committed suicide; and others were confined to insane asylums as punishment.

Thousands of other anti-war anarchist, socialists, and other radical were arrested under the Espionage and Sedition Act of 1917, setting the scene for Attorney-General's Palmer's Red-scare raids, arrests , and de-portations in 1919 and 1920. (This same antiquated law is being used by the Obama administration against government whistleblowers Chelsea Manning, Edward Snowden and seven others in the 21st century.)

The last American CO was not released until November 1920, two full years after the armistice.

In England, even the Duke of Wellington saw an army as "the national and filthy receptacle … for the misfits of society," forcing government to en-act a law to enable an army on an annual basis. 16,000 COs refused England's 1916 Conscription Act during the Great War. During World War II in Britain alone, 60,000 men and 1,000 women applied for conscientious objector sta-tus. Arrests of COs began in March 1916. In all, 5,739 CO men and 500 CO women served prison time by military courts martial. 850 served 20 months or more and some nearly three years. At the expiration of sentence, COs could again be ordered and prosecuted a second and third time.

Although COs were remanded to civilian prisons such as Wandsworth, Wormwood Scrubs and Dartmoor, they were made to wear uniforms, black with white arrows, identifying them as military prisoners and often served in separate sections of the prisons. Some Canadian COs served their time in British prisons, too.

The 1917 conscription act was immensely unpopular in Canada, es-pecially among the Québecois. Large demonstrations on Easter weekend in 1918 resulted in a protester being killed and another arrested for failing to carry his draft papers. Crowds attacked the office of the army registrar and pitched files out into the snow. The federal government responded with soldiers: four civilians were killed.

Some English COs were actually sent to the battlefields in France. When they refused to pick up arms, they were sentenced to death, later commuted to 10 years at hard labor due to protests at home. Although the armistice came at the end of 1918, some COs were not released until mid-1919.

Although no figures are available for COs in New Zealand, those who advocated against conscription were charged with sedition.

Nowhere as numerous, COs were also sentenced to prison in France, Russia, Austria-Hungary, Serbia and Bulgaria, Scandinavia, Switzerland, and the Netherlands.

The United States began to plan for peacetime conscription by 1926.

In the inter-war years 1936-1939, the Spanish Republican majority or Loyalists was attacked by Franco's fascist rebels, the Nationalists, resulting in the Spanish Civil War. Hitler's Germany, Mussolini's Italy, and Salazar's Portugal armed the fascists; the Soviet Union supplied the loyalists...for cash. International Brigades of 59,380 volunteer soldiers were organized into national battalions from 52 countries to fight the fascists.

The very monstrousness of the civil war caused many pacifists, including David Dellinger who drove a Quaker ambulance from France, to question the strength of their commitment to nonviolence. 16% of foreign brigadiers, nearly 10,000, were killed and 12.9% badly wounded. In all, 500,000 were killed, 10% of all soldiers. The result: Franco ruled Spain with an iron fist for the next 36 years and embarked on a killing spree against the leftist and anarchist Republicans.

The history of military volunteers is far better recorded than that of nonviolent activists. However, even in Spain, there were *insumisos* (defiant ones, the conscientious objectors) working for peaceable alternatives. Notable Spanish pacifists such as José Brocca saw no choice but to act against fascism.

Brocca organized peasant agricultural workers to maintain food supplies, helped with the evacuation of children from war zones, both Republican and Nationalist, arranged for their schooling, and offered humanitarian efforts for war refugees, including an underground railroad escape route to France. Much of these relief efforts were assisted by War Resisters' International and Fellowship of Reconciliation.

Dra. Amparo Poch y Gascón was co-leader of the Liga Española de Refractarios a la Guerra, a group of absolutist war resisters. She also was active in the Orden del Olivo (Order of the Olive Branch), the Spanish section of WRI during the civil war.

The imprecise figures of World War II dead hovers between 35 and 60 million. In other words, nobody even cared enough to count. The fiscal cost to the U.S. for World War II was $296 billion, equal in 2013 to $5 trillion, 35.8% of the total GDP.

Although there were isolated instances of nonviolent resistance to fascism, particularly in regards the extermination of the Jewish population, in half a dozen European nations, most citizens were apathetic and acquiescent. Only where the local population resisted repression did authorities turn a blind eye rather than provoke confrontation.

In World War II, COs were still arguing freedom of conscience and involuntary servitude against the Selective Training and Service Act of 1940 though these had been previously rejected by the courts in WWI. The courts did find, however, that those not taking the step forward to receive the military oath remained solely under civil law, and 15,000 men were committed to prison terms of up to six years in Federal prisons during World War II, some of them blacks who refused to fight in a segregated Jim Crow army, Puerto Rican nationalists, interned Japanese-Americans, and Native Americans who did not consider they had any duty to fight and kill for a government which subjected them to daily abuses and denial of rights. Rather than the Draconian military sentences of WWI, COs faced a maximum of five years in civil prisons. And the U.S. military was still firmly segregated by race. Meanwhile, the draft law generated 1.2 million soldiers by six months prior to the Japanese attack on Pearl Harbor.

Of these, 8,000 considered themselves to be conscientious objectors to all wars, 0.15%, but only precisely 10% of the total number, 1,500, were granted presidential pardons as late as 1948. Over 16,000 more were sent to work at payless slave labor in Civilian Public Service camps throughout the country. The CPS camps were administered by the traditional peace churches and each CPS objector had to pay his own monthly keep in penance for bearing moral scruples.

The final Billings decision was written in 1944 by Supreme Court Justice William O. Douglas. Arthur Goodwyn Billings applied for CO status but was rejected by his draft board because he was an agnostic and Gandhian.

He reported for induction but refused to be fingerprinted or to take the oath. The government claimed Billings was subject to military law. "The 1940 draft law specifically said, 'No person shall be tried by any military or naval court in any case unless such person *has been actually inducted* [emphasis supplied].' The Selective Draft Act of 1917 contained precisely the opposite provision: 'All persons drafted into the service of the United States shall, from the date of such draft, be subject to the laws and regulations governing the Regular Army.'

Although convicted by both trial court and Circuit Court of Appeals, they were reversed by the highest court. However, the Supreme Court said, "We have no doubt of the power of Congress to enlist the man-power of the nation for prosecution of the war and to subject to military jurisdiction those who are unwilling, as well as those who are eager, to come to the defense of their nation in its hour of peril. But Congress did not choose that course in the present emergency. It imposed a separate penalty on those who defied the law – prosecution by the civilian authorities . . . "

Billings' *convictions* were frequently cited by lower courts in the early war years but later courts, especially during the American war on Vietnam relied on the final verdict.

"One more thing. The District Court judge in this case just could not restrain himself and added this in his written decision: 'Were Billings given his just deserts [*sic*], he would be consigned to the German and Japanese murderers, where common, decent, human actions and sympathy abide not.'" [Thanks to Jerry Elmer for clarification of this important case.]

Before World War II, 37,000 draft-age men pledged themselves conscientious objectors to war. Thus the first alternative Civilian Public Service Camp was opened in December 1940, a full year before the Pearl Harbor attack and U.S. declaration of war. This followed the passage of the Selective Training and Service Act of 1940.

The World War II draft generated 10 million soldiers by the time the bomb was dropped. Of 34,506,923 WWII Selective Service registrants, 72,354 draftees applied for CO status, 2/10 of one per cent! According to the U.S. Bureau of Prisons, 6,086 COs went to prison, making a CO one of every six federal prisoners. Of these, excluding Jehovah's Witnesses, only 1,675 were absolutist objectors. 11,950 COs joined 150 CPS camps scattered across America.

By far, the most tragic case was cited in Kohn. George Elder, a hobo and American native Indian was arrested in 1942 for failing to notify his draft board of his change of address. The judge was so enraged by Elder's pacifist sentiments that he had Elder committed to a mental institution. Although the examining psychiatrist found Elder intelligent and lucid, he was found to be suffering from *dementia præcox* , the inability to distinguish reality from illusion. Elder was not released from Philadelphia's Byberry Mental Institution until 1970, at age 68, after being hospitalized for 28 years.

When the 1940 draft law expired in 1947, the U.S. had no conscription for only 15 months. Registration was required again in 1948 and continued for another 25 years. By 1949, government had indicted 62 men for refusal to register and others, notably Larry Gara, for counseling refusal.

Korea was divided as a spoil of war between the Soviet Union and the United States in 1945. The American "police action" in Korea lasted from mid-1950 to mid-1953. 220,000 men were drafted to fight by the end of 1950. In all, more than 1.8 million American soldiers fought the Chosin war. Well over a million Koreans were killed in the war and 44,692 American soldiers died. This was not M.A.S.H.

Those are the human costs. The U.S. fiscal costs were 4.1% of America's total GDP – $30 billion; adjusted to 2013, equivalent to $360 billion.

Following the war, the number of conscientious objectors to America's first peacetime draft grew exponentially, from 1.64% in 1952 to 9.17% in 1956.

Dozens were imprisoned as Communists under the Smith Act because of the histrionics late Senator Joseph McCarthy. Those not US-born, particularly anarchists, were summarily deported, many to home countries they could not remember. 110,000 Japanese-Americans had their properties and monies seized by the government and were interned in camps. The Japanese camps are still maintained in readiness by the Federal government for use on all of us under the detention provisions of the McCarran "Red" Act. There will not be any warning, just as there was none for the Japanese.

The U.S. war on Vietnam killed uncounted millions of Vietnamese civilians, in addition to 1,134,787 combatants including those soldiers of U.S. allies South Korea, Australia, New Zealand, and Thailand.

The United States mostly warred with other white men. However, the hidden racist component had reared its head with racial segregation in the military and came into full flower when we fought the Japs, Nips, and Zipperheads. Korea proved to be another racist war, this time assisting our allies, the Biscuitheads, Bucketheads, DAK (Dumb Ass Koreans), Dog Breaths, Kinks, Moose, Shovelheads, and Underbites.

By Vietnam, "the enemy" was not even regarded as human, as recorded by the Winter Soldier Investigation into American war crimes sponsored by Vietnam Veterans Against the War in 1971. VCs, Charlies, Dinks, Ducks, Gooks, and McGooks when they had been killed, Slants, Sloats, Slopes, and Tunnel Rats could simply be hunted and slaughtered with no fear of retribution.

In the present day, Iraqis, Afghanis, and other Muslims have been dehumanized as Beekeepers (women), Crunchies, Headbangers, Mozzies, Muzzies, Ragheads, Rugriders, Whackies, and Hajjis. Who's next?

By 1963 the Vietnam draft was responsible for one-third of all military enlistments and 41% of its officers. In 1962 and 1963, between 6,300 and 9,400 young men were being drafted per month; by the end of 1965, 35,000 to 40,000 *every month*. In 1966, 767,935 men sat for the Selective Service Qualification Test.

27 million men were available in the draft pool. Of these, over two million were drafted, 8,720,000 enlisted or volunteered. 16 million did not serve in the military; of these, 15 million received deferments, exemption, or disqualifications. Of those men on active duty, about two million actually were sent to Vietnam, about 10 per cent of the total U.S. male population who reached 18 during the Vietnam period.

Selective Service local boards were 66.3% made up of old white men with military backgrounds. 71% were 50 or older; 22% over over 70. No women served as members and precious few blacks.

As the Selective Service System was created by executive order of the President, it was ruled by administrative fiat and draftees could not avail themselves of the Constitutional right to judicial oversight and remedy. Between 1965 and 1975, 22,467 young men were prosecuted; 8,756 were convicted, 4,001 imprisoned. In 1969 there were 1,744 prosecutions; by 1972 that number had risen to 4,906.

In 1967, draft prosecutions resulted in a conviction rate of 75%; 89% were sentenced to jail with an average sentence of 32 months. However, the percentage of SSA prosecutions dropped steadily by year as did convictions and sentences. By 1970, only 36.3 percent were convicted with 45% jailed; by 1975, less than 16.6 percent were convicted and less than nine percent were sentenced to prison terms. By 1974, prison terms had dropped to a low of 14.5 months.

Recognition for COs also increased incrementally. By 1970, 25.55 percent of inductees were granted objector status. That rose to 42% in 1971. By 1972, 12% of draftees were being prosecuted for refusal.

One hundred seventy thousand draft-age men were granted CO deferments during the Vietnam years; another 300,000 were denied. Nearly 600,000 evaded the draft and 200,000 were charged with draft "crimes." At least 200,000 draft exiles and 100,000 military deserters escaped to Canada between 1962 and 1973. A further 20,000 decamped for third countries or lived underground in America through the war years.

A young man could kill at age 18 but not vote, or drink, until 21.

Canada opened its gates to American draft resisters and deserters. Canadian Prime Minister Pierre Elliot Trudeau is famously quoted as saying, "Canada should be a refuge from militarism," echoing an appeal by Mennonites. Between 1962 and 1973, a total of more than 200,000 accused draft resisters and 100,000 military deserters fled to Canada, 80,000 in 1972 and 1973 alone. Some of these Americans may have returned to the US after the war on Vietnam but many settled in Canada and irrevocably changed the face of politics and activism in Canada. Canadian tolerance trumped American aggression.

In 1968, 40,000 U.S. soldiers deserted; by 1969 that number had increased to 53,000 – one deserter every ten minutes! A total of half a million U.S. soldiers deserted during the Vietnam era, 57% of whom had voluntarily enlisted.

By Vietnam, waging war had gotten way more efficient. Although the fiscal costs for U.S. involvement against Vietnam only represented 2.3% of our GDP, military expenditures totaled $111 billion or more than $700 billion in 2013.

As of March 1970, more than 90 people declared their participation in draft board raids, resulting in the destruction of more than half a million records. We may find this hard to imagine in the computer age but burning draft files, pouring blood or black paint really did result in the removal of a potential soldier from the system. 40% of all draft records in Minnesota were destroyed.

While our nation was busy fighting its undeclared wars, our covert wars also never stop. Lest any state feel they had the right to sovereignty and self-determination, CIA spooks got to work destabilizing Albania, Angola, Brazil, Bulgaria, Cambodia, Chile, Colombia, Congo, Cuba, Dominican Republic, East Timor, Ecuador, El Salvador, Haiti, Italy, Greece, Grenada, Guatemala (twice), Haiti, Indonesia (twice), Iran, Laos, Nicaragua, Peru, Uruguay, Zaire and overthrowing governments we just didn't like. And let's not leave out U.S. influence over Canada and Mexico.

If these tactics failed to put those foreigners in their place, the CIA resorted to assassination. Political actors in Argentina, Cambodia, Chile, China, Congo, Costa Rica, Cuba, Dominican Republic, France, Egypt, Haiti, India, Indonesia, Iran, Iraq, Jamaica, Lebanon, Libya, Morocco, Nicaragua, Panama, the Philippines, North and South Korea, South Vietnam, Venezuela, West Germany, Zaire were soft targets for extrajudicial murder or its attempts not even to mention Saddam Hussein and Osama bin Laden.

The CIA's specialty in tradecraft lies in lies, lies to prop up dictatorships, lies to organize *coups d'etat*. America's more recent tactics embrace fomenting populist movements, such as the "Arab Spring"s and the color revolutions as well as subverting human rights organizations to get rid of the CIA dictators we grew tired of. Every continent. Did I leave anybody out?

The practice of conscription was halted in 1972, more than two years before U.S. withdrawal from Vietnam, canceling the 1948 peacetime draft. The illegal war was discredited and resisters vindicated.

As his first official act as President, Jimmy Carter pardoned all those indicted for Selective Service Act violations, on January 22, 1977. Registration stopped in 1975. With typical government folly, draft registration was reinstated in July 1980, a policy called "deep standby" by President Carter following the Soviet Union's invasion of Afghanistan. 30,000 demonstrators marched in Washington to oppose registration.

In only five years, more than 800,000 young men had 'silently' failed to register...but 12 million had complied. More than three times as many refused to register between 1980 and 1984 as did during the entire war on Vietnam 1964-1973, estimated at 250,000. Only 20 vocal refusers were prosecuted in the decade 1980 to 1990. Of these, five indictments were quashed and convictions resulted in an average sentence of only 42 days although one resister, Paul Jacob of Little Rock, was sentenced to the maximum five years and others to two years in prison. Gilliam Kerley of Madison plead "not guilty by reason of sanity." Also prosecuted was Phetsamay Maokhamphio, a Laotian refugee.

In 1984, Congress repealed the Youth Corrections Act by which non-registrants could have their felony convictions expunged on completed of their sentence. In 1985, Congress raised the maximum fine for non-registration to $250,000. The Federal government's new, improved strategy, the Solomon Amendment, is to refuse student loans, grants or work-study as did several state governments as punishment for noncoöperation. However, churches, peace groups and tertiary institutions generated their own funding for nonregistrants who were denied aid.

The U.S. government claims 90% compliance with registration by age 20. Selective Service considers registration a powerful diplomatic deterrent and a powerful weapon alongside bombers and missiles, certainly good enough reason to refuse it.

Following two warning letters, Selective Service forwards nonregistration cases to the Justice Department which, nearly invariably, does nothing about them. If a nonregistrant, however, makes enough noise, they send out letters, followed by referral to the F.B.I. to investigate before convening a grand jury to indict the miscreant. Sounds *expensive*, doesn't it? Initially, a five-year statute of limitations applied to Federal crimes which would have provided *de facto* exemption for silent nonregistrants. However, in 1971, Congress had raised the statute for draft offenses to age 31.

Military conscription is only necessary in states which have lost their legitimacy and therefore their ability to inspire loyalty. The alternative is noncoöperation.

Mobilization of Selective Service registrants in a "national emergency" could occur in as little as two weeks on orders of the president. "You're in the army, son."

War Resistance Walk, Canada 2008.

Even in a volunteer military, several dozen men and women refused to deploy to Iraq by December 1990. By the time of the cease-fire in 1991, 2,500 soldiers had sought CO discharges and at least 42 Marines were sentenced from six to 36 months in the brig.

Elizabeth May, Green Party of Canada chair, states, "The UN Handbook on Refugees is clear: soldiers who refuse to participate in wars that have been condemned by the international community should be considered refugees. Canada has a proud history of welcoming conscientious soldiers who lay down their arms in the name of peace, and we should welcome today's objectors with the same pride we had when we welcomed Vietnam War resisters."

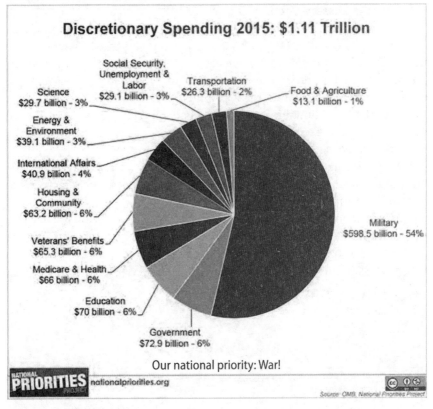

Inevitably, one must be reminded of Ground Zero, the name applied to a nuclear detonation. Of the 350,000 residents of Hiroshima, at least 140,000 were vaporized in an instant on August 6, 1945, others burned alive in the ensuing firestorm, and a further 100,000 dying of radiation sicknesses. Of a population of 250,000 in Nagasaki on August 9, 1945, at least 80,000 were killed immediately. In April 2016, the US Secretary of State visited Hiroshima's Peace Park and refused to apologize for this heinous act.

These figures are far different from the 3,000 Americans who perished in New York City on September 11, 2001. However, both acts were premeditated murder on a colossal scale, war crimes of the greatest magnitude. That one was perpetrated by politicians and the other by "terrorists" makes no difference to the dead. All these innocents died in vain if we do not, once and for all, put an end to war.

The Doomsday Clock maintained by the Bulletin of the Atomic Scientists was set at seven minutes to doomsday; it's even worse in 2012 – five minutes to go. It's difficult not to make a correlation with the World Population Clock: 7.2 billion by 2014.

There are more of us to annihilate, more of us to fight but, in both cases, the U.S. is at the top of this food chain of violence. The world's total annual military budget is nearly $1.7 trillion, consuming 2.3 % of global gross domestic product. America's biggest export is war. Ω

The look of freedom: University of Mosul Library

☮ ☮ ☮

APPENDICES

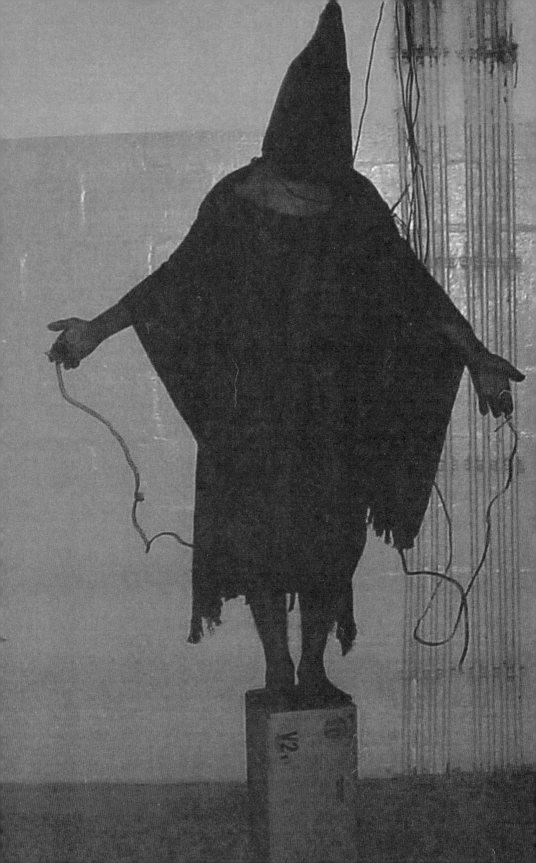

☮ ☮ ☮

Each Stone a Prison

CJ Hinke

Conscientious objectors and other political prisoners in the United States may be sent to any Federal penal and correctional institution. These are generally maximum-security facilities. However, there are often medium- and minimum-security prison camps and farms attached. The largest, at Allenwood, Pennsylvania held the largest number of conscientious objectors without fences, bars, guns, or walls, as in all minimum custody camps. COs may also be held in county jails for considerable periods of time.

In the 21st century, government expects prisons to be profit-making industries and relies extensively on private prisons traded by public stock shares.

Also administered by the Bureau of Prisons are multiple sites in various states of readiness to provide for the internment of prisoners under the provisions of the Internal Security Act should "war, or a state of national emergency" be declared by the President.

In 1967, at least some of these camps were those which had been used for the internment of Japanese-Americans during World War II. 120,000 Japanese-Americans were interned from 1942 by executive order of President Roosevelt. In 1944, the U.S. Supreme Court ruled mass internment constitutional.

The U.S. Immigration and Customs Service operates over 100 Federal detention facilities to "service" non-citizens, putting its suspects on "ICE."

The Department of Homeland Security administers its empty internment camps from 78 "Fusion Centers" located in every state.

In 2012, the National Defense Authorization Act codified modern internment without trial and suspension of habeas corpus guarantees by executive order. (Think Gitmo and Abu Ghraib for Americans.) At least 15 such executive orders have been enacted by presidents over the past 30 years, providing for the detention of Americans. More than a dozen nine Federal laws, dating to World War I, back them up. Currently, the Federal Emergency Management Agency oversees an extensive network of empty U.S. concentration camps in nearly every state, ready and waiting…for you! Although the numbers and locations of these camps is secret, each one is estimated to hold 20,000 prisoners, although some are thought to be dramatically larger. Allenwood is but one of these sites.

No doubt these extrajudicial prisons have been added to, expanded and extended by 2016 to many hundreds in readiness in every state. Ω

☮ ☮ ☮

☮☮☮

THE DESERTER

Winifred Mary Letts (1916)

There was a man, - don't mind his name,
Whom Fear had dogged by night and day.
He could not face the German guns
And so he turned and ran away.
Just that - he turned and ran away,

But who can judge him, you or I ?
God makes a man of flesh and blood
Who yearns to live and not to die.
And this man when he feared to die
Was scared as any frightened child,

His knees were shaking under him,
His breath came fast, his eyes were wild.
I've seen a hare with eyes as wild,
With throbbing heart and sobbing breath.

But oh ! it shames one's soul to see
A man in abject fear of death,
But fear had gripped him, so had death;
His number had gone up that day,

They might not heed his frightened eyes,
They shot him when the dawn was grey.
Blindfolded, when the dawn was grey,
He stood there in a place apart,
The shots rang out and down he fell,
An English bullet in his heart.
An English bullet in his heart !

But here's the irony of life, -
His mother thinks he fought and fell
A hero, foremost in the strife.
So she goes proudly; to the strife
Her best, her hero son she gave.
O well for her she does not know

He lies in a deserter's grave.

☮☮☮

⊛⊛⊛

LOCK 'EM ALL UP:
Spinning money from misery

CJ Hinke

The principal prison villains, Corrections Corporation of America ("Improving our communities"), G4S ("Securing your world"), and the GEO Group operate prison warehouses in five countries. These publicly-traded, for-profit companies share all major banks and many universities as investors.

They are joined by these corporate thieves and schemes exploiting slave labour in US prisons. Ω

DIVEST NOW!

1) **G4S** is the largest security company in the world. £6.683 billion in revenue, £195.90/share GFS (LON).

2) **Corrections Corporation of America** owns and manages private prisons and detention centers. $1.736 billion in revenue, $31.93/share CXW (NYSE).

3) **GEO Group** warehouses prisoners in North America, Australia, and the United Kingdom. $1.61 billion in revenue, €30.02/share GEG (FRA).

4) **Aramark Corporation** ("Enrich and nourish people's lives") - supplies food to 600 US prisons; charged with meal shortages, unsanitary food, and smuggling contraband inside, sex with inmates $14.33 billion in revenue, $33.47/share ARMK (NYSE)

5) *Global Tel*Link* ("Trusted and economical options for staying in touch with their loved ones") – monopoly on prison telephones, $1.13 per minute

6) **Corizon Correctional Healthcare** ("Success through evidence-based medicine") – prison "healthcare," inmate deaths

7) **Corporate call centers** – customer service and reservations for 75¢/hour

8) **GardaWorld** – Prisoner "Transportation security and logistics"

9) **Clothing manufacture** – including Victoria's Secret

10) **Exmark**, a Microsoft corporation, and others – 35¢/hour for recycling Dell products and shrinkwrapping Microsoft gear

11) **Bail bondsmen** – guarantee an arrestee's bail, typically $90,000, and keep 10% even if you're acquitted

12) **Food processing** – including Signature Packaging Solutions to package Starbucks holiday blends

13) **Farm labor** – displacing Mexican workers

REFERENCES

Beryl Lipton, "The Private Prison Primer," MuckRock, Part 1:April 5, 2016. https://www.muckrock.com/news/archives/2016/apr/05/private-prison-primer-what-are-we-really-signing/. Part 2, April 7, 2016: https://www.muckrock.com/news/archives/2016/apr/07/private-prison-primer-what-are-we-really-signing-p/.

Yves Engler, "Garda: Canada's 'Blackwater'. The World's Largest Privately Held Security Firm," Global Research, April 7, 2016. http://www.globalresearch.ca/garda-canadas-blackwater-the-worlds-largest-privately-held-security- firm/5519365.

John Kiriakou, "Forcing the Innocent to Plead Guilty, An American Disgrace," Reader Supported News, April 16, 2016. http://readersupportednews.org/opinion2/277-75/36406-focus-forcing-the-innocent-to-plead-guilty-an-american-disgrace

⊛⊛⊛

MILITARY CONSCRIPTION WORLDWIDE

CJ Hinke

Incredibly, in the 21st-century, more than half of the world's nation-states practice military conscription. According to many sources,
the countries profiled on this list are still be enforcing military conscription.

> *"You may not be interested in war, but war is interested in you."*
> – Leon Trotsky

In all cases, registration is required but military service may not be;
this practice would certainly yield a number of draft refusers. In some cases, other forms of national service are compulsory which also generates
principled refusal.

Starred * countries list provisions for alternative service or conscientious objection which exemption would also result in absolutist refusers;
in some cases, the right to conscientious objection is constitutional.

Article 2(2)(a) of the 1930 International Labour Organization
("ILO") Convention No. 29: Forced Labour Convention http://www.
ilo.org/wcmsp5/groups/public/@asia/@ro-bangkok/documents/
genericdocument/wcms_346435.pdf exempts from its prohibition on
forced or compulsory labour (Article 1(1)), "any work or service exacted
in virtue of compulsory military service laws for work of a purely military
character." The reference to "military service laws" indicates that for the
exemption to be valid, it must be set out in law.

Failure by governments to provision conscientious objection or
alternative service contravenes two primary and fundamental United
Nation conventions, the 1948 *Universal Declaration of Human Rights*
(Article 18) http://www.refworld.org/docid/3ae6b3712c.html and
the 1976 *International Covenant on Civil and Political Rights* (Article 18)
https://treaties.un.org/doc/publication/unts/volume%20999/volume-
999-i-14668-english.pdf, to which almost all these nation-states are party.
Thus, the right to conscientious objection is an inherent derivative right
based on "freedom of thought, conscience, and religion" (para 1) as "the
right to manifest one's religion of belief" (para 3).

However, Article 8(3)(c)(ii) of the ICCPR exempts from the prohibition on forced or compulsory labour (found in Article 8(3)(a)), "Any service of a military character and, in countries where conscientious objection is recognized, any national service required by law of conscientious objectors.

In the 1999 HRC decision in Foin v. France, CCPR/C/67/D/666/1995 http://www.refworld.org/docid/4a3a3aebf.html and 2000 decision in Venier and Nicholas v. France, CCPR/C/69/D/690/1996 http://www.unhcr.org/refworld/pdfid/50b8ec0c2.pdf, the UN Human Rights Council stated that under Article 8 of the ICCPR States may require service of a military character http://www.unhcr.org/refworld/docid/4a3a3aebf.html, para 10.3.

In 1960, every nation-state member of the European Union conscripted for military service with the sole exceptions of Andorra, Iceland, Ireland, Liechtenstein, Malta, Monaco, and San Marino. In 1967, the European Parliamentary Assembly adopted its first resolution supporting the right to conscientious objection.

In 1967, the European Parliamentary Assembly supported the right to conscientious objection with Resolution 337. The Assembly reaffirmed this commitment in 1977 with Recommendation 816 http://assembly.coe.int/nw/xml/XRef/Xref-DocDetails-en.asp?FileID=15752&lang=en in 1977.

Starting in 1975 with the Helsinki Agreement, and reaffirming in 1983, 1990 (twice), 1991, 1994, 1999, 2002, 2003, 2009, 2010 (twice), 2013, 2014, and 2015, the Organisation for Security and Co-operation in Europe (OSCE), a binding council of 57 states in Central Asia, Europe, and North America, committed to freedom of conscience and belief http://www.forum18.org/archive.php?article_id=1351.

The 1978 UN General Assembly was explicit in its Resolution 33/165 http://www.un.org/documents/ga/res/33/ares33r165.pdf which recognize "the right of all persons to refuse service in military or police forces." In 1981, UNHRC again supported conscientious objection in its Resolution 40 (XXXVII). In 1982, this was restated in Resolution 1982/36.

In 1983 UN published its report *Conscientious Objection to Military Service*, E/CN.4/Sub.2/1983/30/Rev.1, 1985 (the "Eide and Mubanga-Chipoya report") http://www.refworld.org/pdfid/5107cd132.pdf, regarding persecution in the context of conscientious objection to conflicts which violate basic rules of human conduct.

The United Nations' Declaration on Human Rights Defenders A/RES/53/144 http://www.ohchr.org/Documents/Issues/Defenders/Declaration/declaration.pdf was begin in 1984 and formally adopted in 1998 by the General Assembly on the 50th anniversary of the Universal Declaration of Human Rights.

In 1987, the European Committee of Ministers issued Recommendation R(87)8 https://www.coe.int/t/dghl/standardsetting/ hrpolicy/Other_Committees/DH-DEV-FA_docs/CM_Rec(87)08. en.pdf, which invites governments of member states to bring their national legislation and practice in line with the principle, "Anyone liable to conscription for military service who, for compelling reasons of conscience, refuses to be involved in the use of arms, shall have the right to be released from the obligation to perform such service, on conditions set out in the Recommendation. Such persons may be liable to perform alternative service ... which is not punitive by its nature or duration."

The UN Human Rights Commission on March 5, 1987 in Resolution 1987/46 http://www.refworld.org/docid/3b00f0ce50.html resolved that "conscientious objection has to be considered as a legitimate exercise of the right to freedom of conscience and religion."

This was reaffirmed in UNHCR Resolution 1989/59 http://www. refworld.org/docid/3b00f0b24.html, stating" all Member States have an obligation to promote and protect human rights and fundamental freedoms and to fulfill the obligations they have undertaken under the various international human rights instruments, the Charter of the United Nations and humanitarian law" and " called upon Member States to grant asylum or safe transit to another State" for conscientious objectors.

In 1990, the country representatives to the Organisation for Security and Cooperation in Europe (OSCE) at the Second Conference on the Human Dimension agreed on the importance of introducing civilian non-punitive alternative service for COs.

UNHRC's 1991 Resolution 1991/65 http://www.wri-irg.org/ node/6409 recognised "The role of youth in the promotion and protection of human rights, including the question of conscientious objection to military service."

In 1993, the Inter-American Commission on Human Rights (IACHR) ruled in a decision on merits that the conscription process must be challengeable in a court of law http://www.refworld.org/ docid/5020dd282.html.

The UNHRC's 1993 Resolution 1993/84 http://www.wri-irg.org/ node/10691 was also explicit in reminding Member States of the previous UN resolutions.

This was reiterated in 1995 by UNHCR Resolution 1995/83 http:// www.wri-irg.org/node/9174 recognising "the right of everyone to have conscientious objections to military service as a legitimate exercise of the right to freedom of thought, conscience and religion."

In 1996, the Council of Europe accepted human rights NGOs' recommendations CM(97)57, on CO recognition https://rm.coe.int/CoERMPublicCommonSearchServices/ DisplayDCTMContent?documentId=09000016804dc9bc.

UNHCR did so again in 1998 by UNHCR Resolution 1998/77 http:// www.wri-irg.org/node/6136 which restated "that States, in their law and practice, must not discriminate against conscientious objectors in relation to their terms or conditions of service, or any economic, social, cultural, civil or political rights; reminding "States with a system of compulsory military service, where such provision has not already been made, of its recommendation that they provide for conscientious objectors various forms of alternative service which are compatible with the reasons for conscientious objection, of a non-combatant or civilian character, in the public interest and not of a punitive nature"; and "emphasizes that States should take the necessary measures to refrain from subjecting conscientious objectors to imprisonment and to repeated punishment for failure to perform military service, and recalls that no one shall be liable or punished again for an offence for which he has already been finally convicted or acquitted in accordance with the law and penal procedure of each country."

In 2000, the right to conscientious objection was included in the *Charter of Fundamental Rights of the European Union* http://www.europarl. europa.eu/charter/pdf/text_en.pdf Article 10(2).

In 2001, the Council of Europe and the European Parliament stated "The right of conscientious objection is a fundamental aspect of the right to freedom of thought, conscience and religion" before the UN Human Rights Council. In May 2001, the Parliamentary Assembly recalled these minimum standards by adopting Recommendation 1518/2001 http:// www.wri-irg.org/node/20890 in which member states were again invited to the standards of legislation and practice in recommendation R987/8.

This standard was concluded by the EU Rapporteur for Legal Affairs and Human Rights in Document 8809, revised May 4, 2001 http://www.assembly.coe.int/nw/xml/Xref/X2H-Xref-ViewHTML. asp?FileID=9017&lang=EN. The Recommendation also means to ensure "the right for all conscripts to receive information on conscientious objection and the means of obtaining it."

In 2002, UNHRC adopted Resolution 2002/45 http://www.wri-irg. org/node/6415 which called upon "States to review their current laws and practices in relation to conscientious objection to military service" according to Resolution 1998/77 and to consider the information outlined in the report of the High Commission."

Also in 2002, The United Nations General Assembly adopted its "Optional Procol to the Convention on the Rights of the Child on the involvement of children in armed conflict" A/RES/54/263 http://www. ohchr.org/EN/ProfessionalInterest/Pages/OPACCRC.aspx against child soldiers and other children at risk in war zones.

The European Committee of Social Rights has several times commented that alternative service lasting long than one-and-a-half times longer than military service constitutes violation of Article 1.2 of the 1961 European Charter for Social Rights. (Conclusions XVI-Vol. 1, November 2002 on Complaint 8/2000.) http://www.wri-irg.org/node/20796.

The UN Commission on Human Rights reiterated these by Resolution 2002/45 http://www.refworld.org/docid/5107c76c2.html and its High Commissioner published Report E/CN.4/2004/55 http://www.refworld.org/pdfid/415be85e4.pdf on 'best practice' in 2004.

In 2004, UNHRC adopted Resolution 2004/35 http://www.refworld.org/docid/415be85e4.html for the protection of conscientious objectors and, in 2006, UNHRC Resolution 2/102 was seconded by 33 UN Member States.

In 2005, the right to conscientious objection was included in the Ibero-American Convention on Young People's Rights https://www.unicef.org/lac/IberoAmerican_Convention_on_the_Rights_of_Youth(1).pdf Article 12(3).

In 2006, UN High Commissioner for Human Rights issued Analytical Report 4/2006/51, Regarding Best Practices in Relation to Conscientious Objectors to Military Service http://www.ohchr.org/Documents/HRBodies/HRCouncil/RegularSession/Session23/A.HRC.23.22_AUV.pdf.

In 2012, the UN Human Rights Council tabled before the UN General Assembly Resolution 20/2 http://www.ohchr.org/Documents/HRBodies/HRCouncil/RegularSession/Session20/A-HRC-20-2_en.pdf, "Promotion and protection of all human rights"... "including Conscientious objection and seconded by 34 UN Member States, many of them conscripting nations. This direction was most recently repeated by UN Human Rights Council's 2013 Resolution 24/17 https://documents-dds-ny.un.org/doc/UNDOC/LTD/G13/172/35/PDF/G1317235.pdf?OpenElement, referring to UNHRC's 2012 Resolution 20/2.

In 2013, UN Human Rights Council published its Analytical report on conscientious objection to military service: Report of the United Nations High Commissioner for Human Rights, A/HRC/23/22 http://www.refworld.org/docid/51b5c73c4.html. The UNHRC adopted Resolution 24/17 A/HRC/RES/24/17 supporting CO http://www.refworld.org/cgi-bin/texis/vtx/rwmain?page=search&docid=53bd05754&skip=0&query=Conscientious%20Objection and again with A/HRC/24/L.23 http://www.refworld.org/cgi-bin/texis/vtx/rwmain?page=search&docid=526e3e114&skip=0&query=Conscientious%20Objection, tabled before the UN General Assembly.

In 2014, the HRC also published its Guidelines on International Protection No. 10 http://www.unhcr.org/529efd2e9.pdf regarding refugee claims by conscientious objectors and deserters. Hundreds of conscientious objectors from dozens of countries have applied for asylum in third countries using Article 1A (2) of the 1951 UN Convention and/or the 1967 *Protocol on the Status of Refugees.*

In 2016, the European Convention on Human Rights found that failure to apply CO status in European member states violated Article 9, "freedom of thought, conscience, and religion" (Application No. 66899/14, 15 September 2016) http://www.ebco-beoc.org/sites/ebco-beoc.org/files/attachments/2016-10-14%20Press-Release_Greece.pdf, and Article 10, "freedom of expression" (Application No. 2458/12, 15 November 2016) https://religion-weltanschauung-recht.net/2016/11/15/egmr-savda-v-turkey-no-2-no-245812/, of the European Convention.

Conscription has now been abolished in 25 EU countries, leaving 16 states still enforcing military conscription. Azerbaijan, Belarus, and Turkey make no provision for conscientious objectors. Romania and Ukraine recognize only religious objectors; Armenia, Cyprus, Greece, Lithuania, and Moldova discriminate in practice against non-religious COs. In 26 European countries, not one complies fully with the EU recommendations and in 16, military authorities are responsible for CO applications. In only seven countries can CO applications be made by serving volunteers, conscripts, and reservists.

Amnesty International lists all worldwide CO prisoners as its "prisoners of conscience." However, AI's country figures do not include the aggregate total number of all such objectors.

Are any politicians listening or is this all just lip-service? As can be seen from the list of countries below, most governments simply ignore human rights recommendations or condemnations.

Criteria for definition of draft "evasion" include the rich who pay substitutes to do their military service. All countries which have armies also have deserters from military service. Aiding or hiding deserters is also a criminal offence and often parents or other family members are prosecuted.

All countries have small numbers of Jehovah's Witness and other sectarian refusers. Politicians prey on the young and weak. We support all means of refusing military service both public and covert.

Countries marked with a check √ are listed on the War Resisters' International *World Survey Of Conscription and Conscientious Objection To Military Service* http://www.wri-irg.org/co/rtba/.

I have included countries where conscription remains in law but at present is not enforced. These statistics, where available at all, may not accurately reflect the actual numbers of refusers; statistics range from 1993-2005. In many cases, resident foreigners are also eligible for conscription, notably the USA.

I have not included "press-gang" forced enlistment by rebel paramilitaries. The practice is widespread in countries where such conflicts exist.

Please note that no information has been recorded for many countries. The author calls on readers to provide any further information to make this survey more complete.

This is the 21st century's Wall of Shame, the real rogue states enslaving young men for war.

√ **ABKHAZIA & SOUTH OSSETIA [GEORGIA]**

√ **ALBANIA***
Repeat prosecutions

√ **ALGERIA**

√ **ANGOLA**

√ **ARMENIA*** –
16,000 evaders
450 Jehovah's Witness prosecutions upheld by EU Court of Human Rights (2009)
Civilian alternative service implemented and approved for 71 JWs
Last 28 JWs released from prison in 2013

√ **AUSTRIA*** –
UN Human Rights Committee condemns alternative service longer than military service

√ **AZERBAIJAN*** –
2,611 in prison (2002), repeat sentences
UN recommends legal recognition of CO
Jehovah's Witness persecution and CO prisoners

√ **BELARUS*** –
30% refuse conscription, Jehovah's Witness deterrent show trials and prisoners
1,200-1,500 evaders/deserters per year
99% of conscripts feign illnesses or go into hiding
CO only for religious objection, alternative service double length
Soldiers cannot change their minds and become COs

√ **BENIN**

√ **BHUTAN**

√ **BOLIVIA** –
80,000 evaders
Draft exiles & refugees abroad

√ **BOSNIA***

√ **BRAZIL***

√ **BERMUDA***,

BULGARIA –
Conscription abolish in 2008
Registration from 18 to 32 reinstituted in 2016, indicating return to compulsory military service

√ **BURUNDI**

√ **CAPE VERDE**

√ **CENTRAL AFRICAN REPUBLIC**

√ **CHAD***

√ **CHILE** –
10,000 nonregistrants

√ **CHINA**

√ **COLOMBIA***
50% draft evasion
Forced enlistment, COs charged with desertion
Forced enlistment of child soldiers, indigenous and Afro-Colombians by paramilitaries
Military & police disobedience & desertion 6,362 serving
UN recommends legal recognition of CO

√ **CONGO***

√ **CUBA**

√ **CURAÇAO & ARUBA**

√ **CYPRUS (NORTHERN)** –
Schools militarized by Turkish Army soldier-teachers
No provision for CO or alternative service
Civilian COs tried by military courts
CO defections to Republic of Cyprus
Military reserve training until age 40
Condemned by European Court of Human Rights, ignored by government
Cyprus (Republic of)
CO application made to military

√ **DENMARK*** –
25 draft refusers per year

√ **DOMINICAN REPUBLIC**

√ **ECUADOR** –
10% of conscripts desert

√ **EGYPT** –
4,000 draft evaders

√ **EL SALVADOR*** –
Draft exiles & refugees abroad

√ **EQUATORIAL GUINEA**

√ **ERITREA** –
12 draft prisoners, secret trials, indefinite detention, torture
No medical care, deaths in custody
Prison & summary execution for fleeing the country

Revokes citizenship, business & driver's licences, passports, marriage certificates, national identity cards, denial of exit visas

54 Jehovah's Witnesses in prison without charge or trial 14+ years

Forced enlistment, including child soldiers, indefinite and arbitrary service, sometimes a decade

Rape, torture, extrajudical killings, inhumane conditions in military camps

Forced labour in State and private enterprises

UN Human Rights Council ruled Eritrea violentes the "right to life" of its nationals, charged the country with "enslavement," ignored by government

√ ESTONIA*

√ FINLAND*

Conscription from age 18 to 60

Alternative service double military, condemned by UN Human Rights Council, 50 absolutist prisoners

Some house arrest sentences

Jehovah's Witnesses exempt

√ GABON

√ GEORGIA* –

2,498 deserters

After abolition in June 2016, conscription was restored in 2017

Alternative service double military service

√ GERMANY*

√ GHANA

√ GREECE* –

Conscripts into Army, Navy, Air Force, including foreign residents of Greek descent

Hundreds of public draft refusers, Gulf Wars objectors

Automatic administrative fines of €6,000 plus interest for installments, often repeat fines. Court costs of €200 assessed

Failure to pay results in property forfeiture and denial of business licence

Repeat prosecutions condemned by UN Human Rights Council, UN Human Rights Committee,

European Court of Human Rights, ignored by Greek government

After prison, five years suspension of civil rights: denied voting, election to parliament, work in civil service, obtain passport or business licence

Soldiers or former soldiers not permitted to declare CO, trials for 'insubordination' in military courts

Amnesty for objectors declared before 1998

CO recognition only for baptized Jehovah's Witnesses

UN Human Rights Committee condemns alternative service double military service, discrimination against COs

"Illogical and arbitrary" punitive rescission of CO for failure in discipline during alternative service

Numerous draft exiles abroad

√ **GUATEMALA** –
350 COs, 75% of conscripts desert,
frequent extrajudicial executions

√ **GUINEA**

√ **GUINEA-BISSAU**

√ **HERZEGOVINA*** –
1,500 COs

√ **HONDURAS** –
29% draft evaders, 50% deserters

√ **INDONESIA**

√ **IRAN** –
Numerous draft and deserter exiles, may not return until after age 40

√ **IRAQ** –
Capital punishment for desertion, amputation of an ear, branding of the forehead
Islamic State of Iraq and Syria/Islamic State of Iraq and al-Sham (ISIS)/
Islamic State of Iraq and the Levant (ISIL)/Da'esh
Forced recruitment, abduction, and conscription, including child soldiers
from age six
Abducted Yazidi minority women raped and forced to marry jihadis and soldiers
Numerous deserters, including foreign recruits
Mass desertion due to disaffection

√ **ISRAEL**
Exponential number of refuseniks against war of Palestinian occupation
Draft refusal starts in high school
COs face military courts-martial, repeat sentences
Women may be COs but not men
Numerous draft evaders, draft exiles & refugees
Israeli Arab citizens are draft-exempt, except for Druze

√ **IVORY COAST**

√ **JORDAN**

√ **KAZAKHSTAN** –
40% draft evaders, 3,000 deserters
UN recommends legal recognition of CO

KOSOVO [SERBIA] –
Status undetermined

√ **KUWAIT** –
Widespread draft evasion

√ **KYRGYZSTAN**

√ **LAOS** –
Widespread draft evasion

√ **LATVIA***

√ **LEBANON**

√ **LIBYA**

√ **LITHUANIA*** –
Conscription reinstated in 2015. UN recommends legal recognition of CO and opportunities for alternative service

√ **MADAGASCAR**

√ **MALI** –
Widespread desertion

√ **MAURITANIA**

√ **MEXICO**

√ **MOLDOVA*** –
1,675 COs, hundreds denied

√ **MONGOLIA**

√ **MONTENEGRO*** –
Widespread draft evasion, 26,000 evaders charged, 150,000 draft exiles

√ **MOROCCO** –
2,250 deserters, five officers executed

√ **MOZAMBIQUE** –
Forced enlistment, mass desertion

√ **MYANMAR***

√ **NAGORNO-KARABAKH [AZERBAIJAN]**
Jehovah's Witness prisoners

√ **NETHERLANDS***
Refusals of duty to Afghanistan

√ **NIGER**

√ **NORTH KOREA** –
Death penalty for draft evasion and desertion

√ **NORWAY*** –
2,364 COs, 100-200 absolutist refusers
No prison time for refusers
Drafted women since 2014

√ **PARAGUAY*** –
Forced enlistment
6,000 COs, 15% of conscripts

√ **PERU** –
Forced enlistment

√ **PHILIPPINES** –
Two historical nonregistrants
Forced enlistment by rebel paramilitaries

√ **Poland*** –
Roman Catholics denied CO status
(Poland is 87.5% Catholic)

√ **Qatar** –
Reintroduced conscription in 2014

√ **Russian Federation*** –
1,445 COs annually by application to military, 17% rejection
Supreme Court protection (1996)
Alternative service double military
Buddhists, Jehovah's Witnesses excluded
30,000 draft evaders and 40,000 deserters
Soldiers not allowed to declare CO, Draft exiles & refugees

√ **Senegal**

√ **Serbia***
9,000 COs
26,000 draft evaders and deserters
150,000 draft exiles abroad
No conscription as of 2011.

√ **Seychelles**

√ **Singapore**
No legal status for CO
Hundreds of Jehovah's Witness & Adventist refusers,
36 months military detention
Refusal of flag salute, national anthem & oath of allegiance
Absolutist refusers fined and sentenced
12-36 months
Repeat sentences
At least 4,200 draft evaders
Social sanctions, including loss of permanent residence or citizenship
for the refuser and family, denial of re-entry Permits

√ **Slovenia***

√ **Somalia** –
Recruitment, abduction, and conscription of child soldiers by both government and paramilitaries. COs considered deserters

√ **South Korea**
13,000 CO prisoners, 400-700 per year,
5,000 draft refusers, repeat sentences
Draft refugees & exiles abroad
599 JW prisoners
UN Human Rights Committee recommends all COs be released from prison, have criminal records expunged,
and recognise CO in law

South Sudan

√ **SPAIN*** –
Dozens of public draft refusers, opposition to Gulf Wars
No conscription as of 2001.

√ **SRPSKA*** –
Widespread draft evasion & desertion

√ **SUDAN** –
2.5 million draft evaders, forced enlistment, including universities
Men of conscription age prohibited from travel abroad

SWEDEN –
Military conscription 1901-2010
New draft for men and women expected in 2019

√ **SWITZERLAND*** –
2,000 COs per year. 100 absolutist refusers per year, 8-12 month sentences
Trials by military courts-martial
Vegan found unfit ordered to report again
3% punitive annual military income tax for failure to join military each year

√ **SYRIA** –
Mass draft evasion, forced enlistment, including child soldiers, at military checkpoints
Summary execution of soldiers who refuse to fire on unarmed civilians or residential areas
Jews are exempt
Anti-government paramilitaries also using forced enlistment, including child soldiers
Condemned by UN Human Rights Council, ignored by government

√ **TAIWAN**

√ **TAJIKISTAN**
Widespread draft evasion and desertion. CO considered evasion
Arbitrary arrests, inhuman treatment, and torture of conscripts
and their parents
50% of military forced recruitmenmt
Cndemned by UN Human Rights Council, ignored by government

√ **TANZANIA**

√ **THAILAND** –
30,000 draft evaders, incidences of public draft refusal
Some draftees are seconded to Royal Thai Police, used as officers' domestic servants or working in their businesses
Hazing and humiliation of conscripts is rife
Beatings of conscripts by officers frequent, sometimes to death
900 21-year olds failed to register in a single province
A new law by the 2014 military coup conscripts 300,000 men
Allows conscription of 12 million registrants
70 JW draft refusers, no prosecutions

√ **TRANSDNIESTRIA MOLDOVAN REPUBLIC*** [MOLDOVA]

√ **TUNISIA*** –
Forced enlistment, widespread desertion

√ **TURKEY** –
74 public draft refusers, repeat sentences, considered deserters
European Court of Human Rights found repeat convictions "civil death" and
degrading treatment, ignored by Turkish government
Muslim COs
Disparaging military or "alienating public from military service" a crime
60,000 draft evaders per year
Objectors imprisoned as deserters
Draft refugees & exiles abroad

√ **TURKISH OCCUPIED TERRITORIES (NORTH CYPRUS)** –
14 declared COs

√ **TURKMENISTAN** –
Significant draft evasion, 20% desertion, 2,000 deserters
Beatings, threats of rape, torture, solitary confinement
9 JW prisoners, held incommunicado from family
11 under house arrest, some suspended sentences, Sentences up to four years
Sunni & Wahhabi Muslims suffer brutal treatment, torture & starvation for CO
Govt denies deaths in penal custody
European Parliament Intergroup on freedom of Religion or Belief and
Religious Tolerance
condemns treatment of Jehovah's Witnesses, found to violate
UN's Covenant on Civil and Political Rights Articles 7, 10 (1), and 18(1),
ignored by government

√ **UGANDA** –
Forced enlistment, including child soldiers
Widespread desertion

√ **UKRAINE*** –
Only religious COs: Seventh Day Adventists, Baptists, Adventists-Reformists,
Jehovah's Witnesses, Charismatic Christians
2,864 COs
Incidence of public absolutist refusal, 3-5 year sentences
Often charged with treason –13 years
10% compliance, 48,624 non-religious draft evaders
Specific refusers to war with Donetsk in the East & Crimea in the South
Cizre canton recognised CO in Kurdish region
Draft refugees in hiding and abroad

UNITED ARAB EMIRATES –
Reintroduced conscription in 2014

UNITED KINGDOM –
Prince calls for military conscription in May 2015

√ **USA*** –

Tens of millions of draft evaders fail to register, fail to report address changes

Thousands of absolutist refusers, only 20 prosecutions, sentenced from 35 days-six months

Conspiracy charges for those who aid, abet, counsel

Five years prison, $250,000 fine

Draft registration for women is anticipated

Military refusers and deserters

Deserters charged with wartime offence

Draft and deserter exiles

Stop-Loss: military's 18-month involuntary extension of service considered 'back-door' conscription

Rampant heroin addiction overseas

√ **UZBEKISTAN***

√ **VENEZUELA** –

Forced enlistment, widespread draft evasion and desertion

34 public absolutist refusers, 180 CO deserters per year

Compulsory registration in Supreme Court challenge

√ **VIETNAM** –

Widespread draft evasion and desertion

√ **WESTERN SAHARA**

√ **YEMEN** –

Significant draft evasion and desertion

√ **ZIMBABWE***

Conscription not enforced.

The numbers of draft refusers, where known, vary widely among the countries. In some, there may be only a handful. This handful also deserve to be protected – you could be one of them! In every country practicing military conscription, there are draft refusers and draft prisoners. Wherever a country maintains an army, from the most liberal of countries to the most repressive, there are conscientious objectors and deserters. Ω

☮☮☮

WARS WILL CEASE WHEN MEN REFUSE TO FIGHT

nansen

PEACE PLEDGE UNION

6 ENDSLEIGH STREET, LONDON, W.C.1.   01-387 550

☮☮☮

THE WAR RESISTERS' INTERNATIONAL DECLARATION

SIGN HERE: http://www.warresisters.org/joinwrl

• English: "War is a crime against humanity. I am therefore determined not to support any kind of war and to strive for the removal of all causes of war."

• German: "Krieg ist ein Verbrechen gegen die Menschheit. Ich bin daher entschlossen, keine Art von Krieg zu unterstützen und für die Beseitigung aller seiner Ursachen zu kämpfen."

• Spanish: "La guerra es un crimen contra la humanidad. En consecuencia, me comprometo a no apoyar ningún tipo de guerra y a luchar por la eliminación de todas las causas de la guerra."

• French: "La guerre est un crime contre l'humanité. C'est pourquoi je suis résolu(e) à n'aider à aucune espèce de guerre et à lutter pour l'abolition de toutes les causes des guerres."

• Bosnian/Croatian/Serbian: "Rat je zločin protiv čovječanstva i čovječnosti. Stoga se odlučno protivim bilo kom obliku rata, te se zalaćem za uklanjanje svih njegovih uzroka."

• Dutch: "Oorlog is een misdaad tegen de mensheid. Daarom ben ik vast besloten geen enkele vorm van oorlog te steunen en te ijveren voor de opheffing van alle oorzakenervan."

• Norwegian: «Krig er en forbrytelse mot menneskeheten. Jeg er derfor fast bestemt på ikke å støtte noen slags krig, og å virke for å fjerne alle grunner til krig».

• Polish: "Wojna to przestępstwo przeciw ludzkości. Dlatego też jestem zdecydowany nie popierać żadnego rodzaju wojny i usiłować usunąć wszelkie przyczyny wojny."

• Portuguese: "A guerra é um crime contra a humanidade. Em consequência disso, comprometo-me a não apoiar nenhum tipo de guerra e a lutar pela eliminação de todas as causas da guerra."

• Finnish: "Sota on rikos ihmiskuntaa vastaan. Siksi olen päättänyt olla tukematta minkäänlaista sotaa ja kamppailla sotien kaikkien syiden poistamiseksi."

• Turkish: "Savaş insanlığa karşı işlenen bir suçtur. Ben bu yüzden, hiçbir türlü savaşı desteklemediğimi ve savaşa yol açan sorunları ortadan kaldırmaya çalışacağımı bildiririm."

Please contribute your language!

☮☮☮

World War II soldier Eddie Slovik is the only American soldier to be court-martialled and executed for desertion since the American Civil War.

☮ ☮ ☮

DESERTION: A LONG, PROUD TRADITION

It's not a job, it's an adventure, or
wearing your own clothes is the new camo

CJ Hinke

Potsdam Memorial to the Unknown Deserter

There are as many reasons to desert military service as there are deserters. All countries' militaries like to snatch young men when they are uneducated, inexperienced, and unemployed. It takes a soldier far greater courage to throw down his weapon than to kill a stranger.

There are deserters in every country that has an armed forces. Armies demand blind obedience and human beings crave liberty.

Why do men desert? Certainly not from cowardice. It takes far more courage to break from the pack and its reliance upon rabid nationalism. 36% of men facing battle for the first time were more afraid of being labeled a coward than of being wounded or killed. War-sick has been called by many names by psychologists. In the US Civil War, DaCosta's disease or soldier's heart; in World War I, shell-shock, conversion disorder or fugue state, flight responce; in World War II, battle fatigue, battle exhaustion; in Vietnam, combat fatigue, combat exhaustion, combat stress reaction; to the oh-so-modern post-traumatic stress disorder shared by Gulf soldiers and drone pilots.

All these diagnoses have at one time been banned and mentions censored, even in medical journals. The goal of treatment being, of course, to send soldiers back to war. 600,000 were discharged from the US Army alone for neuropsychiatric complaints. As noted by *Fortune* magazine, at the start of World War II, "25 years after the end of the 'Great' War, nearly half of the 67,000 beds in Veterans Administration hospitals are still occupied by the neuropsychiatric casualties of World War I." More than one-quarter of all World War II casualties were psychiatric.

Deserters are hardly cowards. Many simply were not willing to kill after joining the military. Others experienced an ideological crisis. Some had needy families at home. Country right or wrong? What nonsense!

"Desertion" is a pejorative term in human society. We think of them as "returners" from the madness of all war. We're waiting for them to come home, proud that they never had to kill anybody.

Although the US penalty for desertion during wartime remains death, no American deserter has served more than 24 months since September 11, 2001.

The Nuremburg Principles *require* a soldier to refuse any orders which may result in the commission of crimes against humanity. (And what else is war!)

WAR OF 1812 (1812-1815)
12.7% of all American troops deserted in comparison to 14.8% during peacetime. This was largely due to the death penalty for such "treason." Many faced summary execution.

MEXICAN-AMERICAN WAR (1846-1848)
8.3%, 9,200 US soldiers deserted.

US CIVIL WAR (1861-1865)
The north's Union Army faced far greater desertion than the south's Confederacy. More than 87,000 deserters were recorded from only three northern states, 180,000 deserters in total by war's end.

The south is said to have lost 103,400 to desertion through the war, including whole units of soldiers. However, as many as 278,000 of 500,000 troops were missing by war's end. Mark Twain deserted from both sides.

William Smitz of the North's Pennylvania Volunteers was the last deserter shot by firing squad in 1865.

SPANISH-AMERICAN WAR (1898)
Black American soldiers deserted in the US war on Filipino indigenistas.

WORLD WAR I (1914-1918)
240.000 British and Commonwealth soldiers were court-martialed and 346 were executed for desertion, cowardice, quitting a post, refusing an order, or casting away arms out of 3,080 death sentences during the "War to End All Wars," including 25 Canadians and 22 Irishmen. They are commemorated by the Shot at Dawn Memorial https://en.wikipedia.org/wiki/Shot_at_Dawn_Memorial in Staffordshire. The memorial was modeled on 17-year old Private Herbert Burden http://news.bbc.co.uk/2/hi/uk_news/england/4798025.stm, blindfolded and tied to a stake.

Great Britain retained the death penalty for 'cowardice' from 1279 to 1930. Such offences included mutiny, striking a superior officer, refusing to obey an order, sleeping on watch, treachery, and desertion.

Almost all of these deserters' names were not added to war memorials. Some, though not nearly all, have been pardoned posthumously by the British government. A few refused a blindfold when facing a firing squad, choosing to look them in the eye. (And these are cowards?!?)

More than 600 French soldiers were executed for desertion.

15 German soldiers were executed for desertion.

28 New Zealand deserters were sentenced to death and five https://en.wikipedia.org/wiki/List_of_New_Zealand_soldiers_executed_during_World_War_I were executed. These soldiers were posthumously pardoned in 2000.

The US military recorded 21,282 deserters and President Woodrow Wilson commuted all 24 death sentences for deserters.

RUSSIAN REVOLUTION (1919)
US and French soldiers rebel, desert and mutiny rather than fight Russian revolutionaries.

QUIT INDIA MOVEMENT (1930)
British Garwhal Rifles units of Hindu soldiers refuse to fire on Muslim demonstrators in Peshawar.

WORLD WAR II (1939-1945)
More than 21,000 American deserters were tried and convicted of desertion during "The Good War." Although 49 were sentenced to death, only one, Private Eddie Slovik https://en.wikipedia.org/wiki/Eddie_Slovik, a soldier who had volunteered to clear mine fields, was executed by musketry on January 31, 1945 at Sainte-Marie-aux-Mines in France. His final declaration was, "I'll run away again if I have to go out there."

Supreme Allied Commander and later US President, Dwight D. Eisenhower, confirmed Slovik's death sentence, claiming "it was necessary to discourage further desertions." Slovik stated, "They're shooting me for the bread and chewing gum I stole when I was 12 years old."

Slovik's execution was hidden from French civilians. He was bound at arms and torso, knees, and ankles and hung from a spike on a six-by-six post against the stone wall of a French farmhouse. 12 soldiers were issued M-1 rifles, only one of which contained a blank round. After the first volley, Private Slovik didn't die; he died as the soldiers were reloading. Eddie Slovik was the first American deserter to be executed since Lincoln was President. He was 24.

Slovik was buried in a numbered grave in Row 3, Grave 65 of Plot "E" alongside 95 US soldiers executed for rape and murder, until 1987 when President Ronald Reagan ordered the return of his remains. He is buried in Detroit, next to his wife, Antoinette. She had petitioned seven US presidents for his return until she died in 1979, never having received GI medical benefits.

World War II saw 1.7 million US courts-martial, one-third of all American prosecutions. In May 1942 alone, there were 2,822 desertions from duty.

More than 1,500 Austrian soldiers deserted the German Wehrmacht. A campaign to remember them was started in 1988 with the theme, "Desertion is not reprehensible, war is." In 2014, they were honoured by a monument, the Memorial for the Victims of Nazi Military Justice https://en.wikipedia.org/wiki/Memorial_for_the_Victims_of_Nazi_Military_Justice. The sculpture sits in Vienna opposite the Austrian Chancellory and President's office. It is inscribed simply with just two words, "all alone."

In Germany, more than 15,000 soldiers were executed for desertion by the Nazi regime. They were commemorated in 2007 by the Deserteur Denkmal http://sites-of-memory.de/main/stuttgartdeserters.html in Stuttgart. It is dedicated "To the deserters from all wars."

WAR ON VIETNAM (1955-1975)
At least 500,000 US soldiers deserted, including 71% who fled to Canada, France, and Sweden. Of the 3,127-30,000 deserters in Canada, more than 59% had voluntarily enlisted…and changed their minds.

IRAN (1979)
Shah's soldiers refuse to fire on student demonstrators.

RUSSIA'S WAR ON AFGHANISTAN (1980s)
The Soviet Union, throughout its history 1917-1991, executed 158,000 deserters and jailed 135,000 Red Army officers. A further 1.5 million Soviet prisoners of war under the Nazis were sent to Siberian gulags on their repatriation due to disaffection in the ranks.

60,000-80,000 ethnic Soviet border troops from the Muslim Central Asian regions deserted during the Afghan Civil War 1979-1989. 85,000 Afghan troops also deserted during this period.

APARTHEID SOUTH AFRICA (1980s)
Soldiers refuse to enforce racist apartheid policies against demonstrators.

INDONESIA'S WARS (2000s)

Numerous indigenous soldiers deployed to suppress native rebellions in Irian Jaya (Papua New Guinea), Aceh, Kalimantan, Maluku. Timor-Leste, and East Java desert.

WARS ON AFGHANISTAN, IRAQ, AND MANY MORE (2001-PRESENT)

Since 2000, the Pentagon estimates more than 40,000 troops have deserted from all branches of military service. In 2001 alone, 7,978 deserted.

More than 5,500 American troops deserted in 2003-2004. In 2005, 3,456 soldiers deserted. By 2006, that number had reached 8,000.

In 2006, the UK military reported over 1,000 deserters.

US Army Sergeant Bowe Bergdahl https://en.wikipedia.org/wiki/Bowe_ Bergdahl was charged with desertion and "misbehavior" before the enemy after abandoning his post in Afghanistan in 2009. He was held captive by the Taliban for five years before being exchanged in 2014 for six high-ranking Afghans held by the US in their extrajudicial prison base at Guantánamo Bay, Cuba. One died before the exchange so five Taliban were released by the US, the army chief of staff, deputy minister of intelligence, a former minister of the interior, and two senior commanders. The Taliban originally demanded $1 million and the release of 21 Afghan prisoners along with a Pakistani scientist who killed US soldiers. (President Obama actually *does* 'negotiate with terrorists'. The Commander-in-Chief took a publicity photo-op with Bergdahl's parents in the Rose Garden.)

It appears the young sergeant is being prosecuted because, were he not, he could demand compensation from the US government due a prisoner of war. (The US can spend trillions on wars, and pay for a court-martial but refuses to compensate one soldier!) Bergdahl faces a life sentence at court-martial.

So what was this home-schooled Idaho boy who studied fencing and ballet, never owned a car and rode everywhere by bicycle doing in the military, anyway? Hint: the military maw will take any cannon fodder it can get! Bowe went from a year-long retreat at a Buddhist monastery direct to infantry school at Fort Benning. Like Pvt. Slovik, Sgt. Bergdahl, announced his intention to "walk away into the mountains of Pakistan.," taking only his compass.After he began to learn Pashto, Bergdahl spent more times with Afghans than the soldiers of his 'counterinsurgency' unit. He wrote his parents he was "ashamed to be an American" and considered renouncing his US citizenship, a small detail buried by the White House. His parents wrote back, "OBEY YOUR CONSCIENCE!"

64% of Canadians were polled to ask their government to accept US military refugees after two motions for compassion were passed in Parliament in 2008 and 2009. However, these legislative efforts were non-binding. The Canadian government has adopted a harsh policy of deporting deserters to the US, in marked contrast to the Vietnam period, and many young Americans simply go underground in Canada. Hundreds of American deserters have fled to Canada. Not one of these resisters has received refugee status.

In defense of American deserters, Canada's War Resisters Support Campaign stated, "The struggle to achieve political refugee status for U.S. war resisters in Canada can be seen as one of many efforts worldwide to defend the primacy of international law. The Geneva Conventions on War and the Nuremberg Principles make clear that soldiers have not only the right, but also the *responsibility to refuse to participate in war crimes*. Such war crimes include illegal wars of aggression, indiscriminate or purposeful killing and wounding of civilians, and torture and abuse of prisoners." UN Secretary-General Kofi Annan stated in 2004 that the war on Iraq was illegal under the UN Charter. The UN High Commissioner for Refugees(UNHCR) guaranteed international protection for deserters in *Guidelines on International Protection No. 10: Claims to Refugee Status related to Military Service within the context of Article 1A (2) of the 1951 Convention and/ or the 1967 Protocol relating to the Status of Refugees*, December 3, 2013, HCR/ GIP/13/10, http://www.refworld.org/docid/529ee33b4.html. Thus far, the Canadian government has refused to abide by these international standards.

The BBC commented on the precedent-setting case of Iraq war resister Jeremy Hinzman https://en.wikipedia.org/wiki/Jeremy_Hinzman in 2004: "Americans in trouble have been running to Canada for centuries... in the wake of the American Revolution...[and in the] Underground Railroad that spirited escaped American slaves to freedom...."

OCCUPIED PALESTINE (2002-PRESENT)
Israeli refusenik conscripts refuse to carry out policies of occupation and oppression against Palestinians. Large-scale trials and prison sentences.

Although I counseled, aided and abetted hundreds of Vietnam draft refusers throughout the 1960s as part of the Student Peace Union, The Resistance, and the Central Committee for Conscientious Objectors, I had little contact with American deserters. It is telling that every branch of the US military has a Deserter Information Point hotline. I first advocated desertion in a large, public Gensuikin demonstration in front of the huge US military base deploying troops to Vietnam in Naha, Okinawa, in 1969. I arrived by ship and left in a private plane.

Soldiers were once someone's little boy or girl, someone's big brother or sister, someone's star, the apple of their parents' eye. These are the good people who become our soldiers. Soldiers die and all their families get is a folded flag, a thank you for your sacrifice.

I still advocate, counsel, aid and abet desertion by *anyone* in military service *anywhere*. Deserters are not only national heroes. They are global heroes who have refused to kill civilians and soldiers on foreign soil.

You can do no greater good than refusing to kill. Admit it: you made a mistake. If you are in the military, *anybody's* military, do the right thing: RUN AWAY! Ω

☮☮☮

Acting Costa Rican President José "Don Pepe" Figueres Ferrer takes a sledgehammer to the Cuartel Bellavista military barracks, 1948.

The 22 countries which have abolished their militaries or were founded without one are uniformly tiny, isolated, and often island nations. In many cases, these states maintain national police or paramilitary forces for internal protection (some might say from their own citizens in the event of a popular uprising to effect regime change), maritime defence patrols, or are defended by their former colonial masters. Some might say they are at little risk of invasion because there's nothing more to take and few to fight back!

Although countries with armies may be more complex and have extensive economic and foreign policy agendas, there is no reason why they, too, could not take the first step in abolishing their large and costly militaries. One country's standing army can only be an implied threat against other nations. When a country has an army, there is every incentive to put it to aggressive use.

Bluntly stated, war is illegal under international law. All member states of the United States signed its Charter http://www.un.org/en/

documents/charter/chapter1.shtml: in 1945 "All Members shall refrain in their international relations from the threat or use of force against the territorial integrity or political independence of any State, or in any other manner inconsistent with the Purposes of the United Nations." The 'purposes' in Chapter I of the Charter are focused on the need "to maintain international peace." The Preamble to the Charter emphasise its purpose: "to save succeeding generations from the scourge of war, which twice in our lifetime has brought untold sorrow to mankind."

Reiterating this principle in 1970, the UN passed its *Declaration on Principles of International Law Concerning Friendly Relations and Co-operation Among States in Accordance with the Charter of the United Nations* http://www.gibnet.com/library/un2625.htm: "No State or group of States has the right to intervene, directly or indirectly, for any reason whatever, in the internal or external affairs of any other State. Consequently, armed intervention and all against its political, economic and cultural elements, are in violation of international law."

If this were not compelling enough evidence for the total illegality of war, nations have also signed to the *General Treaty for Renunciation of War as an Instrument of National Policy* https://en.wikipedia.org/wiki/Kellogg–Briand_Pact, sometimes known as the "Peace Pact of Paris" or the "Kellogg-Briand Pact" of 1928. Article II stipulates: "The High Contracting Parties agree that the settlement or solution of all disputes or conflicts of whatever nature or of whatever origin they may be, which may arise among them, shall never be sought except by pacific means. It was this treaty under which Nazis were prosecuted at Nuremburg.

Incidentally, all these compacts remain on the official website of the US Department of State where is stated, "[T]he fact that a State's domestic law does not provide for a penalty with respect to a violation of international law does not relieve a person from responsibility for that act under international law." This means that every soldier, every officer, every contractor, every politician must be found guilty of crimes against humanity.

If not preparing for war, why does any country have any army? If wars are illegal, certainly so should be armies!

As the modern world works, with the cooperation of the United Nations, countries with or without standing armies are unlikely to be invaded by their neighbours. More is to be gained by economic agreement. Sell me yours and I'll sell you mine.

However, there are a lot of vested interests and huge profits to be made in arms sales and military conflict which the biggest players are loath to give up. Corporate profits must be increased, lobbyists must be supported, bonuses must be paid, and the economy must keep inflating. After all, only the ordinary soldiers and civilians suffer while the politicians and fatcats keep stuffing their wallets.

Although they still have a standing military, South Africa's apartheid state developed nuclear weapons and, to date, is the only nation with enough good sense to give them up, in 1989, and dismantle their six warheads. (Nine brain-damaged ostriches remain to keep the 'assurance' in "Mutually-Assured Destruction.") Argentina, Brazil, South Korea, Sweden, and Taiwan all have standing militaries but abolished their plans for nukes, Following the breakup of the Soviet Union in 1991, Kazakhstan, Belarus, and Ukraine dismantled their resident nuclear arsenals.

[Dr. Strangelove, or, How I Learned to Stop Worrying and Love the Bomb]

There are nine nations with atomic weapons. Five of them, the US (4,500-7,700 warheads), Russia (4,700-8,500 warheads), United Kingdom (150-215 warheads), France (290-300 warheads), and China (260 warheads), are signatory to the UN's Nuclear Non-Proliferation Treaty of 1970..., pay it no attention and act with impunity. India (90-120 warheads) and Pakistan (120-130 warheads) also have the bomb but haven't signed any regulatory treaties.

North Korea and Israel (60-400 warheads) both have nukes and seem to be no more rogue states than the big ones. Bear in mind detonation, accidental or malicious) of just one of these warheads signals the end of life on earth. When politicians discuss the issue of nuclear security, they try to tell the public "terrorists" are the danger. However, governments themselves are the real terrorists threatening to blow up all of us.

This nuclear "club," (as in what a caveman carries), consists of countries which either stole the weapons technology or were given it by the

US. None of these governments mention ever giving up their nukes. Meanwhile, Russia and the US are modernising and expanding their atomic arsenals, the US by around $3 trillion, by order of their War Prize president. America intends to add nuclear cruise missiles to its existing arsenal of long-range nuclear bombers, land-based intercontinental ballistic missiles, and missile-launching submarines.

Just one big country needs to start this trend. Envision a world without war, where differences are solved through mutually beneficial agreement. War is often excused with some feeble excuse that violence is human nature.

In the 21st-century, it's just a bad habit. Long term, wars solve nothing by the imposition of military force because the roots of conflict have never been resolved.

Give up armies and finally have enough money to create a satisfied citizenry and working economy. Free education through trades apprenticeships and tertiary, universal free healthcare including teeth, eyes, medications and lifelong disability and treatment; full childcare and eldercare; free public transportation; long-term maternal and paternal work leave and holidays long enough to mean something; full free housing for all; interest-free home mortgages; genuine social security even when one stops working at any age; and even, yes, an annual income from the surplus guaranteed to each man, woman, and child from birth to death.

You – yes, I'm talking to *you*! – are the taxpayer who pays for your country's military. That's a good first place to start supporting peace as an individual. Stop paying war taxes, more than 53¢ of every tax dollar paying for wars past, present, and future in the United States.

All countries need to do to build that perfect world is give up their militaries. Ill-defined concepts of national security and national pride mean nothing – people do.

Imagine a world with no war, then make it happen. Start with your country! How about Thailand first? Ω

☮☮☮

☮ ☮ ☮

A Guide to Writing Prisoners of Conscience

Freedom Now
http://www.freedom-now.org/

Letter writing campaigns have become an important aspect of modern human rights advocacy. This is especially true in the case of "prisoners of conscience" (individuals who have been detained for peacefully exercising a fundamental human right, such as the right to freedom of religion or free expression).

Current and former prisoners of conscience have emphasized the importance of these letters – not only because they bring desperately needed encouragement and solidarity – but also because the letters puts prison authorities on notice that the international community is watching.

Such attention can help protect prisoners of conscience who are often at great risk for mistreatment by the regimes that have locked them away from the outside world.

Below are some suggested tips to keep in mind while writing to prisoners of conscience and language from an example letter. It is important to remember, however, that this letter is from YOU!

Keep it personal: The personal connection is what makes letters of support so powerful; feel free to tell the prisoner why their story moves you. Handwritten letters, if possible, are the best way to make a personal connection.

Keep it non-political: Often prisoners of conscience are detained for criticizing their government or its policies; however, it is best to avoid direct references to the government or the political situation in the country. Instead, focus on the important work the prisoner was doing before his or her arrest.

Keep it positive: Prisoners of conscience frequently face difficult circumstances, which can include harsh prison conditions, solitary confinement, and even torture. It is essential to avoid dwelling on such conditions and instead convey our support, solidarity, and hope for the future.

Keep it simple: Letters of support don't need to be long or complicated – often a simple message of support or a short postcard is perfect. Just the act of writing sends a powerful message to the prisoner and the government holding him or her!

EXAMPLE LETTER:

Dear Father Ly,
I am writing to share with you my solidarity and support as you continue the struggle for human rights and religious liberty in Vietnam.

Your story is a true inspiration. As a rights advocate myself, I can only imagine the faith required to maintain a commitment to ones principles in the face of such adversity. Despite your own repeated imprisonment, you have selflessly continued to advocate for the rights of others and the future of your country. As long as you remain in prison, please know that the international community will continue to advocate for your immediate and unconditional release.

Please accept my most sincere and best wishes as I keep you in my thoughts and prayers.

Sincerely,
Patrick Griffith

Freedom Now

☮☮☮

☮ ☮ ☮

THE PERSONAL EFFECTS OF RESISTANCE

prepared by the Draft Law Group of
Yale University Law School

In this section we are going to consider some of the less direct but often lifelong effects of a felony conviction. Students have the special problem of whether their institution can be counted on to admit or readmit them following such a conviction.

(1) Government employment: Conviction of a draft offense might weigh heavily against an applicant for any federal job; in many situations it would probably be conclusive against him. Courts have up to now refused to exercise any judicial control over the selection of federal employees. So long as the hiring official does not explicitly reject an applicant for an unconstitutional reason (e.g., race), the courts are unlikely to get into the business of reviewing the selection process. Even if the courts did intervene, a felony conviction would probably be held to be allowable ground for rejection.

Federal employees, in contrast to applicants, are subject to some statutory protections as to the grounds upon which they can validly be dismissed and as to the procedures which must be followed before they can be dismissed. (Editor's Note. Several favorable court rulings have been obtained on this basis.) But a felony conviction would very probably satisfy the statutory standards. Furthermore, even in the unlikely event that the courts did hold a draft offense to be an invalid ground for dismissal, the employing agency often can find an alternative reason for dismissal, and so far the courts have been very reluctant to question the sincerity of the stated grounds. So long as a plausible reason is stated, courts will probably continue to show a reluctance to move into an area which they regard as an appropriate one for the exercise of executive discretion.

State employment is generally subject to the same considerations as is federal employment.

2) Occupations licensed by the states: All of the states license a large number of occupations and for most of these a felony conviction is at least evidence that the applicant for a license is not qualified to receive a license; a past conviction under these licensing statutes will hurt the applicant more or less, depending upon the type of occupation, the nature

of the crime committed, and the relationship between the crime and the activity licensed. In general, teachers, attorneys, dentists, physicians, and accountants are subject to the most rigorous qualification requirements; conviction for a draft offense would be very likely to preclude one from following these occupations in most states.

Editor's Note: Imagine how disturbing it would be to find your veterinarian or embalmer was a felon! A convict can be a prison librarian but not a community librarian. The Watergate 'plumbers' only later became felons! Would you want your dog to learn new tricks from a felon?!? Of course, bear in mind in 1952, there were only 48 states. In the 21st century we are so over-regulated that it probably requires state licensure for any job you could dream up. Activists are free thinkers. Our advice? Don't worry about the man. Create your own work. Ω

The fact that conviction for a felony may seem to be a ridiculous criterion for admission to some of these occupations does not mean that it is not in fact an existing criterion. For example, in California in 1962 a felony conviction was relevant to 39 occupations, among which were barbers and guide dog trainers.

The Supreme Court may well uphold denial of a license because of a felony conviction when the occupation is closely related to the public health, safety, and morals: for example, teachers, doctors, lawyers, accountants, and the like. For an example from law, the Court upheld the refusal of the Illinois Bar to admit a conscientious objector in spite of the fact that the applicant had committed no crime. Although this case might be decided differently today, commission of a draft offense would probably be considered sufficient grounds for rejection. Failure of a physician to produce subpoenaed documents before the House Un-American Activities Committee was upheld as valid grounds for state suspension of his medical license.

However, in some states there is beginning to be some movement away from treating criminal convictions as an absolute bar. In California, where the test for admission to the bar is that the candidate "be of good moral character," the State Supreme Court has held that mere intentional violation of the law (the case involved various acts of civil disobedience in connection with civil rights disputes) does not of itself negate good character. The applicant had a number of misdemeanor convictions, but the Court explicitly analogized the problem before it to the question whether a draft offense (a felony) makes one unqualified to vote. The Court suggested that exclusion of such persons from the practice of law would raise serious constitutional questions.

(3) Private employment: At the present time there are generally no restrictions on private employers' use of a felony conviction as a basis for rejecting an applicant or dismissing an employee.

A citizen who has been convicted of a crime may constitutionally be deprived of his right to vote. Qualifications for voters in both state and federal elections are set by the *state* in which the individual resides. Those states whose statutes or constitutions do not explicitly disqualify voters for violations of laws like the Selective Service Act are limited to Maine, Vermont, Pennsylvania, and possibly Rhode Island. The California Supreme Court has held that violation of the Selective Service law cannot constitutionally be made the basis for disqualification. All the remaining states disqualify either for the commission of "felony" or "infamous crime"; in a large number of these states disqualification depends on the maximum sentence which could have been imposed for the offense. Anyone desiring further information should consult with a lawyer who is familiar with the laws of the state in which he is interested.

It should be noted that it is only recently that the Supreme Court has started to invalidate state voting qualifications; it is possible that the Supreme Court will follow in the footsteps of the California courts and limit the felony disqualification to those convicts whose crimes are of a nature such that to permit them to vote could "reasonably be deemed to constitute a threat to the integrity of the elective process." The latter test is certainly not ambiguous but it is directed at crimes like bribery of election officials, and presumably would not include Selective Service violations.

A conviction for refusal to report for, or submit to, induction does not bar a second conviction if the registrant refuses to submit when ordered to do so after release from prison. The same is true if a conscientious objector repeats his refusal to report for civilian work. Such subsequent convictions have been held not to violate the prohibition against double jeopardy. Apparently the Department of Justice has generally declined to prosecute for successive refusals in recent years. However, the 1967 Act contains two provisions which may cause a change in the Department's policy. One appears to make an order to report for induction after completion of a sentence mandatory in all cases. The other requires the Department to report any failure to prosecute to Congress, with an explanation.

The above paragraph refers to consecutive prosecutions for repeated offenses, but it should also be noted that any single prosecution may involve more than one offense. In such a case, the maximum penalty of five years or $10,000, or both, may be imposed for each offense. For example, if a person burns his draft card, refuses to report for his physical, and fails to appear for induction, he may be charged with three separate offenses. The maximum penalty applies to each offense; so in this case the resister is theoretically liable to a sentence of 15 years and-or a $30,000 fine. It is even possible that if one returns both his notice of classification and his registration certificate to his local board these two offenses could be charged against him separately. The fact that one is liable to the maximum sentence on each charge does not mean that he will receive the accumulated maximum, however, since most judges follow the practice of imposing sentences to run concurrently rather than consecutively. But the first consecutive sentences meted out in many years were recently imposed by a federal judge in Georgia: maximum sentences on two counts for a total of 10 years and $10,000 (the defendant had previously jumped bail, which may well have affected the sentence).

THE PROFESSIONAL HEALTH CARE PERSONNEL DELIVERY SYSTEM

In 1987, under the authority of Title 50 U.S. Code Appendix Section 460(h), Public Law 100-180, Selective Service began assembling a list of "professionally qualified" draft registrants between the ages of 20 through 54 in 57 medical specialties on an immediate stand-by basis:

Physicians

1. Aerospace Medicine
2. Thoracic Surgery
3. Orthopedic Surgery
4. Anesthesiology
5. General Surgery
6. Neurosurgery
7. Urology
8. Otolarnygology
9. Psychiatry
10. Allergy
11. Neurology
12. Dermatology
13. Radiology
14. Colon-Rectal Surgery
15. Pathology
16. Opthalmology
17. Internal Medicine
18. Emergency Medicine

Dentists

1. Oral Surgery
2. Prosthodontics
3. Periodontics
4. Endocrinology
5. General Dentistry

Miscellaneous Allied Specialists

1. Physiology
2. Entomology
3. Clinical Psychology

4. Medical Technology

5. Audiology/Speech Therapy

6. Environmental Health

7. Podiatry

8. Dietetics

9. Physical Therapy

Registered Nurses

1. Medical/Surgical Nursing

2. Surgical Nursing

3. Certified Registered Nurse Anesthetist

4. Mental Health Nursing

Medical Care Technicians

Licensed Practical/Vocational Nursing and Other Medical Care and Treatment Personnel

Other Specialists/Technicians

1. Dental Laboratory

2. Medical Administration

3. Radiology

4. Respiratory Therapy

5. Medical Laboratory

6. Dental Assistance

7. Operating Room

8. Pharmacy

9. Dietetic

10. Medical Supply

11. Medical Equipment Repair

12. Psychiatric

13. Physical Therapy

14. Environmental Health

15. Orthopedic

16. Veterinary

17. Occupational Therapy

18. Optical

19. Opthalmology

20. Optometry

The only defense, of course, is never to register and stay off that list!

☮☮☮

☮ ☮ ☮

Jail Break

Jackson MacLow
for Emmett Williams and John Cage)
from *WIN Magazine*, August 1966

Tear now jails down all.
Tear all now down Jails.
Tear now all Jails down.
Tear jails now all down.
Tear jails now down all.
Tear now jails all down.
Tear now down all jails.
Tear all down Jails now.
Tear jails down all now.
Tear jails all down now.
Tear all jails down now.
Tear jails all now down.
Tear Jails down now all.
Tear down now all jails.
Tear now all down jails.
Tear down now jails all.
Tear now down Jails all.
Tear down all jails now.
Tear down jails all now.
Tear all Jails now down.
Tear all now Jails down.
Tear all down now jails.
Tear down jails now all.
Tear down all now Jails.

All jails now down tear.
All now tear down jails.
All jails down tear now.
All now jails down tear.
All now down tear jails.
All jails now tear down.
All tear now jails down.
All Jails down now tear.

All down now tear jails.
All tear down jails now.
All tear jails down now.
All now down jails tear.
All down tear now jails.
All down tear jails now.
　　All down now jails tear.
　　All down jails now tear.
All down Jails tear now.
All tear jails now down.
All now tear jails down.
All tear down now jails.
　　All jails tear now down.
All now jails tear down.
　　All jails tear down now.
All tear now down jails.

Jails tear down all now.
Jails tear down now all.
Jails down now all tear.
Jails now tear down all.
Jails now tear all down.
Jails tear now down all.
Jails tear now all down.
Jails all tear now down.
Jails tear all now down.
Jails all tear down now.
Jails all down tear now.
Jails now down all tear.
Jails tear all down now.
Jails down all tear now.
Jails down now tear all.
Jails now all tear down.
Jails down tear all now.
Jails now all down tear.
Jails down tear now all.
Jails all now tear down.
Jails down all now tear.
Jails all now down tear.
Jails now down tear all.
Jails all down now tear.

PEOPLE: Five who speak clearly, listen closely to each other and all environing sounds & let what they hear modify how they speak. In WAY 1 they must be able to improvise together, let performance flow a their own impulses determine how they speak, WAY 2 needs a precise conductor and 5 speakers who follow him accurately. MATERIALS: 120 small cards. 5 equal squares of poster board [8 to 28 inches a side, paint/ink, pen/brush: for WAY 1, 10 envelopes each large enough lo hold 24 cards with room for easy removal a Insertion of cards.

PREPARATION: Type permutations on cards, Experiment to find size easiest to handle; size, colors, letter shapes most visible in performance situation. Make 5 square signs, each with one of the 9 words on it, For **WAY 1** attach 2 envelopes to each sign back and put the 24 cards whose ttext begins with the sign's word in one.

PERFORMANCE: WAY 1: The speakers line up, holding signs parallel in the order **TEAR DOWN ALL JAILS NOW**. Each draws a card, listens closely to other speaker & environment until he & the situation are ready, then speaks the words as a connected sentence making good sense.

> *Down tear now jails all.*
> *Down now tear jails all.*
> *Down tear all jails now.*
> *Down all now tear jails.*
> *Down jails tear all now.*
> *Down jails all tear now.*
> *Down now all jails tear.*
> *Down all jails now tear.*
> *Down all tear now jails.*
> *Down jails now tear all.*
> *Down now jails all tear.*
> *Down jails now all tear.*
> *Down tear jails now all.*
> *Down tear all now jails.*
> *Down now jails tear all.*
> *Down now tear all jails.*
> *Down jails tear now all.*
> *Down all tear jails now.*
> *Down tear jails all now.*
> *Down all jails tear now.*
> *Down tear now all jails.*
> *Down all now jails tear.*
> *Down jails all now tear.*
> *Down now all tear jails.*

Speed, loudness & voice coloration are free. He puts the card in the empty envelope a draws another, &c., until he's read each card once. It ends after last speaker finishes. WAY 2: Lined up as above, speakers face conductor, who shuffles the 120 cards & draws one, pointing in turn, in the permutation's order, to each word's bearer, who says the word, connecting it with the others so the sentence makes sense tho said by 5. WAY 2 needs long intense rehearsal; ends when all 129 permutations are read. WAY 2 performed (2nd Jail Poets' Reading, Living Theatre, 9 Sept. 1963) by Judith Malina, Tom Cornell, Paul Prensky, & 2 others,

conducted by JML. WAY 1 firstst performed in rain (reading against USSR jailing of writers, 30 April 1966: WIN II., 9: 6-7) by JML, Blackburn, Rothenberg,
Antin and the Rt. Revd. Michael F. Itkin.

Now all down tear jails.
Now down all tear jails.
Now tear down jails all.
Now jails all down tear.
Now jails all tear down.
Now jails tear down all.
Now down jails all tear.
Now all tear jails down.
Now all tear down jails.
Now down all jails tear.
Now jails down all tear.
Now tear down all jails.
Now tear all down jails.
Now all down jails tear.
Now tear jails down all.
Now jails down tear all.
Now down tear all jails.
Now tear all jails down.
Now all jails down tear.
Now tear jails all down.
Now jails tear all down.
Now down tear jails all.
Now down jails tear all.
Now all jails tear down.

☮☮☮

☮ ☮ ☮

EPILOGUE

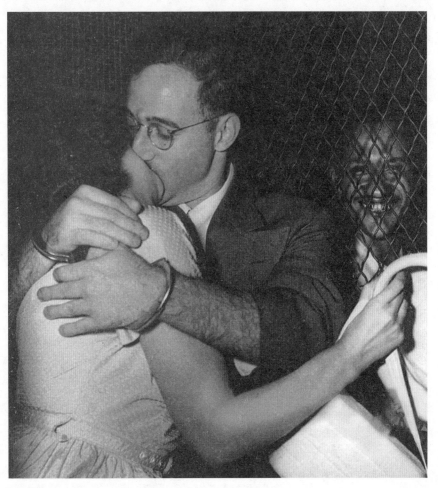

THE ROSENBERG FUND FOR CHILDREN

The Peacemaker Sharing Fund, Peacemakers, and The Peacemaker are all defunct in the 21st century. There have been several subsequent efforts to support movement families.

Robert Meeropol is the younger son of convicted atomic spies, Ethel and Julius Rosenberg. He and his younger brother, Michael, were adopted by Abel and Anne Meeropol after Robert's parents, Ethel and Julius Rosenberg, were executed as atomic spies in 1953 when he was six years old.

In 1990, Robert founded the Rosenberg Fund for Children http://www.rfc.org, a public foundation which provides for the families of targeted and imprisoned progressive activists. He stepped down as RFC director in 2012. Robert's daughter, Jenn Meeropol, now administers the fund.

RFC helps many families whose breadwinner has been imprisoned because of antiwar activity. I can think of no finer cause to which to contribute. Every dollar you give cheers activism.

Please give generously. Ω

☮☮☮

☮☮☮

くろがねの	Kuro-gane no
窓にさしいる	Mado ni sashi-iru
日の影の	Hi no kage no
移るを守り	Utsuru wo mamori
けふも暮らしぬ	Kyo mo kurashinu

Watching
through the iron-barred window
The sunbeams streaming
Today Watching

– tanka poem by Kanno Sugako
an anarcho-feminist journalist executed in Sugamo Prison, 1911, for her
participation in a plot to assassinate the Japanese Emperor.

It may be raining, but the sun is shining for me…
- David Greenglass

(Convicted of espionage with Ethel and Julius Rosenberg and Morton Sobell
for the transmission of the atomic bomb secrets to the U.S.S.R. in 1953, upon
his release in 1966. He escaped the death penalty by providing false testimony
about Ethel, his sister, and Julius, his brother-in-law, leading to their execution.)

☮☮☮

IF YOU ARE DRAFT-AGE, YOUR CHILDREN OR YOUR STUDENTS ARE DRAFT-AGE ...

I DON'T WANT TO BE DRAFTED. WHAT SHOULD I DO?"

1. If you haven't registered for the draft, don't.

2. Don't panic. The government can't prosecute you unless they can prove that you knew you were supposed to register, which requires them to get you to sign for a certified letter, or to send FBI agents to personally notify you and give you a chance to register. Make them work: Don't register unless the FBI finds you and tells you that you have to.

3. Don't give the government evidence against yourself. "You have the right to remain silent. Anything you say will be used against you." Don't sign for any letters from the government, and don't talk to the FBI. Tell your parents, family, and friends to do the same.

4. If you have to register, give the address at which an induction notice will be least likely to reach you. Don't tell the Selective Service System if you move. Don't give the Postal Service a forwarding address to pass on to the Selective Service System (and other junk mailers).

5. Ignore any letters about the draft from the Selective Service System, Department of Defense, or Department of Justice that you don't have to sign for. They may sound scary, but unless you have to sign for them, they are junk mail.

6. Don't sign for any letters from the Selective Service System, the Department of Defense, or the Department of Justice. You are not required to accept or sign for their letters, and you don't have to give the mail carrier a reason why you refuse a letter.

7. Tell your parents or anyone else who lives at the address you gave when you registered not to sign for any letters for you from the Selective Service System, the Department of Defense, or the Department of Justice. Tell them not to talk to any Feds who come looking for you or asking questions about you. They are not required to say anything to the Feds, or answer any questions. Anything they say can, and will, be used against them as well as against you.

8. Don't report for induction. As with registration, they can't prosecute you unless they can prove that you got an induction order, which they can't do unless you sign for a certified letter, or unless they send the FBI to serve you with an order in person. Make them work: Don't report unless the FBI finds you and tells you that you have to.

9. Organize and speak out against the draft. Let people know that you don't want to go.

10. Know that you are not alone. Most people don't want to register for the draft, don't want to fight, and don't want to kill or be killed. Millions of people have violated the draft registration laws.

11. Read this: "Conscientious Objectors and the Draft" http://www.uua.org/documents/washingtonoffice/ conscientiousobjectors_brochure.pdf.

War will exist until that distant day when the conscientious objector enjoys the same reputation and prestige that the warrior does today.

President John F. Kennedy

Albert Camus

☮ ☮ ☮

NEITHER VICTIMS
NOR EXECUTIONERS

Albert Camus

Yes, we must raise our voices. Up to this point, I have refrained from appealing to emotion. We are being torn apart by a logic of history which we have elaborated in every detail--a net which threatens to strangle us. It is not emotion which can cut through the web of a logic which has gone to irrational lengths, but only reason which can meet logic on its own ground. But I should not want to leave the impression... that any program for the future can get along without our powers of love and indignation. I am well aware that it takes a powerful prime mover to get men into motion and that it is hard to throw one's self into a struggle whose objectives are so modest and where hope has only a rational basis--and hardly even that. But the problem is not how to carry men away; it is essential, on the contrary, that they not be carried away but rather that they be made to understand clearly what they are doing.

To save what can be saved so as to open up some kind of future--that is the prime mover, the passion and the sacrifice that is required. It demands only that we reflect and then decide, clearly, whether humanity's lot must be made still more miserable in order to achieve far-off and shadowy ends, whether we should accept a world bristling with arms where brother kills brother; or whether, on the contrary, we should avoid bloodshed and misery as much as possible so that we give a chance for survival to later generations better equipped than we are.

For my part, I am fairly sure that I have made the choice. And, having chosen, I think that I must speak out, that I must state that I will never again be one of those, whoever they be, who compromise with murder, and that I must take the consequences of such a decision. The thing is done, and that is as far as I can go at present.... However, I want to make clear the spirit in which this article is written.

We are asked to love or to hate such and such a country and such and such a people. But some of us feel too strongly our common humanity to make such a choice. Those who really love the Russian people, in gratitude for what they have never ceased to be--that world leaven which Tolstoy and Gorky speak of--do not wish for them success in power politics, but rather want to spare them, after the ordeals of the past, a new and even more terrible bloodletting. So, too, with the American people, and with the peoples of unhappy Europe. This is the kind of elementary truth we are likely to forget amidst the furious passions of our time.

Yes, it is fear and silence and the spiritual isolation they cause that must be fought today. And it is sociability and the universal intercommunication of men that must be defended. Slavery, injustice, and lies destroy this intercourse and forbid this sociability; and so we must reject them. But these evils are today the very stuff of history, so that many consider them necessary evils. It is true that we cannot "escape history," since we are in it up to our necks. But one may propose to fight within history to preserve from history that part of man which is not its proper province. That is all I have to say here. The "point" of this article may be summed up as follows:

Modern nations are driven by powerful forces along the roads of power and domination. I will not say that these forces should be furthered or that they should be obstructed. They hardly need our help and, for the moment, they laugh at attempts to hinder them. They will, then, continue. But I will ask only this simple question: What if these forces wind up in a dead end, what if that logic of history on which so many now rely turns out to be a will o' the wisp? What if, despite two or three world wars, despite the sacrifice of several generations and a whole system of values, our grandchildren--supposing they survive--find themselves no closer to a world society? It may well be that the survivors of such an experience will be too weak to understand their own sufferings. Since these forces are working themselves out and since it is inevitable that they continue to do so,there is no reason why some of us should not take on the job of keeping alive, through the apocalyptic historical vista that stretches before us, a modest thoughtfulness which, without pretending to solve everything, will constantly be prepared to give some human meaning to everyday life. The essential thing is that people should carefully weigh the price they must pay....

All I ask is that, in the midst of a murderous world, we agree to reflect on murder and to make a choice. After that, we can distinguish those who accept the consequences of being murderers themselves or the accomplices of murderers, and those who refuse to do so with all their force and being. Since this terrible dividing line does actually exist, it will be a gain if it be clearly marked. Over the expanse of five continents throughout the coming years an endless struggle is going to be pursued between violence and friendly persuasion, a struggle in which, granted, the former has a thousand times the chances of success than that of the latter. But I have always held that, if he who bases his hopes on human nature is a fool, he who gives up in the face of circumstances is a coward. And henceforth, the only honorable course will be to stake everything on a formidable gamble: that words are more powerful than munitions.

☮☮☮

FEAR OF IMPRISONMENT

Much thought we have advanced in shedding fear of imprisonment, there is still a disinclination to seek it and anxiety to avoid it. We must remain scrupulously honest and non-violent, and at the same time be anxious almost to find ourselves in the gaols of the Government. It must be positively irksome, if not painful for us, to enjoy so-called freedom under a government we seek to end or mend. We must feel that we are paying some unlawful or heavy price for retaining our liberty. If therefore when being innocent we are imprisoned, we must rejoice because we must feel that freedom is near. Is not freedom nearer for the imprisonment of hundreds who are now cheerfully undergoing it for the sake of the country? What can be better for non-co-operators of Bombay than that though innocent, they should be imprisoned for the sake of the guilty?

– Mahatma Gandhi

☮☮☮

**CELEBRATE INTERNATIONAL CONSCIENTIOUS OBJECTORS'
AND WAR RESISTERS'DAY MAY 15**

CELEBRATE PRISON JUSTICE DAY AUGUST 10

CELEBRATE PRISONERS FOR PEACE DAY DECEMBER 1

Whether these men will arise or not I do not know. It is probable that most of them are even now thinking things over, and that is good. But one thing is sure: their efforts will be effective only to the degree they have the courage to give up, for the present, some of their dreams, so as to grasp more firmly the essential point on which our very lives depend. Once there, it will perhaps turn out to be necessary, before they are done, to raise their voices.

The only way to deal with an unfree world is to become so absolutely free that your very existence is an act of rebellion.

– Albert Camus

☮☮☮

413

Supporting US prisoners for peace

Abolitionist Law Center, P.O. Box 8654, Pittsburgh, Pennsylvania 15221 Email: info@absolitionistlawcenter.org. Web: https://abolitionistlawcenter.org.
(Support for political and politicized prisoners for the purpose of abolishing class- and race-based mass incarceration.)

American Friends Service Committee, 1501 Cherry Street, Philadelphia, Pennsylvania 19102. Web: http://afsc.org..
(The AFSC maintained a program of prison visitation and a CO Services Division, which is was involved in the compilation of a prison handbook for draft resisters.)

[Defunct?] **AFSC Youth and Militarism Program**, 1515 Cherry Street, Philadelphia, Pennsylvania 19102. Tel: (215) 241-7176. Email: youthmil@afsc.org. Web: http://www.youth4peace.org.
(Support for counter-recruitment in education.)

Amnesty International U.S.A., 5 Pennsylvania Plaza, New York, New York 10001. Tel: (212) 807-8400. Web: http://www.amnestyusa.org.
(The U.S. section of Amnesty discussed at length the problem of conscientious objectors in prison in their own country. Although each section is required not to take action on the part of those imprisoned within their country, the U.S. section offered support to COs in prison anyway. They published *Amnesty Action* monthly.)

Buddhist Peace Fellowship, PO Box 3470, Berkeley, California 94703. Tel: (510) 239-3764. Email: info@bfp.org. Web: http://www.buddhistpeacefellowship.org.
(Support for Buddhist COs of all disciplines.)

Campus Antiwar Network Web: http://campusantiwar.net/
(Countering militarism and recruitment on campus.)

Church of the Brethren Brethren Service Center, 500 Main Street, PO Box 188, Windsor, Maryland 21776. Tel: (410) 635-8710, (800) 366-5896
(Ministered to Brethren COs and maintained a counseling and visitation program. The Church currently publishes *Call of Conscience*, to develop in young people attitudes about peace and war, including draft registration.)

Church of the Brethren Office of Public Witness, 337 North Carolina Ave. SE, Washington DC 20003. Tel: (717) 333-1649. Email: nhosler@brethren.org. Web: http://www.brethren.org/peace/
(The Brethren Office of Public Witness provides support for acts of conscience.)

Catholic Worker Movement, Maryhouse, 55 East Third Street, New York, New York 10003 and 36 East First Street, New York New York 10003. Tel: (212) 777-9617. Email: info@catholicworker.org. Web: http://www.catholicworker.org/, http://www.catholicworker.org.
(The CW maintains a House of Hospitality for the poor and wretched of New York City as well as 206 communities in the U.S. and 25 communities in 11 countries. Manned by Catholic Worker volunteers, it is where many Catholic prison COs started to put Christ's teachings into practice. CW publishes *Catholic Worker*, still a penny a copy, monthly. A *Catholic Worker* archive is held by Marquette University.)

Center on Conscience & War [National Interreligious Board for Conscientious Objectors], 1830 Connecticut Ave. NW, Washington, DC 20009. Tel: (800) 379-2679. Web: http://www.centeronconscience.org.
(Advocates for rights of conscience, opposes military conscription, and serves all conscientious objectors to war. Publishes *The Reporter for Conscience' Sake* quarterly http://www.centeronconscience.org/pubs/the-reporter-online.html. NSBRO maintained a counseling and visitation service for the more traditional conscientious objector on religious grounds. NSBRO remains one of the best resources around, both historically and in support of current military resisters)

[Regrouping] Central Committee for Conscientious Objectors, Oakland, California

(CCCO maintained an excellent counseling and prison visitation service by interview, mail, and telephone. They had offices in Philadelphia and Chicago and published the *Handbook for Conscientious Objectors* (Twelfth and last edition, 1981), and *NewsNotes of the Central Committee for Conscientious Objectors* bimonthly, *Counter Pentagon* and *Objector* monthly, as well as producing very good counselors' and attorneys' guides to the law.)

CIVIL LIBERTIES DEFENSE CENTRE, 783 Grant Street, Suite #200, Eugene, Oregon 97402 Tel: (541) 687-9180, Web: https://cldc.org/about/contact/.
(Supporting political prisoners.)

COALITION FOR ALTERNATIVES TO MILITARISM IN SCHOOLS (CAMS) Web: http://www.militaryfreeschools.org/
(Supporting counter-recruitment.)

COMMITTEE OPPOSED TO MILITARISM AND THE DRAFT, P.O. Box 15195, San Diego, California 92175. Tel: (760) 753-7518. Email: COMD@comdsd.org. Web: http://www.comdsd.org.
(Publishes numerous resources including *Draft NOtices* quarterly.)

[Defunct] Connections, c/o Cathy Kornblith, 70 Liberty Street, San Francisco, California 94110
(Connections, formerly Prison Widows, was a collective of prison visitors attempting to better communication between prisoners and the outside.)

COUNTER-RECRUITMENT DISCUSSION GROUP http://groups.yahoo.com/group/counter-recruitment/
(Board for counter-recruitment strategy.)

COURAGE TO RESIST, 484 Lake Park Avenue, #41, Oakland, California 94610. Web: http://couragetoresist.org/.
(Supporting military resisters including Chelsea Manning, WikiLeaks whistleblower over 'Cablegate'. A 2014 report by the U.S. Army's War College said Courage to Resist impedes recruiting and retaining soldiers: Courage to Resist [has] "a negative affect [sic] on potential Soldiers [sic] in our formations, and the centers of influence in our schools, communities, and religious institutions". Please give generously. Quakers [AFSC], Mennonites [MCC], Iraq Veterans Against the War, Veterans for Peace and the YouTube video "Before You Enlist" English: http://www.youtube.com/watch?v=kcz7NFrPUg0, Spanish: http://www.youtube.com/watch?v=yLUWoukGWEM are also honored.)

CRIMINON INTERNATIONAL, 431 North Brand Blvd. #309, Glendale, California 91203. Tel: (818) 546-1921. Email: president@criminon.org. Web: http://www.criminon.org/.
(Scientology ministry for rehabilitation in prisons.)

CRITICAL RESISTANCE, 1904 Franklin Street, Suite 504, Oakland, California 94612. Web: http://criticalresistance.org/.
(For prison abolition.)

EDUCATION NOT MILITARIZATION, 332 South Michigan Avenue, Suite 1032 - V152, Chicago, Illinois 60604. Tel: (734) 216-1814. Email: Coordinator@ChicagoVFP.org. Web: http://educationnotmilitarization.org.
(A counter-recruitment project of Chicago Veterans for Peace.)

[Defunct]FEDERAL PRISONS PROJECT, Berkeley, California
(The FPP attempted to engage and maintain a liaison with the federal Bureau of Prisons on behalf of imprisoned conscientious objectors.)

FELLOWSHIP OF RECONCILIATION, Box 271, Nyack, New York 10960. Tel: (914) 358-4601. Email: for@forusa.org. Web: http;//www.forusa.org/.
(The FOR has became increasingly interested in the problems faced by draft resisters in prison and provided public education through seminars throughout the U.S. The FOR publishes Fellowship quarterly.)

FORTUNE SOCIETY, 29-76 Northern Boulevard, Queens, New York 11101. Web: http://fortunesociety.org.

(The Society is available for the guidance and counseling of all former prisoners, as well as making public contact with the prisons in an attempt at reform through public interest.)

THE GENERAL COUNCIL OF THE ASSEMBLIES OF GOD, 1445 Boonville Avenue, Springfield, MO 65802. Email: ksurface@ag.org. Web: http://www.ag.org.

(Support for Pentecostal and other religious COs.)

GI RIGHTS HOTLINE/GI RIGHTS NETWORK, Military Discharges and Military Counseling, 1830 Connecticut Avenue NW, Washington DC 20009. Tel: (877) 447-4487. Email: girights@girights.org. Web: http://girightshotline.org/.

(Supports military resisters both in the US and overseas with centers in seven states, the District of Columbia, and Germany.)

GLOBAL NONVIOLENT ACTION DATABASE. Web: http://nvdatabase.swarthmore.edu/.

GUÅHAN COALITION FOR PEACE AND JUSTICE, Guam. Email: lisanti@yahoo.com. Web: http://www.weareguahan.com/

(Supporting resisters on Guam's US military bases.)

PROYECTO GUERRERO AZTECA PEACE PROJECT. Tel: (760) 746-4568.

(Supports counter-recruitment for Latino students.)

[Defunct?]**INTERFAITH PRISONERS OF CONSCIENCE PROJECT,** PO Box 770608, Lakewood, Ohio 44107. Tel: (216) 780-9262. Email; ipoc@sbcglobal.net.

International Center on Nonviolent Conflict, P.O. Box 27606, Washington DC 20038. Tel: (202) 416-4720. Email: icnc@nonviolent-conflict.org. Web: https://www.nonviolent-conflict.org.

INTERNATIONAL NONVIOLENT INITIATIVES (INI), PO Box 515, Waltham Massachusetts 02454. Tel: (781) 891-0814. Email: woodward@brandeis.edu.

IRAQ VETERANS AGAINST THE WAR, P.O. Box 3565, New York New York 10008. Tel. (646) 723-0989 Email: maggiemartin@ivaw.org / matthoward@ivaw.org / iramali@ivaw.org. Web: http://www.ivaw.org/.

(Supports military resisters.)

JEWISH PEACE FELLOWSHIP, P.O. Box 271, Nyack, New York 10960. Web: http://www.jewishpeacefellowship.org/.

(Publishes Shalom monthly.)

JEWISH VOICE FOR PEACE, 1611 Telegraph Ave., Suite 550, Oakland California 94612; 147 Prince St., Suite 17, Brooklyn New York 11201. Web: http://www.jewish-voiceforpeace.org, http://www.december18th.org.

(Support for Jewish refuseniks and Israeli resisters to Palestinian war of occupation.)

[Defunct] **LIBERATION,** Glen Gardner New Jersey and New York

(Edited by David Dellinger, Liberation was one of the oldest and largest monthly journals of radical pacifism in the United States. Since its inception in 1955 Liberation carried the cause of prisoners for conscience. A complete archive of the magazine is maintained by the Swarthmore College Peace Collection. Dave was described in DeBenedetti as the antiwar movement's William Lloyd Garrison.)

MADRES CONTRA LA GUERRA. Web: http://madrescontralaguerra.blogspot.com.

(Support for Puerto Rican resisters.)

MENNONITE CENTRAL COMMITTEE, 21 South Twelfth Street, Post Office Box 500, Akron, Pennsylvania 17501. Web: http://www.mcc.org.

(Ministered to Mennonite COs and maintains a counseling and visitation program. Published *Mennonite Conscientious Resisters' Newsletter* and *Mennonite Non-Cooperator' Newsletter.* Also hosts the Intercollegiate Peace Fellowship, published *Peace Notes* Web: http://intercollegiatepf.mennonite.net.)

MENNONITE CHURCH PEACE AND JUSTICE SUPPORT NETWORK. Web: http://www.pjsn.org/.

METTA CENTER FOR NONVIOLENCE, PO Box 98, Petaluma, California 94953. Tel: (707) 774-6299. Email: info@mettacenter.org. Web: http://mettacenter.org.

[Defunct] **MIDWEST COMMITTEE FOR DRAFT COUNSELING,** Chicago.
(CCCO's midwest branch office 1976-1997.)

MILITARY FAMILIES SPEAK OUT, 1716 Clark Avenue PMB 122, Long Beach CA 90815. Tel: (562) 597-3980 Email: mfso@mfso.org. Web: http://www.mfso.org.

MILITARY LAW TASK FORCE, National Lawyers Guild, 730 N. First Street, San Jose, California 95112.Tel: (415) -566-3732 / (619) 233-1701. Web: http://nlgmltf.org/.
(Legal support for military resisters.)

MOVIMIENTO ESTUDIANTIL CHICANO DE AZTLÁN (MEChA). Web: http://www.nationalmecha.org/.
(National Latino/a student organization with regional chapters supporting counter-recruiting.)

NATIONAL COALITION TO PROTECT STUDENT PRIVACY. Web: http://www.studentprivacy.org.

[Defunct] **NATIONAL RESISTANCE COMMITTEE,** San Francisco. Published *Resistance News*.

NATIONAL WAR TAX RESISTANCE COORDINATING COMMITTEE, PO Box 150553, Brooklyn, New York 11215. Tel: (718) 768-3420 or (800) 269-7464. Email: nwtrcc@nwtrcc.org. Web: http://nwtrcc.org.

NATION OF ISLAM, 7351 South Stony Island Avenue, Chicago, Illinois 60649. Web: http://www.noi.org.
(Ministered to imprisoned Black Muslim draft resisters.)

NATIONAL NETWORK OPPOSING THE MILITARIZATION OF YOUTH, c/o American Friends Service Committee Wage Peace Program, 65 Ninth Street, San Francisco, California 94103. Tel: (760) 634-3604. Email: admin@nnomy.org Web: http://nnomy.org and Leave My Child Alone Web: http://www.leavemychildalone.org
(Programs of AFSC and the Unitarian Universalist Association.)

NATIONAL WAR TAX RESISTANCE COORDINATING COMMITTEE, P.O. Box 150553, Brooklyn, New York 11215.Web: http://www.nwtrcc.org/.

[Defunct] **NEW ENGLAND COMMITTEE FOR NONVIOLENT ACTION,** Voluntown, CT.
(New England CNVA was a direct action community in the Connecticut woods which organized and based its projects from there at Polaris Action Farm. CNVA has been the leader in radical pacifism and as their message reached more and more people, attacks on the isolated farm grew more serious, especially by the paramilitary Minutemen. CNVA maintained, in the face of attack, a full program of projects, education, construction, maintenance and survival, clerical work, and farming. NECNVA published *Direct Action for a Nonviolent World* at least monthly. The farm is where many imprisoned for draft resistance found their hope for re-entry.)

NONVIOLENCE INTERNATIONAL, 4000 Albemarle Street, NW, Suite 401, Washington, DC 20016. Tel: (202) 244-0951. Email: info@nonviolenceinternational.net, Web: http://nonviolenceinternational.net/.

NONVIOLENT PEACEFORCE, 2610 University Avenue West, Suite 550, St. Paul, Minnesota 55114. Tel: (612) 871-0005. Email: info@nonviolentpeaceforce.org.

THE NUCLEAR RESISTER, P.O. Box 43383, Tucson, Arizona 85733. Tel: (520) 323-8697. Email: nukeresister@igc.org. Web: http://www.nukeresister.org. Prisoner addresses: http://www.nukeresister.org/inside-out/. Writing from prisoners: http://www.nukeresister.org/the-inside-line/.
(The only resource on activists in prison.)

Orthodox Peace Fellowship, P.O. Box 6009, Raleigh, North Carolina 27628. Web: http://www.incommunion.org/.
(Publishes *In Communion*.)

THE PEACE ABBEY, 2 North Main Street, Sherborn, Massachusetts 01770. Web: http://www.peaceabbey.org/.
(Maintains a registry of conscientious objectors and presents the annual Courage of Conscience Award.)

PEACEFUL VOCATIONS, PO Box 12282, Forth Worth, Texas 76110 Web: http://peacefulvocations.org/
(Works against military recruitment in education.)

[Defunct] *THE PEACEMAKER*, Cincinnati, Ohio
(Peacemakers conducted the Peacemaker Orientation Program in Nonviolence and a Reunion and Continuation every summer. They also maintained the Peacemaker Sharing Fund, for the support of imprisoned draft resisters and their families in times of need and hardship. *The Peacemaker* was published every third week by Peacemakers in the Cincinnati area.)

[Defunct] PRISONERS EMERGENCY SUPPORT COMMITTEE, A Quaker Action Group, Philadelphia, Pennsylvania
(The Committee was formed by the families of prisoners at the farm camps of both Allenwood and Lewisburg to create a needed public link for the first organized noncoöperatlon to take place in the two prisons since World War II, taking the form of both hunger and work strikes among imprisoned resisters,   met by harsh punishment by the prison authorities.)

[Defunct] PRISONER'S INFORMATION AND SUPPORT SERVICE, Boston, Massachusetts
(Organized primarily by former prison resisters, PISS was vital in encouraging communication from the prisons and providing library, workshop, and counseling services for prisoners, former prisoners, their families and friends, and those who are about to be imprisoned. They published *P.I.S.S. News Notes* occasionally.)

PRISON FELLOWSHIP, 44180 Riverside Parkway, Lansdowne, Virginia 20176. tel: (800) 206-9764. Web: https://www.prisonfellowship.org/.
(Evangelical Protestant ministry providing counselling, education, and other opportunities widely spread through U.S. prisons.)

PROJECT ON YOUTH AND NON-MILITARY OPPORTUNITIES, P.O. Box 230157, Encinitas, California 92023. Tel: (760) 634-3604. Email: projyano@aol.com. Web: http://www.projectyano.org.

REFUSER SOLIDARITY NETWORK, P.O. Box 53474, Washington, D.C. 20009. Tel: (202) 232-1100. E-mail: info@refusersolidarity.net. Web: http://www.refusersolidarity.net.
(Support for Israeli refuseniks.)

[Defunct] RESIST, Room 4, 763 Massachusetts Avenue, Cambridge, Massachusetts 02139
(Resist maintained a personal and financial supporting link between the community and the Resistance. They organized adult support for draft resistance and offer personal assistance to draft resisters. They published A CALL TO RESIST ILLEGITIMATE AUTHORITY occasionally.)

RESISTANCE STUDIES JOURNAL. Email: editor@resistance-journal.org. Web: http://resistance-journal.org/.

RESISTERS/NATIONAL RESISTANCE COMMITTEE, 1130 Treat Avenue, San Francisco, California 94110. Tel: (415) 824-0214. Email:.edward@hasbrouck.org. Web: http://hasbrouck.org/draft/.
(Provides information on draft registration, draft resistance, the military draft, and the medical draft.)

[Defunct] **RESISTERS FAMILY SUPPORT AND VISITATION FUND, PEACE AND SOCIAL ACTION PROGRAM**, New York Yearly Meeting of the Religious Society of Friends, 217 Second Avenue, New York, New York 10003. Web: http://www.nyym.org.

(The Program organized a celebration of conscience at Allenwood Federal Prison Camp involving imprisoned resisters and 1500 supporters. Since that action, they established a fund for the needs of imprisoned drafter resisters and their families.)

RESOURCE CENTER FOR NON-VIOLENCE. 612 Ocean Street, Santa Cruz, California 95060. Tel: (831) 423-1626. Email: rcnvinfo@gmail.com. Web: http://www.rcnv.org/.

(Military counseling and resister support.)

ROSENBERG FUND FOR CHILDREN, 116 Pleasant Street, Suite 348, Easthampton, Massachusetts 01027. Web: http://rfc.org.

Mission Statement "The Rosenberg Fund for Children was established to provide for the educational and emotional needs of children whose parents have suffered because of their progressive activities and who, therefore, are no longer able to provide fully for their children. The RFC also provides grants for the educational and emotional needs of targeted activist youth."

Background "The RFC was founded by Robert Meeropol, who was orphaned at age six when his parents, Ethel & Julius Rosenberg, were executed at the height of the McCarthy Era. In 1990 Robert figured out how he could repay the progressive community that helped him survive. He started the RFC to help children of targeted activists in the U.S. today- children who are experiencing the same nightmare he and his brother endured as youngsters." Carry It Forward/Celebrating the Children of Resistance: http://www.youtube.com/watch?v=fahmAcS59Xk.

SOLDIER, SAY NO/RIGHT TO RESIST. Email: SoldierSayNo@yahoo.com. Web: http://www.peacehost.net/ssn/;   http://soldiersayno.blogspot.com

(Support for military resisters, with Canada options.)

SPEAK4PEACE/THE CO PROJECT, P.O. Box 1417, Stanwood WA 98292. Email: co-project@speak4peace.com . Web: http://www.speak4peace.com/home.html.

STOP THE DRAFT. Web: http://www.stopthedraft.com.

(News and resources.)

STOP THESE WARS. Web: http://www.stopthesewars.org.

(Real war and peace news for veterans and active military.)

STUDENT PEACE ACTION NETWORK, 1100 Wayne Avenue, Suite 1020, Silver Spring, Maryland 20910. Tel. (301) 565-4050 ext. 322 (800) 228-1228 Email: SPAN@peace-action.org. Web: http://www.studentpeaceaction.org.

(130 chapters supporting counter-recruitment in schools.)

STUDENT PEACE ALLIANCE, 1616 P Street NW, Suite 100, Washington DC 20036. Tel: (202) 684-2553. Email: SPA@peacealliance.org. Web: http://www.studentpeacealliance.org.

(100 chapters opposing militarism in schools.)

UNITED PENTECOSTAL CHURCH INTERNATIONAL, 8855 Dunn Road, Hazelwood, MO 63042. Email: rjohnston@upci.org or main@upci.org. Web: http://www.upci.org.

(Support for Pentecostal and other religious COs.)

[Defunct?] **UNIVERSITY CONVERSION PROJECT**, Kent State University, Ohio & Cambridge, Massachusetts.

(Maintained the War Research Info Service to oppose ROTC (Reserve Officer Training Corps) presence on   university campuses. [See Albanese.])

VETERANS FOR PEACE, 216 South Meramec Avenue, St. Louis, Missouri 63105. Tel: (314) 725-6005. Email: vfp@veteransforpeace.org. Web: http://www.veteransforpeace.org.

(Veterans for Peace provides support to military resisters. VFP's homepage provides a counter of the costs of W.S. wars since 2001. Guaranteed to make your head spin!)

VIETNAM VETERANS AGAINST THE WAR, P.O. Box 355, Champaign, Illinois 61824. Tel: (773) 569-3520. Email: vvaw@vvaw.org. Web: http://www.vvaw.org/.
(Supporting military resisters.)

WAGING NONVIOLENCE, 500 Washington Ave., #52, Brooklyn New York 11238. Email: contact@wagingnonviolence.org. Web: http://wagingnonviolence.org/.
(Web-based peace news. Free newsletter subscriptions available.)

WAR RESISTERS LEAGUE (WRL) 168 Canal Street #600 New York, NewYork 10013. Tel: (212) 228-0450. Email: wrl@warresisters.org. Web: http://www.warresisters.org/.
(The WRL is officially the U.S. branch of the War Resisters' International, but maintains many separate programs of its own. The WRL is a pioneer in both education and direct action and maintained communication with many draft prisoners and those who expected to be imprisoned. They publish *WIN: Through Revolutionary Nonviolence* quarterly.)

WATCHTOWER BIBLE AND TRACT SOCIETY OF THE JEHOVAH'S WITNESSES, 25 Columbia Heights, Brooklyn, New York 11201. Web: http://www.jw.org/en/.
(Ministered to Jehovah's Witnesses imprisoned for draft resistance.)

WE WON'T GO PLEDGE, Mountain View Voices for Peace. Web: http://www.mvvp.org/wewontgo/.

WIN PEACE AND FREEDOM THROUGH NONVIOLENT ACTION, 168 Canal Street #600 New York, NewYork 10013. Web: http://www.warresisters.org/win.
(From its beginnings as a biweekly of revolutionary pacifism, *WIN Magazine* (Workshop in Nonviolence) still provides joyous and colorful coverage of U.S. peace activism and civil disobedience action quarterly.)

WOMEN'S INTERNATIONAL LEAGUE FOR PEACE AND FREEDOM, 777 UN Plaza, 6th floor, New York, New York 10017. Tel: (212) 682-1265. Email: president@wilpfus.org. Web: http://www.wilpfus.org.

SUPPORTING US DESERTERS IN CANADA

CAMPAGNE D'OPPOSITION AU RECRUTEMENT MILITAIRE. Web: http://www.antire-crutement.info/?q=en.

CANADIAN VOICE OF WOMEN FOR PEACE/LA VOIX DE FEMMES, 579 Kingston Road, Mailbox 125, Toronto ON M4E 1R2. Tel: (416) 603-7915. Email: info@vow-peace.org. Web: http://vowpeace.org.

CENTRE DE RESSOURCES SUR LA NON-VIOLENCE (CRNV), 1945 rue Mullins, bureau 160, Montréal QC H3K 1N9. mTel: +1 (514) 272-5012. Email: crnv@nonviolence.ca. Web: http://www.nonviolence.ca/.

CONSCIENCE CANADA, 8 Chandos Drive, Kitchener ON N2A 3C2. Tel: (250) 537-5251. Email: info@consciencecanada.ca, janslakov@shaw.ca. Web: http://www.consciencecanada.ca.

THE PENTECOSTAL ASSEMBLIES OF CANADA, 2450 Milltower Court, Mississauga ON L5N 5Z6. (905) 542-7400. Email: info@paoc.org. Web: https://paoc.org.

WAR RESISTERS SUPPORT CAMPAIGN/CAMPAGNE D'APPUI AUX OBJECTEURS DE CONSCIENCE, Box 13, 427 Bloor Street West, Toronto ON M5S 1X7. Email: (Toronto) resisters@sympatico.ca, (Vancouver) vanresisters@yahoo.ca, (Victoria) vlannon@pacificcoast.net. Web: http://resisters.ca/.
(Supporting U.S. military resisters since 2004. Let them stay!)

SUPPORTING INTERNATIONAL CONSCIENTIOUS OBJECTORS, DESERTERS, AND PRISONERS OF CONSCIENCE

INTERNATIONAL

EUROPEAN NETWORK FOR CIVIL PEACE SERVICES. Email: contact@en-cps.org. Web: http://www.en-cps.org/.

RED ANTIMILITARISTA DE AMÉRICA LATINA Y EL CARIBE, Web: http://ramalc.org
(Coordinator of Caribbean, Central, and South American war resisters.)

SERVICIO PAZ Y JUSTICIA AMÉRICA LATINA. Contact: http://serpajamericalatina.org/mapa/. Web: http://serpajamericalatina.org/.

WAR RESISTERS' INTERNATIONAL, 5 Caledonian Road, London N19DY ENGLAND. Tel: +44 20-7278-4040. Email: info@wri-irg.org. Web: http://www.wri-irg.org.
(The WRI provides an international expression of concern and support for conscientious objectors and political prisoners throughout the world and maintains current and historical statistics on conscription in many countries and supports those imprisoned for their resistance to it. They publish *The Broken Rifle* quarterly in English, French, Spanish and German.
WRI's excellent handbook, *The Conscientious Objector's Guide to the International Human Rights System*, created jointly with the Quaker United Nations Office, the Centre for Civil and Political Rights, and Conscience and Peace Tax International, is available here: http://co-guide.org in English and Spanish.)

AUSTRALIA

GLOBAL NONVIOLENCE NETWORK, P.O. Box 68, Daylesford, Victoria 3460 Australia. Email: flametree@riseup.net. Web: https://globalnonviolencenetwork.wordpress.com.

WAR RESISTERS' LEAGUE (WRL) PO Box 451, North Hobart TAS 7002 AUSTRALIA. Email: pdpjones@mpx.com.au. Tel +61 3-6278-2380.

AUSTRIA

ARBEITSGEMEINSCHAFT FÜR WEHRDIENSTVERWEIGERUNG UND GEWALTFREIHEIT (Working Group on Conscientious Objection to military service and for Nonviolence) (Arge WDV), Schottengasse 3a/1/59, 1010 Wien AUSTRIA. Tel: +43 1-535-9109. Email: argewdv@verweigert.at. Web: http://www.verweigert.at/.

BEGEGNUNGSZENTRUM FÜR AKTIVE GEWALTLOSIGKEIT (Center for Encounter and Active Non-violence) (BFAG), St Wolfgangerstr 26, 4820 Bad Ischl (Pfandl) AUSTRIA; Tel: +43 6132-4590. Email: mareichl@ping.at. Web: http://www.begegnungszentrum.at/.

BELARUS

CAMPAIGN FOR ALTERNATIVE SERVICE. Web: http://ags.by/ссылки/.

BELGIUM

AGIR POUR LA PAIX (formerly Action pour la Paix and Mouvement International de la Réconciliation/ Internationale des Résistant(e)s à la Guerre), 35, Rue Van Elewyck, 1050 Bruxelles BELGIUM. Tel: +32 2-648-52-20. Email info@agirpourlapaix.be. Web: http://www.agirpourlapaix.be.

ACTION JEUNESSE POUR LA PAIX YOUTH ACTION FOR PEACE, 3 avenue du Parc Royal, 1020 Bruxelles BELGIUM. Tel: +32 2-478-9410. Email: yapis@xs4all.be.

EUROPEAN BUREAU FOR CONSCIENTIOUS OBJECTION (EBCO), 35 Van Elewyck Street, B-1050 Brussels BELGIUM. Tel: +32 2-648-5220. Email: ebco@ebco-beoc.org. Web: http://www.ebco-beoc.org/.
(Support for EU COs, excellent reports.)

INTERNATIONAL FELLOWSHIP OF RECONCILIATION (IFOR), La Maison de la Paix, 35, rue Van Elewyck, 1050 Ixelles Bruxelles BELGIUM. Web: http://www.ifor.org/.

NONVIOLENT PEACEFORCE, Rue Belliard 205, 1040 Bruxelles BELGIUM. Tel: +32 2-648-0076. Email: headoffice@nonviolentpeaceforce.org. Web: http://www.nonviolentpeaceforce.org.

VREDESACTIE, Patriottenstraat 27, 2600 Berchem BELGIUM. Tel: +32 3-281-6839. Email info@vredesactie.be. Web: http://www.vredesactie.be/.

BENIN

ASSOCIATION POUR LA SENSIBILISATION, LA PROMOTIONET LA DÉFENSE DES DROITS HUMAINS, BENIN Email: aspddhbj65@yahoo.fr.

BOSNIA AND HERZEGOVINA

KAMPANJA ZA PRIGOVOR SAVJESTI U BiH (Campaign for Conscientious Objection in BiH) Džemala Bijedića 309, 71000 Sarajevo BOSNIA & HERZOGOVINA. Tel. +387 33-61-84-61. Email: info@prigovorbih.org.

BRITAIN

ALDERMASTON WOMEN'S PEACE CAMPAIGN (AWPC), c/o 5 Caledonian Road, London N1 9DX ENGLAND. Tel: +44 07969-739812. Email: awpc@gmx.co.uk. Web: http://www.aldermaston.net/.

AMNESTY INTERNATIONAL, 1 Easton Street, London WC1X 0DW ENGLAND. Web: http://www.amnesty.org.
(Amnesty maintains constant vigilance in their campaign to free political prisoners all over the world. They published *Amnesty International Review* quarterly.)

ANGLICAN PACIFIST FELLOWSHIP, 11 Weavers End, Hanslope, Milton Keynes MK19 7PA ENGLAND. Tel: +44 1908-510642. Email: ajkempster@aol.com. Web: http://www.anglicanpeacemaker.org.uk/.

AT EASE, Bunhill Fields Meeting House, Quaker Court, Banner Street, London EC1Y 8QQ. Web: http://atease.org.uk. Email: info@atease.org.uk
(Providing peace advice and information to members of the UK Armed Forces.)

BROTHERHOOD CHURCH STAPLETON, Pontefract, West Yorkshire WF8 3DF ENGLAND. Tel: +44 1977-620381. Email: cr@c-r.org. Web: http://www.c-r.org/.

CAMPAIGN FOR NUCLEAR DISARMAMENT (CND), 162 Holloway Road, London N7 8DQ ENGLAND. Tel: +44 20-7700-2393. Email: enquiries@cnduk.org Web: http://www.cnduk.org/.

[Defunct] **CENTRAL BOARD FOR CONSCIENTIOUS OBJECTORS**, London ENGLAND
(Although CBCO became inactive because of the elimination of conscription in Great Britain, they maintained a Continuing Committee which provided an excellent historical background on British prison COs.)

CIVIL RESISTANCE. Web: http://civilresistance.info.

CONCILIATION RESOURCES, Burghley Yard, 106 Burghley Road, London NW5 1AL ENGLAND. Tel. +44 20-7359-7728.

Conscience and Peace Tax International, Archway Resource Centre, 1b Waterlow Road, London N19 5NJ ENGLAND. Tel: +44 20-3515-9132. Email: info@ conscienceonline.org.uk, cpti@cpti.ws Web: http://www.cpti.ws, http://www.conscienceonline.org.uk/.
(Support for resisters.)

European Network Against Arms Trade (ENAAT). Web: http://www.enaat.org.

Fellowship of Reconciliation England (FOR-England), Peace House, 19 Paradise Street, Oxford, OX1 1LD ENGLAND. Tel: +44 1865-250781. Email: office@ for.org.uk. Web: http://www.for.org.uk/.

Housmans Bookshop, 5 Caledonian Road, London N1 9DX ENGLAND. Tel: +44 20-7837-4473. Email: shop@housmans.com. Web: http://www.housmans.com.

The Housmans World Peace Database. Web: http://www.housmans.info/wpd/.

[Defunct] **National Council for Civil Liberties**, London ENGLAND
(Maintained various programs to safeguard the rights of British COs.)

Peace Brigades International, Development House, 56-64 Leonard Street, London EC2A 4LT ENGLAND. Tel: +44 20-7065-0775. Web: http://www.peacebrigades.org/.

Peace News, 5 Caledonian Road, London N1 9DX ENGLAND. Tel: +44 20-7278-3344. Web: http://peacenews.info/.
(*Peace News* is refreshing, sophisticated and refined but, despite all that, is a fine weekly journal of international pacifism which reports in great detail about those men imprisoned for draft refusal.)

Peace Pledge Union (PPU), 1 Peace Passage, London N7 0BT ENGLAND. Tel: +44 20-7424-9444. Email: enquiry@ppu.org.uk. Web: http://www.ppu.org.uk/. Learn Peace. Web: http://www.ppu.org.uk/learn/peaceed/pe_ednetcurriculum.html.
(Venerable pacifist support group for COs beginning in World War I.)

Prison Reform Council, 27 Warminster Road, London SE.25 ENGLAND. Web: http://www.prisonreformtrust.org.uk.
(The Council is involved in reforming British prisons.)

Reprieve, PO Box 72054, London EC3P 3BX United Kingdom. Web: http://www.reprieve.org.uk. Email. info@reprieve.org.uk. Tel. +44 (0)20 7553 8140.
(Helping those suffering "extreme human rights abuses at the hands of the world's most powerful governments." Currently working on death penalty, lethal injection, torture, Guantánamo, drones, and secret prisons.)

Resistance Studies Network. Email: l.odysseos@sussex.ac.uk. Web: http://resistancestudies.org.

Tolstoyans, c/o 59 Chapel Road, Ramsgate, Kent CT11 0BS ENGLAND. Tel: +44 18-4358-9027. Email: gez6551@yahoo.co.uk.

Trident Ploughshares, 42-46 Bethel St, Norwich NR2 1NR ENGLAND. Tel: +44 15-4752-0929. Email reforest@gn.apc.org, rbrianlarkin@googlemail.com. Web: http://www.tridentploughshares.org/.

Veterans for Peace UK Web: http://veteransforpeace.org.uk/education/.
(Educating young people about military service, stand with resistiors.)

Chad

Tchad Non-Violence, BP 1266, N'Djamena CHAD. Tel: +235 517-283.

Chile

Grupo de Objeción de Conciencia Ni Casco Ni Uniforme, Bremen 585, Ñuñoa, Santiago CHILE. Tel: +56 2-556-6066. Email: objetores@yahoo.com.

Web http:/nicasconiuniforme.wordpress.com/.

GRUPO DE OBJECIÓN DE CONCIENCIA ROMPIENDO FILAS, Prat 289 Oficina 2-A, Temuco CHILE. Email: rompiendofilas@entodaspartes.org.

NI CASCO NI UNIFORME, SANTIAGO. Email: objetores@yahoo.com, Web: https:// nicasconiuniforme.wordpress.com.

COLOMBIA

ACCIÓN COLECTIVA DE OBJETORES Y OBJETORAS DE CONCIENCIA (AAOOC), Cr. 19 #33A - 26/1 II Bogotá COLOMBIA. Tel. +57 1-560-5058, +57 316-820-8709. Email: objecion@objetoresbogota.org. Web: http://objetoresbogota.org.

JUSTAPAZ, Calle 32 No. 14-32, Pilmer Piso, Bogotá COLOMBIA. Tel: +57 (1)-232-6080 / +57 (1) 301-605-6951 / +57 (1) 301 431-0123 . Email: justapaz@justapaz.org. Web: http://www.justapaz.org/index.php/en-us/.

KOLECTIVO ANTIMILITARISTA DE MEDELLÍN, Medellín – Antioquia, COLOMBIA. Tel: +57 4-31-2215-1091. Email: antimilitarismomedellin@gmail.com.

RED JUVENIL, A.A.52-215, or Calle 47 N 40 53, Medellín COLOMBIA. Tel: +57 239-3670. Email: info@redjuvenil.org.

RED PRO DE PAZ, Calle 35, No. 7 - 25 Piso 10, Bogotá, Cundinamarca COLOMBIA. Tel: +57 (1) 288-8982 / +57 (1) 285-5649. Email: informacion@redprodepaz.org.co. Web: http://redprodepaz.org.co.

CROATIA

CENTAR ZA MIROVNE STUDIJE (Centre for Peace Studies), Selska cesta 112a, 10000 Zagreb, CROATIA. Tel: +385 1-482-0094. Email: cms@cms.hr. Web: http://www.cms.hr/.

CYPRUS

KIBRIS'TA VICDANI RET INSIYATIFI (Cypriot Initiative for Conscientious Objection). Web: http://www.reddet.org.

ΚΥΠΡΑΙΟΙ ΕΝΑΝΤΙΑ ΣΤΟ ΣΤΡΑΤΟ! (CYPRIOTS AGAINST THE ARMY!) Email: cyantiarmy@espiv.net. Web: https://cypriotsagainstarmy.wordpress.com.

DENMARK

ALDRIG MERE KRIG (AMK), Nørremarksvej 4, 6880 Tarm DENMARK. Tel +45 9737-3163. Email: Info@AldrigMereKrig.dk. Web: http://aldrigmerekrig.dk.

ECUADOR

SERVICIO PAZ Y JUSTICIA DEL ECUADOR (Serpaj-Ecuador), Casilla postal 17-03-1567, Quito ECUADOR. Tel: +593 2-257-1521. Email: serpaj@ecuanex.net.ec. Web: www.serpaj.org.ec/.

EGYPT

NO TO COMPULSORY MILITARY SERVICE MOVEMENT, Tel: +49 17631415934. Email: NoMilService@gmail.com. Web: http://www.nomilservice.com/.

FINLAND

ASEISTAKIELTÄYTYJÄLIITTO UNION OF CONSCIENTIOUS OBJECTORS, Peace Station, Veturitori, 00520 Helsinki FINLAND. Tel: +358 9-7568-2444. Email: toimisto@akl-web.fi. Web: www.akl-web.fi/.

COMMITTEE OF 100 IN FINLAND, Peace Station, Veturitori, 00520 Helsinki FINLAND. Tel: +358 9-7568-3551. Email: sadankomitea@sadankomitea.fi. Web: www.sadankomitea.fi/.

SITOUTUMATON VASEMMISTO, Independent Left Mannerheimintie 5 C 7.krs, 00100 Helsinki FINLAND. Web: www.helsinki.fi/jarj/sitvas/.

TOTAALIBLOGI. Email: totaaliblogi@riseup.net. Web: http://totaaliblogi.org.

FRANCE

ACTION NON-VIOLENTE COP21. Email: anvcop21@riseup.net. Web: http://anv-cop21.org.

ALTERNATIVES NON-VIOLENTES, c/o Mundo-M, 47 avenue Pasteur, 93100 Montreuil FRANCE. Tel: +33 6-2123-2398. Email: contact@alternatives-non-violentes.org. Web: http://alternatives-non-violentes.org/.

CENTRE DE RESSOURCES NON-VIOLENCE SUR LA DE MIDI-PYRÊNÊES, 11 allée de Guérande 31770 Colomiers FRANCE. Tel: +33 5-6178-6680. Email: crnv.midi-pyre-nees@wanadoo.fr. Web: http://www.non-violence-mp.org/.

COLLECTIF DES DÉSOBÉISSANTS, Maison des initiatives et de la citoyenneté (M.I.C), 1 bis rue Méchin, 93450 l'Ile-Saint-Denis FRANCE. Tel: +33 6-6418-3421. Email: contact@la-boutique-militante.com. Web: http://www.desobeir.net.

COLLECTIF DES OBJECTRICES ET OBJECTEURS TARNAIS (COT), Sophie Flaquet - Arvieu - 81190 Tanus FRANCE. Tel: +33 56-338-3955. Email: cot@cot81.com.

COMITÉ LOUIS LECOIN, Pour que plus aucun objecteur de conscience ne puisse connaître la prison. Web: http://www.louis-lecoin.fr.

INSTITUT DE FORMATION ET DE RECHERCHE DU MOUVEMENT POUR UNE ALTERNATIVE NON VIOLENT. Email: http://www.ifman.fr/index.php/contact. Web:http://www.ifman.fr/.

INSTITUT DE RECHERCHE SUR LA RÉSOLUTION NON-VIOLENTE DES CONFLITS (IRNC), 14 rue des Meuniers, 93100 Montreuil FRANCE. Email: irnc@irnc.org. Web: http://www.irnc.org/Diaporamas/index.en.htm.

MOUVEMENT INTERNATIONAL DE LA RÉCONCILIATION (MIR), 68 rue de Babylone, 75007 Paris FRANCE; Tel: +33 1-4753-8405. Email: mirfr@club-internet.fr. Web: http://mirfrance.org.

MOUVEMENT DE L'OBJECTION DE CONSCIENCE (MOC), c/o MOC-Nancy, BP 363, F-54007 Nancy FRANCE. Tel: +33 3-8328-7590. Email: mocnancy@ouvaton.org. Web: http://mocnancy.ouvaton.org/.

MOUVEMENT POUR UNE ALTERNATIVE NON-VIOLENTE (MAN), 114 rue de Vaugirard, 75006 Paris FRANCE. Tel: +33 1-4544-4825. Email: man@nonviolence.fr. Web: http://nonviolence.fr/.

NON-VIOLENCE ACTUALITÉ (NVA) CENTRE DES RESSOURCES SUR LA GESTION NON-VIOLENTE DES RELATIONS ET DES CONFLITS, BP 20241 45202 Montargis FRANCE. Tel: +33 2-3893-6722. Web: http://www.nonviolence-actualite.org/index.php/fr/in-english.

REFRACTAIRES NON-VIOLENTS À LA GUERRE D'ALGERIE. Web: http://www.refractairesnonviolentsalgerie1959a63.org/.

REVUE SILENCE EXPLORATEUR D'ALTERNATIVES, 9, rue Dumenge, F 69317 Lyon 04 FRANCE. Tel: +33 4-7839-5533. Web: http://www.revuesilence.net.

[Defunct] **SECRETARIAT DES OBJECTEURS DE CONSCIENCE**, 3 Impasse Chatiers, 75-Paris FRANCE

(The Secretariat coordinated work camp programs as alternative service for conscientious objectors under the French draft and also maintained a vital link for imprisoned COs serving lengthy sentences.)

UNION PACIFISTE DE FRANCE (UPF), Boîte Postale 196, 75624 Paris 13 FRANCE. Tel: +33 1-4586-0875. Email: union.pacifiste@wanadoo.fr. Web: http://unionpacifiste.org/.

GEORGIA

PEOPLE TO PEOPLE, Apt 45-Building 13, Vazha-Pshavela 6, Tbilisi 186 GEORGIA. Tel: +995 3230-6162. Email: ptptg@posta.ge.

WAR RESISTERS' INTERNATIONAL – Georgian Section (WRI Georgia) 89/24 Agmashenebeli Ave, 12th floor, Tbilisi 202 GEORGIA. Tel: +995 3295-1003. Email wri@caucasus.net.

GERMANY

ANTI-KRIEGS-MUSEUM, Bruesseler Strasse 21, 13353 Berlin GERMANY. Tel: +49 30-4549-0110. Email: Anti-Kriegs-Museum@gmx.de: Web: https:www.anti-kriegs-museum.de/.

ARCHIV AKTIV FÜR GEWALTFREIE BEWEGUNGEN, Normannenweg 17-21, 20537 Hamburg GERMANY. Tel: +49 40-430-2046. Email: email@archiv-aktiv.de.

 Web: http://www.archiv-aktiv.de/.

BUND FÜR SOZIALE VERTEIDIGUNG (Federation for Social Defence) (BSV) Schwarzer Weg 8, 32423 Minden GERMANY. Tel: +49 571-29456. Email: office@soziale-verteidigung.de. Web: http://soziale-verteidigung.de.

CONNECTIONE.V.INTERNATIONALEARBEITFÜRDERKRIEGSDIENSTVERWEIGERER UND DESERTEURS (International Support of Conscientious Objectors and Deserters), Von-Behring-Str. 110, D-63075 Offenbach GERMANY. Tel. +49 69-8237-5534. Email: office@Connection-eV.org. Web: http://connection-ev.org/en_index.php.

DEUTSCHE FRIEDENSGESELLSCHAFT-VEREINIGTE KRIEGSDIENSTGEGNER (DFG-VK), Werastraße 10, 70182 Stuttgart GERMANY. Tel: +49 711-5189-2626. Email: office@dfg-vk.de. Web: http://www.dfg-vk.de/.
(The Verband coordinated work camp programs for German conscientious objectors under the West German draft law and continues as part of War Resisters' International with many local peace groups. There were those COs who went to prison for refusal, but no information could be obtained at the time of this writing.)

DEUTSCHE FRIEDENSGESELLSCHAFT - INTERNATIONALE DER KRIEGSDIENSTGEGNER (DFG-IdK) Jungfrauenthal 37, 20149 Hamburg GERMANY. Tel: +49 40-453-433. Email: mail@dfg-idk.de. Web: http://www.dfg-idk.de/.

EVANGELISCHE ARBEITSGEMEINSCHAFT FÜR KRIEGSDIENSTVERWEIGERUNG UND FRIEDEN (EAK). Email: info@asfrab.de.

FORUM PAZIFISMUS ZEITSCHRIFT FÜR THEORIE UND PRAXIS DER GEWALTFREIHEIT,Werastraße 10 70182 Stuttgart GERMANY. Tel. +49 711-5188-5603. Web: http://www.forum-pazifismus.de.

GALTUNG-INSTITUT FOR PEACE THEORY AND PEACE PRACTICE, Markgrafenstraße 42a, 79639 Grenzach-Wyhlen GERMANY. Tel. +49 762-4912-9137. Email: info@galtung-institut.de. Web: https://www.galtung-institut.de/en/.

GANDHI-INFORMATIONS-ZENTRUM, Postfach 210109, 10501 Berlin GERMANY. Email: mkgandhi@snafu.de. Web: http://www.nonviolent-resistance.info/index.htm.

GLOBAL ECUMENICAL NETWORK FOR THE ABOLITION OF MILITARY CHAPLAINCY, Postfach 28 03 12, 13443 Berlin GERMANY. Tel: +49 511-446-482. Email: global-network@militaerseelsorge-abschaffen.de. Web: http://globnetabolish-militarychaplaincy.webnode.com/.

GRASWURZELREVOLUTION BREUL 43, 48143 Münster GERMANY. Tel: +49 251-482-9057. Email: redaktion@graswurzel.net. Web: www.graswurzel.net/.

INITIATIVE MUSIKER/INNEN GEGEN DIE AUFTRITTE DER MILITÄRMUSIKKORPS, c/o Dietmar Parchow, Austraße 77, D-72669 Unterensingen GERMANY. Email: musikergegenmilitaermusik@idk-berlin.de. Web: http://musiker-gegen-militaermusik. jimdo.com/startseite/our-demand-in-english/.

INSTITUT FÜR FRIEDENSARBEIT UND GEWALTFREIE KONFLIKTAUSTRAGUNG (Institute for Peace Work and Nonviolent Conflict Transformation) (IFGK), Hauptstr 35, 55491 Wahlenau/Hunsrueck GERMANY. Tel: +49 65-43-980-096.

Email: BMuellerIFGK@t-online.de. Web: www.ifgk.de/.

INTERNATIONALE DER KRIEGSDIENSTGEGNER/INNEN (IDK), Postfach 28 03 12, 13443 Berlin GERMANY. Email: info@idk-berlin.de. Web: www.idk-berlin.de.

KAMPAIGN GEGEN WERPFLICHT ZWANGSDIENSTE + MILITAR, Email: info@asfrab. de. Web: http://www.kampagne.asfrab.de.

MILITARY COUNSELING NETWORK GI-RIGHTS HOTLINE IN GERMANY, Richard-Wagner Str. 48, 67655 Kaiserslautern GERMANY. Tel: +49 151-5672-7550. Email: gi-cafe-germany@gmx.net.

NETZWERK FRIEDENSSTEUER. Email: http://www.netzwerk-friedenssteuer.de/index.php/kontakte. Web: http://www.netzwerk-friedenssteuer.de/.

NONVIOLENT-PEACEFORCE, Schwarzer Weg 8, Minden 32423 GERMANY. Tel: +49 571-29456. Email: info@nonviolent-peaceforce.de. Web: http://de.nonviolent-peaceforce.de.

NONVIOLENT RESISTANCE. Web: http://castor.divergences.be/?lang=en.

ÖKUMENISCHE INITIATIVE ZUR ABSCHAFFUNG DER MILITÄRSEELSORGE, Heiner Schuster, Werner-Messmer-Straße 1, D-78315 Radolfzell GERMANY. Tel. +49 511-446-482. Email: kontakt.bremen@militaerseelsorge-abschaffen.de Web: http:// www.militaerseelsorge-abschaffen.de.

SATYAGRAHA FOUNDATION FOR NONVIOLENCE STUDIES. Web: http://www. satyagrahafoundation.org/.

GREECE

ASSOCIATION OF GREEK CONSCIENTIOUS OBJECTORS (Συνδεσμοσ Αντιρρησιων Συνειδησησ), Tsamadou 13, 10683 Athens GREECE. Tel: +30 69-4454-2228. Email: greekCO@hotmail.com. Web: http://www.antirrisies.gr/.
"You can find us every first Sunday of the month, after 20.00, at the "Immigrant Hangout" Tsamadou 13A in Exarcheia neighborhood, Athens."

KEADEA - Movement for Peace, Human Rights, and National Independence, Akadamias 35, 10672 Athens GREECE. Tel: +30 210-3560-2430. Email: keadea@ otenet.gr.

HONG KONG

ASIAN HUMAN RIGHTS COMMISSION, Ground Floor, 52 Princess Margaret Road, Ho Man Tin, Kowloon HONG KONG. Tel: +852 2698-6339. Web: http://www. humanrights.asia.
(Pan-Asian human rights support for resisters.)

HUNGARY

ALBA KÖR - ERÖSZAKMENTES MOZGALOM A BÉKÉÉRT ALBA CIRCLE (Nonviolent Movement for Peace in Hungary) (Alba-Kör) Bati Mark, Arpad fejedelem utja 30, H-1023 Budapest HUNGARY. Tel: +36 30-914-6610. Email: alba@albakor.hu. Web: http://www.albakor.hu.

INDIA

EKTA PARISHAD. Email: info@ektaparishad.com, vinod@ektaparishad.com. Web: http://ektaparishad.com.

GANDHI RESEARCH FOUNDATION, 299, Tardeo Road, Nana Chowk, Bombay 400 007 INDIA. Tel: +91 22-2387-2061. Email: info@mkgandhi.org.

GANDHIAN SOCIETY VILLAGES ASSOCIATION (GANSOVILLE) Amaravathi Pudur PO, Pasumpon District, Tamil Nadu 623301 INDIA. Tel: +91 86-458-3234.

SWADHINA, 34/C Bondel Road, Kolkata 700019 INDIA. Tel: +91 33-247-0934. Email: mainoffice@swadhina.org. Web: http://www.swadhina.org.in/.

WAR RESISTERS OF INDIA/WEST, c/o Swati & Michael, Juna Mozda, Dediapada, Dist Narmada, Gujarat 393040 INDIA.

IRELAND

INNATE - AN IRISH NETWORK FOR NONVIOLENT ACTION TRAINING AND EDUCATION, 16 Ravensdene Park, Belfast BT6 0DA NORTHERN IRELAND.Tel: +44 28-9064-7106. Email: innate@ntlworld.com. Web: http://www.innatenonviolence.org/.

IRISH CAMPAIGN FOR NUCLEAR DISARMAMENT, PO Box 6327, Dublin 6 EIRE (IRELAND). Tel: +353 86-362-1220. Email: irishcnd@gmail.com. Web: http://indigo.ie/~goodwill/icnd.html.

ISRAEL

ADDAMEER (Conscience) Prisoner Support and Human Rights Association مؤسسة الضمير لرعاية الأسير وحقوق الإنسان, P.O. Box 17338, Jerusalam ISRAEL / 3 Edward Said Street, Sebat Bldg., 1st floor, Suite 2, Ramallah, West Bank PALESTINE. Tel. +972 (0)296 04 46, +972 (0) 297 01 36. Email: info@addameer.ps. Web: http://www.addameer.org.
    (Supporting Palestinian political prisoners.)

BREAKING THE SILENCE (שוברים שתיקה), POB 51027, 6713206 Tel Aviv ISRAEL Email: info@breaking the silence.org.il English: http://www.breakingthesilence.org.il Hebrew: http://www.shovrimshtika.org
    (Supporting Israeli draft and military resisters.)

CONSCIENTIOUS OBJECTORS AGAINST THE OCCUPATION. Web: https://www.facebook.com/refusingIDF/.

COURAGE TO REFUSE (אומץ לסרב), POB 16238 Tel Aviv, Israel Tel. +972-3523-3103 Email: info@seruv.org.il Hebrew: http://www.seruv.org.il English: http://www.seruv.org.il/English/
    (Supporting Israeli draft and military refuseniks.)

END CONSCRIPTION CAMPAIGN. Web: http://www.endconscription.org.

NEW PROFILE (פרופיל חדש), c/o Sergeiy Sandler, POB 48005,Tel Aviv 61480 ISRAEL. Tel: +972 3-696-1137. Email: newprofile@speedy.co.il. Web: http://www.newprofile.org/.

REFUSER SOLIDARITY NETWORK. Web: http://www.refusersolidarity.net.

SAMIDOUN PALESTINIAN PRISONER SOLIDARITY NETWORK سمدون شبكة تضامن السجناء الفلسطينيين. Email: samidoun@samidoun.ca. Web: http://samidoun.net.
(Supporting Palestinian political prisoners and solidarity with international prisoners.)

URFOD - REFUSE, YOUR PEOPLE WILL PROTECT YOU. Web: https://www.facebook.com/urfod?fref=ts.

YESH GVUL MOVEMENT (לובג שי תעונת). "There is a limit !" Web: https://www.facebook.com/Yesh.Gvul.1982/.
(Supporting military resistance in Israel.)

ITALY

ASSOCIAZIONE SIGNORNÒ!, via della Guglia 69a, 00186 Roma ITALY. Tel: +39 6-678-0808. Email: signorno@hotmail.com.

LEGA DEGLI OBIETTORI DI COSCIENZA (LOC) Sede Nazionale, via Mario Pichi 1, 20143 Milano ITALY. Tel: +39 2-837-8817. Email: locosm@tin.it.

MOVIMENTO NONVIOLENTO CASA PER LA NONVIOLENZA, via Spagna 8, 37123 Verona ITALY. Tel: +39 45-800-9803. Email: azionenonviolenta@sis.it. Web: http://www.azionenonviolenta.it/.

JAPAN

GLOBAL PEACE CAMPAIGN, 1047 Naka, Kamogawa, Chiba 296-0111 JAPAN. Email: Yumi Kikuchi yumik@fine.ocn.ne.jp Tel: +81 470-97-1011 Fax: +81 470-97-1215

NIPPONZAN MYOHOJI, 7-8 Shinsen-Cho, Shibuya-Ku, Tokyo 150 JAPAN. Tel: +81 3-3461-9363. Email: info@nipponzanmyohoji.org. Web: http://nipponzanmyohoji.org.

WRI JAPAN, 666 Ukai-cho, Inuyama-shi, Aichi-ken 468-0085 JAPAN. Tel: +81 568-615-850.

MACEDONIA

MIROVNA AKCIJA PEACE ACTION JOSESKI ICE (Мировна Акција), ul <Andon Slabejko> Br. 138, 75000 Prilep MACEDONIA. Tel: +389 48-22616. Email: mirovna@mirovnaakcija.org. Web: www.mirovnaakcija.org/.

MALAYSIA

PENTECOSTAL WORLD FELLOWSHIP, Calvary Convention Centre, No 1 Jalan Jalil Perkasa 1, Bukit Jalil, 57100 Kuala Lumpur, MALAYSIA. Email: pentecostalworldfellowship@gmail.com. Web: http://www.pentecostalworldfellowship.com.

NEPAL

COMMUNITY SELF-RELIANCE CENTRE (CSRC), Tokha Muncipality, Post Box No. 19790 Kathmandu NEPAL. Tel: +977-1-436-0486/435-7005. Email: landrights@csrcnepal.org. Web: http://www.csrcnepal.org/.

HUMAN RIGHTS WITHOUT FRONTIERS, Post Box No. 10660, Maitidevi-33, Kathmandu NEPAL. Tel: +977 1-444-2367. Email: hrwfnepal@mail.com.np. Web: www.hrwfnepal.net.np/.

NATIONAL LAND RIGHTS FORUM (NLRF), BhumiGhar, Tokha-10, Dhapasi Kathmandu NEPAL. Tel: +977-1-691-4586. Email: land@nlrfnepal.org. Web: www.nlrfnepal.org/.

NETHERLANDS

INTERNATIONAL FELLOWSHIP OF RECONCILIATION (IFOR), Postbus 1528, 3500 BM Utrecht NETHERLANDS. Web: http://www.ifor.org/.

MUSEUM VOOR VREDE EN GEWELDLOOSHEID (Museum for Peace and Non-Violence), Turfmarkt 30 2801 HA Gouda NETHERLANDS. Email: info@vredesmuseum.nl. Web: http://www.vredesmuseum.nl/.

PAIS, Vlamingstraat 82, 2611 LA Delft NETHERLANDS. Tel: +31 15-212-1694. Email: info@vredesbeweging.nl. Web: www.vredesbeweging.nl/.

STOP WAPENHANDEL, Rekening NL11 TRIO NETHERLANDS. Tel. +31 390-407-380. Email: info@stopwapenhandel.org. Web: http://www.stopwapenhandel.org/English.

WOMEN PEACEMAKERS PROGRAM (WPP), Laan van Meerdervoort 70, 2517 AN Den Haag NETHERLANDS. Tel: +31 70-345-2671. Email: info@womenpeacemakersprogram.org. Web: http://womenpeacemakersprogram.org.

NEW ZEALAND

WHITE POPPIES FOR PEACE http://www.whitepoppies.org.nz.
(New Zealand campaign to remember all victims of war not only soldiers. Proceeds support peace scholarships.)

NIGERIA

ALTERNATIVES TO VIOLENCE PROJECT NIGERIA, 5 Ogunlesi Street off Bode Thomas Road, Onipanu, Lagos NIGERIA. Tel: +234 1-497-1359. Email: prawa@linkserve.com.ng.

HUMAN RIGHTS, JUSTICE AND PEACE FOUNDATION (HRJPF) 93, Market Road, First Floor (Back), Aba, Abia State NIGERIA. Tel: +234 803-505-6312. Email: hrjpfoundation@yahoo.com. Web: http://www.kabissa.org/directory/HRJPF.

NORWAY

FOLKEREISNING MOT KRIG (FMK) PO Box 2779, Solli, 0204 Oslo NORWAY. Tel: +47 2246-4670. Email: fmk@ikkevold.no. Web: http://www.ikkevold.no/.

FORUM 18 NEWS SERVICE, Postboks 6603, Rodeløkka, N-0502 Oslo NORWAY. Web: http://www.forum18.org.
(Forum 18 supports 1966) supporting conscientious objection, focusing on Eastern Europe and former Soviet states.)

PALESTINE

JENIN CREATIVE CULTURAL CENTRE, Al-yamony Building 4th floor, Above Al-bait Baitak Restaurant, Jenin, West Bank, PALESTINE. Tel: +972 4-2423-42442. Email: jenin3c@yahoo.com. Website: http://jenincreativeculturalcenter.wordpress.com/ .

PAPUA NEW GUINEA

LEITANA NEHAN WOMEN'S DEVELOPMENT AGENCY, P.O. Box 22, Buka, Bougainville PAPUA NEW GUINEA. Tel: +675 973-9062. Email: leitananehan@daltron.com.pg.

PARAGUAY

MOVIMIENTO DE OBJECIÓN DE CONCIENCIA (MOC-Paraguay) Calle Iturbe N° 1324 entre Primera y Segunda Proyectada - Asunción PARAGUAY. Tel: +595 981-415-586. Email moc_py@yahoo.com. Web: http://www.moc-py.org/.

PORTUGAL

ASSOCIAÇÃO LIVRE DOS OBJECTORES E OBJECTORAS DE CONSCIÊNCIA (ALOOC) Rua D. Aleixo Corte-Real, 394, 3ºD, 1800-166 Lisboa PORTUGAL. Email: alooc. portugal@gmail.com.

TRANSCEND INTERNATIONAL. Tel: +351 226-065-617, +351 914-945-965. Email: antonio@transcend.org.

ROMANIA

SIBIENII PACIFISTI, Str. Mitropooliei, 2400 Sibiu ROMANIA. Tel: +40 692-18178.

RUSSIA

CITIZEN AND ARMY / FOR A DEMOCRATIC ALTERNATIVE SERVICE. Web: http://ags.demokratia.ru/.

SOLDIERS' MOTHERS (Солдатские Матери), ул. Разъезжая, 9, St. Petersburg 190000 RUSSIA. Tel. +7 906-263-1717, +7 911-772-3440. Email: voen@soldiersmothers.ru, Web: http://soldiersmothers.ru.

SCOTLAND

SCOTTISH CAMPAIGN FOR NUCLEAR DISARMAMENT, 77 Southpark Avenue, Glasgow G12 8LE SCOTLAND. Tel: +44-141-357-1529. Email: scnd@banthebomb. org. Web: http://www.banthebomb.org.

SERBIA

WOMEN IN BLACK AGAINST WAR (Žene u Crnom protiv Rata), Jug Bogdanova 18/5, 11000 Beograd SERBIA. Tel: +381 11-623-225. Email: stasazen@eunet.yu. Web: http://zeneucrnom.org/index.php?lang=en

POKRET ZA MIR PANČEVO, PF 186, 26000 Pancevo, Vojvodina SERBIA. Tel: +381 13-45009. Email ppm@bozic.co.yu.

SINGAPORE

YELLOW RIBBON PROJECT, 407 Upper Changi Rd North, Singapore 507658 Tel. +65-6251-3597 / 6214-2832 / 6513-1597 Email: yellow_ribbon_proj@yahoo.com. sg Web: http://www.yellowribbon.org.sg
(Scholarships for ex-prisoners, job bank, and one thousand community partners.)

SOUTH AFRICA

END CONSCRIPTION CAMPAIGN. Tel: +27 11-717-1973. Email: catherine@saha.org. Web: http://www.saha.org.za/ecc25/index.htm.

THE RESISTANCE PROJECT. Tel: +27 21-465-3551. Email: gallery@mutifilms.co.za. Web: http://resistance-project.com.

SOUTH KOREA

WRI-KOREA, Mudang-Rl, 405 Hongdong-Myoun, Hongsung-Gun Choong-Chung-Namdo SOUTH KOREA. Tel: 82-2-991-5020. Email: wrikorea@hotmail.com. Web: http://www.wrikorea.wo.to/.

WORLD WITHOUT WAR, 3F, 422-9, Mangwon-dong, Mapo-gu, Seoul, 121-230 SOUTH KOREA. Tel: +82 2-6401-0514. Email: peace@withoutwar.org. Web: http://www.withoutwar.org/.

431

SOUTH SUDAN

ORGANIZATION FOR NONVIOLENCE AND DEVELOPMENT (SONAD). Tel: +249 9-1212-5374. Email: sulafasonad12@gmail.com. Web: http://www.sonad.org/.

SPAIN

ACTIVISMO SIN VIOLENCIA. Email: info@nonviolenceinternational.net. Web: http://noviolenciaactiva.com.

ALTERNATIVA ANTIMILITARISTA MOC (AA.MOC), c/o San Cosme y San Damián 24-2, 28012 Madrid SPAIN. Tel: +34 91-475-3782. Email: moc.lavapies@nodo50.org. Web: www.antimilitaristas.org/.

ANTIMILITARISTES MOC-VALÈNCIA, C. Roger de Flor 8, baix-dta, 46001 València SPAIN. Email: retirada@pangea.org. Web: http://www.antimilitaristas.org,

ASSEMBLEA ANTIMILITARISTA DE CATALUNYA, c/o De La Cera 1 bis, 08001 Barcelona SPAIN. Tel: +34 93-329 -0643. Email: mocbcn@pangea.org.

CANARIAS POR LA PAZ / ALTERNATIVA ANTIMILITARISTA MOC. Web: http://canariasporlapaz.blogspot.de.

LA CASA DE LA PAZ, c/o Aniceto Saénz,1 local 3, Plaza del Pumarejo, 41003 Sevilla SPAIN. Web: http://www.lacasadelapaz.org.

CENTRE D'ESTUDIS PER LA PAU J.M.DELÀS, c/o Rivadeneyra, 6 10è 08002 Barcelona SPAIN. Tel: +34 93-317-6177. Email: info@centredelas.org. Website http://centredelas.org/.

EDUCARUECA. Email: yalajb@educarueca.org. Web: http://www.educarueca.org.

INTERNATIONAL INSTITUTE FOR NONVIOLENT ACTION, Plaça Catalunya, N° 9, 5é 08002 Barcelona. Tel: +34 93-551-4714. Email: communication@novact.org.

KONTZIENTZI ERAGOZPEN MUGIMENDUA (MOC-EUSKAL HERRIA), Iturribide 12-1 D, 48006 Bilbao SPAIN. Tel: +34 94-415-3772. Email: betxea@euskalnet.net.

PLATAFORMA POR LA DESOBEDIENCIA CIVIL. Web: http://desobediencia.es.

RED ANTIMILITARISTA Y NOVIOLENTA DE ANDALUCÍA. Web: https://redantimilitarista.wordpress.com.

SIN KUARTEL BILBOKO TALDE ANTIMILITARISTA KEM-MOC, la calle Fika n° 4, 48006 Bilbao SPAIN. Tel. +34 94-415-3772. Email: sinkuartel@gmail.com. Web: http://www.sinkuartel.org.

TALLER DE PAZ PEACE FACTORY, c/o Gaspar Fernandez 1, Apartado de Correos 728, Jerez de la Frontera SPAIN. Tel: +34 956-346-652. Email: smunozn@clientes.unicaja.es.

SRI LANKA

NONVIOLENT DIRECT ACTION GROUP (NVDAG) Post Box 2, 29 Kandy Road, Kaithady-Nunavil, Chavakachcheri SRI LANKA. Tel: +94 112-177. Email: delsmskr@eureka.lk.

SWEDEN

KRISTNA FREDSRÖRELSEN, Ekumeniska Centret, Starrbacksgatan 11, 17299 Sundbyberg SWEDEN. Tel: +46 8453-6840. Email: info@krf.se. Web: http://www.krf.se/.

OFOG, Linnégatan 21, 41304, Gotemborg SWEDEN. Tel: +46 733-815-361. Email: info@ofog.org. Web: http://www.ofog.org.

SVENSKA FREDS- OCH SKILJEDOMSFÖRENINGEN (Swedish Peace and Arbitration Society) (SPAS) Box 4134, Svartensgatan 6, 10263 Stockholm SWEDEN. Tel: +46 8702-1830. Email: info@svenska-freds.se. Web: http://www.svenska-freds.se/english/.

SWITZERLAND

CENTRE POUR L'ACTION NON-VIOLENTE (Centre for Nonviolent Action) (formerly Centre Martin Luther King) (CENAC) Rue de Genève 52, 1004 Lausanne SWITZERLAND. Tel: +41 21-661-2434. Email info@non-violence.ch. Web: http://www.non-violence.ch.

GROUPE POUR UNE SUISSE SANS ARMEÉ (GSSA). Web: http://www.gssa.ch/wp/.

GRUPPE FÜR EINE SCHWEIZ OHNE ARMEE (GSoA), Postfach 103, 8031 Zürich SWITZERLAND. Tel: +41 1-273-0100. Email: gsoa@gsoa.ch. Web: www.gsoa.ch/.

INTERNATIONAL PEACE BUREAU, 41, rue de Zürich, CH-1201 Geneva SWITZERLAND. Tel. +41 22-731-6429. E-mail: mailbox@ipb.org. Web: http://www.ipb.org/.

QUAKER UNITED NATIONS OFFICE, 13 Avenue du Mervelet, 1209 Geneva SWITZERLAND. Tel: +41 22-748-4800. Email: quno@quno.ch. Web: http://www.quno.org/.

WOMEN'S INTERNATIONAL LEAGUE FOR PEACE AND FREEDOM, Rue de Varembé 1, Case Postale 28, 1211 Geneva 20 SWITZERLAND. Tel: +41 22-919-7080. Email: secretariat@wilpf.ch. Web: http://www.wilpf.ch.

THAILAND

FOR FRIENDS ASSOCIATION สมาคมเพื่อเพื่อน Web: http://www.ffathailand.com/ Facebook: https://www.facebook.com/สมาคมเพื่อเพื่อน-FFA-549291405250407/
(Supporting Thai political prisoners.)

INTERNATIONAL BUDDHIST COUNCIL, Kasetsart University, Kamphaengsaen Campus, Bakhon Pathom 73140 THAILAND. Email: agrtws@ku.ac.th.

INTERNATIONAL NETWORK OF ENGAGED BUDDHISTS (INEB), 666 Charoen Nakorn Road, Banglumpuland, Klong San, Bangkok 10600 THAILAND.. Tel: +66 2-860-2194, +66 2-860-1277, +66 81-803-6442. Email: secretariat@inebnetwork.org. Web: http://www.inebnetwork.org.
(Interfaith support for Thai COs and military resisters. Publishes *Seeds of Peace* triannually.)

NONVIOLENT CONFLICT WORKSHOP (NVCW), Box 31, Udomsuk Post Office, Bangkok 10260 THAILAND. Tel: +66 87-976-1880. Email: canceloyw@gmail.com, nvcw.gs@gmail.com. Web: http://www.facebook.com/nvcw.gs.

THAI LAWYERS FOR HUMAN RIGHTS (TLHR) (ศนู ยท์ นายความเพื่อสิทธิ มนุษยชน). Tel: +66 96-789-3172, +66 96-789-3173. Email: tlhr2014@gmail.com. Web: http://www.humanrights.asia/countries/thailand/thaicoups/pdf/en-after-coup-thai-human-rights-situation-report.

TURKEY

İSTANBUL ANTI-MILITARIST İNISIYATIF (ISTANBUL ANTIMILITARIST INITIATIVE) (IAMI), Istanbul TURKEY. Tel: +90 536-895-9290. Email: uygarabaci@hotmail.com.

NONVIOLENCE SIDDETSIZLIK. Web: http://www.siddetsizlik.org/.

NONVIOLENT EDUCATION AND RESEARCH CENTER, Kuloğlu Mah. Güllabici sokak No: 16 Daire:3 (2nd floor) 34433 Cihangir, Istanbul Avrupa TURKEY. Tel: +90 212-244-1269. Email: office@nvrc-sarm.org. Web: http://www.nvrc-sarm.org.

VICDANI RET DERNEĞI (VR-DER) (Conscientious Objection Association), Söğütlüçeşme Caddesi No. 76 Sevil İş Hanı Kat:5, 108 Kadıköy TURKEY. Tel: +90 216-345-0100. Email: vicdaniretdernegi@gmail.com. Web: http://vicdaniret.org/.

UGANDA

JAMII YA KUPATANISHA FELLOWSHIP OF RECONCILIATION IN UGANDA (JYAK), P.O Box 198, Kampala UGANDA. Tel: +256 77-149-5903, +256 47-166-0791. Email: jyak.peace@gmail.com.

WALES

CAMPAIGN FOR NUCLEAR DISARMAMENT CYMRU, Llys Gwyn, Glynarthen, Llandysul, Ceredigion SA44 6PS CYMRU (WALES). Tel: +44 12-3985-1188. Email: heddwch@cndcymru.org. Web: http://www.cndcymru.org.

ZIMBABWE

GAYS AND LESBIANS OF ZIMBABWE (GALZ), Private Bag A6131, Avondale, Harare ZIMBABWE. Tel: +263 4-741-736. Email: director@galz.co.zw. Web: http://galz.co.zw.

☮ ☮ ☮

You can't expect to stay informed if you're being brainwashed by mass media's corporate propaganda. Pick reliable alternative media:

Activist Post	http://www.activistpost.com
AlterNet	http://www.alternet.org
Article 19	http://www.article19.org
Countercurrents	http://www.countercurrents.org
Counterpunch	http://www.counterpunch.org
Dissident Voice	http://dissidentvoice.org
Electronic Frontier Foundation	https://www.eff.org
Freedom House	http://www.freedomhouse.org
Global Research	http://www.globalresearch.ca
Global Voices	http://globalvoicesonline.org
GV Advocacy	http://advocacy.globalvoicesonline.org
Inter Press Service	http://www.ipsnews.net
OpEd News	http://www.opednews.com
Rabble	http://rabble.ca
Raw Story	http://www.rawstory.com
Salon	http://www.salon.com
Vice News	https://news.vice.com

☮ ☮ ☮

☮ ☮ ☮

CONSCIENTIOUS OBJECTORS IN PRISON: A Comprehensive Bibliography

CJ Hinke

D ue to limitations of space, we are not able to include the references which helped to create *Free Radicals: War Resisters in Prison*. As an alternative, the complete bibliography, the most comprehensive in its field is available at: https://prisonwarresisters.wordpress.com for view or downlaod as a PDF.

The bibliography attempts to provide activists, peace movement strategists, the general reader, academic researchers and scholars with useful references to conscientious objectors and political prisoners throughout the world. Ω

☮ ☮ ☮

☮ ☮ ☮

ACKNOWLEDGMENTS

Acknowledgment with gratitude is made to the following individuals and publications who contributed their efforts to these pages:

e.e. cummings, XXX, "i sing of Olaf glad and big" from W (ViVa), in e.e. cummings, Poems 1923 - 1984, New York: Harcourt, Brace and Company, Copyright 1954, used with permission of poet Marianne Moore, from the original uncensored manuscript.

CJ Hinke, "The Last Draft Dodger: We still won't go!," original contribution, 2015

CJ Hinke, "The View From 1969," original contribution, 1969.

Thomas and Marjorie Melville, "Preface," original contribution, 1968, used with permission.

Daniel Berrigan, "Foreword," original contribution, 1968, reprinted in Dateline Ithaca, No. 59, October 23, 1968, used with permission.

CJ Hinke, "The World at War in the 21st Century," original research, 2016.

CJ Hinke with Koozma J. Tarasoff, "Shaking, Quaking, And Spirit-Wrestling, Uncompromising pacifists: Shakers and Doukhobors," original research, 2014.

CJ Hinke with Andrei Conovaloff, "Russian Spiritual Christians In America: The Innocence of Lambs," original research, 2014.

CJ Hinke, "Russia's Jewish Draft Pogrom"s, original research, 2015.

Eugene V. Debs, "My Prison Creed," from Walls and Bars, Chicago: Socialist Party, Copyright 1927, used with permission.

Earle Humphreys, "Four Hutterites In Military Confinement," from The Hutterites: A Story of Christian Loyalty, Fordville, North Dakota: Forest River Colony (now Forest River Community), undated, used with permission.

Carl Haessler, Carl, "In Camp," original contribution, 1967, used with permission.

CJ Hinke, "AWAKE! Jehovah's Witnesses and War," original research, 2013.

CJ Hinke, "Should I Stay Or Should I Go? Conflicted Christians: The Seventh-Day Adventists," original research, 2013.

CJ Hinke, "NOT Universal Soldiers: Unitarian Universalist COs," original research, 2013.

Bureau of Prisons, "Federal Prisons and the War," from Prison Progress, produced by The Atlantian, United States Penitentiary, Atlanta, Georgia, 1943, used with permission.

Lowell Naeve, "Envelopment," from The Phantasies of a Prisoner, Denver: Allan Swallow, Copyright 1958, used with permission of the author.

Philip Jacob and Mulford Q. Sibley, "Prosecution, Trials and Imprisonment of Conscientious Objectors," from Fellowship, Volume XV, Number 1, January 1949, prepared by the Pacifist Research Bureau from their book, Conscription of Conscience: The American State and the Conscientious Objector, 1940-1947, Ithaca, New York: Cornell University Press, Copyright 1952, used with permission of the authors.

Howard Schoenfeld, "The Danbury Story," an original contribution which has appeared in different versions in several other sources. Copyright 1970 by the author, used with permission.

James Peck, "Ending Jimcrow: Two Wars Later," original contribution, 1969, used with permission.

Lowell Naeve, "1969 – I've Changed My Mind," from an original letter to the editor and in addition to his book, *Field of Broken Stones*, in collaboration with David Wieck, Glen Gardner, New Jersey: Liberation Press, 1950, and Denver: Allan Swallow, 1959, used with permission.

Wallace Nelson, " I Don't Close Jail Doors," original contribution, 1968, used with permission.

Ernest Bromley, "The Story Of Corbett Bishop," from an article titled "18-year old Kills Corbett Bishop," in *The Peacemaker*, Volume 14, Number 8, June 3, 1961, used with permission of the author.

Lowell Naeve, "Written after two years in Upper Hartford Cell House, Danbury Federal Prison," from *Field of Broken Stones*, op.cit.

Joel, Orin, Paul, Sid, and William N. Doty, "Letters from the Four Doty Brothers," from original letters to their parents from prison in the files of The Central Committee for Conscientious Objectors, Philadelphia, used with permission of the authors.

Karl Shapiro, "The Conscientious Objector," in *Trial of a Poet and Other Poems*, New York: Reynal & Hitchcock, 1947, used with permission of the Estate of Karl Shapiro.

Arlo Tatum, "The Second Time Around," excerpts from a conversation with the editor, 1969, used with permission.

Karl Meyer, Karl, "The Nonviolent Revolution And The American Peace Movement," excerpts from the pamphlet published in Chicago by St. Stephen's House, 1960, used with permission.

Hinke, CJ, "PEACE – What (some) Muslims Want, Muhammad Ali: 'Float like a butterfly, sting like a bee'" , original research, 2013.

Julian Beck, Julian, "Letters From Jail," original letters from prison to Karl Bissinger, reprinted in *Ikon*, Volume I, Number 2, April 5, 1967. Copyright 1965 by The New York Times Company, used with permission of the author.

Marjorie Swann, "Experiences At Alderson," original contribution, 1969, used with permission.

Arthur Harvey, "Prison And Me," original contribution, 1968, reprinted in *The Greenleaf*, June 1, 1968, and *The Peacemaker*, volume 21, Number 9, July 20, 1968, used with permission of the author.

John Phillips, "How I Was Carried To A Cell In A Wheelchair And Evicted From Prison In A Laundrycart, With Some Observations Made In The Intervening Period," from original contributions, 1968, the latter portion of which was reprinted in *The Peacemaker*, December 30, 1967, and by *Prisoners' Information and Support Service News Notes* (P.I.S.S.), Boston, 1968, under the title, "How I Was Evicted from Federal Prison," used with permission of the author.

F. Paul Salstrom, "A Prison Journey," excerpted from an original contribution, 1968, used with permission.

Darryl Skrabak, "What Will It Be Like When You Get Out?," from a pamphlet published by the American Friends Service Committee, Portland, Oregon, 1968, and reprinted in *P.I.S.S. News Notes*, Number 4, January 1969, used with permission.

Michael Vogler "The Scene At Springfield," excerpted from an article in *P.I.S.S. News Notes*, Number 2, June 1968, used with permission of the author.

Robert Gilliam, "To Stand Where One Must Stand," from an original collection of letters from prison to Jennie Orvino, published in *The Catholic Worker*, Volume XXXIV, Number 6, July-August 1968, used with permission of the author. For more Jennie Orvino: http://jennieorvino.com.

Michael Wittels, "Stockade Life," from an original letter and notes, 1968, used with permission.

Suzanne Williams, "The New Absolutist," from original letters from prison to her mother, 1968-1969, used with permission.

Jeffrey Segal, "Jail Is A Bummer," from an original letter from prison published in *New Left Notes*, Volume 3, number 40, January 8, 1969, used with permission of the author.

Dorothy Lane, "2 Monologues," from a poem published in *WIN Magazine*, Volume III, Number 1, January 13, 1967, used with permission of the poet.

Simon Townsend, "Objector In The Guardhouse," original contribution of an un-published letter and another published in *The Australian*, Melbourne, May 22, 1968, used with permission of the author.

Phil Ochs, "Draft Dodger Rag," 1965, used with permission.

Netiwit Chotiphatpaisal, "My Declaration On My 18Th Birthday," Rise Up Thai Students Network, September 3, 2014 http://powerlessboy.asia/entries/general/my-declaration-on-my-18th-birthday-i-am-a-conscientious-objector, used with permission of the author.

CJ Hinke, "Military Lies In Our Schools: 'Hey, teacher, leave them kids alone'," original research, 2016.

CJ Hinke, "Military Conscription Worldwide," original research, 2015.

CJ Hinke, "Resistance in America," original research, 2016/

CJ Hinke, "Desertion: A Long, Proud Tradition," original research, 2015.

CJ Hinke, "Imagine there's no army…," original research, 2015.

CJ Hinke, "Each Stone a Prison," original research, 2016.

CJ Hinke, "Lock 'em all up: Spinning money from misery," original research, 2015.

Freedom Now, "A Guide to Writing Prisoners of Conscience," used with permission. http://www.freedom-now.org/a-guide-to-writing-prisoners-of-conscience/

Draft Law Group, "The Personal Effects of Resistance," from a pamphlet titled, "The Draft Law and Antiwar Protests," New Haven: Yale University Law School, March 1968, used with permission.

Jackson MacLow, "Jail Break," (for Emmett Williams and John Cage), published in *WIN Magazine*, Volume II, Number 14, August 1966, used with permission of the poet.

Kanno Sugako, "EPILOGUE," [Public domain].

Albert Camus, "Neither Victim Nor Executioner," Combat, 1946 [Public domain]

Mohandas K. Gandhi, "Fear of Imprisonment," "Epilogue: A Quiet Afterthought," published in *Stonewalls Do Not a Prison Make*, edited by V.B. Kher, Ahmedabad, India: Navajivan Publishing House, copyright 1964, from an article published in Young India, January 1921, used with permission.

CJ Hinke, "Supporting prisoners for peace, war resisters, and deserters," original correspondence, 2016.

CJ Hinke, "Conscientious Objectors In Prison: A Comprehensive Bibliography," original research, 2016.